Y0-CBR-005

# Marxism
# in the Modern World

Edited by Milorad M. Drachkovitch

# Marxism
# in the Modern World

*Contributors*

Raymond Aron        Richard Lowenthal
Arthur A. Cohen     Boris Souvarine
Theodore Draper     Adam B. Ulam
Merle Fainsod       Bertram D. Wolfe

*Stanford University Press, Stanford, California*
*London: Oxford University Press*

The Hoover Institution on War, Revolution, and Peace,
founded at Stanford University in 1919 by Herbert
Hoover, is a center for advanced study and research on
public and international affairs in the twentieth century.
The views expressed in its publications are entirely
those of the authors and do not necessarily reflect
the views of the Hoover Institution.

Stanford University Press, Stanford, California
© 1965 by the Board of Trustees of the
Leland Stanford Junior University
Printed in the United States of America
Cloth ISBN 0–8047–0254–3
Paper ISBN 0–8047–0255–1
First published 1965
Last figure below indicates year of this printing:
79  78  77  76  75  74  73  72  71  70

# Preface

On October 5, 6, and 7, 1964, a conference organized by the Hoover Institution on War, Revolution, and Peace, on the general subject of "One
Hundred Years of Revolutionary Internationals," met at Stanford University. Thirty-five European and American scholars, mainly historians
and political scientists, presented papers and comments on a variety of
subjects related to the revolutionary movements that for a hundred years
have claimed direct ideological kinship with the International Workingmen's Association—the First International—founded in London on September 28, 1864. The conference participants sought to analyze dispas-
sionately the variety of Marxist movements that have so profoundly
affected the destiny of mankind during the last century.

The essays collected in this volume are for the most part slightly revised
and updated versions of the papers presented and discussed during the
second day of the conference. The papers from the other two days of the
conference will appear in two separate volumes, each of which, it is
hoped, will form a coherent, topical whole.

In presenting this book to the public I wish to express my sincere grati-
tude to Mr. Gene Tanke and Mrs. Muriel Davison of Stanford University Press, whose editorial competence and intellectual alertness have
been a great help in tying together this volume.

M. M. D.

May 1, 1965


Except for two dozen slight modifications and a postscript by Richard
Lowenthal on pages 271–73, the text of this printing is the same as that
of the original edition. The other volumes deriving from the Institution's 1964 conference have now been published; they are *The Revolutionary Internationals, 1864–1943* (Stanford University Press) and *Marxist Ideology in the Contemporary World: Its Appeals and Paradoxes*
(Frederick A. Praeger, Inc.).

M. M. D.

August 10, 1966

# Contents

# Contributors

RAYMOND ARON, a graduate of the Ecole Normale Supérieure, is Professor of Sociology at the University of Paris and a member of the Académie des Sciences Morales et Politiques. Books of his that have appeared in the United States include *The Century of Total War* (1954), *The Opium of the Intellectuals* (1957), *France: Steadfast and Changing* (1960), *Introduction to the Philosophy of History* (1961), and *The Great Debate* (1965).

ARTHUR A. COHEN studied at the University of Chicago and at Stanford. He is the author of numerous articles on Chinese Communism and *The Communism of Mao Tse-tung* (1964). He is currently engaged in research for the United States government on the policies of the Peking regime.

THEODORE DRAPER has been a Research Associate of the Russian Research Center at Harvard University and a Senior Fellow of the Research Institute on Communist Affairs at Columbia University and is now a Senior Research Fellow of the Hoover Institution on War, Revolution, and Peace at Stanford University. He is the author of *The Roots of American Communism* (1957), *American Communism and Soviet Russia* (1960), *Castro's Revolution: Myths and Realities* (1962), and *Castroism: Theory and Practice* (1965).

MERLE FAINSOD served as Director of Harvard University's Russian Research Center from 1959 to 1964. He is at present the Carl H. Pforzheimer University Professor at Harvard and Director of the Harvard University Library. He is the author of *Smolensk under Soviet Rule* (1958) and *How Russia Is Ruled* (rev. ed., 1963).

RICHARD LOWENTHAL went to Britain as an exile from Nazi Germany and traveled widely after the war as a foreign correspondent for the London *Observer*. Since 1953 he has specialized in the comparative study of totalitarian movements and particularly in the study of relations between the Communist parties of different countries. He was a co-author, with G. F. Hudson and Roderick MacFarquhar, of *The Sino-Soviet Dispute* (1961) and is the author of *World Communism: The Disintegration of a Secular Faith* (1964).

BORIS SOUVARINE, a French writer of Russian descent, was intimately involved in the early work of the Communist International. In 1921, as a delegate of the French Communist Party to the Comintern's Third Congress, he was elected to

the Presidium and the Executive Committee. In 1924 he became the first high official of the Comintern to be expelled from the organization specifically for opposing
the policies of the Zinoviev-Kamenev-Stalin faction, and later he broke with
Trotsky and Communism in general. He has served since 1957 as the editor of
*Le Contrat social,* and is the author of *Stalin: A Political Survey of Bolshevism*
(1939).

ADAM B. ULAM is Professor of Government at Harvard University and has been
a Research Fellow at Harvard's Russian Research Center since 1948. Among his
books are *Titoism and the Cominform* (1952), *The Unfinished Revolution* (1960),
*The New Face of Soviet Totalitarianism* (1963), and *The Bolsheviks* (1965).

BERTRAM D. WOLFE is at present a Senior Research Fellow at the Hoover Institution on War, Revolution, and Peace at Stanford University. His most recent aca-
demic appointment was as Distinguished Visiting Professor of Russian History at
the University of California (Davis). His published works include *Communist
Totalitarianism* (1956), *Khrushchev and Stalin's Ghost* (1957), *Three Who Made
a Revolution* (rev. ed., 1964), and *Marxism: One Hundred Years in the Life of a
Doctrine* (1965).

Milorad M. Drachkovitch

# Introduction

The title of this volume notwithstanding, the generic term "Marxism" is only inferentially connected with the doctrine and movement that Marx and Engels developed and originally led in the nineteenth century. More precisely, this book deals with the historical destiny of Marxism in our century. One could say that our starting point, both chronologically and substantively, is 1902, the year Lenin's slender volume *What Is To Be Done?* appeared. After its publication, and a fortiori after its revolutionary application fifteen years later, the face of Marxism had fundamentally changed, along with the face of the political world. The emergence of Leninism as the precursor of the other Communist "isms" analyzed in this volume points to three aspects of Marxism in this century that have been expressly or implicitly examined in all the essays: first, the strictly "voluntarist" Marxism of Lenin and his successors, as opposed to the "determinist" social physics of the mature Marx and Engels; second, the recurrent "revision" of Marxism by every subsequent Communist "ism"; and third, the metamorphosis of Marxism from a nineteenth-century ideology into a twentieth-century system of political power.

Leninist voluntarism has legitimate roots in some aspects of nineteenth-century Marxism, and Lenin's claim that "the living soul of Marxism was its revolutionary content" can be substantiated by many of the pronouncements of Marx and Engels. On the other hand, Lenin's theories of 1902 and the Bolsheviks' practice of 1917 do obvious violence to the hard core of scientific Marxism and its impersonal laws of history. In strangling Russia's incipient parliamentarism, and in denying capitalism any chance to develop within the framework of bourgeois democracy, Lenin refuted Marx's dictum that "no social order ever disappears before all the productive forces for which there is room in it have been developed." In this sense Karl Kautsky, the learned and universally recognized ideological leader of all Marxists before 1914, theoretically had only to quote Marx to prove that the Bolshevik Revolution was un-Marxist and in many ways anti-Marxist. And Pavel Axelrod, another orthodox Marxist and Lenin's close comrade-in-arms in the formative period of Russian Social Democracy, claimed later that the Bolsheviks owed their success to the putschist ideas of Marx's bitterest enemy, Bakunin. Whoever might have been ideologically right in the controversy, the formerly unified bloc of Marxist revolutionary socialism was irretrievably split as a consequence of the October Revolution.

Revolutionary voluntarism produced all the post-Lenin Communist triumphs, too. Stalin ruled and transformed Russia after 1928 by putting into practice the ideas of his more inventive opponents, but stamped with his own extraordinary political imprint. Khrushchev's de-Stalinization certainly reflected the pressures of a maturing and complex Soviet society, but the way in which de-Stalinization was inaugurated and conducted was highly personal. No scientific Marxist theorems can explain the unique history of Titoism, shuttling between political impotence and total control in Yugoslavia, and between the most intransigent revolutionary élan and what Tito's opponents in the international Communist movement call pure opportunism. China and Cuba never entered the minds of any nineteenth-century Marxists—and of very few in the first half of this century—as candidates for socialist pre-eminence, and the success of Communism in these two countries is hardly conceivable without the voluntarism of Mao Tse-tung and Fidel Castro. One could therefore say that the destiny of Marxism in our century is easier to explain in terms of Thomas Carlyle and his heroes than in terms of Karl Marx and his economic laws.

Communist free will is closely linked with the revision of Marxism. The concept of revisionism, usually associated with the German reformist Socialist Eduard Bernstein, can as justifiably be imputed to the post-1902 Lenin. One could hardly find a greater political discrepancy than that between Lenin's *What Is To Be Done?* and the last important political writing of Engels—his 1895 preface to a reissue of Marx's *The Class Struggles in France, 1848–1850.* In this strictly democratic document, Engels singled out universal suffrage as the decisive weapon of the proletariat. In his view, the final victory would be won by a broad socialist party which—first in Germany, then in other countries—would win over a majority of the different social strata and march irresistibly to power by winning a majority at the polls. In contrast to Engels's democratic optimism and faith in the working class came Lenin's elitist pessimism, his revisionist interpretation that workingmen were not revolutionary-minded, and that their class consciousness had to be brought to them from without by a new organization of professional revolutionaries, led by educated but estranged representatives of the propertied classes—the intellectuals—who had mastered the theory of socialism.

The liberties Lenin took with Marxism became more pronounced under his successors. Stalin liquidated Lenin's most trusted and brilliant comrades-in-arms, and Stalinism, as a political and economic system, became the incarnation of the totalitarian state that orthodox Marxists had visualized as the final stage of capitalist barbarism. Tito in his turn achieved prominence by de-Stalinizing his regime—that is, by revising Marxism-Leninism-Stalinism. In this complex, ambiguous, and unfinished process he was followed by his hot-and-cold friend Nikita Khrushchev. Mao Tse-tung's revolutionary career as a trained Leninist who led peasant guerrillas to victory in the name of the proletariat, and his own style of economic experimentation, were revisions of all previous Communist seizures of power and attempts at social engineering. Finally, the originality of Fidel Castro lies in the fact that he, a non-Communist at the moment of seizing power, has hurriedly pushed Cuba along one of the most militant Communist paths while eliminating, one after another, the Communist old guard.

The passage of Marxist movements from opposition to power brought with it a qualitative distinction between nineteenth- and twentieth-century Marxism. The Marxism of Karl Marx, as Raymond Aron argues in this volume, was essentially a science of capitalism. Fortunately or unfortunately for his pupils in this century, Marx's blueprint for socialism was either nonexistent or irrelevant. Lenin felt the full burden of this world when he realized, after seizing power, the extent to which Marx, the invaluable and acid critic of the bourgeoisie, was useless and even dangerous as an adviser for socialist construction. Every Communist "ism" discussed in the following pages represents a huge effort of improvisation and experimentation, an effort made in the name of Marx but certainly not according to Marx.

Thus, Marxism has become a two-edged sword for all Communist systems. In the name of Marx Communist parties have "expropriated the expropriators," abolished private ownership of the means of production, nationalized economic life, and socialized the existence of individual citizens. Thoroughgoing Communist revolutions have been carried out in the name of basic postulates that Marx himself did not and could not work out in detail. But at the same time Communist states have developed characteristics that either resemble (if not exaggerate) some of the aspects of capitalism that Marx had mercilessly exposed, or represent new facts and realities incompatible with the logic of Marx's criticism and his vision of a future social order. The obsession with *power*—the essence of modern Communism, according to Milovan Djilas—is at the root of all the evils that modern totalitarian states generate: the alienation of man in a milieu beyond his control; the absence of democratic freedoms and equality in societies in which strictly elitist, self-perpetuating minority parties monopolize all power and deprive citizens of the right to opposition; and the use of militarism and frenetic nationalism as tools for the discipline and mobilization of the masses. The paradox of twentieth-century Marxism consists, then, in the applicability of the criticisms of Marx to the social systems founded in his name.

By giving precedence to politics over economics, the Marxist "isms" have not only turned Marx's seemingly scientific doctrine on its head; they have engendered the Communist pluralism that Richard Lowenthal discusses in the concluding essay of this volume. The limited utility of Marx's compass to Communist rulers is borne out particularly by the mutual Sino-Soviet accusations of "great-power chauvinism"—something all orthodox Marxists once attributed exclusively to the existence of antagonistic capitalist states. A movement born in a different century, under the specific conditions of Western European society in full environmental change, was bound to undergo substantial modifications in traveling through the accelerated time of modern history and through the space of divergent countries, continents, and civilizations. Communist successes in this century, unrelated as they have been to the analyses and expectations of the founding fathers of Marxism, could not but generate heterogeneous political entities. By trying to harness the force of nationalism—domestically and internationally—the Communists have set in motion a fateful and unpredictable historical process. On the one hand, the Communists' domestic pronouncements are couched increasingly in patriotic, populist terminology. All the Communist states try to exploit the nationalism of the emerging nations in Africa and Asia, as well as the nationalist ferment in Latin America. The Chinese Communists, in particular, apparently see in these areas a good chance of establishing a worldwide anti-Western front under their aegis. On the other hand, the dynamics of nationalism can make international solidarity difficult. Rumanian nationalism is unpalatable to the Soviet rulers even if it is used by the Rumanian Communists to strengthen their own domestic power. And Chinese Communist proselytism worries the Russian Communists despite its Marxist vocabulary. Nationalism—the strongest emotional force of this century—will thus in all probability determine the fate of Communism, either by fostering its further expansion or by precipitating its greater fragmentation. George Orwell's vision of a Communist-ruled world in which three totalitarian systems wage perpetual, side-shifting warfare seems less fantastic in the light of the exchange of invectives between Stalin and Tito and Mao and Khrushchev. Conversely, de-Stalinization may prove so irresistible that for the first time in Russia's post-1917 history the will of its leaders may be unable to prevent the evolution of Russian society in a direction that would transform the future of the world.

One hundred years after the founding of the First International, the Communist movement has acquired a complex identity that Marx could not have anticipated, and many features that he would certainly disown. The following essays illuminate much of the history of Marxism in this century. And after some of the best analytical minds in the Western world have examined that history from today's perspective, even the future may seem less opaque.

# Marxism
# in the Modern World

Raymond Aron

# The Impact of Marxism
# in the Twentieth Century

The word "impact" is difficult to translate (or to define, if one regards it as French). Does it mean influence, shock, challenge? Probably the English word suggests all these meanings—and in doing so indicates the immensity of the ground we should have to cover if we had the absurd ambition to try, in a single essay, to answer the question, or rather the multiple questions, posed by the title at the top of this page.

The term "Marxism," moreover, is hardly less equivocal than "impact." Indeed, Marxism may denote: (1) the ideas of Marx himself, as reconstructed by the historian who seeks to understand them in relation to the man and his times; (2) the ideas of Marx as interpreted by various "Marxist" schools in relation to their own times, their own problems, their own goals; (3) the social movements, the parties in opposition, and the parties in power that claim to be acting or governing in accordance with Marxist ideas. Between the second and third definitions, i.e., between the *ideas* that spokesmen for Marxist movements attribute to Marx and the movements themselves, there is necessarily a dialectical relationship. Every movement creates its own Marxism, or reads the writings of Marx in its own way, just as every religious sect has its own way of reading Holy Writ, although of course the texts themselves influence the being and consciousness of the reader, and hence the way he reads them.

Even if we hold to the first definition, the term Marxism is still not free from ambiguity. Equally objective historians do not necessarily come to the same general conclusions—for two main reasons, both of which stem from the peculiar nature of Marxism. First, the historian hesitates between theories that are often crude and historical and sociological analyses that are rich and subtle. In every one of his historical studies Marx discerned a number of classes, even though on the theoretical level he asserted that capitalist society tends to polarize into two classes, the proletariat and the bourgeoisie. Similarly, in his historical studies, he did in fact recognize and take note of the role played by the state, by parties, even by individual men, while in theory the state is only a tool in the service of the economically dominant class. Finally, certain basic concepts —"the relations of production," "infrastructure," "superstructure," "in the final analysis"—seem destined to remain the source of endless controversy, of a theological rather than scientific nature.

The linking of *materialism* and *the dialectic* and the differences in style and vocabulary between the so-called youthful writings (before the *Poverty of Philosophy* and the *Communist Manifesto*) and those of the mature period inevitably promote controversy. There are, to put it simply, two philosophical methods of interpreting Marxism: one in which dialectic and Hegelian influence dominate, the other in which materialism dominates. Either the laws of the dialectic are an objective description of natural (cosmic, theological, biological, human) development, or else the dialectic is related to the wellspring of human action—history is dialectical because men deny reality and reach toward a future that, when it becomes objective reality, is in turn denied by later generations. These two philosophical methods are not fundamentally incompatible; the Hegelianized Marx of Georg Lukács is still a materialist—at least in the sense that the contradictions of capitalism, and the objective dialectic they give rise to, still play a central role in *History and Class Consciousness*. Even so, the materialism propounded by Lenin in his book *Materialism and Empirio-Criticism* and the materialism of the young Lukács, or of the Sartre of *Raison dialectique,* have hardly anything in common but the name.

This duality of philosophical interpretation was deepened, renewed, brought up to date, if you will, by the publication some thirty years ago (in 1932) of all Marx's early manuscripts, particularly the *Economic and Philosophic Manuscripts of 1844* and *The German Ideology* of 1845, the first antedating, the second postdating, the beginning of his collaboration with Engels. Although even by the time he wrote *The German Ideology* Marx repudiated the style and vocabulary of the 1844 manuscript; although he read and approved Engels's *Anti-Dühring,* which more than any other book by the two men is the source of classical Marxism and dialectical materialism; although the concept of alienation (*Entfremdung*) has almost disappeared in the great books of Marx's maturity— despite all this, an entire literature developed, first in Germany between 1919 and 1933, then in France after the Second World War, which tried to rethink Marxism in the light of manuscripts that Marx himself had never published.

This "Hegelianized" or "existentialized" Marx, though sometimes presented to us by historians of Marxism (Father Calvez, for example), is not independent of historical circumstance; he, too, fulfills an ideological function, like the materialist Marx of Lenin, Stalin, and Maurice Thorez. Of course, no social movement of any importance has made use of "existentialized Marxism," which is too difficult for the non-philosopher to understand, and which would strip Marxism of the double aura of *science* and *prescience*. In Sartrism scientific necessity is unintelligible, opaque to the mind, brute fact, not apodictic. But the intelligibility founded on freedom of constitutive dialectic would seem to imply that the future is unforeseeable. *History and Class Consciousness,* which is even more committed to the thesis of objective necessity and the foreseeability of social revolution, was never acceptable to Marxist-Leninist doctrinaires; it confines the primacy of economics to modern society, and, when all is said and done, undercuts the certainty of foresight by emphasizing the *efficacy* of class consciousness, the discovery by the historical subject of its historical calling.

To narrow our topic as much as possible, I shall put aside the first meaning of Marxism, i.e., Marxology, and give my attention to Marxist social movements and the doctrines that they propound. My remarks will center around the controversies between factions inside a given party, and between different parties that deem themselves equally loyal to Marx's thinking. Since these controversies arise from the clash between circumstance and doctrine, the title of this study might well be "Marxism at Grips with the Twentieth Century," or "On the Triumph of Marxism in a Century That Refutes Some of Its Main Ideas."

Marxists, like all believers, are inclined to be quarrelsome, and the ambiguity of their faith reinforces this natural inclination. The theory of scientific socialism is first and foremost a *science of capitalism.* Marx analyzes the capitalist system and the way it functions in the light of a general concept of history and human society. He brings out its intrinsic contradictions, and he announces its inevitable destruction by the working class, which, as it becomes conscious of itself and of the exploitation of which it is the victim, organizes for revolutionary action. It is not impossible to extract from *Das Kapital* some indication of what a socialist economy should be like. But the fact remains that Marx, like all of his contemporaries, knew nothing of the problems of centralized planning, and that the pre-1917 Marxists gave much more thought to capitalism and its contradictions than to the role of money, prices, and interest in a socialist economy. If, as I believe, classical Marxism is essentially a theory of capitalism and thus of contemporary history, it is understandable that controversies between Marxists should be at once theoretical and

4

practical: What action should be taken in circumstances unforeseen in the shared doctrine? What decision would most closely conform to the doctrine? How can today's decision or action be brought into line with a century-old doctrine, which, having become Holy Scripture, can be shaped to any purpose but cannot officially be revised? Is the socialism of the Soviet Union in agreement or in conflict with a doctrine that contains no description of the system to succeed capitalism?

It is hardly surprising that believers who were at the same time men of action have given contradictory answers to these questions.

The history of Marxist movements in the twentieth century is divided into four periods, and we have now entered the fifth. The first lasted until 1917: There was no Marxist state, only Marxist parties, all (or at least all the major ones) European. The Second International was dominated by the German Social Democrats. Neither Lenin nor Kautsky was aware that at the hour of decision they would both discover the precariousness of their agreement, the depth of their hostility.

October 1917: The victory of the Bolshevik Party marked the first great schism inside the Marxist movement. The Second and the Third Internationals took separate roads, which were never to meet. The paths of reform and revolution were neither convergent nor parallel, but divergent. Pre-1917 classical Marxism might have had as its motto "Revolution through Reform." The post-1917 Marxists—gradually, even if they caught on slowly—lost their illusions; their slogan became "Reform or Revolution."

The second period ended with Stalin's rise to absolute power. From 1917 to 1930 the split between the two Internationals was completed, but doctrinal discussion among the factions of the Russian Party had not been smothered. The Communist parties of the Third International were subject to the absolute authority of Moscow, but Moscow was not yet a monolith. The Bolshevik Party had right and left wings, though the controversies that preceded industrialization were little known in the West at the time. Today, as we get further away from them, they are attracting new interest in the light of the events of the last thirty years.

From 1930 to 1953—a period we shall call, with Nikita Khrushchev, that of the cult of personality—Trotsky's famous prediction came true. The Party took the place of the class, the Central Committee that of the Party, and finally the General Secretary that of the Central Committee. One man became the historical subject incarnate, and from then on the class could express its freedom only by passively submitting to an all-powerful ruler.

The fourth period opened with the death of the sovereign, or, if you prefer, with the Twentieth Congress of 1956. The Party leaders, the comrades and heirs of Stalin, publicly confessed that they had been lying for years, out of fear; that socialist legality had been disregarded; that monstrous crimes had been committed; that innocent Party workers by the tens of thousands had been shot or sent to concentration camps. And the truth about the concentration camps and about the Great Purge was, at least in part, admitted in the Soviet Union, and was spread unreservedly across the rest of the world. Simultaneously, the countries of Eastern Europe regained limited autonomy. Under Khrushchev, Yugoslavia, which had been excommunicated during the preceding phase and subjected to an economic blockade for several years, once again became a Communist state in good standing—without, however, rejoining the bloc.

The quarrel between Moscow and Peking has opened a fifth phase, not only because of the historic importance of China, but because some of the basic tenets of Marxism-Leninism—especially those concerning relations among Communist states and between Communist and capitalist states (in other words peace, war, and imperialism)—have been called into question. Can the final struggle between the Communist camp and the capitalist camp take some form other than armed conflict? Won't a nonviolent transition to Communism become the rule, rather than the exception? Can a Communist country be imperialist? Can nationalism make enemies of two Communist countries? Would a world composed exclusively of Communist countries necessarily be a peaceful one? All these questions arise as soon as one considers the implications of the quarrel between Moscow and Peking.

In each one of these five periods, the Marxists have been engaged in impassioned controversies, which are summarized briefly below. We must then consider what interest these controversies have had for non-Marxists, and what influence they have exerted on the outside world.

### The First Phase

The leading working-class parties of continental Europe became more or less Marxist at the end of the last century. The British Labour Party had never been so, and only a few intellectuals among its leaders had espoused Marxian beliefs—although they were never "converted" as the German and Russian Social Democrats were. Even on the continent, commitment to the doctrine of the *Communist Manifesto* and *Das Kapital* varied in nature and scope from country to country. I have always had doubts about the authenticity of Jaurès's Marxism. Karl Kautsky's was dreadfully serious (*toternst*, as the Germans would say).

The Second International, dominated by the German Social Democrats, was shaken by two public debates, on which attention was focused at the time. During the same period, the Russian Social Democrats were engaged in two debates that were no less impassioned, but that were known at the time only to the insiders (and most of the leaders of the Second International did not belong to the little group of insiders). Subsequent events were to endow these debates with prophetic value.

One of the Second International's debates concerned the revisionism of Eduard Bernstein, the other what action the labor movement should take to prevent war. Although Bernstein was condemned by the German Social Democrats and the Congresses of the International, today we think of him, far more than of his adversary Karl Kautsky, as the forebear and theoretician of twentieth-century democratic socialism. Because on the essential points—the evolution of the capitalist system, the influence of social reform—it is obviously Bernstein who after two World Wars and the Great Depression has turned out to be right. Reforms wrested by trade unions or Socialist parties from capitalist societies do not lead to revolution. They transform capitalism, they humanize it, but they do not unsettle it.* Once this is apparent, either one must prevent the working class's progressive involvement in the private-property system and stake everything on an elite core of professional revolutionaries (Lenin's solution), or one must admit formulas such as Bernstein's: "The goal is the movement itself. ... The sum total of the reforms *is* a revolution." At most, the Revolution that makes everyday action seem less prosaic can be seen as the myth in the eyes of the workers and party stalwarts. Bernstein's revisionism, like present-day democratic socialism, was founded on the assumption that the evolution of capitalism would be non-catastrophic, or, in other words, on the following two hypotheses: (1) the contradictions in capitalism will not keep intensifying, or, if they do, the ruling classes will be able to take the necessary steps to save the system; (2) the working class, or more broadly the masses, themselves are beneficiaries, and not victims, of the development of the forces of production.† If these two hypotheses are borne out (as they seemed to be before the First World War, and have seemed to be since the Second World War), reformism regularly tends to win out over revolutionary radicalism. Besides, Marxism is sufficiently flexible to stand warrant for a reformist doctrine.

In retrospect Kautsky was in an impossible position between Lenin and Bernstein, whose analyses of the situation had more in common than

---

* At least when capitalism is defined as essentially private ownership of the means of production.

† Or, in non-Marxian terms, of economic growth.

they cared to admit, but from which they drew exactly opposite conclusions. At the time Kautsky represented the center—and all its contradictions. The party workers were becoming too bourgeois not to denounce "Blanquism" and those working for a violent seizure of power, but they were insufficiently converted to democratic rhetoric to accept the theory underlying their practice. The Socialists were willing to act as though Bernstein were right, but they continued to think as though Kautsky were speaking the truth. In 1917 these two men found themselves in the same camp once more.

The debates of the International on the war question had revealed a helplessness that was tragically confirmed by the events of July–August 1914. The largest of the European Socialist parties, the German Social Democrats, never believed they could prevent war by means of a general strike and had never intended to try. Whatever reason is given for this refusal—resignation to the inevitable course of history, justified by a determinist philosophy; hope that revolution would follow the war; patriotism, nationalism, or imperialism among sections of the working class and the Socialist Party—the fact remains that the Second International had denounced capitalism in advance as responsible for any future war, but had been unable to agree on means to prevent that war. In August 1914 the German Social Democrats debated the advisability of voting for or against war credits, not the chances of a general strike or popular revolt. The situation in France was the same. The French workers, like the German workers, had a country to defend—the French against Germany, the Germans against Russia.

During this same period, the Russian Social Democrats, a minority party at the Second International, generated polemics and schisms by the dozen, amid the somewhat scornful indifference of their West European comrades. Today, of course, we know that the debates of the Russian Social Democrats prefigured later events: Was Lenin right to oppose the trade-unionist tendency of the working class, if it was to be left to shift for itself by the creation of a Party composed of professional revolutionaries and organized on the principle of "democratic centralism"? Or was Trotsky right to predict and denounce the substitution of the Party for the class—and, ultimately, the substitution of the General Secretary for the Party? Or were they both right at the same time, the one on the plane of effectiveness, the other on the nature of the system that a victorious Leninist party would establish? Furthermore, could a revolution in a country like Russia, still in the early stages of industrialization, become a socialist revolution without a transitional period of bourgeois democracy? Or, in more general terms, did all countries have to go through the same stages that Western Europe had gone through? Finally —and this last question was not taken up again in the West until after the Second World War—did not a system of public ownership and state planning risk a return to what Marx called the Asiatic method of production instead of an advance to the superior method of socialism?

Of the two ideas on which Communism was based, Lenin conceived one (the elitist party of professional revolutionaries, organized on the principle of democratic centralism), Trotsky the other ("the weakest link in the chain"). Both concepts were indispensable for the transition from Marxism to Marxism-Leninism. According to Lenin, under capitalism the working class itself organizes in order to press its claims, not in order to start a revolution. It is the elite party that plays, and must play, the role of activist avant-garde, and its chances of success are dependent on the vulnerability of the capitalist system. And it is not in the most advanced industrial countries, but in the backward countries, that this vulnerability is greatest.

Trotsky had at first rejected the Leninist concept of democratic centralism, and Lenin had rejected the Trotskyist concept of a permanent revolution that in a barely industrialized country would gradually become a socialist revolution through an alliance of the workers and the peasants. The merger of these two ideas gave to Bolshevism its explosive force. We should add here that neither of the founders of Bolshevism felt he was betraying the Marxist heritage. Lenin never doubted for an instant that the Party was not only the avant-garde but also the incarnation of the working class and its historic mission. Trotsky, for his part, regarded capitalism as one historic entity, whith encompassed all capitalist countries; even if the revolution had snapped only "the weakest link in the chain," i.e., the least industrialized country, it was the system as a whole that had been struck.

Lenin and Trotsky believed themselves sincere Marxists even as they were scrapping essential portions of Marx's thought. They repudiated his vision of a parallelism between development of the forces of production and the succession of social systems; they forgot the famous formula which holds that, "No social order ever disappears before all the productive forces for which there is room in it have been developed, and new, higher relations of production never appear before the material conditions of their existence have matured in the womb of the old society."[*] They implicitly dropped the primacy of economic forces in historical evolution.

---

[*] In the Preface to *A Contribution to the Critique of Political Economy* (1859).

The points of controversy among twentieth-century Marxists are apparent in this first phase. According to classical Marxism, the development of capitalism leads spontaneously to revolution. But if the standard of living of the masses rises instead of falling, if those entrusted with the historic mission are content with social reform and political democracy; in short, if economic progress thwarts the catastrophes that would be the revolution's salvation, "What Is To Be Done?" On the other hand, Marxism is a theory of capitalism, but there are actually a number of capitalisms, and the Second International, according to the famous formula, was nothing more than a letter-box. When capitalist countries make war upon one another, what is the duty of the workers, of Marxists, of the leaders of the International? *Prosperity* and *nations* are the two obstacles on which the unifying impulse of Marxist movements has regularly shattered.

At the beginning of the century, the Marxism of the Second International played only a minor part in the cultural life of Europe, including Russia. It would be difficult to name one economist, one sociologist, one historian of great stature, who explicitly called himself a Marxist. A Kautsky is not in the same class with a Max Weber, or even a Georg Simmel. Nevertheless, the Marxists of the pre-1914 German, Austrian, Italian, and Russian schools did participate in the development of the social sciences, did belong to the same universe as the non-Marxists, were "valid interlocutors" in the never-ending discussions on the destiny of modern societies. It would not be wrong to say, it seems to me, that the best of Marxism had been assimilated by Western culture. As for its political and prophetic ingredients, they were left to the "Marxists," i.e., to doctrinaires and leaders of workers' movements. By 1914 these movements had ceased to frighten the bourgeois governments.

The revolution of 1917 opened a new era.

## Victory and Decline: 1917–30

Prior to 1917, European and Russian Socialists had discussed in the abstract, so to speak, problems to which the events that began in 1914 gave a tragic urgency. There was no longer room for speculation, only action. One had to take sides—for or against the war, for or against the Bolshevik Revolution.

In 1914 the Second International ceased to exist. Every Socialist party, on its own and in its own way, had accepted the obligation of national defense, even if it had not subscribed to the Sacred Union. As for the ten days that shook the world in 1917 (i.e., the seizure of power by Lenin and company), they produced what one French historian has called the Great

Schism: the final break between Socialists and Communists, between the Second International (more dead than alive) and the Third International, between reformers and revolutionaries.

Two questions dominated the debate. Was the Russian Revolution the one that Marx and the Marxists had anticipated and evoked with fervent wishes? Had the Messiah come or not? Whatever the verdict on Bolshevism, the Socialist parties outside Russia also had to decide whether they should submit unconditionally to the authority of the Third International, which meant, actually, to the Bolshevik Party of the USSR.

In theory the non-Russian Socialists had three options. They could condemn the revolution of October 1917 out of hand and denounce the dictatorship of the Party *over* the proletariat, which was falsely represented as a dictatorship *of* the proletariat. They could abstain from passing definite judgment on the revolution of 1917 but reject the statutes of the Third International and the subordination of the international working-class movement to a party merged with a national government—that of the USSR. Or, finally, they could submit to the demands of the Third International, conceding that the Socialist movement had indeed become inseparable from the destiny of the Bolshevik Revolution, and that obedience to the one Marxist party that had succeeded in coming to power was both inevitable and justified.

In France and elsewhere a good many Socialists took the second position, at least verbally, during the period between the founding of the Third International, or of a national Communist party, and the conclusion of the Nazi-Soviet pact of 1939. But the dialectic of competition inevitably led to hostility between the champions of the Second and Third Internationals, a hostility that was but thinly veiled at the time of the Popular Fronts. The Communists denounced the "social traitors," and, even as they cooperated with them, sought to infiltrate joint organizations with their own men, to take over key positions, to win over the activists and voters of the party they had pledged to work with. How could the Socialists have failed to arraign in their turn the Communists and their methods?

Hopelessly at odds, Socialists and Communists alike were the prisoners of a false consciousness, which Marxists had once been pleased to unmask in their adversaries. The false consciousness of the Social Democrats consisted of dressing up reformist practice in revolutionary ideology, in representing essentially national policies as international ones in speeches and congresses. The false consciousness of the Communists consisted of painting over a line of action inspired by a revolutionary voluntarism with a doctrine positing objective laws of history, of hiding an actual primacy of politics and party beneath a jargon of "relations of production" and "class struggle." The false consciousness of the Social Democrats has been commented upon and criticized many times, recently by the Social Democrats themselves. It is not necessary for me to dwell upon it further. The false consciousness of the Communists, on the other hand, has been acknowledged and explained much less frequently.

Marxist doctrine is one of both theory and practice, a dialectic between consciousness and action. It is in danger, therefore, of leaning toward objective determinism, in which case it would favor adaptation (or resignation) to the inexorable laws of history. But it also is liable to lean in the other direction, toward voluntarism, and substituting Party decree for the will of the masses or evolutionary trends. Bolshevism was a "voluntarist" reaction to the "determinist deviation" of the Second International, unless you prefer to call Bolshevism a voluntarist deviation, or heresy. One defines orthodoxy only by taking a position, since the sacred texts are ambiguous and since events have ruled out the centrist synthesis ("revolution through reform").

True, the war and its aftermath did foster revolutionary situations, but these derived neither from the development of the forces of production nor from the economic contradictions of capitalism. In the final analysis, events depended neither on the means of production nor on class relations, but on the Party. In practice the Bolsheviks substituted the primacy of political action for the primacy of the forces of production. They concealed this revision by retaining the vocabulary of the class struggle, and by identifying the Party with the class.

Once again Bolshevik Marxism made the most of ambiguities inherent in Marx's thinking. In his historical and sociological research, Marx had often recognized the relative freedom of action and effectiveness of political events, national states, wars, and armies—nothing prevented the Communists from acting in accordance with one doctrine and speaking in accordance with another without being aware of the contradiction. A technique for revolution and seizure of power, Bolshevism invoked the laws of history, which it freely adapted to the needs of its propaganda and to the course of events. The supreme triumph of voluntarism came with the first Five-Year Plan, when Stalin set goals at once unattainable and unquestionable, unleashing the terrible crisis of agrarian collectivization.

The disputes between Bolsheviks during this period (1917-30), although scarcely known in the West at the time, were as interesting as the debates that had accompanied the "Great Schism." Before 1930 the Bolsheviks argued among themselves over the organization of the state and the building of socialism. Westerners are realizing that factions inside the party were opposed to the totalitarian regimentation of all organizations, especially the trade unions. Other methods of industrialization, of "capital accumulation," were put forth. At the time people in the West were not sufficiently aware of the problems involved in choosing a technique of economic development to grasp the real scope of these controversies.

By contrast, the clash (more of myths than practices) between "socialism in one country" and "permanent revolution" caused a tremendous stir. The personalities of the leading contenders, the apparently worldwide significance of what was at stake, the renewed antinomy between the International and nations—all this helped to transfigure the interchange between Trotsky and Stalin, to lend it a tragic magnitude. In retrospect it is difficult to separate the polemics, an aspect of the struggle for power, from the purely theoretical discussion. Even if we assume that Trotsky and Stalin did hold differing views of the relations between the Soviet Union on the one hand and the Communist parties and the world revolutionary movement on the other, even if we suppose that in China or Germany Trotsky would have taken a different tack, circumstances allowed but limited room for maneuver. Since both saw the USSR as the first socialist state and the center of world socialism, both would have had to work toward the development of socialism's temporary homeland while awaiting the opportunity to seize power elsewhere.

After 1917 the worldwide influence of Marxism changed in character. Marxian thought lost what Soviet reality (or illusion) gained. There was less talk of absolute or relative pauperization, of the law of gradual decline in the rate of profit—more about the meaning, the setbacks and successes, of the Russian Revolution. Neither the Marxists nor the non-Marxists as yet made any effort to interpret this revolution by the method used by Marx himself in *The Eighteenth Brumaire of Louis Bonaparte*.

Then, too, I have the feeling that on the intellectual plane the victory of 1917 contributed to the decline of Marxism. The survivors of the Second International prolonged their labors without renewing their ideas. No new Mondolfos or Labriolas appeared in Italy, no new Kautskys or Hilferdings in Germany, no Jaurès in France. Only the Austrian school, with the Kantian Marxism of Max Adler, still had a certain vitality. Classical Marxism had lost its power of attraction. Bolshevik activists and apologists were recruited among men of letters or scientists. Neither Paul Langevin, a great scientist, nor Louis Aragon, a great writer, had any effective knowledge of economics or sociology. The

Social Democrats, rightist revisionists, were condemned to participate in the management of bourgeois society; Marxism, the pessimistic science of capitalism, was not of much help to them, teaching as it does the irreducibility of the contradictions that they, as managers of bourgeois society, had the immediate task of mitigating. The Communists, left revisionists or voluntarists, were led gradually into dogmatism. Masters of a supposedly socialist country, the Bolsheviks had to justify their actions in terms of the doctrine in whose name they had triumphed. But the doctrine was of little more help to them in the managing of their new state than it was to the Social Democrats in their management of the bourgeois state. The Social Democrats resorted to the expedient of projecting the reconciliation of events and predictions, of their practice and their theory, into the distant future. The Bolsheviks, however, had to proclaim, if not achieve, this reconciliation at every moment. By the time Stalin gained absolute power, around 1930, only the orthodox version of the doctrine was tolerated, and it was imposed on the Third International by one omnipotent man. And the facts themselves were doctored as necessary to make the orthodoxy true.

### The Period of the Personality Cult

Debate ceased inside Russia in the early thirties, when the era of the Great Lie began. Until 1953 Stalin, and Stalin alone, decided what was the correct interpretation of Marxism and what the dogma would contain. The realm of "state truths" was enlarged to an inordinate extent, eventually including such day-to-day matters as the necessity of tractor stations, the percentage of national income to be set aside for investment (fixed at 25 per cent), and even scientific thought (one thinks of Lysenko, Mitchurin, the condemning of bourgeois genetics and Einstein's relativity). Stalin's pronouncements on linguistics and his final treatise on economics were immediately incorporated into the dogma, to become the subject of endless commentary by Communist "ideologues" in Russia and abroad.

Of all the Bolsheviks only Trotsky, his life in constant danger, pursued from his exile the debate against Number One, who had become master of both the party apparatus and the state. To the bitter end the organizer of the Red Army remained loyal to Lenin, and demanded that he himself be given his due for his role in the 1917 revolution. Until the end of his life he claimed that the Soviet Union was a proletarian state—despite the process of "bureaucratization" he himself had mercilessly denounced. From the study of the French Revolution, he borrowed the concept of the Thermidorian reaction, which he often used to describe Stalin's

regime. In opposition to this, he demanded a return to free discussion
inside the party, a freedom which had, in fact, existed under Lenin and
for the first few years after his death, but which even in Lenin's day had
been denied to Mensheviks and Socialist Revolutionaries. When in power
Trotsky had not always been more inclined to "liberalism" and moderation than Stalin. Undoubtedly he would not have eliminated his rivals
after spectacular trials in which the defendants, Lenin's comrades-in-
arms, confessed to fictitious crimes before thoroughly disabused judges.
The regime's style was set by the personality of Stalin, a personality at
once mediocre and monstrous. But it was Trotsky himself who had had
the premonition that Lenin's concept of "democratic centralism" would
lead to the replacement by one man of the Central Committee, the Party,
and even the proletariat. This leader of the revolution had perhaps never
been so great as in misfortune. Pursued across the world by a vengeful
despot, his children dying mysteriously one after another, he never abdi-
cated. He kept on hoping for other revolutions, which he expected to
follow the Second World War; the Soviet Union, now the victim of
bureaucratic degeneration, would be regenerated; instead of being confined to a single country, socialism would once again be an international
movement. Trotsky wrote somewhere that if history took a different
course, it would then perhaps be necessary to resign oneself to regarding the Marxist hope of social revolution as a myth belied by the supreme
judge: History.

Trotsky's polemics have an element of pathetic greatness, but they remain on the fringe of that History which Marxists never tire of invoking.
Soviet reality was not what the revolutionaries had imagined it would be
before they seized power. No, indeed—but in the name of what could
they call their dreams right and reality wrong? Forced industrialization?
Trotsky himself had favored it. Stalin had appropriated, and in his own
way carried out, the platform of the left opposition; so again, on what
principle could one renege? Everyone found quotations from Marx to
justify his proposals, but in fact Marx could not possibly have anticipated
—much less solved—the problems of economic development in a predominantly agrarian country governed by a party in the name of a dictatorship of the proletariat. Within the Bolshevik cadre the Trotskyist
opposition did not lack for arguments, but none was decisive. It would
have been necessary to call into question Lenin, democratic centralism,
"the weakest link in the chain," and finally the Revolution itself.

In any event, there was no way for Trotsky to alter his fate after 1930.
There were only two possible positions left for a Marxist—the Social
Democrats' or the Communists', the reformists' or the revolutionaries'.

True, both were open to criticism. The Social Democrats could have been more effective reformers; the Stalinists could have been less cruel in building socialism. The critics of the social democracies could go on living in them, but the Stalinists' critics instantly became traitors or agents of the Gestapo. Trotsky, who had organized and commanded the Red Army, was nothing more than the theorist and leader of an international sect that was torn by doctrinal bickering echoing the quarrels of the pre-1917 Russian Socialists. But the repetition was comic—or tragicomic.

The party of Stalin remained a monolith for some twenty-five years, but it did not have the same "impact" on the West before and after the Second World War.

During the thirties the Great Depression lent a measure of actuality to the old Marxist theories about the inevitable catastrophe in which capitalism, doomed by History, would be swallowed up. But the one who came up with a theoretical interpretation of semipermanent unemployment, of insufficient aggregate demand, of excessive savings, was not a Marxist, and it does not appear that John Maynard Keynes ever read *Das Kapital* very carefully, or took the distinction between value and prices very seriously. Even so, in his *General Theory of Employment, Interest, and Money* he did allude to a current of thought to which he himself adhered, to the pessimist school that foresaw the decline or paralysis of capitalism. The American economists speculating on the "maturity" of capitalism (e.g., Alvin H. Hansen) were also, in this sense, Marx's heirs.

Now, while the Great Depression was leading some bourgeois economists to rediscover and renew Marxist ideas (Marxist in the broad sense of the term), scarcely any Marxist economists or sociologists were making original analyses of the historical situation. To profit from the progress that had been made in economic thinking since Ricardo and Marx, one would have had to dispense with the conceptual apparatus of *Das Kapital*. Bourgeois economists refreshed their knowledge, whereas Marxist economists were content to proclaim that Marx's predictions had come true, and that the bourgeois governments would be incapable of overcoming the contradictions inherent in capitalism or of curing its evils.

Instead of making the working-class revolution inevitable, the crisis of capitalism swelled the ranks of other revolutionary parties—national and anti-Marxist parties. This fact had a double significance. In 1914 the workers as well as their leaders had demonstrated that they had a country, a fatherland; the non-worker masses, struck by the Great Depression, repeated the demonstration. Only a minority of the working class was willing to follow a party that acknowledged its subservience to a foreign party that had been merged with a foreign government. The non-proletarian masses, for their part, rallied not to workers' parties but to parties that borrowed their techniques in the name of an authoritarian national ideal. That the Fascists and National Socialists had the backing of Big Money is beyond doubt. But to reduce the victories and regimes of Mussolini and Hitler to phases or forms of monopoly capitalism is to fall victim to a detective-story concept of history and to misconstrue obvious facts. A capitalist society, even one shaken by an unprecedented crisis, does not spontaneously polarize into two blocs, one bourgeois, the other proletarian. Both the middle and the working classes become divided. The moderate middle-class parties draw closer to the anti-Bolshevist working-class party. And the Bolsheviks find themselves in temporary alliance with the extremists of the right against formal or bourgeois democracy. Here again voluntarism prevails—in the sense that the decision by the men in Moscow of the line to be followed by the German Communist Party determines events whose "laws" one would seek in vain.

A Marxian analysis, i.e., one that seeks to relate the attitudes of different social groups to socioeconomic circumstances, was by no means unsuited to the ups and downs of European politics between the two World Wars, provided one took the same liberties with the method that Marx himself had taken in his historical writings. The connection between socioeconomic circumstances and political attitudes and positions is always discernible, but it is not strictly predetermined or at the very least not predictable. Prejudices, value systems, ideological convictions come between the crisis or proletarization process and the reactions of individuals and social strata. True, these reactions are influenced by what "monopolistic capitalism" does, but monopolistic capitalism cannot create out of nothing the emotions it exploits. After he has taken over the state, the charismatic leader makes decisions himself, and he does not necessarily obey those who have allowed him to come to power.

Despite the mediocrity of Marxist thought during the years of the personality cult, Communism—or, more precisely, the Soviet experience —exerted a profound influence on the political life and ideological controversies of the West. The cause of this apparent paradox is simple. Before 1939 most of those who rallied to the Soviet cause were ignorant of Stalinist reality, or refused to look at it. They were reacting to the crisis in the West, and seeking in the East an ideological fatherland because they were in revolt against their own society. Never was the Soviet regime more cruel than between 1930 and 1938, the years of agrarian collectivization and the Great Purge; never did it seduce more minds, even in the United States. After 1945 the Soviet Union was crowned with the halo of its army's victories, transfigured by its power in the eyes of worshippers of History. The very madness of the despot contributed to the bewitchment of the faithful and of fellow travelers. In regimenting the speech of millions of men—even of free men—Stalin became a kind of high priest, the Father Ubu of a sacred and bloody mystic rite.

Between the periods 1930–39, on the one hand, and 1945–55, on the other, there is one major difference. Prior to 1939 democrats regarded National Socialism as the immediate danger. The imperialism of the Third Reich gave rise to the Popular Front and Franco-Soviet rapprochement, and made a common struggle of the bourgeois democracies and the Soviet Union against "fascist" countries probable. After 1945, however, the fascist threat had ceased to exist, except in Communist propaganda, and the Soviet take-over of Eastern Europe spread fears that the Russian Empire and a Communist ideocracy would be extended to the Atlantic.

Too, the postwar years in continental Europe, especially in France and Italy, were filled with the tumult of ideological debate. A rather strange debate, one might add. In theory we anti-Communist democrats should have been debating with the spokesmen for ideological orthodoxy. But how could one seriously debate with intellectuals, almost all of whom were shameless mediocrities, and all of whom were bound to a discipline that is always restricting, no matter how much the party line fluctuates. For want of a worthwhile interlocutor among the Communist true believers, we had to look around for some among the fellow travelers. These, for their part, tried to strike up a dialogue with the orthodox, or at least be recognized by them as allies. Depending on the circumstances, they were either cast into the outer darkness or tacitly tolerated. We laid before the Communists the facts verified by Khrushchev's speech to the Twentieth Party Congress, but any mention of them prior to 1953 was taken as a sign of prejudiced anti-Communism. With the subtle Marxism of Maurice Merleau-Ponty or Jean-Paul Sartre a philosophical dialogue was possible.

Dogmatic crystallization of Stalinized Bolshevik Marxism after 1930; mediocrity of Social Democratic thought, torn between an ever-more-theoretical adherence to the Marxism of Marx (in the centrist version of the Second International) and reformist policies that would have required an understanding of the capitalist system: this was the outcome of the Great Schism between Communists and Socialists, of the refusal of both to accept a course of history that did not fit the framework of their philosophy. Missing from this sketch is an element the political importance of which is almost negligible, but which rates mention in the history of ideas: Hegelianized Marxism, now leaning toward the Bolsheviks, now toward the Social Democrats, now locked in opposition to both—the last a curious position for a philosophy that claimed to be a union of theory and practice.*

Unquestionably it was Lukács who founded this movement with a book that he has several times disavowed, *History and Class Consciousness*. The materialist interpretation of history is applicable primarily to capitalist societies; the class is the historical subject; the proletariat alone can be aware of total reality because it is on the proletariat that capitalist society works out its inhumanity and contradictions; thus, the proletariat can see capitalist society from the vantage point of the future, whereas the bourgeoisie clings to a condemned order. As historical subject, the class is not objective reality, but action; it fulfills itself only through action, i.e., in the Party. The Marxist concepts *alienation* and *reification* allow simultaneous criticism of capitalist culture and analysis of the socioeconomic dialectic of the capitalist system.

This Marxism of left-wing intellectuals (whom we shall henceforth call Marxians) blossomed first in Weimar Germany between the defeat and Hitler's rise to power. Karl Korsch, the Frankfurt circle (*Zeitschrift für soziale Forschung*), Max Horkheimer, Wiesengrund-Adorno, Herbert Marcuse, were all Marxians of this stripe. Publication of Marx's early manuscripts, particularly of the unpolished and hence fascinating fragments published under the title *Economic and Philosophic Manuscripts*, confirmed, as it were, the authenticity of their Marxism—and this at the very moment that the chief representatives of the school had to emigrate to the United States. Lukács himself was influenced by the German social scientists Wilhelm Dilthey, Georg Simmel, and Max Weber, as well as by the great philosophers from Kant to Hegel. His research on esthetics is probably more important than his specifically Marxian theories. Even so, to this day he is the last European thinker of any importance in the Communist world. He has often had to confess his errors and has often been condemned to silence. He was a member of Imre Nagy's government, and, back in Hungary, has regained some freedom of expression thanks to the regime's new revisionism.†

---

* When the review *Les Temps modernes* was founded, Merleau-Ponty suggested at a meeting of the board of editors that they all agree and promise not to join any political party, to have philosophical but not partisan commitments.

† Ernst Bloch and Hans Mayer have come over to the West. Wolfgang Harich has just been released from his East German prison after serving most of his sentence of ten years at hard labor.

France succeeded Germany in the rise of Hegelianized Marxism and progressive intellectuals on the threshold of Communism. Moreover, the dominant philosophy in France since 1945 has been essentially Germanic in origin. The Neo-Kantian philosophy or semireligious spiritualism of Louis Lavelle and René Le Senne has gone out of style. The master thinkers of the younger generation, through the writings of Sartre and Merleau-Ponty, have been Edmund Husserl and Martin Heidegger, among the moderns, and beyond them Hegel and Marx.

Before 1940 neither Merleau-Ponty nor Sartre was particularly interested in politics. Neither was a Marxist, or had even seriously studied Marxism. And nothing in the writings of either man shows any knowledge of economic problems, or any reflection on the nature of modern societies and possible social systems. Only after the war did the pressure of events make them both heed the call of politics and launch a strange dialogue with each other and with the Communists, a dialogue pursued in several books and public statements that were always being refined and changed in spite of two constant traits: sympathy for the Communist cause and refusal to join the Party or, what is more, to espouse the orthodox Communist doctrine in either Stalin's or Khrushchev's version.

It is not possible within the framework of this brief study to discuss in detail Merleau-Ponty's books *Humanisme et terreur* and *Aventures de la dialectique* or Sartre's *Les Communistes et la paix* and *Critique de la raison dialectique,* and it is even less possible to analyze the conflict between the two friends caused by *Aventures de la dialectique.* Since we are investigating the "impact" of Marxism in this century, these postwar French philosophers must figure in our study. They are the descendants of Hegel and Marx; their own position is determined by their relation to the Marxism represented by the Soviet Union and world Communism; they strive to interpret the historical situation philosophically.

Their problem, reduced to its essentials, was the following. On the strictly political plane their sympathies were with the Communist cause, because in their eyes it was the only, and the only possible, incarnation of historical reason. Marxism, wrote Merleau-Ponty, is not one philosophy of history among others, but *the* philosophy of history. If it is wrong, the very concept of historical reason is invalidated, and history (in Shakespeare's words) becomes nothing more than "a tale told by an idiot, full of sound and fury, signifying nothing." From this it follows that even if for the time being the Soviet Union is a harsher regime than the bourgeois democracies, even if it does suppress freedoms that they protect, one must still be predisposed in its favor. Acceptance of bourgeois democracy is the renunciation of hope. Thus Sartre, in his article denouncing Soviet intervention in Hungary, did not on that count retract his identification of Communism with hope. "This monster dripping with blood," he wrote, is indeed the present face of socialism. This principle (or prejudice) makes one of three positions possible: membership in the Communist party; pro-Communism without membership in the Communist party; non-Communism that is not anti-Communist. Neither of these two philosophers has gone so far as to join the Party. To do so would have cost them their literary freedom, if not their freedom of thought. Under Stalin, or even Khrushchev, they could not have echoed the official doctrine without prostituting themselves. They would have been forced into silence or self-repudiation.

But another factor stood in the way of their joining. Technically speaking, Merleau-Ponty's philosophy is compatible with the dialectical, Hegelianized Marxism of Lukács or the young Marx. It is obviously not compatible with the dialectical materialism of the *Anti-Dühring*, of Lenin, and of Stalin. It is still less compatible with a determinist view that makes human history subject to laws comparable to the laws of nature (even if these laws do have "dialectical" properties, as Engels called them, such as quality and quantity and contradictions). The same thing applies, only more so, to the philosophy of Sartre. Both men start from historical perspectivism, which one derives from the phenomenology of perception, the other from the ontology of consciousness. Historical man, according to Merleau-Ponty, is situated in a given society at a given time. His view of the past changes with his situation. In Sartre's vocabulary, the mind is itself translucid, and creates, as it were, its own situation by the act of focusing on an object. For both men, the difficulty lies in getting back to totality from perspectivism or the individual consciousness, which Sartre regards as the perfect model of dialectic.

It is the Revolution, which marks the end of prehistory, that would make historical totality possible, by establishing a society in which human beings would achieve mutual recognition and which would reveal the meaning of the long journey. But what Merleau-Ponty had the most trouble in finding a philosophical basis for was precisely the possibility of such a radical break with all known past and present societies. Why would a socialist revolution suddenly put an end to all alienation? Why would there be a difference in kind between socialist society and all others? Why did the advance toward mutual recognition necessarily have to progress through violence, rather than reform?

In *Aventures de la dialectique*, Merleau-Ponty himself implicitly admitted these difficulties; whereas he had once assigned the Soviet Union a privileged place because of the ultimate goal of the socialist movement, he now adopted a position he described as "acommunism." There was no question of fighting Communism, so long as the Soviet Union did not try to extend its system beyond its borders by military force, but neither could there be any question of placing it beyond normal criticism. In speaking of a generalized economic science, he indicated a direction in which many others, better informed than he about economic and social mechanics, had long been traveling. Nearly half a century after the revolution neither Communism nor the Soviet Union can be defined either by the writings of Marx or by the intentions of Lenin and his companions. The Soviet Union is an established regime, whose Communism is a "point of spiritual honor"—"the spirit of a spiritless time," in Marx's words. It must be judged for what it is, not for what its leaders think it is, and certainly not for what they would like the world, including the Soviet citizenry, to think it is.

Despite his condemnation of Russian intervention in Hungary, Sartre today still calls himself a Marxist (in a certain sense of the word) and pro-Soviet (if we understand by that not approval of every act of the Soviet Union but agreement in principle with the so-called socialist camp, the incarnation of truth of our time). True, in his *Critique de la raison dialectique,* which depicts Marxism as the unsurpassable philosophy of our time, he derides the very notion of a dictatorship of the proletariat: "The very idea is absurd, a bastard compromise between the active sovereign group and the passive seriality." A dialectic that goes from free, transparent, individual action to the group via practico-inertia, and returns to practico-inertia when the group is institutionalized, is difficult for Communists to accept, even when they try a little Hegelizing. A dialectic whose model is individual praxis will always seem marred by some individualism, or to be carrying the seed of petty-bourgeois individualism. Nor is the concept of dialectical reasoning, radically different from scientific or positivist reasoning, acceptable to Engels's heirs.

Merleau-Ponty died before the publication of *Critique de la raison dialectique,* a gigantic effort to combine existentialism and Marxism, a philosophy of personal destiny and a philosophy of collective destiny. It seems unlikely that the effort has succeeded in surmounting the contradiction (although the second volume, devoted to *History,* has not yet appeared). The individual consciousness, a perfect entity in itself, transparent before any encounter with the Other, does not fuse with Others except at moments of collective exaltation, as in the seizure of the Bastille. Then the "I" disappears into a "We"; I am the Other because the Other is I—all are one, first in one action, then in one oath. But a tranquil society, free from turmoil, is not such a *group.* Not only is it not a fused *group,* it is not even an institutionalized group. It is a conglomerate or juxtaposition of *groups* and *series.* Inevitably, alienation is likely to be constantly re-created—the day after it has been overcome. Hence the promise of Volume Two may not satisfy the Communists. "It will seek to establish that there is one human history, with *one* truth and *one* way to interpret it. Not by considering the material content of this history, but by demonstrating that a practical multiplicity (whatever it be) must constantly become a totality, internalizing its multiplicity at every level." In his mature years Marx wanted to demonstrate that there was *one* human history, *one* historical truth, *one* way to interpret it; but not (like Hegel) by retracing the adventure of Spirit, or viewing each epoch as a stage in its coming, but by bringing out the (determinist) necessity of the historical process—in other words, precisely what Sartre himself considers the negation of intelligibility and freedom.

The Hegelian existentialist Marxist movement seems to me to have passed its peak and to be in decline, even in France. In the United States those who carry on the Marxist tradition fall into two groups, the second apparently the larger. The first group criticizes capitalism as an economic system, accusing it of exploiting the masses, or of not fully utilizing the forces of production, or of churning out useless merchandise, or of sacrificing millions of victims along the way—all this, and more besides, at the same time. The second group moves from socioeconomic criticism to cultural criticism, making its target either mass culture (the stupefying of the individual by culture industries) or the monstrous crimes committed in our era (wars, concentration camps, genocide), attributing these to capitalism by identifying a system defined by specific characteristics (private ownership of the means of production, market mechanism) with a concrete historical entity. If, having lost either their faith or their Mecca, many Marxists hold out against conservatism and denounce a false culture, it would be wrong to think that these disappointed, unrepentant Marxists have a monopoly on such criticism. They have simply joined the large army of those who do not expect a revolution, i.e., replacement of private ownership of the means of production with collective ownership, to miraculously change man's lot. Which does not mean that Marxists must now be resigned to the evils they have hitherto denounced. All they have to do, instead of dreaming of revolution, is think about reform.

## The Legacy of De-Stalinization

Between 1945 and 1953 the Soviet Union and the entire Soviet bloc seemed so monolithic that observers ended by losing any sense of historical perspective. Fascinated by Stalinism, they wound up regarding this almost aberrant episode as the essence of the Communist movement. Within the Second International the Russian Social Democrats were notorious for their propensity to factional conflict and schism. Once launched upon revolutionary action and finally in power, the Bolsheviks quarreled every time a big decision (October coup d'état, peace of Brest-Litovsk) had to be made. Though Lenin, obsessed with the example of the French Revolution, had solemnly warned against crossing the "blood line," they wound up killing one another right and left, or, rather, were practically all slaughtered at the orders of the man they had chosen as General Secretary of the Party. The struggle for power was intensified by the practice of turning the preferences and ambitions of each faction into ideology.

When the Stalinist façade collapsed after 1953, the Communists became their old selves once again; delivered from the fear inspired by a ubiquitous police force and a despot who was publicly adored and privately hated, they reverted to their true nature and resumed their historical-ideological debates—debates that were the more numerous and impassioned because several other countries were now laying claim to the same doctrine, and each of these countries, even if it was itself a monolith (which was not the case), spontaneously wished for some autonomy vis-à-vis Big Brother.

The official dogma, which was inordinately extended during the period of the personality cult, has shrunk to several simple propositions: public ownership of the means of production; identification of the Party with the class; insistence upon an irreducible contradiction between class societies and socialist societies (defined by the power of the Bolshevik Party); the inevitable decay of capitalism and final victory of socialism; rejection of ideological coexistence, i.e., of any questioning of theses that party leaders declare to be doctrinal truth at any given moment. The more limited this truth becomes, the more room there is for social, political, and economic debate within the Communist framework.

Some of this debate, however, cannot help touching the dogma itself, and shaking it. Here, it seems to me, are the main controversies which Khrushchevism gave rise to and which threaten the integrity of the dogma itself.

*The Controversy about the Past.* Once the personality cult has been acknowledged, once the crimes of the Great Purge and the concentration camps have been confessed, how can one maintain Party infallibility? How can one claim superiority for the Soviet system over all others? How is one to explain the cult itself? Western Marxists find it easier to answer these questions than orthodox Marxists. We shall always find an Isaac Deutscher to explain that the barbarism of the Russian people could be uprooted only by barbarous methods, a theorist of development to suggest that the Soviet concentration camps are the equivalent of child labor during the first decades of the last century in England. Peter Wiles will stage an ironic dialogue between the theoretician of historical determinism and the simple historian; the latter will have an answer for all the arguments of the former, and will suggest, without demonstrating it, that the horrors of agrarian collectivization and the Great Purge were unnecessary for development and would not have occurred if not for Stalin.

None of these interpretations is wholly acceptable to the Soviet Communists. That one man alone can be responsible for such events ill accords with the vision of a history governed by objective laws. That economic systems and planning techniques depend upon the level of development is a thesis dangerously close to a view of history more appropriate to a Rostow than to a Communist. The Russians would not willingly subscribe either to the explanation that "barbarism has to be fought by barbarous methods," the obstacle here being, if not their Marxism, at least their national pride.

Hence there is no way for the Communists to return to their former dogmatism once they have admitted the facts of the personality cult. The despotism of one man *over* the Party, or *with* it, has demonstrated that power in the hands of the Party does not necessarily mean the liberation of the proletariat.

*The Economic Controversy.* Correctly or incorrectly, the Communists have derived certain economic ideas from *Das Kapital*: Price should not be a function of scarcity but of the cost of production (to be calculated, if possible, in terms of hours of labor); the constant rate of interest should not play an active role, but at most should encourage businesses not to overstock; indicators intended for the heads of business enterprises should be objective, quantitative, expressed in units of value. If a profit indicator is introduced, the prices must be *real prices,* and not arbitrarily fixed by planning agencies. Personally, I do not think that such reforms are incompatible with *Das Kapital,* in which Marx did suggest what would amount to a noncapitalist economy, but never analyzed its methods in detail. The fact remains that the reforms advocated by the more daring Soviet economists tend toward re-establishment of some sort of market, hence toward a Soviet economy whose functioning is more like that of Western economies.

*On Intellectual Freedom.* During the period of the personality cult, party dogma was at once so broad and so imperative that agreement between the orders issued by the regime and the words spoken by the intellectuals was spontaneous and immediate. The latter did not pretend to fix their own margin of freedom; once the party had spoken, they knew what they had to say. Even in relation to painting, music, and sculpture, the theory, if not the actual practice, was beyond doubt or criticism. This is no longer true today. In his speech on culture Khrushchev abjured setting up his own taste as a criterion of beauty. But the boundaries between intellectual freedom and the categorical condemnation of ideological coexistence are uncertain. At what point does social criticism, as expressed in a novel or a comparison of the Soviet and Western systems, become the heresy of "ideological coexistence"? In a sense it is more difficult to allow some intellectual freedom than to suppress it completely.

*Relations between Communist Countries.* Marxism is weak on the subject of international relations. The Leninist theory of imperialism, a simplification of English ideas (in particular J. A. Hobson's), has been incorporated in the Marxist canon. Imperialism is viewed as the inevitable expression of monopoly capitalism, just as the state is considered a mere instrument of oppression in the hands of the ruling class. By deduction from these axioms it follows that Communist countries are all brothers and that none of them can be imperialist because all conflicts between countries have economic causes and stakes, and since these causes and stakes disappear with the disappearance of capitalism, conflicts between Communist countries are inconceivable. In actual fact, relations between Communist countries involve the same risk of conflict as relations between non-Communist countries. The frontier between Rumania and Hungary, the fate of Transylvania, affects the two nations —rulers and populations—regardless of their socioeconomic system. Communist China does not agree that Outer Mongolia is part of the Soviet Union, and is perhaps not happy about conceding it the Maritime Territory either.

On the economic plane, trade between Communist countries has led to some disputes. The terms of trade for goods whose prices are arbitrarily set in each country are open to arbitrary manipulation. After 1956 Khrushchev admitted that Polish coal had been acquired at an artificially low price, and agreed to make supplemental payments to Poland. Even referring to the world price on the capitalist market is no guarantee of fairness.

Being allies and members of the same bloc leaves Communist countries many opportunities for disagreement with one another. The small ones may want to assert their independence of Big Brother; or they may have a different idea of what is in the bloc's interest; or the national interest of one bloc member may clash with what the Soviet Union considers the bloc's higher interests. Yugoslavia broke away to protect its control of domestic affairs, China because it did not want to be subordinate to the Soviet Union and because it considered Khrushchev's strategy contrary to its own interests and to the interests of Communism and Marxist-Leninist ideology.

Even so, relations between Communist countries are not exactly the same as relations between Western countries. Adherence to a common ideology helps both to unite and to divide them. United by the feeling of having common enemies, they are divided in the ideological formulation of their positions. They have not learned how to accommodate to their way of thinking and acting differences of opinion and antagonisms that are considered normal in countries not ruled by ideology.

*War and Peace.* This is the last and most serious controversy. If nuclear armaments have ruled out war as the last phase of the historic transition from capitalism to socialism, how can the feeling of a death struggle between the two blocs be sustained? And how can the hope of victory be kept alive in the Communist parties of the industrialized countries?

The issue of peaceful-coexistence versus final-victory-of-Communism repeats on an international level the reform-versus-revolution dialectic of the Second International. At the beginning of the century the question was whether reform would or would not lead to revolution. Bernstein and Lenin both were inclined to give a negative answer, though the practical conclusions they drew from this were diametrically opposed. Today the Chinese and the Russians are wondering, the former openly, the latter secretly, whether without a war peaceful coexistence will ever lead to the destruction of capitalism. The Chinese are no more lighthearted than the Russians about the prospect of atomic war. But they are less hesitant than the Russians to support wars of national liberation, and more hesitant than the Russians to rule out once and for all, in so many words, a decisive war between the two camps.

*Communism and the Underdeveloped Countries.* To the five currently acknowledged subjects of debate we should perhaps add a sixth: How can one account for the variety of systems flourishing in the Third World? On this point Communists would seem to have no choice but to return to 1917, i.e., to the day events obliged them to abandon the thesis that the development of the forces of production parallels the development of socialism. The classical Marxism of the Second International did not anticipate history's skipping, or jumping over, the capitalist phase, since socialism was supposed to be nurtured by capitalism, as capitalism had been by feudalism. Men ask only the questions they can answer. The vision of parallel growth of the forces of production and the development of social systems was replaced by Trotsky's image of the weakest link in the chain. If you take not one capitalist country but the whole capitalist world as your field, the explosion of revolution in a single barely industrialized country seems less of a blow to the doctrine. Even so, the spokesmen for the new state felt it necessary to expound the paradoxical thesis that the fatherland of socialism still had to "catch up" with the United States, thus indirectly admitting that the most progressive system in the world was at the same time economically behind.

To the extent that the "building of socialism" progressed, the paradox tended to disappear. After the Second World War the Soviet Union became one of the two greatest military powers on earth, and if its percapita output still lags behind that of Western European countries, it is nonetheless second only to the United States in gross national product. Socialism is now identified with economic and military power, rather than a high standard of living.

Since the twenties, the Communists, encouraged by their own experience, have been staking their hopes on the "underdeveloped" countries of the Third World. Since they accepted Lenin's analysis of imperialism, they readily believed that revolt by colonial or exploited countries—particularly the two largest, India and China—against imperialist domination would be a fatal blow to the capitalist system.

In a sense their assessment of the revolutionary potential of Asia has been borne out by events, though, like good Marxists, the Soviet leaders were banking on the working class, not the peasant mass, to be the ultimate instrument, if not agent, of the so-called proletarian revolution. But Communist expectations have been radically belied on one very essential point: loss of their colonial empires has not weakened the capitalist mother countries in the least, and has not caused their standard of living to collapse. On the contrary, since 1945 growth rates in the West have been higher than they ever had been in the previous century or first half of this century. At the same time, no depression has occurred, and cyclical fluctuations, although they may still occur, have been less severe.

The creation or re-creation of some sixty countries in the short span of some twenty years, some by dint of their own efforts, others as a gift, raised two kinds of questions for orthodox Marxist-Leninists. First, how should these countries be classified? What categories did they fall into? How did they stand in relation to the two principal systems of our time, capitalism and socialism? Second, what method of development should they adopt? Did the Soviet Union have a concept of development to oppose to the Western concept (or the several Western concepts)?

To the first question the answer given during Stalin's reign was simple, even primitive: Either the independent countries would rally to the socialist camp and adopt a Communistic government, or they would continue to be the victims (voluntary or involuntary) of capitalist exploitation. Stalin's Manichaeism—capitalism or Communism, there is nothing in between—was matched, incidentally, by Dulles's unshakable stand, neutrality is immoral. When Stalin's successors decided to pursue a more flexible foreign policy and to exploit the rivalries and tensions among capitalist countries or between them and the newly independent countries to their own end, this crude black-and-white picture of the world was dropped. The "national bourgeoisie" was considered "progressive" to the extent that it tried to win or maintain national independence and to shake off the imperialist yoke. In the struggle against imperialism the masses, and above all the proletariat (i.e., the Communist party), were the most valiant fighters, but they could and should allow the struggle to be directed temporarily by the national bourgeoisie. But what happens the day after independence is won?

The Moscow theoreticians find it difficult to set up a typology because of the number of applicable criteria, even within the framework of their own system of thought. Seen from Moscow, an underdeveloped country can be classified according to:

   (a) its attitude toward the two blocs;
   (b) the class in power;
   (c) the status or position of the Communist party;
   (d) the technique of economic development it adopts, and its economic relations with the capitalist world.

For the Soviet theoreticians are guided primarily by their distinction between capitalist and noncapitalist roads to development after independence, without reverting to a simplistic contrast between total socialism (Communist party in power) and total capitalism (Communist party not in power). A system midway between these two has now been identified as National Democracy, whose principal characteristic seems to be, official nonalignment notwithstanding, a diplomacy relatively favorable to the Communist camp, coupled with revolutionary rhetoric embodying themes or phrases taken from the Communists. As of now three countries, Guinea, Ghana, and Mali, have been christened National Democracies; a fourth, Indonesia, has been admitted to the category with some reservations. These countries, or at least the first three, have a single, but not Communist, party; espouse a relatively pro-Soviet neutralism; and play down the role of the market economy and private ownership.

Thanks to this concept of National Democracy, the Soviets have divided underdeveloped countries into three categories:

(1) Independent countries ruled by the national bourgeoisie, in which capitalism is still the dominant influence;

(2) National Democracies that have only one party, espouse pro-Soviet neutralism, and operate planned economies;

(3) Communist countries.

Other writers have arrived at a more complicated classification composed of six types:*

(1) Relatively advanced capitalist countries, whose leaders come from the national bourgeoisie (India, Burma, Ceylon, Syria, Lebanon, Tunisia, Brazil, Mexico).

(2) Countries in which feudal forces continue to operate, capitalism is less developed, and the national bourgeoisie is weaker, but which have a neutralist policy and are struggling for their independence (Iraq, Morocco, Nigeria, Somalia, Sudan, Cambodia).

(3) Countries in which power is held by a reactionary bourgeoisie, often in alliance with great feudal landowners (the Philippines, Turkey, Malaysia, Thailand, Pakistan, many Latin American countries).

(4) Countries on a noncapitalist road to development (Ghana, Guinea, Mali, to some extent Indonesia).

(5) Countries under imperialist domination (former French West Africa, Madagascar, Congo-Leopoldville).

(6) Countries in a feudal state but having a neutralist policy (Nepal, Saudi Arabia, Ethiopia, Afghanistan, Yemen).

It is very likely that some countries will change categories, or may already have done so—owing to shifts in diplomacy or domestic conflicts. What interests us here is the efforts of Communist theorists to elaborate a typology that takes into account four variables—diplomatic orientation, class relationships, political institutions, economic institutions—and the implied admission that many combinations of these variables are possible.

In the same stroke the Communist theorists are resuming the dialogue, such as it is, with Western theorists. On both sides it has been necessary to admit one undeniable fact: If socialism is what the Communists say it is, and the Soviet system is the model, there is no parallel between development of the forces of production (or stages of economic growth, to

* I have taken this classification from an article by Robert F. Lamberg, in *Europa-Archiv 1963*, "Die marxistische-leninistische Theorie von den Entwicklungsländern: Wunschdenken und Verwirrung" (pp. 567–76).

use Western terminology) and the transition from capitalism to socialism. On both sides it has been necessary to acknowledge a second indis-
putable fact: The political systems of the underdeveloped countries are
numerous and diverse, and not all one-party systems are necessarily Communist. One regime that did join the socialist bloc (Cuba) was not established by a Communist party. A typology of the political systems of our
time must be based on combinations of many variables.

The Soviet theoreticians are semiparalyzed in their typological en-
deavors by their obligation to keep rediscovering, no matter what, Marxist-Leninist patterns. They continue to identify the proletariat (often
non-existent) with the Communist party, to use the term "feudal aristocracy" in a sense so vague that it ends up covering any conservative
class or group of large landowners. They assume that state capitalism or
planning is "progressive," refusing to accept certain kinds of evidence,
such as the fundamental difference between the single African parties,
like those of Guinea and Ghana—whatever their terminology—and the
Communist parties of the Soviet Union or Czechoslovakia. Nevertheless,
communication has been re-established, and two ways of interpreting
modern political systems are taking shape: one is that of the Communists, who maintain that the prime factor is the economic regime; the
other is the one popularized by W. W. Rostow, who takes as his point of
departure the phases of economic growth. Each of the two viewpoints
takes into account the other's prime variable. I do not know whether the
book *The Stages of Economic Growth* ought to be regarded as the *Non-
Communist Manifesto* of the twentieth century, but I do know that the
Communists look upon the currently fashionable Western theory of industrial society or theory of growth as a challenge to their own philosophy of history. The Marxists' disputes among themselves have culminated in disputes between Marxists and non-Marxists. Or should we say
between Eastern Marxists and Western Marxists? For is not Rostow's
*Non-Communist Manifesto* in a sense more Marxian, if not more Marxist, than its author suspects?

The confrontation between the Soviet and Western systems, between
those who call themselves socialists and those who do not like to be called
capitalists, has become one of the dominant themes of a historical sociology inspired simultaneously by Marx and Max Weber. A scientific confrontation and, at the same time, a political dialogue.

Indeed, each of these systems perceives and understands itself in the
light of one possible version of Marxism, and makes the other part of its
vision. If we assume that development of the forces of production is the
key factor, then the Western countries are at the forefront of historical

evolution. The Soviet countries must try to catch up with them, and the gap will be narrowed as the Soviet standard of living rises. On the other hand, the key determinant may be the regime—property ownership, regulation or planning, the class or party in power. By Marxist hypothesis, a system of proletarian rule and state planning constitutes "the avant-garde of humanity," to borrow Auguste Comte's formula. Of course, in the matter of per-capita output, this avant-garde will have to catch up with the country that is still a prisoner of capitalist exploitation. But at least wherever the capitalists and exploiters are eliminated, imperialism disappears as well, and the classes that remain will not be enemies.

Even if both these outlooks fit into a Marxist framework, they are not equivalent. In the last analysis, the Communist interpretation rejects the primacy of the forces of production, i.e., of the infrastructure or what is commonly known as the economy. Communism is *voluntarist* and *political*. Revolution depends on human action; seizure of power by the Party inaugurates a new era. Not that the class struggle suddenly ceases with the victory of the Communist party, but at least it changes in character. True, an Eastern Marxist could adopt the Westerner's simple idea that in the twentieth century underdevelopment favors revolution. But he hesitates to do so, because then how could he at the same time claim that the proletariat (very small, sometimes nonexistent) is the revolutionary class par excellence? How can one define the Party and socialism in terms of a class which does not exist, and which will be created only gradually with the building of socialism under the direction of a Communist party?

It is no less true that the Western Marxists' interpretation of the two types of system is equally unreconcilable with Marx's Marxism. A continuous development of the forces of production *without* paralysis of a system based on private ownership and competition obviously conflicts with one aspect of Marx's thought, the aspect the Marxists themselves have always considered fundamental. Even if we rule that the Soviet system is not socialist (because of insufficient development of the forces of production), the fact remains that there are different ways to accumulate the capital necessary for industrialization—it can be accomplished by entrepreneurs or by a party, by collectivizing agriculture and bleeding the peasants, or by allowing the peasants to own land and have a decent standard of living, etc.—and that the choice of method depends on a variety of circumstances, at times even on one man.

In other words, it is impossible fully to reconcile the Marxism of Marx with the course of twentieth-century history if we take authentic Marxism to include at least both a scheme of historical development and a method of analysis. As we have seen, in the absence of parallel development of the forces of production and succession of social systems, the Marxists, now pessimistic, now hopeful, waver between revolutionary voluntarism and resignation to the spontaneous course of historical evolution. ("Capitalism brings war as surely as storm clouds bring the storm." "Economic growth brings catastrophe—or abundance.") They subordinate the forces of production to the class struggle, or the class struggle to the forces of production; i.e., they accept in fact the primacy of political action, or the primacy of the forces of production; in one case they are technicians of revolution, in the other reformists.

If in one sense neither the Western nor the Soviet spokesmen, neither Khrushchev nor Rostow, are strictly faithful disciples of Marx, in another sense they are both Marxists. When in 1955–57 I gave the two courses that have since been published under the titles *Dix-huit leçons sur la société industrielle* and *La Lutte des classes,* a number of ex-Stalinists, disillusioned by the Twentieth Party Congress and the events in Hungary, seized on the theory of industrial society as a position from which they could rebound. Sovietism and capitalism, enemy brothers, resemble each other more than either admits. In the mid-twentieth century the major opposing forces were not different kinds of advanced economies, but advanced economies and underdeveloped economies—a thesis partly true, partly erroneous. Two industrialized societies belong to the same historical era; industrialized and unindustrialized societies belong to different eras; but the French society of 1950, incomparably less developed than the American, was nevertheless part of the same civilization, whereas Soviet society during the personality cult, in the Stalinist era, belonged to another world. The theory of industrial society is in danger of being spoiled by a vulgarized brand of Marxism that is now becoming fashionable. Playing down the differences between systems, explaining away Stalinism as a necessity of industrialization, predicting an inevitable rapprochement of Soviet and Western systems and the industrialization of the entire planet—all this is grist to the mill of vulgarized Marxism, or economism. But the lesson of our century is something entirely different.

A new era in human history has begun, or is about to begin. It matters little what date we give this technical or scientific revolution. In truth it might be better not to use the concept of revolution, which, despite the meaning it has had since the great French Revolution, still reflects something of its cosmological origins. The scientific revolution is not a moment in a cycle; it will not return, in a later phase, to its point of departure. It indicates a *mutation of society,* and not, as some would have it, a *mutation of man.* The mastery that man is in the process of gaining over the forces of nature is so superior to that of past societies that we are entitled to look upon the epoch that began in the sixteenth century, and is coming to fruition today as one long transition from historical societies to scientific societies. The nineteenth-century sociologists' perception of this prefigured the decisive awareness that dawned after the Second World War. But those who grasp the situation today are not prophesying, and know why they cannot do so.

Sociological insight at the beginning of the nineteenth century came in reaction to two major events: the French Revolution and the beginning of industrialization. Every sociologist tended to treat one of these events as essential, to stress its assets or liabilities, to extrapolate the remote future from one of the trends observed at the time, and to imagine its culmination in a positivist or socialist society. Even the probabilist thinkers like Herbert Spencer and Alexis de Tocqueville, who left it to the future to choose between systems—despotism or freedom, a free, commercial society or a controlled, authoritarian society—emphasized one variable and speculated on the outcome. We know, or ought to know, that the outcome is a beginning, the beginning of an unpredictable adventure. Society is not a *totality* ruled by one dominant variable. The so-called capitalist system is not adequately defined by its laws of property ownership, nor by its system of control. So-called capitalist societies are ruled neither by determinism nor by an objective dialectic whose movement is determined exclusively by economic contradiction. No society, no epoch, constitutes a unified entity that can be summarized in terms of one cause, one value. Sociological and historical pluralism is not a confession of ignorance, but a recognition of the true structure of the sociohistoric world.

The relationship between the art, science, politics, and economics of a society can be considered dialectical, but this relationship, while perceptible after the fact, can rarely be predicted in advance. The power over nature that science gives societies neither rules out nor rules in irreligion. It does not remove the "agony of choice" between modes of property ownership and regulation of the economy, any more than it puts an end to politics, i.e., to the authority of the few (inevitable and never fully justified), or to rivalries within and between states. The philosophies of history based upon an all-inclusive determinism are not indemonstrable. They are false. Whether or not one believes in man's metaphysical freedom, the fact is that historical man does appear to be free. In each of his specific activities he is subject to the obligations of that practical or intellectual world which he has chosen to enter. The scholar, as scholar, is not a slave of society, and he is free to seek the truth. The state of the forces of production is not, in itself, a sufficient cause of any specific political or even economic system. Conversely, given an economic system (laws of property ownership, system of control), we cannot deduce with any certainty either its political system or its human relationships—i.e., the degree of exploitation or oppression. Finally, any social order *inevitably* confers on one man or several an absolutely disproportionate power over the destinies of his or their fellows. One can always say that Hitler was an expression of German monopoly capitalism, but if Hitler had been killed in the First World War, would a different expression of this same capitalism have behaved in the same way? Would he, too, have committed genocide?

In reflecting upon his condition, man is tempted to be, by turns, proud and afraid of such indetermination. The freedom of the artist or scientist is our pride; the freedom of the political man means subservience to the constraints of action. The indeterminateness of the system sets limits to rationalization and bureaucracy. It makes the rivalry between parties and ideas meaningful. It makes it impossible to mistake social rationalization for historical Reason. It leaves men collectively and individually responsible for their own destiny, but this responsibility, being every man's, is no man's. The role of mass leaders in our century—of Lenin, Hitler, Stalin, Churchill—elates the adventurer and terrifies the sage. Is it possible for one man, one man alone, to do great good or great evil in certain circumstances? And if tomorrow there be other heroes of the same stature, they will have thermonuclear bombs at their disposal.

The theory of the stages of economic growth, a kind of Western Marxism, does not always avoid the pitfalls of vulgarized Marxism. By what right does one consign all unindustrialized societies to the same category—the traditionalist societies of the Central African tribes, for example, along with China, the oldest empire in history? Do the stages of economic growth offer a much more satisfactory schema than the succession of social systems—when corresponding "stages" can be, and are, reached in one place by nineteenth-century methods, in another place by twentieth-century methods; in one by a system of free enterprise, in another by a system of state planning? Is it right to postulate or suggest that different systems become alike once they have reached the same stage of growth? As if relative opulence can mean only one way of life, as if comfort were sufficient to gratify all human aspirations and to end all ideological and class conflicts. Is not dollar diplomacy, too, which has given birth to takeoff-point diplomacy, based on the simple notion that underdevelopment breeds Communism, and hence economic aid is the answer to the threat of revolution?

If the West has not been impervious to the seductions of Marxism, the Third World is the scene of its greatest triumphs. In Italy and France a fraction of the working class and a number of intellectuals see the world through the distorting lenses of Marxism. Twenty-five years ago Daniel Villey wrote that it was Marx's genius to have guessed the feelings of the proletariat, and to have worked out in advance a spontaneous philosophy for it to adopt. Historical experience moves us to modify this formula. The working classes are not Marxist either in the advanced Anglo-Saxon or Scandinavian countries or in a number of underdeveloped countries in which factory workers enjoy a semiprivileged status in relation to the peasant masses. Even in the Latin countries, where slow development and political and religious traditions have favored it, Marxism seems to decline as the standard of living rises and the economy expands. By contrast, intellectuals in the Latin countries, and even more those in the countries of the Third World, have not lost their attachment to Marxism, and above all to Marxism-Leninism; because Marxism, supplemented by Lenin's theory of imperialism, enables them to understand both exploitation in the colonies and widespread prosperity in the industrialized mother countries, to establish a link between these two phenomena. In fine, the essence of capitalism is seen not in American or European prosperity, but in the mass misery of Algeria, India, and Brazil.

There is indeed a kind of moral affinity (*Wahlverwandschaft*) between the passions of the Third World's intellectuals and Marxism-Leninism. The image projected by capitalism in countries colonized or dominated by big companies, or by white minorities established on conquered territory, does resemble in many respects Marx's general picture of capitalism. Moreover, Lenin's idea that capitalism *necessarily* leads to imperialism, or could not exist without foreign markets and excess profits from colonies—and on this point he reverses Hobson's thesis, to which he owes so much in other respects—is readily accepted by intellectuals whose own homeland is poor and weak. Thereafter they can attribute their poverty and weakness to their old masters, who have waxed rich and strong at the expense of those they oppressed and exploited. From this point of view the misery of the Third World is a direct result of the West's prosperity, for which it was first the indispensable prerequisite.

In this simplified form, the theory is false. Capitalism can grow in intensity. The mother countries which have lost their empires continue to grow richer. Right-wing decolonizers have learned the cost of domination, and prefer to keep their investment capital at home. To prove that the industrialized countries of the northern hemisphere are today exploiting the underdeveloped countries of the southern hemisphere, one must now resort to subtler arguments: the terms of trade, for example, or the disparity between the prices of raw materials and the prices of finished industrial products. But it is still true that, in the past, colonial exploitation could have contributed to European industrialization, and probably did in certain cases, and that when they withdrew, the colonizers more often than not left the territories they had ruled over in an underdeveloped state.

But with the introduction of a third participant in the Marxist dialogue between East and West we have come to the fifth and final period, that of the second Great Schism, not between the Second and Third International, not between Social Democrats and Bolsheviks, but between Russians and Chinese—or should we say between the Third and Fifth International, between the new revolutionaries and the new revisionists?

## The Present Phase

The debate between the Seventh Floor of the State Department and the Kremlin is semiclandestine, semipublic. Which of the two systems, the Soviet or the Western, will grow more like its rival? Which interpretation of history will ultimately be borne out by history? The interpretation that sees Communism as a harsh method of industrialization useful in underdeveloped countries? Or the one that heralds the extension of Soviet socialism to the entire world, even though it first appeared in an unindustrialized country? Will Communism grow bourgeois, and state planning more flexible? Will both systems be transformed simultaneously, each one influencing the other by its very existence? Will the dialectic of hostility and imitation continue until the two systems finally become identical, or will there be no ultimate resolution, merely unending interaction?

The Chinese are disrupting this dialogue even as it is becoming more amicable. Though the polemics between Moscow and Peking, like all polemics between Bolsheviks, follow specific rules that make them difficult to interpret, one can guess some of the new issues at stake in the debate between Marxist-Leninists (and not, as in the earlier stages, between Marxists). The first is the Chinese accusation that the Soviet Union was becoming bourgeois. Khrushchev freely admitted that good goulash is no detriment to socialism, and that a pair of substantial leather shoes is much more desirable than wooden ones. Such goals are surely not unbefitting a Marxist. When all is said and done, Marxism was betting on the abundance that capitalist development of the forces of production would make possible. In an oft-quoted passage in *The German Ideology* Marx himself says that if there is still poverty in the days following the revolution, "the same vile business will start up again." The accumulation of means of production cannot be, in itself, the end of socialism; it is but a means.

When capitalist regimes are in power, prosperity is a threat to Marxism because it is likely to snuff out the revolutionary ardor of the masses; in a subtler sense, it is also a threat to Communist regimes in power. First, different Communist countries are at very different stages of development. Should not the more advanced countries come to the aid of the less favored? Is it right for some to harvest the fruit of their labors while others are still in the throes of capital accumulation? What obligations accompany the brotherhood that Communist parties never cease proclaiming?

More serious still, the unequal development and hence unequal living standards of the Communist countries irresistibly suggest an interpretation of history that is more in keeping with Western Marxism than with Eastern, more with Rostow's than with the Kremlin's. If a country's living conditions depend not on the system but on the value of per-capita output, a competition in growth rates replaces the implacable struggle between systems. Whoever wins the competition, victory can only be very relative. The victor is merely *going faster* than the vanquished; there has been no contest between good and evil.

And that is not all. For the "building of socialism" to mean something more than a mere increase in production it has to retain some human or moral significance. Authentic socialism requires socialist men. Neither Marx nor Lenin ever said what the New, or Socialist, Man would be like. It is certain, though, that this man was not to resemble the man found in a bourgeois society. Now, there is nothing to indicate that Soviet youth, enjoying social privileges, are any less eager than Western youth for the goods industrial civilization has to offer: comfort, cars, dachas. Not that there are not Komsomols ready to make sacrifices for a noble cause; there are. But the United States also finds volunteers for the Peace Corps by the thousand.

The disabused observer will reply that revolutionary faith does not stand up well under the wear and tear of time, that the utter impersonality of human relations at work and in everyday life needs to be offset by the intimacy of the family circle and leads to a kind of individualism or family-centered selfishness. Perhaps that is the destiny of modern societies. But this transformation, however inevitable, does lend weight to the charge of "embourgeoisement" brought by the brother parties, who are still very close to their revolution, very fervent, and very puritanical— puritanical because of their fervor, and also, perhaps, because of their poverty. They cannot conceive of socialism outside the discipline of collective organization, and they look with suspicion upon the first signs of relative prosperity in the Soviet Union, a prosperity that is qualitatively less different from the West's than ideologues may have wished.

Did Khrushchev deserve to be called a revisionist, a term first applied to Bernstein and since then always used by Marxists in a pejorative sense? The situation in 1965 is so different from that of 1900, one might simply dismiss the question. Bernstein observed that capitalism was not conforming to Marxist predictions, and from this drew certain inferences. Concerning socialism there are no Marxist predictions that events might disprove, and therefore one cannot accuse Khrushchev of noting such contradictions and drawing conclusions from them. Still, it is not impossible to see an analogy between the denunciation of Bernsteinian revisionism by orthodox Marxists at the beginning of the century and the denunciation of Khrushchevian revisionism by the Chinese more than half a century later.

First of all, one Marxist is always the revisionist of another Marxist. An ideological movement inevitably involves a right and a left; the left thinks it alone is faithful to the inspiration of the prophet and accuses the right of betrayal. In Kautsky's eyes, Bernstein was a revisionist. Kautsky in turn became a revisionist, and even a renegade, when he refused to see the October Revolution as the first step on the road to the millennium. In Trotsky's eyes, Stalin himself, the proponent of "socialism in one country," was a "Thermidorian," i.e., a traitor to the revolution. How could Khrushchev, if he took his two theses of peaceful coexistence and buttered bread seriously, seem like anything but a revisionist to the dour, pure Chinese?

The analogy, it seems to me, goes further still. Khrushchev discovered the impossibility of keeping alive revolutionary tension in a stabilizing Communist regime, just as Bernstein recognized the impossibility of keeping alive revolutionary tension in a so-called proletarian party under a progressive capitalist regime. The Chinese were able to accept certain elements of de-Stalinization the more easily because they resorted to subtler governing procedures and did not have the equivalent of concentration camps and the Great Purge. But de-Stalinization has gradually brought with it seeds of liberalism and the (still timid) adaptation of certain Western techniques of managing an economy.

Here again, one cannot say that the Chinese are orthodox and the Russians revisionists. Marx had the temperament of a rebel, and unless he himself held power, it is hard to imagine him subjecting his thought and pen to the orders of any state, even a state that called itself Marxist. He

wanted to go beyond formal freedoms, while preserving them. Khrushchevian liberalism, however, was still very relative. The right, or rather
duty, of the Party to direct intellectual and artistic life, to make writers
and artists bow to the exigencies of politics, was not called into question.
Ideological coexistence was rigorously condemned, which means that
Communist ideology was true, endowed with Universal Truth, and that
so-called bourgeois ideologies were radically wrong. In spite of everything, Khrushchev's Russia was opening its doors to Western influences,
and, compared to Stalin's Russia, might have seemed liberal. Far from
permeating everyday life and shaping men's minds, the doctrine, still the
official state truth, degenerated into an "ideology" (in the derogatory
sense in which Marx used the term). A conscious or unconscious justification for reality, Marxism was less the basis for an ideocracy than the
camouflage for a satisfied bureaucracy.

And this bureaucracy, concerned for rationality, moved further and
further away from the primitive methods used in earlier stages of planning. After making progress between 1953 and 1958, agriculture brought
new disappointments each year to the leaders in the Kremlin. Culti-
vation of the virgin lands of Central Asia proved a costly error. Despite
all the reforms, centralized authoritarian planning was running into ever-
greater difficulties. All the European Communist countries, not only the
Soviet Union, are openly debating the reforms necessitated by the increasing complexity of an advanced economy. Now, these reforms can be
labeled "revisionist" if we are agreed that a system is socialist only to the
extent that planning is centralized and authoritarian. Indeed, most of
the reforms being contemplated do entail borrowings from the market
economy, or from the spirit of such an economy: restoration of a margin
of free decision to the heads of enterprises; abandonment of arbitrary
price-fixing by the authorities, with consideration to be given the relative
scarcity of a product; more widespread use of interest; possible replacement of quantitative indicators with a profit indicator, as the more daring
reformers have suggested. All these measures, whether adopted or under
discussion, are steps toward rationalization in the eyes of the economists;
to the ideologues, they may seem, and should seem, tainted with revisionism.

I have no doubt that the Chinese will be disposed to take every bit as
much liberty with dogma as the Russians are now doing should the need
arise. The fact is that because of the difference in the levels of development of the Communist economies (if one may be allowed to apply to
the Communist world the law that Lenin formulated for the capitalist
world), the Russians and Chinese are pursuing different policies. But,

unable to refrain from putting in ideological terms practices that arise more from circumstance than from doctrine, they accuse each other of deviation. Having criticized the Communes and the Great Leap Forward, the Russians inevitably appear as opportunists to the Chinese. The latter, by the implacable logic of dialectics, are dogmatists in the eyes of the Russians.

I do not claim, of course, that ideological debates are *the cause* of the split between Peking and Moscow. Perhaps it is a classical conflict between the interests of two great powers. Perhaps the Soviet Union, like Holy Mother Russia, fears the Chinese masses, "miserable and innumerable." Perhaps the territorial ambitions of Communist China have disturbed the men in Moscow. Or maybe the experience, in 1958, of the Chinese military operations in the Formosa Strait have made the Russians fear that the brother party will drag them into conflict with the United States. The preceding pages do not attempt any historical explanation of the Sino-Soviet quarrel. In keeping with the aim of this study, they attempt to interpret debates between Marxists, debates which give expression to the dialectic of a historical doctrine at grips with history itself.

We have not yet mentioned what the leading contenders consider the essential issue: world revolution. Did Khrushchev take no interest in the spread of socialism, as the Chinese claim? Was he more interested in an accommodation with the imperialists (i.e., with the United States of America) than in supporting wars of national liberation (which in Western language means attempts by Communist parties to come to power by force)? The Russians have replied that the Chinese are ready to set fire to the world, to unleash a thermonuclear war in which hundreds of millions of men would perish, whereas they themselves refuse to sacrifice the living to the dream of a socialist civilization to rise upon the ruins of an atom-smashed universe. We have no ground for imputing any intention of war to Mao Tse-tung. Peking's diplomacy, moreover, has never been imprudent, and several years ago the official truth in Moscow was that a nuclear war would bury capitalism, not civilization.

The Sino-Soviet quarrel really repeats within the Communist world the Second International's experience in the capitalist world. Whether in opposition or in power, the workers, the Communists, the proletarian parties, all have a homeland, a country. The Communists are no exception. By dint of his omnipotence, Stalin succeeded for several years in maintaining the appearance of a monolithic Soviet bloc (although he could not prevent the defection of Yugoslavia). China was too big and too proud to take Moscow's word as law. Stalin's successors did not have sufficient prestige to impose their will without recourse to force. De-Stalinization dealt a death blow to the myth of Party infallibility (especially Bolshevik infallibility). In Europe, Rumania is refusing to abide by Comecon's directives; Albania is siding with Peking—mainly, it would seem, to keep Moscow at arm's length. The parties are "brothers," but each one wants to have as much autonomy as possible. Everything suggests that Communism cannot avoid becoming national even though Communists may continue to invoke the universal truth of Marxism-Leninism.

Whether it be a matter of defining common policy toward the imperialist enemy or of reconciling the different economic interests of the different members of the bloc, the Communist countries do not get much help from the doctrine that theoretically unites them. And perhaps the invocation of an ideology makes common action even more difficult. That the Chinese are prepared to take greater risks than the Russians in supporting wars of national liberation may be true. In the absence of ideology divergent strategic assessments would not generate so much passion. That the Russians wanted to preserve their monopoly on atomic weapons in the Communist camp, as the Americans did in the Western camp, is perfectly understandable. But countries calling themselves brothers cannot confess their selfishness; they must hide it under ideological formulas. Agreeing to disagree is easier for countries that are not bound by a common ideology.

What will be the impact of this polymorphic, polycentric Communism on the outside world? (I am assuming that Khrushchev's successors, even if they avoid a total break with Communist China, will not restore the unity of the Communist world.) I would hesitate to make categorical judgments on this point.

In the prosperous West, the Communist parties, especially the Italian Party, which is less sclerotic than the French Party, will benefit from the autonomy fostered by the decline of Moscow's authority. Instead of being a kind of closed countersociety within Western society, the Communist parties will probably try to become revolutionary once again, by playing the reform game. The French Party, crystallized in its conservatism as though it had been in power for forty years, *may*, under pressure and constraint, break out of the Stalinist prison it has locked itself into. The Italian Party may follow the Nenni Socialists' example. "Popular Front" may be the next watchword. The European Communists have everything to gain from super-Khrushchevism, from increasing "nationalization" of their parties, in the service of a theoretically universal truth.

Of course, the same disintegration of the Communist bloc that on the

political level gives the Communist parties a chance in the West is a blow
to the power of the Soviet camp. The ideology will probably seem less
convincing, less compelling, when it has multiple versions. But this assumption has yet to be proved. Religions did not cease to spread once
they broke up into rival churches. Castro was not a Communist when he
seized power, and today his relation to Moscow and Peking is more that
of head of an autocephalous church than faithful worshiper at either of
their churches. Other autocephalous regimes may appear in the Third
World tomorrow. From now on, we shall have Communism without
obedience to Moscow. The diplomatic scene will grow more and more
complicated, and diplomats will pine for the good old days when the
confrontation of just two blocs made it easy to distinguish between
friends and enemies.

This story, like all true stories, is unfinished. It has no ending, no conclusion, but this does not proscribe all forward and backward glances.

It would be quite pointless to ask ourselves whether Marx, who near
the end of his life was already saying that he was not a Marxist, would
or would not be a Marxist-Leninist today. We shall never know. A
thinker, especially one like Marx, a philosopher of history, is bound too
tightly to the problems, ideas, and values of his own time to be transfer-
able to a different epoch, even as a game, without loss of his essential
being, of that which made him what he was. Having rebelled against the
cruelties of capital accumulation at the beginning of the nineteenth century, would Marx have turned his rebellion against the bureaucrats of
the Kremlin or the magnates of American corporations a century later?
Would he have looked around in the Third World, like so many of his
disciples, for opportunities to reanimate his indignation? In any case,
he would have found it difficult to accomplish now his feat of one hundred years ago: today capitalism acclaims those who condemn it. His
books would be translated into all languages, and would be best sellers
or cause a scandal—which amounts to the same thing—and would com-
mend him to the attention of the Swedish Academy.

Nor is it possible to assess Marx's share of the responsibility for the way
Marxism has turned out. No one will ever know what the Russian Revolution would have been like in the absence of Marx's ideas. A revolution
of some kind had become probable, at least when bourgeois Europe
started to destroy itself in a war to the death. But would it have followed
the same course if its leaders had not believed that they were the proletariat incarnate, that they were the avant-garde of world socialism? Or
are we to assume that the revolutionaries would somehow or other have

found or thought up a doctrine to justify their actions? Logically, all things considered, Marxism should have deflected the Bolsheviks from the road that they took in 1917. As it was interpreted before 1917, Marxism suggested that it would be impossible to establish socialism in a country like Russia, which had not yet passed through the stage of capitalist industrialization. In this sense one can say that the Bolsheviks took power and built their allegedly socialist system *in spite of their doctrine.* Other Marxists, the Mensheviks, had warned that an attempt to establish socialism in a country in which most of the population worked in agriculture would result in fifty years of despotism. Events proved them right, but did not save them from defeat and exile. True, most of the Bolshevik leaders themselves became the victims of their victory, and rather quickly.

The Mensheviks were not the only ones whose perception was unavailing. In our century Marxists have frequently fought and won, but they have rarely accomplished what they set out to do. Rarely have men who claimed to act in accordance with a science of history been so surprised by the consequences of their deeds—consequences foretold with great precision by other Marxists. Trotsky had foreseen where democratic centralism would lead. From time to time Lenin, but most often the Mensheviks, foresaw the consequences of an attempt to establish socialism in a predominantly agrarian country. Bukharin had foreseen the consequences of forced industrialization at the expense of collectivized peasants. But what they all failed to foresee was the capacity for progress and self-renewal of the system they have persisted in calling capitalism. Nor did they foresee the demoniac power of a minority determined to stop at nothing. Democratic socialism was built by workers' parties that had been converted from Marxism to pragmatism, whereas no socialist regime built by Communists has yet emerged from totalitarianism.

The lesson should be clear to all who prefer men to ideas, dialogue to violence. But experience proves that it is not. One reason for this is underdevelopment. In countries that lack an entrepreneurial class and an effective government apparatus, thanks to the resistance of the privileged classes, the Bolshevik technique, the mobilization of an entire people by one party in the name of an ideology, seems the only way. But this practical reason is not the only one. Though on the historical plane it is the most important, on the plane of ideas it is secondary. Marxism à la Rostow has no trouble taking into account the Communism of the underdeveloped countries. What is interesting is the obstinacy with which superior minds in the West retain their faith in Marxism. I am thinking of Jean-Paul Sartre, whose case is not unique. Others, too, like Herbert

Marcuse, are apparently beyond cure of the Marxism contracted in their youth. True, it will be objected that Sartre himself has no great love for what Marxism has become. "Marxism has come to a standstill. Precisely because this philosophy wants to change the world, because it is addressed to a Becoming (a philosophical realm), because it is and is intended to be *practical,* a real schism has occurred within it, with the result that theory is rejected on the one hand, action on the other.... The result of the separation of theory and practice was the transformation of the latter into empiricism without principle, the former into pure, congealed knowing.... Marxism, as a philosophical interpretation of man and history, necessarily had to reflect an unquestioning commitment to planning; this fixed image of idealism and violence did idealistic violence to the facts. For years the Marxist intellectual believed that he was serving his party by distorting experience, by overlooking embarrassing details, by grossly oversimplifying data, and above all by conceptualizing an event before he had studied it."[*] Since 1917 the Communists have contributed nothing, or next to nothing, to the humanities and social sciences. Some Marxists, who have at times submitted to orthodoxy and at times broken out of their confinement, have made a modest contribution.

Sartre immediately adds, of course, that Marxism is, nevertheless, the unsurpassable truth of our time. "Marxism's arteriosclerosis is not the result of normal aging. It is caused by a peculiar world situation. Far from being worn out, Marxism is still very young, almost a child. It has barely started to develop. It is therefore still the philosophy of our time. It is unsurpassable, because we have not yet passed beyond the circumstances that created it. Our thoughts, whatever they are, can take shape only upon this humus. They must be contained within the framework it provides, or be lost in a vacuum, or retrogress."[†] I shall not discuss the basically Hegelian idea that one philosophy, and only one, dominates an epoch because it both summarizes its wisdom and expresses its being and will. Applied to Marxism in our time, this is really absurd. To agree with Garaudy, as Sartre does, that "Marxism today is the only system of coordinates that enables one to place and define a thought in any realm whatever, from economics to physics, from history to morals," is simple delirium, whether conscious or not. Neither Marx's Marxism nor the Marxism of the Communists in Moscow or Peking makes it possible to synthesize a universe of knowledge by now grown so rich that it defies any hope of synthesis. Encyclopedic minds no longer exist and, regardless

[*] *Critique de la raison dialectique,* pp. 25–26.
[†] *Ibid.,* p. 29.

of the school they belong to, philosophers cannot possibly encompass the whole of contemporary culture.

What Sartre's formulas come down to is that he thinks of Marxism as a *philosophy*, not as a *science*, even though it was Marx's purpose to elaborate a *scientific* analysis of capitalism. What Marx meant by science is certainly debatable. Let us grant that the term has kept something of its Hegelian meaning. The Marxist science of capitalism does not claim to be an operational science. It claims to be total yet objective, critical yet analytical. Marx gave his *Das Kapital* the subtitle *Kritik der politischen Ökonomie* because he believed that in going back from price to value he was grasping essential phenomena and the inner law of the system, and at the same time exposing what he considered the crippling illusions of bourgeois economists.

Sartre has given up referring to Marxism as a science, the more so because of the horror in which he holds the scientism of Engels and his disciples. He has christened it a philosophy. But, having brushed aside what serves as philosophy for the Marxists, i.e., the—to say the least—rough speculations of the *Anti-Dühring,* the unsurpassable philosophy of Marxism he is left with is nothing but vague general propositions such as, "The essential discovery of Marxism is that labor, as a historical reality and as the utilization of specific tools in a predetermined social and material environment, is the real foundation of organized social relations."* Or, "Men make their history themselves, but in a given environment, which conditions them."† Or, "The material mode of production generally dominates the development of social, political, and intellectual life."‡ Such propositions, each of which calls for extensive criticism, hardly amount to an unsurpassable philosophy. Where, then, in the final analysis, is this unsurpassable philosophy, if we knock out both the speculation of the *Anti-Dühring* and the vague primacy of labor and economic relations? There is a third kind of text that may reveal the secret. "Any formal remarks," writes Sartre, "cannot, of course, begin to add *anything at all* to the clarity of the synthetic reconstruction of Marx's *Das Kapital*. They cannot even begin to be a marginal commentary on it. Indeed, by its clarity that reconstruction rejects all commentary."§ Now, at last, we have it. The unsurpassable Marxism is, on the one hand, the anthropology of man, who creates himself in the course of time through labor and the class struggle; on the other hand, it is a synthetic reconstruction of capitalism, i.e., a total interpretation of modern society,

---

* *Ibid.,* p. 225.                     ‡ *Ibid.,* p. 31.
† *Ibid.,* p. 60.                       § *Ibid.,* p. 376.

containing a critique of what is and an announcement of what will be. A synthetic and at the same time critical science of the present, inspired by atheism and a will to universality: this is the "unsurpassable Marxism" of which Sartre could make existentialism the foundation. What Western Marxists have been unwilling to forgo is, precisely, a philosophy of history that would present itself as a science and that would make what should be and what will be emerge from what is.

The synthetic reconstruction of capitalism attempted by Marx with the conceptual instruments available to him is hopelessly outdated. His historical scheme no longer works, unless we add so many qualifying assumptions that it loses all meaning. In short, the economic and sociological theory of capitalism, which from his thirtieth year he regarded as the essence of his work, has not escaped the common fate of all learned works. It is still a monument, but it has been surpassed, because knowledge progresses and history continues. Hence those who, in spite of everything, still call themselves Marxists, without identifying Marxism with the catechism of Moscow, Peking, Belgrade, or Havana, can only choose between equally precarious solutions. One group travels in the opposite direction over the road that led Marx from the Hegelian left to economics and returns to his early writings, discovering in them an unsurpassable philosophy, though Marx thought he had surpassed it by 1848. The others cling passively to the letter of *Das Kapital,* and in doing so are comparable to biologists who would explain evolution as Darwin did, paying no attention to genetics and mutations, or physicists who would reject relativity, quantum theory, or microphysics.

Indeed Marxism, which seems sclerotic and unsurpassable to Sartre, seems to me both surpassed and alive. Perhaps we are not capable of writing *Das Kapital* in the twentieth century because we have lost the ambition for a synthetic and critical reconstruction of modern society— or the illusion that such reconstruction is possible. But on the fringe of state orthodoxies and vain ratiocinations we have not given up trying to understand man's condition in history and the meaning of modern societies. After 1848 Marx believed that the true way to philosophize was to know the social world in order to change it. Strange Marxists, those who discourse upon alienation or try to change the world without knowing it.

# Leninism

The term Marxism-Leninism, coined after Lenin's death, implied an apostolic succession: from Marx to Lenin to Stalin. Leninism was "the only Marxism of the period of imperialism, proletarian revolution, and the construction of socialism." By virtue of these three defining terms, Lenin was not only the orthodox twentieth-century heir and apostolic successor of Marx, but also the creative extender of Marxism, the applier of its scientific doctrine to the new situations of monopoly capitalism, world war, proletarian revolution, proletarian dictatorship, the soviet system, the building of a socialist order, international Communism, and developing world revolution. That is how Lenin was portrayed by his successors. His opponents, on the other hand, claimed that there was little or no Marxism in Lenin: he was a Blanquist, a Bakuninist, a latter-day Jacobin, or a disciple of Tkachev and Nechaev, but certainly no Marxist.

As for Lenin himself, he honestly accounted himself an orthodox Marxist. He read and reread the works of Marx with seriousness and passion. At every difficult turn and with each new problem or contro-versy, in the words of Krupskaya, "Ilyich consulted Marx." To be sure, an actual word count of quotations would show that he cited Engels much more often than Marx, but he regarded the writings of Engels as a consubstantial part of the sacred canon of Marxism. In any case, he was not aware of any serious differences in the conceptions of Marx and Engels, such as those that have since been suggested by such Marx-ists or Marxicologists as Korsch, Hook, Rubel, and Lichtheim. To Lenin's simple faith, every utterance of either was sacred. That this was no mere tactical pretense is proved by passages in letters to Inessa Armand, which were never intended for publication. Inessa, it seems, had discovered important differences between Engels and, if not the Marx of 1848, at any rate the Lenin of "1848 Marxism," whose ardent disciple she was. In a series of letters written to her in December 1916 and January 1917, Lenin defends Engels against her strictures:

"Engels was right," he says in December. "In my time I have been pained to see many accusations charging Engels with opportunism, and my attitude is skeptical in the extreme. . . . Try, say I, just once to prove that Engels was wrong! ! You will never be able to." In January he adds: "Engels was the father of passive radicalism? ? Not true! Not at all. This you will never be able to show." And again: "I am still 'in love' with Marx and Engels, and will not tolerate in silence any slander against them. No, these are real people! From them we must learn. From *this* ground we must not depart."[1]

## Three Traits of Lenin's Character

Before we go into the kind of Marxism this "love" engendered, it might be well to take note of certain aspects of Lenin's personality. The more I deal with intellectual history, the more I have been forced to conclude that when we study ideas that have moved men, we must consider the character traits of their creators. "What matters," Sir Lewis Namier once wrote of political ideas, "is the underlying emotions, the music to which the ideas are the mere libretto." Certain of Lenin's character traits, insofar as they determined the substance and intensity of his doctrines, will emerge as we consider the doctrines' constituent parts. But here I should like to distinguish three traits that permeate his whole system of thought: his "selflessness," his struggle with his own nature, and his rages.

Elsewhere I have described Lenin as a "selfless egoist." His selflessness has been commented on and stressed by virtually all who have written on him. We never catch him glancing at himself in the mirror of history. His work contains almost no personal autobiography or overt expression of personal feelings and sentiments. He was selfless, too, in the sense that he sought neither the perquisites and privileges nor the cult of adoration that often go with the sort of absolute power he achieved. "To be completely acquitted of egoism by the generality," Bertrand de Jouvenel has written, "rulers need only affect a studied austerity and a strict economy. As if the pleasures of authority were not quite other."[2] In Lenin's case, it should be added, the austerity was natural and not "studied."

But this selflessness was only the outer shell. At the core of Lenin's spirit was an abnormally powerful and unquestioning belief in him-

---

[1] Numbered notes will be found at the back of the book, pp. 275–93.

self and his destiny, an absolute certitude that he was the best and virtually the only true master and exponent of an infallible science called
Marxism. On the inside cover of I. E. Nizhegorodsky's *Sotsializm i
Khristyanstvo,* Lenin wrote for his own eyes: "Out of every hundred
Bolsheviks, seventy are fools and twenty-nine rogues, and only one a
real socialist." And in his *Philosophical Notebooks,* also written for his
own eyes, he set it down that "After a half century, not a single Marxist
has understood Marx!" It is self-evident that he regarded himself as
the one exception.

Accompanying this belief in himself and his destiny was a certitude
of his rightness in every controversy, large or small, a tendency to make
the rejection of his viewpoint in the least of them a pundonor, a splitting
point. Whether it was over the definition of a member of the party, or
a controversy over boycotting elections, a matter of recalling or giving
ultimatums to dubious Duma Deputies, or any one of a score or more
of differences, he was always sure that just this difference was the test
dividing the saved from the damned, and he was always ready for a
split on it. If he changed his mind after he had rallied the faithful on
the point in question, he was just as ready to excommunicate them for
repeating his arguments of the previous day.

This quarrelsome belief in himself and his destiny seemed the more
selfless because he was scarcely conscious of it, never felt the need to
argue for it or demonstrate it, always presented his views not as personal ones but as the only possible, the only correct ones. He almost
seemed averse to using the first person pronoun at all. When he spoke,
it was Marxism, Science, or History that spoke, or it was the party, the
working class, or the "majority," that was issuing the only possible, the
only correct, formulation for the occasion. From this belief followed
the conviction that he must have authority and power in whatever
sphere he happened to be operating: power in the *troika,* the Editorial
Board, the Central Committee, the Party; power in Russia; power in
the international Communist movement. He was not merely ready to
split any organization on any difference that he had come to think important; he was ready to split and discredit and wreck every organization he could not control. He was not vengeful like Stalin; he would
say the most outrageous things to discredit a yesterday's follower who
opposed him, but if the man gave in and repented, he would do his
best to salvage his standing and self-esteem by having him present to
the party the viewpoint of which Lenin had just convinced him.

Thus in 1913, after the vile things he had written of the Vperyodist
Bolsheviks, when he saw a chance of reconciliation he wrote to Gorky:

"Have they understood that *Marxism* is more serious and deeper than they had thought ... ? *If* they have understood—then a thousand greetings to them, and everything personal (such as is inevitably brought in in a sharp struggle) will vanish in a minute. Well, and if they haven't understood, nor learned ... then friendship is friendship and duty duty. Against any attempt to revile Marxism or confuse the policy of the workers' party, we will fight without sparing life itself."[3]

In the same fashion, at a Party Court of Honor where he was on trial for slandering his own comrades in public, Lenin admitted that he had chosen "obnoxious" phrases, "calculated to evoke ... hatred, aversion, contempt ... calculated not to convince but to break up the ranks of the opponent, not to correct the mistake of the opponent but destroy him, to wipe his organization off the face of the earth." His excuse? He thought that the difference on how to nominate candidates for Duma Deputy would become a splitting point. Since he expected a split, that meant war, and in war one acted as if one were at war: "and *I shall always act in that way whenever a split occurs* ... in the event of the development of a split *I shall always conduct* a war of extermination."[4]

It must be added that when Lenin said "extermination" he meant it, and saw nothing wrong in it. When the occasion came, he carried out his pledge in full.

Yet Lenin's character was not so simple and all of one piece as it has been portrayed by those who saw him only after his dogmas, his splits, his passions, his shibboleths, had been legitimated by the bitch goddess, Success, and only after the extent of his aims, destructiveness, and power and his great influence on the history of our time had distorted our view of him.

If we look at Lenin as he seemed to his intimates, comrades, and friends before he came to power, we see a quite different picture: a man at war with himself and all those who were close to him. To Rosa Luxemburg his attitude toward the working class was that of a "night watchman," an "overseer," a distrustful, dictatorial, quarrelsome, divisive sectarian. To the young Trotsky he was a natural autocrat and despot, a man inclined to rule only by terror and a permanent state of siege. Victor Adler thought he was "crazy," when he listened to him on Russian quarrels. August Bebel, whom Lenin deeply admired, "looked daggers" at him in congresses of the International and conferences intended to bring about socialist unity in Russia. Angelica Balabanoff thought that he was not interested in the masses or in socialism, but only in his own "chess moves."[5]

Nor do we have to limit ourselves to Lenin's critics. Krupskaya's hagiographical *Memories of Lenin* is full of evidence of his "nerviness," breakdowns after controversies with his opponents or his own followers, sleeplessness, restlessness, rages, quarrels, characteristic cycles of extreme tension ("rage") followed by prolonged depression, weeks of complete nervous or mental exhaustion when he could do nothing but doze. Her memoirs show his detailed and systematic quarrelsomeness and at the same time his detestation of the exile quarrels of which he himself was the chief fomenter; his inability to find occupation each night after the library closed in whatever city he was living; his search for relief by going to plays only to find that he could not bear to sit through them; his inability to comprehend or take interest in the world around him in England, France, or Germany; and his completely ingrown absorption with the personal and factional feuds, shibboleths, petty power mechanisms, of the little colonies of isolated exiles.

The closer men were to Lenin, the more bitterly he quarreled with them. The great wealth of shared views was never enough to weigh in the balance against the single pundonor or splitting point of the moment. Feuer raises the question whether in reality it was not a war with his own self that he was waging. Something similar is suggested by Peter Struve, who was close to him for a brief period while both were young at the end of the last century. "The terrible thing in Lenin," writes Struve, "was that combination of actual self-castigation, which is the essence of all real asceticism, with the castigation of other people as expressed in abstract social hatred and cold political cruelty.... Lenin was absolutely devoid of any spirit of compromise in the moral or social sense [of tolerance for men and for everything human].... In accordance with this dominant feature in Lenin's character, I at once perceived that his principal *Einstellung* ... was *hatred*."[6]

"All his life," writes Feuer, "Lenin was engaged in a self-surgery of his emotions ... to shape his character to political requirements." This raises the question whether his pedantic and apparently cold and abstract intolerance for certain traits, sentiments, and views in others was not "part of a desperate struggle with himself." Was it not after a cruel blueprint for the remaking of himself that the blueprint was drawn for the remaking, first of the Russian "Oblomov," then of the Russian people, then of all mankind?

Two characteristic examples will suffice to indicate the continuous struggle Lenin carried on with his own spirit to make it conform to his blueprint for a proper political self: Lenin's account of the end of his "love" for Plekhanov and his explanation to Gorky of why he could not listen to good music "too often."

In the first case, Lenin was writing a political report to Martov in November 1900 on his negotiations with Plekhanov and the other "Elders" for the joint publication of a journal. The language of the report is more suited to a Russian novel than a political document, for Lenin had not yet learned to disguise his passions or present them "objectively," with political matter-of-factness:

"Never have I stood before any man with such 'humility' as I stood before him, and never before have I been so brutally 'spurned.' ... Since [Plekhanov] resorts to chess moves in dealing with comrades, there can be no doubt of the fact that he is a bad man ... an insincere man. ... Young comrades court an old comrade out of the great love they bear for him—and suddenly he injects into this love an atmosphere of intrigue.... An enamored youth receives from the object of his love a bitter lesson: to regard all persons 'without sentiment'; to keep a stone in one's sling."

This revealing document occupies some fifteen pages of Volume IV of Lenin's *Works*. His soul would never again be so nakedly exposed. He learned to give his passions "objective" and "political" expression. And two years later he showed that "the enamored youth" had truly learned his lesson well, for then he regarded "without sentiment" that Vera Zasulich whom he had called "clear as crystal," the organizer Axelrod whom he had so admired, that young Martov whom alone he had addressed as *ty,* and Potresov who had been the third man in his *troika*. And six months later he showed that he had kept a "stone in his sling" for his revered teacher Plekhanov, too.

For two years these six had worked together as the closest comrades-in-arms, together striving to shape the whole movement in *Iskra's* image, excluding all others. In this all six editors had been equally self-righteous and intolerant. But when the second Congress of the Russian Social Democratic Labor Party met in July and August 1903, and its delegates, including four editors, outvoted Lenin on the first issue that he was to consider a "splitting point"—the definition of a Party member—he flew into a rage, used a temporary majority to oust Axelrod and Vera Zasulich from the Editorial Board, and posted guards to keep the other editors of *Iskra* out of the "Iskra caucus!"

In his memoirs, Gorky reports Lenin as having said to him: "I know nothing greater than the *Appassionata*.... I always think with pride: what marvelous things human beings can do! But I can't listen to music too often. It affects your nerves, makes you want to say stupid, nice things, and stroke the heads of people who can create such beauty while living in this vile hell. And you mustn't stroke anyone's head—you might get your hand bitten off. You have to hit them over the head without any mercy, even though our ideal is not to use force against anyone. Hm, hm, our duty is infernally hard."[7]

Anyone who has ever listened to the *Appassionata* and considered that just this stormy piece was to Lenin the greatest of all works of music can sense the storms that must have raged within his "cold" spirit. "Surgery of the soul," indeed—a surgery turned outward into cruelty to others, "hitting them over the head without mercy."

Lenin was passionate in combat to the point of uncontrollable rage. But more dangerous to the society over which he was to exercise absolute rule was the dispassionate, controlled rage with which he was later to order arrests and shootings. This literal possession by "rages" was part of Lenin's character from boyhood. Krupskaya writes to members of his family about them as something well-known to all, a given fact to be reckoned with. In a letter to Potresov, dated September 13, 1903, that is to say, shortly after the scandalous split at the Second Congress that was called to unify the Party around *Iskra*, Lenin acknowledged that he had been "possessed" by such a "rage" during the Congress. He apologized for his loss of self-control and suggested that it be overlooked while they considered ways in which they might possibly repair the damage.[8]

In letters to Gorky, he spoke more than once of the furies that possessed him as if they were common knowledge among his intimates. "I became enraged and possessed (*ozlilsya i vbezilsya*)," he wrote to Gorky on February 25, 1908, concerning his break with Bogdanov on the latter's philosophical views, views actually known to Lenin when he and Bogdanov formed their "bloc neutral on philosophy!" Most striking is the case in which a coy and trivial jest by Gorky (he had written that he had no God at the moment because he had not as yet created one) provoked Lenin to write a furious and insulting letter, charging Gorky with "God-creation" and bidding him realize that "God-creation" was "copulation with a corpse." Because Gorky was a renowned writer, highly valued and even overvalued by Lenin, he held the letter until his wrath had cooled. Then he mailed it all the same, with a lame apology for its tone, which had come, he said, from the welling up of his uncontrollable rage. But the interesting point is that Lenin by no means repudiated in his cooler moments the thoughts that had come to him and the things he had said in his rage.

Even so he had written to Potresov (for Martov's and Axelrod's eyes): "I admit that I often acted with frightful irritation and rage. I am quite ready *to acknowledge to any comrade whatsoever this my*

*fault....* But when I consider [now] without any rage... I cannot see
in the outcome anything, absolutely anything, harmful for the Party...
or insulting to the Minority." Yet, to Central Committee lieutenant
Krzhizhanovsky he sent a letter at the same time telling him to "write
Martov, appealing for the last time to reason... and prepare for definite war with the Martovites.... Do not look upon Martov as before.
The friendship is at an end. Down with all soft-heartedness!"[9]

"Down with all soft-heartedness!" This might well serve as the device
for the laboratory in which Lenin performed the "self-surgery of his
emotions." It was, too, an appropriate slogan for the operation by which
he sought to remake the Russian people and all mankind.

### Lenin's Marx

To Lenin, Marxism was a unitary, monolithic system. "In this philosophy of Marxism," he wrote, "cast from a single block of steel, you
cannot eliminate a single substantial premise, a single essential part,
without deviating from objective truth, without falling into the arms
of bourgeois-reactionary falsehood."[10] However, Marx was no monolith, but was full of contradictions and ambiguities. Moreover, his
thought has a history; it developed and altered in time with the changing historical situation in Europe and with the logical and psychological
changes in his own outlook. If we are to judge by the late writings of
Engels and Marx, they looked back at their youthful follies of the 1848
period with a mixture of nostalgic pride and the amusement of later
wisdom. Hence there is a Marx for Lenin, as there is a Marx for Kautsky,
a Marx for Rosa Luxemburg, and a Marx for Axelrod.

While Lenin devoutly believed that every utterance of Marx in every
period was equally part of a sacred canon, a single infallible doctrinal
system, a science, it is noteworthy that he quotes certain pronouncements of Marx and Engels again and again, while others, no less important, he never quotes at all. When his opponents brought these up
against him, he was at pains to explain them away, to "revise" them
("creatively" of course) and to show that they no longer applied in the
new world that Marx, being science incarnate, foresaw but did not live
to see.

Lenin's favorite quotations are bunched chronologically as well as
topically. A study of them shows that they come chiefly from the young
Marx of the period from 1844 to the middle of 1850. Lenin's favorites
are *The Communist Manifesto* and the *Circular Letter (Address) of
the Central Committee to the Communist League* of March 1850. Thereafter Lenin's use of Marx's writings becomes strikingly sparing and

selective. From the First International Lenin uses not the many moderate and democratic documents produced in the prosperous democratic, federalist, reformist, and trade-union-oriented period from 1864 to 1871, but only the utterances of the moment when Marx strangled the International by his claim to centralized power for the General Council, including the power to expel whole national organizations and international tendencies. There are reiterated quotations from Marx's *Civil War in France,* but no hint of the anxious warnings of Marx and Engels against the adventure of the Paris Commune before it was set up, nor of Marx's final sober second thoughts on the legend of the Commune created by his own pamphlet.* Typical of the quotations from the Marx of 1872 that Lenin's opponents had to force into his attention and that Lenin was at pains to explain away was Marx's statement in his speech at The Hague to the effect that in England, the United States, and perhaps Holland, violent revolution and barricades were unnecessary "because there, if they do but want to, the proletariat can win victory at the polls."[11]

For our purposes it is necessary to distinguish clearly two periods of Marx's thought, during which he was reacting to two different periods in the history of the Europe of his day, with September 1850 as the dividing line.

The first opens in Paris in 1844, when Marx became a "Marxist" under the influence of French socialism and the atmosphere of a gathering storm, a storm that was to break in 1848 not only in Paris but all over Europe. This period reaches its climax with the *Communist Manifesto,* the articles of Marx and Engels in the *Neue Rheinische Zeitung* in 1848 and 1849, and the conspiratorial *Address of the Central Committee to the Communist League* of March 1850.

Marx's socialism during this period was the romantic, egalitarian, street-fighting, and seizure-of-public-buildings brand of socialism associated with the names of Babeuf, Buonarroti, and Blanqui. It looked forward to an insurrection that would be started by a conspiratorial elite of self-appointed revolutionaries who would drag the masses into action by their deeds, and, in a single insurrection, start the revolution going in permanence and establish a revolutionary dictatorship that

---

* Marx's final verdict on the Commune is contained in a letter to Domela Nieuwenhuis, dated February 22, 1881, in which he writes: "The Commune was merely the rising of a town under exceptional conditions; the majority of the Commune was in no sense socialist, nor could it be. With a small amount of common sense, they could have reached a compromise with Versailles." Marx/Engels, *Selected Correspondence* (New York, 1935), pp. 386–87.

would remake society into a world without private property, without classes, without class antagonisms, oppression, or exploitation, without war, and without frontiers. This time the romantic storm attack would be supported by "scientific" knowledge, and it would be led by, or in the name of, a new class, more consistently revolutionary than the bourgeoisie. The class that had hitherto fought all the revolutions for others and brought others to power only to be cheated by them would this time take power for itself.

But as the revolutions of 1848 lost out in Paris, Frankfurt, Vienna, Budapest, and Berlin, Marx's mood became black and he introduced a new element into his writing and thinking: he consoled himself for the defeats by threats of terror and revenge. "There is only one way to *shorten* the murderous death agonies of the old society [Marx wrote on November 5, 1848], only one way to shorten the bloody birth pangs of the new society . . . only *one means*—revolutionary terror."

The climax of this mood came in March 1850. The revolution had died down; the continent was silent; the street crowds and armies of insurrectionists had dissolved again into workaday people in a workaday world. Yesterday's captains—Mazzini, Garibaldi, Louis Blanc, Ledru-Rollin, Kossuth, Herzen, Marx, Engels, Willich, and Schapper—found themselves suddenly alone with each other in the stillness of the English beach on which the subsiding storm had stranded them. They attempted to make up for the disappearance of "the people" from the streets by combining their tiny groups into "universal" organizations. For a few months they polarized into two groupings: the Central Committee of European Democracy, made up of all the democrats and moderate socialists from Mazzini to Louis Blanc and Ledru-Rollin, with *Le Proscrit, Journal de la République Universelle* as its public voice; and the coalesced Marxist and Blanquist Communists in the Société Universelle des Communistes Révolutionnaires. (Blanqui himself was, as usual, in jail.)

It was at this moment that Marx wrote his most "Leninist" document, his *Circular Letter of the Central Committee to the Communist League,* of March 1850.[12] The *Circular Letter* is noteworthy both for the extremism of the methods advocated to secure its aims and for the highly centralist and statist formulation of those aims. Its proposals on how to support, use, then outmaneuver and overthrow the democratic petty bourgeoisie, seem to have been written in accord with Lenin's celebrated formula *Kto kogo?*—Who whom? who uses whom? who defeats whom?

Despite the silence of the continent, Marx was convinced that a new commercial crisis in England (long overdue on his timetable), or a new uprising of the Paris workingmen, would lead at any moment to a fresh wave of uprisings. In Germany the Liberals had disgraced themselves in the Frankfurt Assembly as in France the bourgeois leaders of the February uprising had disgraced themselves in June 1848. The leading role would now be assumed by the democratic petty bourgeoisie who use "deceptive socialist slogans" and call themselves "the Red Party"—socialistic "Democrats" in Germany, democratic "Socialists" in France. The members of the Communist League must use these petty-bourgeois Democrats, "march together with them against the faction which they aim to overthrow, and oppose them in everything whereby they seek to consolidate their position." The Communist League, and the workingmen who can be induced to follow them, must form alongside the official Democrats "their own secret and open organization" with local organizations in every community.

Marx assumes without question that the victory of the petty-bourgeois democrats thus supported by the Communists and the workingmen will be swift. They cannot win their victory without the "armed proletariat," which should then resist being disarmed. These must make the consolidation of the new rule as difficult as possible and "dictate to it such conditions as will from the very outset contain within themselves the germ of their [the democrats'] downfall and will make significantly easier the supplanting of their rule by the rule of the proletariat." "The workers must above all else during the conflict and immediately after the struggles ... work against civil* pacification and force the democrats to carry out their present terrorist phrases. Far from opposing so-called popular excesses—the people's revenge against hated individuals or public buildings which are connected with hateful memories—the Communists must take the leadership of such actions into their hands."

The workingmen must force all sorts of concessions from the bourgeois democrats, "the surest means of compromising them." They must show "unconcealed distrust" of the new regime. "Alongside the new official governments they must build at the same time their own revolutionary workingmen's governments, whether in the form of Communal (Municipal) Councils, Communal Leading Committees, workers clubs or workers committees, so that the bourgeois democratic governments not only lose at once the support of the workers behind them, but from the very outset see themselves supervised and threatened by officials behind whom stands the entire mass of the workers.... [For this] the workers

* "Civil," or perhaps "bourgeois"—the word "bürgerlich" has both meanings in German.

must be armed and organized. The arming of the entire proletariat with rifles, guns, pistols, and munitions must be carried out immediately.... The workers must seek to organize themselves independently as a proletarian guard, with their own elected officers and own elected general staff. Arms and munitions must not be permitted to leave their hands under any pretext; every attempt at disarming them must be prevented by force."

The entire *Circular* (eleven pages in *Werke*) breathes the same spirit of conspiracy; plans to "support" the petty-bourgeois democrats—to use an apt phrase of Lenin's—"as the hangman's rope supports the hanged man"; plans to set up a dual power to supervise, control, threaten, and as soon as possible, replace, bourgeois democracy; plans for the arming of a proletarian "Red Guard" as an independent and ultimately insurrectionary force; plans to keep things stirred up, organize "popular excesses," "compromise" the Provisional Government of petty-bourgeois democracy.

No less notable is the extreme centralism and statism of the *Circular*. The democrats will want, as in the French Revolution, to confiscate the lands of the feudal aristocracy and "give the land to the peasants as free property." Against this "the workers must demand that the feudal property remain state property and be transformed into labor colonies." "The democrats will ... work for a federal republic, or, if they cannot avoid a single and indivisible republic, will seek to cripple the central government by the greatest possible autonomy of the communal [or municipal, the German word is *Gemeinde*] governments and provisional governments." Against this the workers must fight for "a single and indivisible German republic ... with the most decisive centralization of power in the hands of the State."[13]

As if to resolve our doubts on how great the influence of Blanqui was on the young Marx of this period, in the self-same month of March 1850, while drafting this *Circular* of "Blanquist" instructions, Marx published in the short-lived *Neue Rheinische Zeitung: Politisch-ökonomische Revue* of Hamburg (Part III, March 1850) the famous passage of praise for the imprisoned Blanqui which has been the subject of so many interpretations: "The proletariat groups itself more and more around *revolutionary* socialism, around *communism,* for which the bourgeoisie itself has invented [or discovered, the German word is *erfunden*] the name *Blanqui.* This socialism is the *declaration of the revolution in permanence,* the *class dictatorship* of the proletariat as a necessary transition point to the *abolition of class differences altogether,* to the abolition of all the relations of production on which they rest, the abolition of all social relationships which correspond to these production relationships, the transformation of all ideas which arise from these social relationships."[14]

There are striking resemblances between this tribute to the perpetual if not permanent revolutionist and revolutionary conspirator, Blanqui, and two other passages from the same period. One passage is in the March *Circular*: "While the democratic petty bourgeoisie will be inclined to bring the revolution to as speedy a conclusion as possible, it is our interest and duty to make the revolution permanent until all the more or less propertied classes are forced from power, the state power is seized by the proletariat, and the partnership of the proletarians of the world has advanced to such an extent that competition between the proletarians has ceased, not just in one country but in all the principal countries of the world, and at least the vital forces of production are concentrated in the hands of the proletariat."

It is this which became the favorite text from Marx of Parvus and Trotsky, and ultimately, in 1917, of Lenin, to solve the problem of a "bourgeois democratic revolution" to be made without the bourgeoisie and without democracy in "backward" Russia by "the proletariat and the peasantry."

The other passage is the programmatic statement of the union of Marxists and Blanquists in April 1850 in the Société Universelle des Communistes Révolutionnaires. It was a conspiracy to the second power, for even the rank and file of the federating secret organizations did not become members of this new Universal Society. It consisted of six men, a general staff for whom the associating societies should serve as armies: Vidil and Adam representing the Blanquists; Marx, Engels, and Willich the London members of the Communist League; and Julian Harney representing what was left of the British Chartists. "The aim of the association," the Statutes said, "is to make an end of all the privileged classes, to subject these classes to the dictatorship of the proletariat by maintaining the revolution in permanence until the complete realization of communism, which ought to be the last form of the constitution of the human family."[15]

Whether whole classes can ever really rule in modern society, whether whole classes can form a "party of the class" or "dictate" as a class, does not concern us here. What does concern us is that in the *Communist Manifesto* Marx spoke of the rule (*Herrschaft*) of the working class as a whole, and in praising Blanqui he spoke of the dictatorship of the class as a whole.

Twice Marx entered into an alliance with the Blanquists: in March 1850 to revive the dying revolution, and in 1872 for his war against the antistatist Bakuninists and the Proudhonists. After the second alliance broke up, Engels wrote of Blanqui in 1874 (with Marx's approval) : "In his political activity Blanqui has been essentially a 'man of the deed,' of faith that a small, well-organized minority, which at the right moment attempts a *coup de main* (*Handstreich*), can stir the masses by a couple of early successes and thus make a victorious revolution. From Blanqui's conception of every revolution as a coup de main, it necessarily follows that a dictatorship is needed after the success of the revolution: the dictatorship, it should be clear, not of the entire revolutionary class, the proletariat, but of the little handful of men who have made the coup, and who themselves are under the dictatorship of a single individual or several individuals.[16] The words could serve as well for a description of Lenin's conception of the seizure of power and the revolutionary dictatorship to follow.

By September 1850 Marx had come to the conclusion that the revolution of 1848 was over. Neither threats, nor terror, nor "universal unions" with Blanquist exiles, nor acts of revolutionary will, could bring it back. His *Circular* of March now seemed absurd to him. But he chose not to acknowledge his own error of estimate or tactics, at least not in writing, repudiating those errors only as they persisted among his comrades of the Communist League. He managed to get a majority of one in the Central Committee, but had almost no support in the League as a whole. "The minority [i.e., the minority in the Central Committee] replaces critical observation with dogmatism, a materialist attitude with an idealist one. It regards its own naked will as the driving force of the revolution instead of the real facts of the situation."[17] With these words Marx broke with his "voluntarism" of yesterday and he and Engels withdrew from the League that had been their "party" since 1847.

The Marx of revolutionary voluntarism and insurrectional conspiracy gave way to the Marx of the endless research in the British Museum, hunting for the secret "law of motion" of capitalist society, which, by its "imminent workings," would all the same make the cataclysm someday inevitable. The "real facts" had to be investigated to determine when the "next crisis" would come.

It is customary for Social Democrats and Marxicologists to draw a sharp line between the young, voluntarist, insurrectionist Marx, and the "mature, scientific" Marx. Insofar as the demarcation is justified, the September 1850 declaration marks the dividing line. Certainly, Lenin had an instinct for bunching his quotations in the earlier period.

It is noteworthy that both Lenin and his democratic socialist opponents have found comfort and sustenance in the *Communist Manifesto*. It is a mixed bag from which all would-be heirs can grab what they seek. In it are voluntarism and fatalism, a theory of a vanguard professional revolutionary elite (only the term is Lenin's), and a specific formula for the rule of a class; conspiracy and propaganda slogans; observations on the "art of insurrection" and the first elements of the "science" that guarantees the insurrection's victory; Blanquism and democratic socialism; Marx's past and Marx's future. It is the very embodiment of the ambiguities in Marxism.

Because Marx never expressly repudiated either the more extreme and outdated parts of the *Communist Manifesto* or the Blanquist *Circular* of March 1850, and because by his eloquence he imposed upon his followers a legendary picture of the Paris Commune, the new social democratic movements that honored his name developed a schizoid personality, which Lenin exploited. On the one hand there was the voluntarism and extremism of the Marxist "classics," a mood suitable only for the holidays of the Second International; on the other, the patient struggle for practical reforms and respect for democratic process in their daily work. The *Circular* of March 1850 lay like an undetonated bomb on the Marxian road, an explosive manual of Leninist strategy and tactics, to be joyously dug up by Lenin in the following century.

In any case, Lenin had his fixed points on which to chart his trajectory and Kautsky had his. Kautsky had a far greater volume of text by actual word count and a far weightier one by content-analysis—much of the *Communist Manifesto* (but not the fire it breathed) and the great bulk of Marx's post-1850 writings. He had besides the express words and the unequivocal support of the "consubstantial" survivor of classic Marxism, the Engels of the last years.

But Lenin had texts enough, too, all of them electrifying: the more stirring and romantic parts of the *Manifesto*; the centralist and statist and "labor army" planks of Marx's Seventeen Point Program of March 1848; the discussion by Engels (in Lenin's day attributed to Marx) of the military tactics proper to "The Art of Insurrection"; the eulogy of Blanqui in *Class Struggles in France*; the use of Blanquist emissaries and alliance with Blanquist conspiratorial clubs of April and June 1850; the apparent recrudescence of the messianic spirit in Marx's first legendary picture of the Paris Commune; the chiliastic ending of the penultimate chapter of *Das Kapital*. And above all, the precise conspiratorial directives, the praise of terror and lynch law, the cynical *kto-kogo* spirit and ultra-extremism of the never-repudiated *Circular* of March 1850. Both Lenin and Kautsky had warrant for charging each other with "distortion," not to say "betrayal" of the heritage.

When Lenin's opponents charged him with compounding his doctrine out of the terrorism of the Narodnaya Volya, the Jacobinism of the "bourgeois" French Revolution, the centralism, revolutionary dictatorship, revolutionary elitism and voluntarism of Blanqui, he accepted the charge with pride. What is Marxism, he asked, if not Jacobinism "fused with the working-class movement"? Had not Marx, too, been in love with the great days of 1789–95? Had he not in the name of the proletariat sought to revive those days in 1848? Had he not celebrated their revival in 1871?

The great years were not dead, only the world had been asleep. Sloughing off the dull accumulation of the years of civil peace, reformism, and capitalist expansion, in the "final crisis," the Apocalypse, the great time would return. Then all the stormy years—1789, 1793, 1848, and 1871—would fuse together. That was Lenin's Marxism. That was what he dreamed he was doing when his own year came, the fateful year, 1917.

## What Kind of Revolution?

For Russian Marxists, the central problem was the nature of the coming Russian Revolution. It was Plekhanov, not Marx or Engels, who made this the central problem.[18] When he broke with the Narodniki, he laid down the premises for the "Marxist" stand in his *Socialism and the Political Struggle* (1883). He took the position that any attempt to establish socialism in Russia without modern industry and a concentrated, enlightened, and organized industrial proletariat would result in the discrediting of the very idea of socialism, and in the creation of a *new class* (Plekhanov's orthodoxy compelled him to say a "socialist *caste*"), something like the Inca rulers of ancient Peru. These "Peruvian sons of the Sun" would act as guardians, bureaucratic socializers, administrators, tribute takers, absolute rulers over the people. The people would be reduced to obeying the centralized supreme command and its bureaucratic agents. Far from being educated for socialism, they would be reduced to more complete subservience to a more powerful state than that of the Tsars, and would lose the very capacity for further progress toward freedom, democracy, and socialism.

For a decade and a half, this work was gospel for Lenin, to be added to the "classics" of Marx and Engels. He repeated Plekhanov's dogmas concerning the industrialization of Russia and the need of a "bourgeois democratic revolution" before the struggle for socialism could be put on the order of the day. Like Plekhanov and Struve, he proved that the capitalist market and capitalist industry were developing with giant strides in Russia.[19]

A typical formulation in his *What Are the "Friends of the People"?* (1894) will suffice to show Lenin's acceptance of his master's formula, and a certain special tone that we may call "Leninist"—a tone that might have been audible even then to those sensitive to the nuances of style that are the man:

"The complete repudiation of petty-bourgeois theories by Marxists does not prevent them from including democratic demands in their program; on the contrary, it calls for stronger insistence on these demands than ever.... The three main postulates that are the stock-in-trade of the representatives of petty-bourgeois socialism [are] lack of land, high land-redemption payments, and the tyranny of the bureaucracy.... Social Democrats will most strenuously insist on the immediate return to the peasants of the land of which they have been deprived, and on the complete expropriation of the landlords.... This latter, which coincides with the nationalization of the land, contains nothing socialistic...but is extremely important in a democratic sense as the only measure that will finally break the power of the landed nobility.... Social Democrats will unhesitatingly join in the demand for the complete restoration of the civic rights of the peasants...the abolition of bureaucratic tutelage over the peasantry, and self-government for the peasantry."

Quoting Plekhanov in place of Marx or Engels in his *ipse dixit,* Lenin concludes this section with the words, "Generally speaking, Russian Communists, the followers of Marxism, should more than anyone else call themselves *Social Democrats* and in their activities never forget the enormous importance of *democracy*."[20]

When Plekhanov learned that Lenin was proposing to solve the land hunger of the peasants by the *nationalization* of the land, he repeated his warning of the danger for Russia of despotic and bureaucratic collectivism à la Inca. Russian despotism, he said, had been built upon the binding of the peasant to the state. "By demanding the nationalization of the land, you are making easier a return to this type of [despotic] nationalization of [both the land and the servile peasant], for you are leaving intact this legacy of our old, semi-Asiatic order."

*Iskra* was founded to organize, unify, and capture ideological hegemony over the socialist movement of Russia. The first and third aims are characteristically "Leninist." But in his first pamphlet published under the auspices of *Iskra* (*What Is To Be Done?*), Lenin put on the flyleaf not a quotation from Marx or Engels but from Lassalle: "Party struggles give a party strength and life.... A party becomes stronger by purging itself."

When *Iskra* had finally succeeded in undermining the influence of its rivals and called its "unifying congress" in 1903, Lenin ended up breaking not only with non-Iskrists and anti-Iskrists, but with the five other members of the *Iskra* Editorial Board as well. All six accounted themselves "orthodox Marxists"; indeed, the program Plekhanov drafted for the Congress (with some minor modifications by Lenin) remained the official program of both Bolsheviks and Mensheviks until the autumn of 1917. Only in 1919 did Lenin draft a new program for his party.

The issue on which he broke with the others, according to Lenin, was "a purely ideological struggle around the basic principles of organization." Henceforth Lenin was to rule his faction alone. Whenever he lost control of his leading committee (invariably handpicked by him), his motto would be *raskol, raskol, i eshchë raskol*. This can be translated "schism, schism, and again schism," or "split, split, and again split"; both translations must be held onto, for Lenin was by temperament both a schismatic and a splitter. More than a *raskolnik* he was the messianic founder and leader of each *raskol,* so that, wherever two or three were gathered together with Lenin, there would be revolutionary socialism or Bolshevism.

Yet the first split (the only one in which he split from his co-equals) was not painless for him, and there is evidence that it required some of Feuer's "soul-surgery." It grieved Lenin personally to be estranged from Martov, the only political figure for whom he ever seems to have felt a deep and intimate affection, which Krupskaya testifies he still expressed on his death bed. It grieved him politically to be separated from his revered master, Plekhanov.

N. Valentinov (N. V. Volsky) was quite intimate with Lenin at that crucial period when, to become the messiah of his own movement, he was deciding to renounce both his master and his most intimate party friend. Valentinov and Lenin took daily walks together while Lenin was talking out the substance and the formulations of the book proclaiming the break, *One Step Forward, Two Steps Backward*. Writes Valentinov in his *Vstrechi s Leninym*: "From the robust man, full of fire and energy that he had been, he became thin, wrinkled, turned yellow; his eyes, naturally alive, roguish, mocking, became at times tender, at times dead. [Often he gave way to despair and talked of abandoning his project altogether].... 'I have never before written anything in a similar mood,' Lenin said. 'I am nauseated by what I have to write.'

"But then *rage* would take possession of him, and he would push on with the work."

Left to himself as chieftain of his own band, with no one near big enough to offer criticism or correction, Lenin began to develop the independent feelings he had always nourished into an independent system of views on the nature of the revolution facing Russia, views that were more in accord with his preference for voluntarism over "Marxist scientific fatalism," with his temperamental impatience at the slowness of history's measured tread, his natural extremism, his concentration on power, his Jacobinism, his greater kinship with such Russians as Tkachev, Nechaev, Bakunin, Chernishevsky, Zaichnevsky than with West European socialists, his Blanquism, his inclination to vanguardism, terror, dictatorship. Yet he was loath to give up the seal of Russian orthodox Marxism associated with the name of Plekhanov.

As before, Lenin kept insisting that what Russia faced was a "bourgeois-democratic revolution." He repeated the old formula again and again, yet somehow it began to seem different. "Is it not clear," he wrote in March 1905, "that it is impossible to achieve these [bourgeois-democratic] reforms in bourgeois society without a revolutionary-democratic dictatorship of the lower classes?" Here is our first glimpse of one of Lenin's original inventions, a "bourgeois revolution" without the bourgeoisie and against it, for the sake of establishing "bourgeois democracy."

In the period of deep reaction, in April 1908, Lenin returned once more to this unique idea. In an article entitled "Toward an Appraisal of the Russian Revolution," he stated the paradox with his accustomed stubbornness. In the West, he explained, "the victory of such a revolution was possible as the victory of a corresponding layer of the bourgeoisie over its opponents.... But in Russia the case is quite otherwise. A victory of the bourgeois revolution is impossible in our case *as a victory of the bourgeoisie*. This may seem paradoxical, but it is a fact. The predominance of a peasant population ... the strength and consciousness already organized in the socialist party of the proletariat—all these circumstances give *our* revolution a *special* character. This peculiarity does not eliminate the bourgeois character of the revolution (as Martov and Plekhanov tried to make out in their more than unsuccessful remarks on the position of Kautsky). This peculiarity is merely determined by the counterrevolutionary character of our bourgeoisie and the need for a dictatorship of the proletariat and peasantry for victory *in such* a revolution. A 'coalition of the proletariat and the peasantry,' which wins *victory* in a bourgeois revolution—that is precisely what is meant by the revolutionary-democratic dictatorship of the proletariat and the peasantry."[21]

Having invented a bourgeois revolution without the bourgeoisie, there was only one more innovation possible to Lenin, and years later, at the Second Congress of the Communist International, he would make it: namely, a proletarian revolution in lands without a proletariat. But of this we shall have more to say later. First we must analyze some of his key formulations of the stirring years 1905–6.

In the year 1905, having discovered that by calling the peasantry "bourgeois" he could devise an ersatz bourgeoisie for his revolution, he permitted himself to dream concerning the spread of this *sui generis* revolution into a world revolution.

"A revolutionary Social Democrat will dream—he must dream if he is not a hopeless philistine—of how, after the vast experience of Europe ...standing as we do on the shoulders of a number of revolutionary generations of Europe, we can dream of how we shall succeed in carrying out all the democratic reforms[22] ... making the Russian Revolution not a movement of a few months' duration, but a movement of many years....And if we succeed in doing that, then...the revolutionary conflagration will spread all over Europe; the European worker...will rise in his turn, and will show us 'how to do it'; then the revolutionary wave...will sweep back into Russia and will convert an epoch of a few revolutionary years into an era of several revolutionary decades; then...but we shall have plenty of time to say what we shall do then ...at the meetings of thousands of workers in the streets of Moscow and St. Petersburg, at the free assemblies of Russian *muzhiks*."[23] Here we are close to the Marx of March 1850, the revolutionary dictatorship of a Blanquist elite, arousing and leading masses of workingmen and peasants, keeping the revolution going in permanence.

Lenin hastened to differentiate himself from the theory of the "permanent revolution" as expounded by Parvus and Trotsky. The revolutionary democratic dictatorship *"cannot be* a government of labor democracy" or have a "Social Democratic majority." This cannot be "because only a revolutionary dictatorship relying on the overwhelming majority of the people can be at all durable....The Russian proletariat, however, constitutes at present only a minority of the population in Russia. It can become a great overwhelming majority only if it combines with the mass of semi-proletarians, semi-small proprietors, i.e., with the mass of the petty bourgeois, urban and rural poor. And such a composition...will find its reflection in the composition of the revolutionary government."[24]

And again: "By making it the task of the provisional revolutionary government to achieve the minimum program [of Social Democracy], the resolution eliminates the absurd, semi-anarchist ideas that the maximum program, the conquest of power for a socialist revolution, can be immediately achieved. The present degree of economic development of Russia (an objective condition) and the degree of class consciousness and organization of the broad masses, of the proletariat (a subjective condition) make the immediate, complete emancipation of the working class impossible. Only the most ignorant people can ignore the bourgeois character of the present democratic revolution; only the most naïve optimists can forget how little as yet the masses of the workers are informed of the aims of socialism and of the methods of achieving it. And we are all convinced that the emancipation of the working class can only be brought about by the working class itself; a socialist revolution is impossible unless the masses become class conscious, organized, trained and educated by open class struggle against the entire bourgeoisie. In answer to the anarchist objections to the effect that we are delaying the socialist revolution, we say: we are not delaying it, but are taking . . . the only means that are possible along the only right path, namely the path of the democratic republic. Whoever wants to approach socialism by any other path than political democracy will inevitably arrive at absurd and reactionary conclusions in the economic and in the political sense."[25]

These words, which were aimed at Trotsky, Parvus, and Rosa Luxemburg, proved to be a true prophecy. In 1917, they would come back to haunt the man who had pronounced them.

In the same vein, Lenin declared categorically that the coming "bourgeois revolution without the bourgeoisie" would nevertheless strengthen the domination of the bourgeoisie. "The democratic changes in the political structure and the social and economic changes that have become a necessity to Russia do not in themselves mean an undermining of . . . the rule of the bourgeoisie; but, on the contrary, they will for the first time properly clear the ground for a wide and rapid, a European and not an Asiatic, development of capitalism."[26]

But, Lenin continued, "the proletariat benefits even more than the bourgeoisie" by these swift and sweeping changes. Hence the bourgeoisie is afraid to win. The proletariat must force it to win, even if, in panic, the bourgeoisie deserts its own revolution. Whereas the Mensheviks wanted to moderate their actions in order not to frighten away the bourgeoisie (that way lies opportunism and treason!), Lenin proclaimed that the bourgeois revolution would become truly sweeping only after the bourgeoisie deserted it. "Whoever really understands the role of the peasantry in a victorious revolution is incapable of saying that the sweep of the revolution will weaken when the bourgeoisie deserts it. For in actual fact, only then will the revolution take on its real sweep ... the widest sweep possible in the epoch of the bourgeois-democratic revolution.... In order that it [the bourgeois revolution] may be carried out unwaveringly to the end, it must rely on such forces as can paralyze the inevitable wavering of the bourgeoisie."

Lenin's use of the word "paralyze" in this sense is interesting and suggestive. He makes his meaning clear in the following propositions:

(1) "The immediate interests of the proletariat ... demand a democratic government."

(2) "The achievement of this democratic republic is possible only as the result of a victorious popular uprising, the [leading] organ of which is a provisional revolutionary government."

(3) "It is necessary to propagate among the widest masses ... the idea of the need for constant pressure on the provisional government by the armed proletariat, led by the socialists, for the defense, the deepening, and the widening of the conquests of the revolution."

If this force is powerful enough, Lenin thinks the Social Democratic Party will force its way into and dominate the provisional government. Then it must make it into a dictatorship, which Lenin describes at the same time as "democratic." This will put into the hands of the revolutionary party a wonderful new weapon, hitherto unknown in history, namely the power to enforce and extend the revolution "from above" by means of a governmental dictatorship. "This," Lenin exults, "is a new and almost unprecedented means of struggle." Since "the great questions of political freedom and class struggle are, in the last analysis, decided by force, we must concern ourselves with the preparation, the organization of these forces, and the use of them not merely for defensive but also for offensive purposes."

This unprecedented force of the dictatorial and democratic state exercised "from above" and backed by the armed force of the masses from below, will be used to crush and annihilate reaction, to "paralyze" the wavering of the bourgeoisie, and then of the petty bourgeoisie, including the peasantry, which is bound to waver in its turn as the revolution continues its relentless march toward its final goals. "Only the workers," Lenin proclaims, are capable of leading other classes in this fight. "And only they will fight consistently, unwaveringly, and to the end."[27]

But what will the "party of the proletariat in power" choose to do if the proletariat, too, wavers? In 1905, this thought was to Lenin still unthinkable. But after he seized power in 1917, he came face to face with the wavering of the proletariat, too. Unwaveringly, he would continue his dictatorship and revolution from above, answering the waverings of the proletariat by outlawing the other socialist parties, forbidding strikes, setting up the first "temporary" ("extraordinary") and then permanent secret police, and bombarding the Kronstadt rebels with big guns.

## Lenin's Conception of the Class War

When the ordinary socialist speaks of *class struggle* he means little more than a struggle for universal suffrage, labor legislation, social reforms, social security, unions, and a party of labor—the attempt to win men of good will from other classes to support of labor's needs and demands. Social revolution is either an accumulation of such changes and reforms until "quantity becomes quality," or a fundamental transformation of the political, economic, and social structure of society by a ruling socialist party after it has won power by democratic means. Force, if it were to be used at all in democracies, or so Engels held in his last years, was to be kept in reserve against the possibility that a ruling minority might attempt to hold on to power by force or stage a violent counterrevolution.

But when Lenin said class war he meant *war*. As his organizational doctrines showed, the operative word was not class, but war. It would, of course, be a war for the good of humanity, but, for the good of humanity, a good part of humanity would have to be dealt with according to the rules of war.

"When we get into power we will establish the dictatorship of the proletariat, although all development goes toward the abolition of the rule by force of one part of society over another. Dictatorship is the rule of one part of society over the whole of society, and, moreover, rule resting directly on force.... The question of the dictatorship of the proletariat possesses such importance that he who rejects it or recognizes it only conditionally cannot be a member of the social democratic party."[28]

"Dictatorship," Lenin declared on December 5, 1919, after he had been dictator for two years, "is a harsh, heavy, and even bloody word." With beautiful simplicity, he bade democratic opponents remember that, "The scientific concept of dictatorship means neither more nor less than unlimited power, resting directly on force, not limited by anything, not restricted by any laws or any absolute rules. Nothing else but that."[29] Indeed, the first giant step in the establishment of a totalitarian power is the destruction of all the restraints of religion, morality, tradition, institutions, and laws that limit the use of force to atomize the nation. In that sense, the history of totalitarian regimes has proved the rightness of Lenin's "scientific" definition.

Lenin had begun work on his "science" of terror even while on the

Board of *Iskra*. In its first number he wrote, "In matters of tactics, Social Democracy does not tie its hands.... It recognizes all methods of
struggle." In *Zarya*, in January 1901, "Trial by the street [what we in
America call lynch law] breathes a living spirit into the bureaucratic
formalism that pervades our government institutions." In *Where To
Begin?* (*Iskra*, May 1901) he rejected "acts of terror only when they are
engaged in isolation from the general struggle and weaken the fighting
detachments which alone can be counted on.... We have never rejected
terror in principle, nor can we ever do so." In *What Is To Be Done?* he
asked, "What type of organization" does *Iskra* require, and answered,
one that "will be ready *for everything,* from protecting the honor, prestige, and continuity of the party... to carrying out a *national armed
insurrection.*"[30]

In 1905, unlike Trotsky, who hastened to Russia to lead actual struggles through the Petersburg Soviet, Lenin showered his followers with
bloody instructions from afar. His first comment on reading of Father
Gapon's procession was to call for "the immediate arming of the workers and all citizens in general,... the annihilation of the governmental
power and institutions."[31] In "The Plan of the Battle of St. Petersburg"
he wrote: "Revolution is war.... The workers will arm themselves....
Each will strain with all his might to get himself a gun, or at least a
revolver."[32]

Subtly Lenin recalled the cry of Zaichnevsky, *To the Axe!* "'Axes?'
says one. 'No, with axes you won't be able to do anything against sabres.
With an axe you can't get to him, perhaps with a knife, but that is
even less. No, what is needed is revolvers... still better, guns.'"

He called for a Congress of his faction, which must proclaim itself
the Party: "The Congress must be simple, short, not many people. A
Congress for the organization of war." Lenin meant war in both senses,
war on *Iskra* and the Mensheviks, and war on the government of Russia.
In a preliminary draft of the Call for the Congress, he suggested as the
Order of Business: "Organization, relation to the periphery,* uprising,
arming the workers (setting up workshops for making dynamite),
agreements with the Social Revolutionaries for an uprising, support of
the revolutionary peasant movement." *Workshops for making dynamite*
on the order of business of a socialist congress—who but Lenin, even
among the rock-hard, could think of that?

In the *Resolution on Armed Uprising,* which he prepared for the
Congress, he wrote: "The Congress resolves... that by preparation of

---

* Lenin's term for organizations infiltrated by his party.

the uprising it understands not only the preparation of weapons and the creation of groups, etc., but equally the accumulation of experience by means of practical attempts at individual armed attacks—for example, attacks of armed detachments on the police and the army... on prisons, government institutions, etc."

His organization in St. Petersburg duly set up a "Military Committee," but Lenin soon became convinced that it was doing "nothing but discussing." There were armed bands, holdups, jail breaks, murder of policemen, in Poland and in the Caucasus, but they were not under the control of his organization. Was his organization good only for talk?

"The bomb has ceased to be the weapon of the solitary bomb-thrower. It has become a *necessary* part of the equipment for arming the people. ...Preparation of bombs is possible everywhere and in all places.... No force can oppose the detachments of a revolutionary army that arms itself with bombs.... In this, frenzied energy is needed, and yet more energy. With consternation, by God with consternation, I see that there has been talk of bombs *for more than a half year,* and not a single bomb has yet been made."

What could Lenin do at "the accursed distance," but write instructions so detailed that they could not be evaded, so simple that they could be followed by anyone, even without the guidance of his committee? The result was a notable document: "Tasks of the Sections of the Revolutionary Army." It was written at a moment when the Tsar was promising a Constitution and when large sections of the opposition were calling off all attacks until they could see whether the Tsar's promises were genuine and meaningful. All the more reason, thought Lenin, to push for an uprising.

The revolutionary detachments, he wrote, should have two related tasks: to engage in military actions on their own, and to assume leadership over mobs. The detachments might be of any size, beginning with two or three persons. They must "arm themselves as best they can (guns, revolvers, bombs, knives, brass knuckles, cudgels, rags with kerosene to start fires, rope or rope ladders, spades for building barricades, barbed wire, tacks against cavalry, etc. and so forth). In no case wait for help from above, from outside, but procure everything themselves.

"They should select leaders or officers, work out signals to hang in their windows, agree upon cries, whistles, passwords, signs by which to know each other amidst tumult or in the dark. Even before they had arms they could assume the leadership of crowds, attack a policeman or a cossack that has gotten separated, and take away his weapons, rescue the arrested and wounded when the police are numerous; climb on roofs or upper floors and shower stones on troops, boiling water, etc."

They should start "theoretical studies" of the art of warfare (for this Lenin had translated General Cluseret). They could invite friendly officers and workingmen who had been in the army to teach what they knew. They needed "practical training," too: procurement of weapons and explosives, selection of good sites for street fighting ("good for giving battle from above, for storing bombs or stones, etc., for pouring acid on the police, etc."); "espionage and reconnaissance to learn the layout of prisons, police stations, ministries, official institutions and banks, to learn how they are guarded, to strike up friendships with guards and service personnel, locate supplies of arms, arsenals, etc." (There is an "etc." or "and so forth" or both in virtually every sentence that catalogues deeds of terror and daring, as if Lenin were afraid that he might forget something, or that overly servile and overly disciplined followers might not go beyond the letter of his instructions.) "The aged, women, children, and altogether weak persons" have their work cut out for them, too. After all, how much strength does it take to spy out locations, pour oil or acid or boiling water from a roof, strew tacks in front of horses?

From the very beginning it was important not to limit oneself to mere preparatory work, but as soon as possible to undertake "military actions" with the aims: "(1) of training fighting forces; (2) spying out the weak spots of the enemy; (3) dealing him partial defeats; (4) liberating prisoners (the arrested); (5) securing arms; (6) getting hold of resources for the uprising (confiscation of government funds, etc., etc.) ... for without training *under fire*, it is impossible to acquire the readiness for uprising."

Since "the slogan of an uprising *has already been proclaimed* and the uprising has already begun" (did not Lenin himself proclaim "the beginning of the uprising" three days after Father Gapon's procession was fired on?), it follows that "to begin attacks under proper circumstances is not only a right but the outright duty of every revolutionary. The killing of spies, policemen, gendarmes, the blowing up of police buildings, the liberating of the arrested, the seizing of government funds for use in the uprising, cannot be premature. Has not the Polish Socialist Party, under Pilsudski, already begun them? Why are we Bolsheviks lagging?" To miss any opportunity now "is the greatest crime for a revolutionary ... the greatest shame for anyone striving for freedom, not in words but in deeds." Those "democrats" who refuse to take part must be branded as "pseudo-democrats."[33]

These directives, and the train of thought that led to them, are unique in the history of modern socialism. Neither in Russian Social Democracy nor in the entire International was there another man who could have given these coldly calculated directives and urged them so ardently. Engels, though he fought on the barricades of 1848 and thereafter, wrote much on military matters, and delighted in the nickname "The General," never wrote anything like them. The Marx of 1848, with his apostrophes to terror, popular vengeance, and the fist, seems but to be "unpacking his heart with curses," compared to these thoughtful, pedantic instructions on acid from rooftops, tacks for horses' hoofs, kerosene rags to start fires, casing of banks to be held up. The ruthlessness of Nechaev, the romantic exaltation of bandit and barricade by Bakunin, the appeal of Zaichnevsky to the axe, are mere violent posturing in comparison. Here is the pedantry, systematization, and "scientific organization" of terror. Up to August 1914, the overwhelming majority in every socialist party rejected both Lenin's methods of organization and his methods of waging the class war. Had they understood more fully what he was saying and believed that he meant it literally, they would have been still more outraged.

But in August 1914 began the terrible years—four long years during which statesmen and generals treated their people as "human matériel," to be expended without stint or calculation in the pursuit of unattainable objectives. Men learned to accept as commonplace the ruthless logic of mutual extermination. They learned to master their fear of death and the revulsion against inflicting it. They developed a monstrous indifference to suffering, their own as well as that of others. Universal war so brutalized European man that, in the words of Reinhold Niebuhr, it became possible to "beguile men into fresh brutalities by the fury of their resentment against brutality."

Lenin's technique of organization and his plans for "class war" began to seem less alien, to arouse less indignation. "Since it was a time of horrors," Raymond Aron would later write, "at least violence might have peace as its objective, and as its enemy the civilization that had made the sterile carnage possible." Now that all things were being subjected to the arbitrament of bayonet and bullet, why not war and peace and the nature of the system out of which the crisis had come? If Lenin still rejected peace in favor of having the world war prolonged and turned into civil war, this fine point of distinction was now less noticeable, for was he not declaring war on the "system that breeds war"? Thus war was Lenin's opportunity, since it made his fantastic prescriptions for the class war seem more timely and less unnatural. Before there could come the reign of what Churchill would one day call "the bloody-minded professors of the Kremlin," there had first to be the bloody mess of Flanders Field, where, as England's wartime leader Lloyd George was to write, "nothing could stop Haig's compulsion to send thousands and thousands to their death against the enemy's guns in the bovine and brutal game of attrition."

## The Sovereign Remedy

The completeness of Lenin's belief in himself was matched by the completeness of his distrust of everybody else. Once in power he tried to check on everything; his correspondence is filled with detailed instructions to lieutenants and time limits for their detailed reports. Uncomfortable in the presence of complexity and ambiguity, partial truth, shadings, pluralism, the not-yet-known or the unknowable, Lenin treated all questions as if they had only one right answer, and a definite "administrative" solution. With the striking exception of his retreat on the NEP, his answer to whatever failures and irrationalities arose from his fantastic blueprint and his excessive centralization and control was yet more control and more administration machinery. A "terrible simplifier," he tended to cut through any complexity or muddle with the simplest of "remedies": *arrest!*

A perpetual conspirator himself, before he came to power he bombarded the Provisional Government with demands for the arrest of the "wealthy conspirators," the "ten capitalist ministers," and a number of bankers and manufacturers, and compulsory publicity for their "secrets." His way of supporting Kerensky against Kornilov was to demand: "Arrest Miliukov, arrest Rodzyanko."[34] In "The Threatening Catastrophe," he demanded the abolition of all commercial secrets (is there any country with more secrets today than the totalitarian regime he founded?) and "the firing squad for hiding anything."[35]

But it was after he took power in the state that was to begin at once to wither away that his imagination ran riot. On November 18, 1917, he called upon the people of Petrograd and Moscow to show initiative by "arresting and handing over to revolutionary tribunals" all those guilty of "damage, slowing up, undermining production ... concealment of supplies ... any sort of resistance to the great cause of peace," to the policies of "land to the peasants" and "workers' control of production and distribution."[36] Every man his own judge! Then he proposed that every man should be his own executioner, too, provided only that he was one of the mob and not one of the "scoundrels, loafers, rich." The instruction came in an article entitled, with unconscious irony, "How

To Organize Competition." Each commune, each village, each town, should show initiative and inventiveness in devising ways of *"cleansing the Russian land of all noxious insects, scoundrel fleas, bedbug rich, and so forth and so forth."*

"In one place they will put into prison a dozen rich men, a dozen scoundrels, a half-dozen workers who shirk on the job.... In another place they will set them to cleaning outside toilets. In a third they will give them yellow tickets [as identity cards] after a term in prison.... so that the entire people ... will act as the overseers of them as *harmful* people (wreckers). In a fourth they will shoot on the spot one out of every ten guilty of sloth.... The more varied, the better ... for only practice can work out the *best* measures and means of struggle."[37]

Clearly, Lenin is being unjust to himself when he wrote: "We will suppress the resistance of the possessing classes by the methods they used" since "other means have not been invented." In the same speech in which he thus belittled his own inventiveness, he invented the term "enemies of the people" for an entire political party, the Kadets. Three days later he outlawed the Kadets and their elected Deputies to the Constituent Assembly. In three weeks he had invented the Extraordinary Commission (Cheka) and the experimental shooting of one in ten.

On January 27, 1918, he demanded that the entire working class join the terror. Workers who did not want to join in the hunt against "speculators" must be "forced to" do so "under threat of the deprivation of their bread cards." Every factory and every regiment must pitch in to set up "several thousand raiding parties of ten to fifteen people each." "Regiments and workshops that do not accurately set up the required number of detachments [the word *accurately* is typical of this pedant of terror] will be deprived of bread cards and subject to revolutionary measures of persuasion and punishment.... Speculators caught with the goods ... will be shot on the spot by the detachments. The same punishment for the members of the detachments convicted of bad faith."

As a Socialist, Lenin had voted for the resolution of the parties of the Second International in favor of abolishing the death penalty for any crime. No one dreamed then that in the twentieth century the death penalty would be restored for theft, crimes against property, or "speculation." But Lenin was furious with his lieutenants for abolishing the death penalty in October 1917. Even before the Civil War began, he had restored it and was calling for "shooting on the spot." "As long as we do not apply terror—shooting on the spot—," Lenin told the representatives of organizations for procuring food on January 14, 1918, "we won't get anywhere."[38]  When the Civil War ended, the death penalty was abolished (on January 17, 1920) but restored in May of the same year. The first Criminal Code of the RSFSR provided the death penalty for seventy crimes. With ebbs and flows, the regime Lenin set up, returning now to "Leninist norms," has once more restored the death penalty for various types of "aggravated speculation," theft, forgery, and crimes against the one real property, state-owned property.

*Ce n'est que le provisoire qui dure.* Lenin did not intend this "accurate" application of terror to chaos to be more than temporary. But there is an embarrassment of riches in Lenin's subsequent writings and speeches in the same vein. Let us skip to the Eleventh Congress, during the gentler age of the NEP, in April 1922. Lenin is talking now of the problem of "purchasing canned goods in a cultured manner": "One must think of this elementary culture, one must approach a subject thoughtfully. If the business is not settled in the course of a few minutes on the telephone, collect the documents and say: 'If you start any of your red tape, I shall put you in prison.' "[39]

Still the sovereign remedy! At the same Congress, Lenin decided that he would not, now that peace had come to the Soviet Union, tolerate any more party groupings, i.e., any party democracy. "Armies in retreat," he said, meaning the NEP, "are accustomed to turn machine guns on the few voices of panic." Whereupon his faithful lieutenant Shlyapnikov, who had been his only active workingman lieutenant during the war and People's Commissar of Labor in Lenin's government, said to the Congress: "Vladimir Ilyich said that we are spreading panic, and that with spreaders of panic it is necessary to deal with machine gun fire. This is the second time that I have heard this, and I feel the machine gun fire aimed at me."[40] Lenin tried to explain that his sovereign remedy was reserved for Mensheviks and such. Yet a few minutes later he returned to Shlyapnikov to remind him and the Congress that he was but three votes short of the necessary two-thirds majority in the Central Committee to put his lieutenant into outer darkness, outside the party, where his fate would have been indistinguishable from that of "the Mensheviks."[41]

## "A Party of a New Type"

Marx had been vague on how the working class takes power, though repeatedly he stressed that it was to be through a party of the entire class, which was to rule as a class. Except when competitors such as Lassalle or Dühring forced him to speak, Marx was deliberately silent on how an entire class could take power and on what they would do with the power after they had taken it. The few remarks he made on this, directly in his *Critique of the Gotha Program,* and at greater length through Engels in *Anti-Dühring,* were taken literally by Lenin and again by Stalin. Their blind faith in these fantastic precepts on the abolition of the market, on labor-time receipts instead of money, on universal, centralized rationing, on the unimportance of the state and the law that were to immediately begin to wither away, was to cost the Russian people dearly.

In Lenin, however, Marx had an innovating disciple, one who was a theoretician, technician, and virtuoso of organization, to take and wield power. Lenin's specialty was the how rather than the why. Conspiracy, centralized organization, military discipline, the ability to stir, manipulate, and coalesce discontent and hatred—a technique, indeed a technology, and a pedantic systematization of the art and science of seizing power, holding power, wielding power, extending power in width and depth—what are these if not the levers of modern totalitarian revolution?

Here indeed was a revolutionist of a new type, determined to form what he himself would call a "party of a new type," to make, as it turned out, a revolution of a new type. But it must be remembered that the role of Lenin and his machine was not to prepare the revolution that overthrew the Tsar, but to take advantage of it when it had occurred quite without him and his machine. He was as astonished at the revolution as the Tsar himself. But his machine was admirably designed to discredit and destroy democracy, itself devoid of a power machine or a power sense. It was from February to October 1917 that Lenin displayed his virtuosity. What he overthrew was what he himself called the "freest government in the world." Power was lying on the streets, and his reckless demagogy was admirably calculated for seizing it. "It was as easy," he said afterward, "as lifting a feather."

The first peculiarity that strikes one in Lenin's organizational doctrine is his centralism, and his extreme distrust not only of whole classes (the intelligentsia, the petty bourgeoisie, the peasantry, and the workers), but even of the rank and file of his own party and his own local organizations.

"What is bad," Lenin asked when he was in control of the Central Organ, "about the complete dictatorship of the Central Organ?" But when he did not have a majority, he could not think of "the subordination of the minority to the majority." Then he would split, build a new *troika,* threaten to resign or to "go to the sailors," that is, appeal to the unruly sailors of Kronstadt against his own party. Chided for suppressing party democracy in his faction, Lenin answered for his followers: "They have no time to think of the toy forms of democracy ... but they have a lively sense of their responsibility and know by experience that to get rid of an undesirable member, an organization of real revolutionaries will stop at nothing."[42]

This is surely one of the most unresponsive answers in the entire literature of politics. Lenin implies that with police rule in old Russia "democracy is a useless and harmful toy." In the context of conspiratorial underground organization, democracy can be completely replaced by the mutual trust of members toward each other, and by their confidence that the self-selected center will know how to get rid of those unworthy of trust. Yet it was precisely Lenin who was never without several police agents high in his confidence.

Lenin soon made it clear that police espionage was only a pretext and his inclination to centralist rule a matter of "principle." A virtue of revolutionary socialism, even in a country like Germany where there was freedom to organize parties and unions, was an inclination to "bureaucratic centralism." "Bureaucratism *versus* autonomy, such is the principle of revolutionary social democracy as against that of the opportunists.... The organization of revolutionary social democracy strives to go from the top downward, and it defends the enlargement of the rights and plenary powers of the Central Body."[43] Of course, he unconsciously assumed that it was he who would exercise those plenary powers in the Central Body. To Lunacharsky he said: "If we have in the CC or Central Organ a majority, then we will demand the firmest discipline. We will insist on every sort of subordination of the Mensheviks to party unity." Lunacharsky asked, "What if it should turn out that we are in a minority?" Lenin "smiled enigmatically" and said: "It depends on the circumstances. In any case, we will not permit them to make of unity a rope around our necks. And under no circumstances will we let the Mensheviks drag us after them on such a rope."[44]

Not until Lenin had been bombarded by opponents for over a half decade did he finally hit on the fictitious label "democratic centralism." In the third year of his rule over Russia, when he could no longer give as justification the Tsar's police, he abolished the very basis of such party democracy as had existed before his control was consolidated, prohibiting party groupings, platforms, gatherings to discuss differences. Then he defined the self-contradictory term democratic centralism to mean "only that representatives from the localities gather and choose a responsible organ.... The responsible organ must do the administering."

And that administering included the right to assign organizers, secretaries, and other officials to the localities who could then come back as "representatives" of the localities. If "democracy" elected someone distasteful to "centralism," then "centralism" could send him to Kirghizia, as it sent Pestkovsky; to Turkestan, as it sent Tomsky; to Norway, as it sent Kollontay.

When Lenin's concept of "democratic centralism" was transplanted to the Comintern, it read: "The main principle of democratic centralism is that of the higher cell's being elected by the lower cell, the absolute binding force of all directives of a higher cell to a cell subordinate to it, and the existence of a power-vested (*vlastnogo*) party center, unchallengeable for all leaders in party life from one congress to the next."[45] What Lenin did with his twenty-one points, his attacks on Serrati and Levi, his splitting of the Italian Party, which eased Mussolini's parade to power, are samples of what "democratic centralism" meant in the Comintern.

Lenin's division of spheres between that which should be centralized and that which should be decentralized would be high comedy if he were not so much in earnest and if the implications for Russia and Communism were not so fraught with tragedy. In his very early (September 1902) "Letter to a Comrade on Our Organizational Tasks," Lenin wrote:

"We have arrived at an extremely important principle of all party organization and activity. In regard to ideological and practical *direction*, the movement and the revolutionary struggle of the proletariat need the *greatest possible centralization*, but in regard to *keeping the center informed* concerning the movement and the party as a whole, in regard to *responsibility* before the party, we need the *greatest possible decentralization*....The movement must be led by the smallest possible number of the most homogeneous groups of trained and experienced revolutionaries. But the largest possible number of the most varied and heterogeneous groups drawn from the most diverse layers of the proletariat (and of other classes) should take part in the movement. And, in regard to each such group, the center must always have before it not only exact data on its activities but also the fullest possible knowledge of its composition.... *Now* we have become an organized party [Lenin exulted] and that means the creation of power, the transformation of the authority of ideas into the authority of power, the subordination of the lower party organs to the higher ones."[46]

*The transformation of the authority of ideas into the authority of power!* Lenin left unstated the premise that the ideas would be his and his the power, but his every party act both before he seized power in Russia and after he had won it made this unstated assumption clear.

At the Second Congress of the Russian Social Democratic Labor Party, delegate Popov had spoken of the future Central Committee in liturgical language as a "Spirit, omnipresent and one." But Lenin cried out from his seat: "Ne dukh, a kulak!" ("Not spirit, but fist!") Thus, even before there was a Party Congress or a Central Committee, Lenin was already dreaming of this, his fist, that would hold all the reins within its grasp, control all the levers and springs of action, check up on everybody and hold everybody to account.[47] And a year before that Congress, he had already written:

"The Committee should lead *all* aspects of the local movement and direct *all* local institutions, forces, and resources.... Discussion of all party questions, of course, will take place in the district circles also, but the *deciding* of all general questions of the local movement should be done only by the Committee. The independence of the district groups would be permitted only in questions of the technique of transmitting and distributing. The composition of the district groups should be determined by the Committee; i.e., the Committee designates one or two of its members (or even nonmembers) as delegates to such and such district and entrusts these delegates with the *setting up of the district group* all the members of which should in turn be confirmed in their positions by the Committee. The district group is a local branch of the Committee and it receives its powers only from the latter."[48]

Thus the Center is the brain, the local organizations the limbs; the Center decides, the locals execute; the Center directs, the locals report and are responsible; the Center designates local leaders and confirms them in their posts. The local leaders in due course would become delegates to a Congress to approve the Center that had designated them. This, in its pristine purity, was Lenin's conception of the Center (provided he was at the center of it)—Spirit and Fist in one. The word *democratic* in "democratic centralism" was simply one more label meant to paralyze or confuse his opponents, like the other labels we shall examine below.

Lenin was never one to avoid repetition when he wanted to hammer something home. Perhaps the best statement of what he meant by democratic centralism, because of its vivid metaphor, reads as follows: "We must centralize the direction of the movement...and *for this reason* ...decentralize *responsibility* of each individual member as much as possible.... This decentralization is the necessary condition for revolutionary centralization, and *its necessary corrective*. . . . In order that the Center may not only give advice, persuade, argue (as has been done up to now), but may really direct the orchestra, it is essential to know exactly who is playing which fiddle and where, who is learning to master which instrument, or has mastered it, and where; who is playing out of tune, where and why . . . and who should be transferred to correct the dissonance, how and where."[49]

Lenin's Archimedean cry for an organization of revolutionaries "to turn Russia upside down" did not cease once Russia had been turned upside down. As before, Lenin continued to call for "organization, organization, organization." But now he had something new to add. To his old dream of centralized organization of the party, he added the dream of total organization of life by the party. Now he would remake the spirit of Russia, its industries, its agriculture, its feelings, its thoughts, its habits, even its dreams, eliminate by total organization all slackness, all waywardness of will. He would perform "soul surgery" now on Oblomov and Ivan Ivanovich. "We must organize everything," he said in the summer of 1918, "take everything into our hands."[50] Thus, to the authoritarianism inherent in an infallible doctrine, possessed and interpreted by an infallible interpreter, who ruled an infallible party, from above, infallibly, Lenin added the further dream that was possible only with total and absolute and exclusive power—the dream of "organizing everything, taking everything in our hands."

This ambition to organize everything tidily, accurately, and totally was actually inherent in his doctrine from the start. We have only to read attentively his outburst against the first and chief of the cardinal sins in his Decalogue: *stikhiinost* (elementalness or spontaneity, that which comes from below, from the depths). In early 1918 he declared that the elemental, uncontrollable spontaneity of the "million-tentacled hydra" òf the petty bourgeoisie (the peasantry), and the workers affected by them, was the "main enemy." And in 1922 and 1923, after four years in power, he repeated this, adding the grim thought: "Petty-bourgeois spontaneity is more terrible than all the Denikins, Kolchaks, and Yudeniches put together."[51]

If it seems strange for a "democrat" to distrust the rank and file and local organizations of his party, it seems still stranger for a Marxist to express distrust of the very class from whom "proletarian consciousness" is to come and whose mission it is to establish socialism. But Lenin found this distrust axiomatic. "Cut off from the influence of Social Democracy," said his first signed article for *Iskra*, "the workingmen's movement becomes petty and inevitably bourgeois."* That single sentence was enough to finish off the entire "class" theory of Marx. But one sentence in his first signed article, it became the central thought of *What Is To Be Done?* There the distrust was spelled out, underscored, and reiterated, tirelessly and monotonously.

An entire chapter deals with the contrast between "The Spontaneity of the Masses and the Consciousness of the Social Democracy." This distinction between spontaneity (*stikhiinost*) and consciousness (*soznatelnost*) brings us to the hard core of Lenin's spirit.[52] Lenin opposed the two words as one might light and darkness. The elemental and spontaneous were embodied in the working class, the peasantry, the petty bourgeoisie, the masses generally, in the way they thought or desired, the way they felt, the way they fought, except where they had control and guidance from consciousness. Consciousness was the Party— or rather, its Center. The Party, without leadership over the masses, was mind without body; the masses, without the leadership, direction, and control of the Party, were body without mind.

As his emphasis on centralism against democracy had led to his inventing the heresy of "opportunism on the organization question," so his emphasis on *soznatelnost* against *stikhiinost* led him to invent the heresy of *khvostism* (tailism), or "slavish kowtowing before spontaneity." The language is strange, the heresy still stranger. Kowtowing is the act of worship in which the devout prostrate themselves before a revered image. To call it slavish and shameful makes it clear that Lenin regarded respect for the desires, the will, the self-activity and the self-development of the masses as evil. But why?

Because the working class was not to be trusted. Left to itself, or merely served by the party, without the party's tutelage and control, it could never in its life attain to so much as the conception of its "mission."[53] Socialism turns out not to be, as Marx held, the existential or quintessential nature of the experience, organization, and consciousness of the working class. Instead, it was a "science" somehow developed by Marx in spite of his misapprehension of the nature of the proletariat, a science understood, mastered, possessed by an intellectual revolutionary elite, and an elite springing not from the working class but from the "educated representatives of the possessing classes." Hence to look to the working class to learn from experience, or merely to aim to serve the working class and help it to organize, to fight, and to learn from its experience, instead of taking it in tow, was worthy only of a "bourgeois politician." That would be to renounce both a political "democratic" revolution and socialism itself. That would be dragging behind the tail of the working class instead of dragging it after you.

The struggles of the working class had never made them into socialists and never would. For this they needed Lenin's "vanguard" of professionals—professionals of theory, of organization, of conspiracy, men
who made revolution and underground activity their full-time occupation. All his life Lenin had steeled himself to hate not only the slippered
sloth and dusk-to-dawn discussions of the Russian intelligentsia, but
also the spontaneous and unreliable flareups and the changing conceptions of self-interest of the Russian masses. From the outset he had
been working on a machine to harness the force of the waves, the tides,
and the storms, a machine to convert their fluctuating, unreckonable
rise and fall into a single, controlled stream of energy. It was his aim
"to collect and concentrate all the drops and streamlets of popular excitement that are called forth by Russian conditions ... into one, single,
gigantic flood." This machine—or at least so Lenin thought—was his
*Apparat*. And at the center of the *Apparat* was *soznatelnost*. There had
not been, there was not, "nor *could there be,* social democratic consciousness in the workers. This can be brought to them only from the
outside. The history of all lands testifies to the fact that alone, by their
own forces, the working class is capable only of working out a trade
union consciousness.... But the teachings of socialism have grown out
of those philosophical, historical, economic theories that were worked
out by the educated representatives of the possessing classes, the intelligentsia. By their social position Marx and Engels, the founders of
contemporary scientific socialism, belonged to the bourgeois intelligentsia, too. This is true for Russia also, where the theoretical doctrine of
social democracy arose in complete independence from the spontaneous, elemental growth of the workers' movement—arose as the natural
and inevitable result of the development of thought among the revolutionary intelligentsia."[54]

The workers had to be "pushed from the outside." There had never
been, nor could there be, too much of this type of manipulation. But
to "flatter" the workers, to arouse in them "a sense of distrust toward
those who bring them political knowledge and revolutionary experience
from the outside," is to be a demagogue. This is a unique Leninist definition of the term. "And a demagogue," Lenin said, "is the worst enemy
of the working class."[55]

"Since there can be no talk of an independent ideology's being worked
out by the workers themselves ... the only choice is: either bourgeois
ideology or socialist. There is no middle term.... Hence *any* lessening
of socialist ideology and *departure* from it signifies ... a strengthening
of bourgeois ideology. But the *spontaneous* development of the work-

ers' movement leads precisely to its subordination to bourgeois ideology."[56]

Lenin is tireless and uncompromising in hammering home his key ideas: "Class political consciousness can be brought to the worker *only from outside*...the sphere of relations between workers and bosses. The sphere from which alone it is possible to derive this knowledge is the sphere of the relations of *all* classes and strata and the state and the government. Therefore the question, What is to be done to bring the workers political knowledge? cannot be answered by 'go to the workers.' To bring the *workers* political knowledge, the Social Democrats must *go into all classes*...send *in all directions* the detachments of its army."[57]

Not coming from the working class, not going to the working class but to "all classes," Lenin continues, "*We* must take upon ourselves the task of organizing such an all-sided political struggle under the direction of our party.... We must...be able to direct all the manifestations of the all-sided struggle, be able at the necessary moment to dictate a positive program of action alike to rebellious students, dissatisfied Zemstvo leaders, dissatisfied religious sectaries, indignant schoolteachers, and so on."[58]

Now it is possible to see where Lenin was heading. It was at a party to direct not merely the working class, but the entire populace, a party that would conceive it its duty to "dictate a positive program" for every class in society. And that *dictate* was no empty rhetoric, Lenin had shown even while a member of the *Iskra* Board. He wrote for the Board a memorandum proposing to show "every kindness" to the peasantry but "not yield an inch" in "our maximum program." When the dictatorship comes, "if the peasants do not accept socialism, we shall say to them, 'It's no use wasting words when you've got to use force.' " On the margin of the memorandum Vera Zasulich wrote: "On millions of people? Just you try!" When he came to power, that is just what he tried.

If socialist "consciousness" comes not from the working class, its experience, its struggles, its growth, and the growth of its understanding, as Marx believed, then the members of the elite band would come chiefly from those layers of society capable of mastering this science, namely students and intellectuals. True, by becoming "professional revolutionaries" they had in a sense declassed themselves, but they did not thereby become members of the working class. Rather they withdrew from their profession or economic function, withdrew from the existing "classes" and from society itself, living in its interstices as masters of a new profession, the profession of social sapper or revolutionary. They were not to be part of the present at all, but its challengers, gamblers staking their all in *va banque* on their bet concerning the future.

As a concession to the "proletarian" element in Marxist doctrine, Lenin perforce expressed the hope that "the best of the workers" might also attain this consciousness and this status. But these, too, would have to leave the factory or workbench and be declassed: "The working-man-revolutionary, for full preparation for his [new] job, must also become a professional revolutionary.... A worker-agitator who shows any talent and is at all 'promising' *should not* work in the factory.... We must see to it that he lives on party support... and goes over to an underground status."[59] Even in power and exercising the "proletarian" dictatorship, Lenin repeated this: "It is clear that the broad masses of the toilers include many people who... are not enlightened socialists and cannot be, for they have to work at hard labor [Lenin uses the term *katorzhno,* derived from *katorga,* penal hard labor] in the factory, and they do not have the time or opportunity to become socialists."[60] Thus, from declassed revolutionary intellectuals and declassed revolutionary workers, the "new class," the bureaucratic ruling class of the Soviet Union, was to be born.

Among professional revolutionaries, whether declassed members of the possessing classes or declassed workingmen, "*all distinctions as between workers and intellectuals* must be obliterated."[61] This "socialist caste" as Plekhanov called it, this "new class" of Djilas, Makhaisky, and Bakunin, this classless band of priest-guardians of doctrine, duties, and power, must "form a clandestine group of leaders to set the largest possible masses in motion," must "dictate the program" to all the discontented of all classes of society and lead them in a single, centralized, disciplined, military, all-Russian struggle against the authorities and the society-in-being without any idea of what they would put in its place.

When Lenin's opponents accused him of wanting merely to use the proletariat for one more nineteenth-century revolutionary conspiracy like those of the Narodnaya Volya, he answered proudly: "The very idea of a militant centralized organization that declares war on Tsarism you describe as Narodovolist.... No revolutionary tendency that thinks seriously of fighting can dispense with such an organization... a powerful, strictly secret organization concentrating in its hands all the threads of secret activities... of necessity centralized."[62]

Yes, he was "flattered" to be identified with the Narodovolists. Like them he sought "to recruit *all* the discontented and hurl this organization into decisive battle. . . . That was their great historic merit." They had made only two mistakes: they had failed to realize that Russia, too, would develop modern heavy industry and with it an industrial proletariat and they had failed to realize that then the *main* mass, the most concentrated, and, by barracks and factory, the most disciplined mass to use as the battering ram against the walls, would be the working class.

Herein lay the "proletarian" core of Lenin's Marxism. This was what made it essential that his elite, recruited from the possessing classes, should appeal to the proletariat and regardless of class origins proclaim itself the *vanguard of the proletariat*. This was what made it absolutely necessary for the revolutionary vanguard of "all society" to claim recognition above all as the vanguard of the class most useful for the struggle. And this justified the claim that the working class was the vanguard of all other classes. Hence his declassed elite from the possessing classes must penetrate the working class and its organizations, not to serve them but to use them, not to follow their will but to inject the will of the vanguard. That is why they must penetrate the "essentially bourgeois" trade unions, with their narrow, selfish concentration on a few more kopeks and a few less hours, and turn them to the uses of revolution. That is the reason why they must indoctrinate the working class with the principle that its role was to destroy, not to improve or reform, the world in which they lived. This was the true proletarian doctrine and the true proletarian role, whether the proletarian accepted or rejected it. For this the elite must seek to control and channel the workers' struggles, divert them from their "spontaneous" and "elemental" purposes to the vanguard's conscious purpose. Only the latter was in accord with science and history. Indeed, the workingmen and their organizations would be measured by a standard impossible for them to develop by themselves: for them *consciousness* could be measured precisely by the degree to which they accepted the leadership, the guardianship, the purposes, the decisions, and the program of this elite band of professionals of revolution.

Thus Lenin's "vanguard" was the vanguard of the proletariat by definition. The proletariat could have no other. The vanguard's doctrine was the doctrine of the proletariat by definition. And its organization was the "highest form" of organization of the working class by definition. By definition, too, it was the officers' corps and general staff of the future revolutionary armies of the working class and all other classes. It must drill them by skirmishes, recruit or conscript them in ever-greater numbers, urge them on into clashes, harden them in battle, teach them the arts of dropping boiling water from rooftops and tacks under horses' hoofs, setting fires with kerosene rags, and killing isolated policemen or raiding sporting goods stores and weapons deposits to obtain guns. (Lenin never dreamed that total war would suddenly put arms into every man's hands—"I doubt that Franz Josef and Nikolasha will do us that favor," he had written to Gorky during the Balkan wars.)

To take power, Lenin had flattered the proletariat and promised them "workers' control." But in power he told them that "just because the revolution has begun, that does not mean that the people have turned into saints." Far from it. Workers' control and ownership became counterrevolutionary syndicalism. One of the primary duties of the "proletarian power" was "to resist the inevitable petty-bourgeois waverings of the proletarian masses," to combat the "demoralization" that war, and the Party's own war against the Provisional Government, had introduced into the masses. "Only by an extraordinary, difficult, prolonged, stubborn road can we overcome this demoralization and conquer those elements who are augmenting it by regarding revolution as a means of getting rid of their own shackles by getting out of it as much as they can."[63] What these ominous words forecast for the "ruling" class is another story.

This is not the place to decide whether and to what extent Marx is responsible for his unique disciple. Here it is enough to say that Lenin's idea of the relation of class to party and Marx's can only be reconciled to each other intellectually—or rather, verbally—by four acts of Leninist legerdemain, four feats of semantic juggling, four fundamental deceptions achieved by four arbitrary acts of redefinition.

The first is the confounding of the proletariat with the people. The second is the confounding of the party with the proletariat. The third is the confounding of the party machine (Central Committee, Politburo, Presidium, Orgburo, Secretariat, *Apparat*) with the party. The fourth is the confounding of the *Vozhd* or Leader with the Central Committee and the *Apparat*.[64] Though Stalin and Khrushchev are entitled to credit for their further "creative development" of these four inventions, all four are the creations of Lenin.

This man, who regarded himself as the most orthodox of orthodox Marxists, the only one to have understood Marx in fifty years, could rightly claim that he was building a "party of a new type"—a party Marx and Engels would have been astonished to contemplate. It was not only new in type; it was unique and exclusive. For while there might be other parties claiming to be socialist, there was room in society for only *one* Party which claimed to be *the* vanguard of the working class and of all other discontented classes, and which, once in power, would appoint itself the vanguard of the "ruling class," in whose name it would rule over all classes, not excluding the proletariat. For then, with the aid of exclusive and dictatorial power, at long last it could compel the working class to accept its revolutionary leadership, its doctrine, and its consciousness.

There have been attempts to find predecessors and influences for Lenin in Babeuf, Blanqui, Bakunin, Pestel, Nechaev, Tkachev, Chernishevsky. Yet when the relevant fragments from the writings and actions and aspirations of these men are added together, they do not add up to a Lenin. He is indeed unique in his conceiving and begetting his machine, in systematizing and developing his doctrine, and then—and this alone gives him his great historical importance—when power lay fragmented and in the streets, in suddenly perceiving that this was his opportunity, casting all doctrine and scruple behind him, seizing power and atomizing Russian society under his ruthless and completely self-confident dictatorship. "The point of the uprising is the seizure of power: after that we will see what we can do with it." And after that the main point was to hold power, to consolidate power, to make whatever changes in doctrine, to undertake whatever acts of concession, persuasion, and terror seemed necessary, to hold on to power and to "organize everything." This was the heart of his mystery. And this made what might otherwise have been one more page in the book on which are inscribed the names of Blanqui, Bakunin, Nechaev, and Tkachev, into the story of a great man in history, a man who changed the world into which he was born beyond all recognition.

Lenin's classless elite, recruited from students and intellectuals who are children of the possessing classes, might well seize power not, as Marx expected, where the economy was most advanced and the working class most "conscious," cultured, organized, numerous, and politically most active; it might seize power just as easily, nay, even more easily, where the economy was backward, the workers neither mature nor conscious nor politically active, and all political parties of all classes rudimentary or nonexistent. Indeed, the more fragmented and the less organized and educated a society, the easier for a little classless band of the discontented to seize power in the name of socialism and the proletariat.

This vanguard-elite theory would later make it possible for restless students, officers, or intellectuals to seize power in the name of the proletariat even where the proletariat was in its infancy. In the name of this doctrine, Mao could seize power "for the proletariat" by means of peasant armies. Ho Chi Minh might do the same in a land where the only workers were plantation hands and handicraftsmen plying their ancient trades. All that was needed was a power vacuum; a supply of arms (the Second World War took care of that); a supply of malcontents (and where are there no malcontents?); an *apparat* to seize power; some fragments of Lenin's doctrine; and Stalin's example. Once in power they can do as Lenin, Stalin, and Khrushchev have done: use the "proletarian power" to rule society as a whole, to put all industry, all weapons, all means of communication, into the hands of the ruling "party," to develop a power as total as the wayward spirit of man and the development of technology and controls permit.

# Stalinism

The term Stalinism was not in public use under Stalin, at least not in the Soviet Union or in the international Communist movement. It was used in a derogatory sense by Stalin's adversaries, to indicate a distinction between the practices, and later the theories, of Stalin and Lenin. The word Stalinism or the expression Marxism-Leninism-Stalinism was sometimes seen in the Soviet press, but only occasionally; neither one took root. Indeed, for a long time it was only abroad that "Stalinism" had any currency, and even today it has hardly gained a foothold in the Communists' everyday language. Under Stalin one spoke only of Marxism-Leninism, just as under Lenin the term was never Leninism, but simply Marxism. Stalinism is not mentioned in any of the Soviet *Encyclopedias* or *Political Dictionaries of Communism,* in which other "isms" abound. Even Marxism-Leninism did not exist in the first two editions of the *Little Soviet Encyclopedia* (1930 and 1937) or in the *Great Soviet Encyclopedia* of 1938, or in the *Political Dictionary* of 1940. This official synonym for Stalinism was not fully sanctioned by Soviet reference works until after the Second World War.

According to one definition of Stalinism well-known in the West, that in S. V. Utechin's *Everyman's Concise Encyclopedia of Russia,* Stalinism is the "theory and practice of Stalin's near-totalitarian rule in the Soviet Union, the satellite states of Eastern Europe, and in the world Communist movement." This definition is correct but should be slightly modified, for the practice preceded the theory. What we have essentially is a conglomeration of practices, some of which have ex post facto been erected into theories, but most of which have been left without any theoretical formulation or, rather, hidden under formulas that belie reality. Utechin continues: "Orthodox Communist propaganda denies that Stalinism exists as a distinct body of theory, maintaining that Stalin simply developed and enriched the teachings of Marx and Lenin; since the

Twentieth Congress of the Communist Party it is also permissible to say that Stalin made mistakes. The theory of Stalinism is in fact a combination of Leninism and National Bolshevism." Utechin mentions the principal characteristics of Stalinism, rightly observing that for the most part they are "dogmatic postulates in form and fictions with respect to content, conceived to reinforce the conformity of public behavior." At the same time he emphasizes, and rightly so, the importance of these fictions to the Communist system of rule, fictions in which no one in the Soviet Union believes and which are dropped when they cease to serve the regime in power; and he differentiates them from myths, though they can become myths abroad.[1] For a picture of Stalinism somewhat less concise than that of a "concise" encyclopedia, we must look first at the practice, then at the theory, as they evolved historically.

Stalinism can logically be distinguished from Marxism and from Leninism, similarities of vocabulary and form notwithstanding, since Stalin emptied the earlier concepts of their original meaning. When traditional Bolsheviks started to use this term, there were accumulating signs of a change in methods, a change disturbing to the party leadership, and hence to the legal government, for the party had long since become one with the higher state bureaucracy and subjected to the control of an "oligarchy" (Lenin's own word). Stalin certainly did not create out of thin air the system of coercion that he used and abused to establish his personal autocracy. He inherited from Lenin an oligarchy in which the instruments of persuasion and dissuasion, of pressure and suppression, assured perpetuation of the regime established by the October Revolution. The expedients adopted during the Civil War, the exceptional measures required by exceptional circumstances, became the permanent conditions of Soviet life after the Kronstadt uprising of 1921.

By the time of Lenin's death, the party had already been transformed into a strictly disciplined military hierarchy. The soviets were mere ornaments, the trade unions appendages, of the government machine. Judicial procedure was completely subordinated to *raison d'état,* which was determined by the party. The secret police was everywhere, with absolute freedom to work any injury upon a defenseless population—the party alone was still immune to its arbitrary interference. But at the Tenth Party Congress, in 1921, Lenin "put the lid on the opposition," i.e., he abolished all freedom of criticism between Communists, all internal democracy. He subjected the party to the state of siege he had already imposed on the country. The "democratic centralism" extolled by the leaders was a sham. The "dictatorship of the proletariat" became more and more a dictatorship exercised against the proletariat. If in

1867 Wilhelm Liebknecht could characterize the Reichstag as "the fig leaf of absolutism," with all the more reason can we compare the Congresses of the Soviets and their Executive Committees to so many fig leaves of a new despotism, a despotism more oppressive, better organized, more efficient, than that of the old regime.

This was the situation in 1924, when Stalin, rid of the burden of Lenin's presence, acquired that extra elbowroom he needed to extend his influence and consolidate his personal authority. He had no original ideas at the time. (Nor, for that matter, did he ever distinguish himself in the realm of political thought, and his contribution to party doctrine was even less notable.) In a variety of circumstances—in disputes among Social Democrats and later among Communists, for example—his attitude tended to be conciliatory and moderate, a kind of golden mean between extremes, a "reasonable" attitude, suggestive of what is known as bourgeois prudence. He did not pretend to be an ideological innovator. In his capacity as General Secretary of the party, he confined himself to administration, to dominating the immense party "apparatus," which held in its grip the whole network of government agencies and all forms of the country's social, economic, and intellectual life. At least he never betrayed any other ambition than to appear as the great master of "practical tasks." But it was soon found that under the system of leadership and government that had been established, practical matters went hand in hand with theoretical considerations. Having gradually invested the position of General Secretary with an absolute power unmentioned in the Soviet Constitution, Stalin had to develop a theory to justify the fact. The result was the birth and nurturing of that shapeless, hard-to-define phenomenon on which the label "Stalinism" would ultimately be pinned.

In 1923, while Lenin was still alive, a conflict was secretly taking shape at the summit of the Communist oligarchy, with Trotsky and his supporters opposing the rest of the Central Committee on economic policy and on the ways and means of exercising the party's dictatorship. After the forces in the party that had opposed the Leninist line after 1917 had been defeated and dispersed; after rigorous measures had been directed primarily against the "Workers' Opposition" and the "democratic centralist" group; after it had been forbidden to form "factions" (a prohibition tantamount to the suppression of all discussion among party members)—after all this, there nevertheless arose a group that opposed the ruling clique, notably the triumvirate of Zinoviev, Kamenev, and Stalin, and accused it of incompetence and shortsightedness (if not blindness) in its conduct of affairs. At the end of 1923 the internal conflict flared into the open, in the form of bitter polemics in *Pravda* attacking

Trotsky. Stalin was prudent enough to let Zinoviev and Kamenev lead the main attack. Trotsky, however, belatedly concerned over the growing bureaucratization of the party, called into question the excessive power of the secretariat and the "hierarchy of secretaries." Goaded by this opposition, the Central Committee adopted resolutions promising reform and "workers' democracy," and announced a "new course" for the party. Kamenev publicly stressed that these resolutions satisfied Trotsky on all essential points. There was no question of any ideological disagreement in this clash between "tendencies"; the only issues were the internal problems of the party and the socioeconomic difficulties of that year. On both sides the antagonists claimed to be adhering to the same Marxism that Lenin had Russianized, and thus to the same Leninist tradition.

But in October 1924, Trotsky published a collection of his writings dating from 1917, to which he appended an introduction taking Zinoviev and Kamenev to task for their temporizing attitude during the October Revolution and attributing to this spirit of temporization the failure of the 1923 revolution in Germany. The result was a furious campaign against "Trotskyism"—a fiction invented for the occasion by the two men Trotsky had assailed. Stalin took an active part in this campaign, but at the same time he restrained his henchmen in their thirst for reprisals. For the time, he thought it enough to humble a potential rival without depriving the party of his services, whereas the other two wanted to oust the man whose prestige they envied and whose future activities they feared. To throw Trotsky out of the party under the conditions prevailing in 1924 would have been to deliver him into the hands of the GPU and consign him to a miserable end. But that apparently was not Stalin's intention, although in 1925 Trotsky was expecting to be killed one way or another.[2]

A brief recapitulation of these vicissitudes is necessary for an understanding of the origins of Stalinism, which was conceived as the antithesis of the previously created myth of Trotskyism. The competition for the political heritage of Lenin crystallized in attempts to seize the position of General Secretary. Since none of the leaders had any hope at this point of equaling Lenin's stature, they all agreed to say that a collective or collegial leadership was what the situation required. Stalin asserted in 1925 that Trotsky could keep his place in the Politburo provided that he cooperated with his partners, and as late as 1926 Trotsky deemed it unthinkable to put together a Politburo without Stalin.[3] Ideology was thus absent from these internal struggles, and was only read into them at a later date.

The primacy of Trotsky would necessarily have meant changes in the office of Secretary as well as the transfer of Stalin called for in Lenin's Testament, a directive that the Central Committee, including Trotsky, chose to ignore by refusing Stalin's resignation. From 1923 on, Zinoviev and Kamenev, for their part, had tried to reform the office of Secretary by appointing two other Secretaries with authority equal to Stalin's. In 1925, with no greater success, they tried to get Stalin out of the Secretary's job by naming him Commissar for War. The discord created by their ill-concealed intentions gave rise to a new opposition directed at Stalin and his clan, the "left" opposition. Like earlier formations of its kind, it was mowed down by the party machine, at the Fourteenth Congress, held in December 1925, and in 1926 it formed an alliance with the Trotskyites. The "Trotsky-Zinoviev bloc" could not confine its program to the replacement of Stalin as Secretary; it had to come up with some positive alternative to the policies of the Central Committee that it was challenging. This is how two factions conventionally designated as "left" and "right" took shape. Stalin, with the advice of Rykov and Bukharin, assumed the role of theoretician in what now had the appearance of an ideological struggle.

Stalin had picked up from Lenin the notion of a dictatorship of the proletariat, a term borrowed by Lenin from Marx and Engels, who meant it in a sense exactly opposite to the one given it by Lenin and Stalin, in whose hands it became the dictatorship of a party. Marx alluded only twice to a very brief dictatorship of the proletariat: he mentioned it incidentally in five lines of a personal letter, and again in his critical notes on the Social Democratic Gotha Program. As for Engels, he described the Paris Commune of 1871 as the model of such a dictatorship: a federalist system of free communes, with a plurality of non-Marxist political parties, free elections, and universal suffrage—the very antithesis of the Soviet regime. This dominant theme of Marxism-according-to-Lenin thus takes up about fifteen lines in the 38 large octavo volumes of the Russian edition of the works of Marx and Engels, and, when examined in context, contradicts the arbitrary Leninist interpretation passed on to Stalin. The same is true of the theoretical trappings that Bukharin was the first to furnish the "right-wing" faction. Two brief quotations from the 55 volumes of the incomplete works of Lenin, amounting to some fifteen very sketchy and tentative lines, provide Stalin with theoretical justification for establishing socialism in one country, a concept that became the dominating thesis of Stalinism.

The word socialism has so many meanings (among others the one Hitler gave it) that disputes over it between people who are not talking about the same thing seem pointless. But it does seem certain that if Lenin had wanted to treat of socialism in the Marxian sense of an egalitarian classless society devoid of a governing power, he would have had something more to say on the subject than a brief and vague allusion buried in an article on a hypothetical United States of Europe. Furthermore, when before his death Lenin specified "the conditions necessary for the construction, through cooperation ... of the complete socialist society," he listed conditions that did not, of course, exist in the Soviet Union, where there was no authentic (i.e., voluntary) cooperation. Hence there was no relation between Lenin's abstract concept and the crude and falsified version of it embodied in Stalinist dogma.

Both the left and the right were at pains to drape in ideological clothing a conflict whose true stake was the job of General Secretary. The right, in power, condemned the views of the left on industrialization and planning, branding them extreme and likely to generate peasant resistance; it linked these views to an old theory of Trotsky's about "permanent revolution," which dated from the revolution of 1905 and which Lenin had at one time rejected, only to adopt it again in 1917.[4] According to this theory, the revolution anticipated in Russia could not be stopped at the stage of bourgeois democracy, but would necessarily spread and deepen until it brought the proletariat to power; the inevitable repercussions throughout the world would accelerate the universal revolution. Neither Stalin nor Bukharin ever conceived the slightest objection to the so-called Trotskyite theory before the fight for supremacy that followed Lenin's illness and death—Bukharin, indeed, had even given it his retrospective approval. No member of the Communist oligarchy disputed the identification of the party with the proletariat. But to justify the official policy of stimulating agricultural production by granting material advantages to the peasants, it was necessary to denounce the "planners" of the left for fanning the flames of class struggle by pushing industrialization at the expense of agriculture. The source of this "deviation" was traced to Trotsky, on the pretext that his concept of permanent revolution did not take into account the interests of the peasant class, but merged all social categories into one.

Now, it was Trotsky who, in 1923, was the first to say of the Russian peasant: "We must see to it that next year he is more prosperous than this year." And he advised against increasing taxes, "so that the peasant economy can expand and the peasant be richer in future." In 1925 he still advocated enlarging "capitalist-merchant relations in the countryside," and reinforcing the "capitalist farm economy," and he emphatically opposed "de-kulakizing the kulaks."[5] Nothing, therefore, separated

Trotsky from Bukharin, who during this same period exclaimed: "To the peasants, to all the peasants, we must say: 'Enrich yourselves, develop your economy, and have no fear of being dispossessed.'" Nor did he differ markedly from Stalin, who was, logically enough, contemplating a return to small-scale ownership of rural land, which would limit the nationalization program. But in 1926 left and right were bent on opposing each other, and Stalin, like Bukharin, was accused of "kulakophile tendencies," whereupon Stalin accused Trotsky and his supporters of "underrating the peasantry." Ironically, Stalin was promptly dubbed "Tsar of the kulaks" by opponents who claimed to be adhering to "Bolshevism-Leninism." However, his fleeting liberal inclinations on matters of agricultural progress and peasant prosperity were not destined to become a permanent feature of Stalinism; a new round of disputes at the oligarchy's summit placed him at loggerheads with Bukharin and Rykov, who took seriously the "new course" in the countryside, as Trotsky had taken seriously the "new course" in the party. Stalin succeeded in overcoming the new opposition as he had all previous opposition, and by the same methods: appropriating as his own the views of the left on industrialization and planning, just as he had made himself spokesman for the right on agricultural policy and economic development.

That Stalin was able to vanquish his opponents of left and right so easily, to the point of exterminating them all, including leaders much more eminent than he in the history of the party; that he was able to perform an about-face as astonishing as that of massacring by the millions peasants of all conditions after championing their well-being— these are aspects of Stalinism that no theory explains. Stalin exploited to the hilt the fiction originated by Lenin and shared by Stalin's adversaries that the party is identical with the proletariat, and that the Central Committee, and thus the party Secretariat, are the Class Chosen by History incarnate—the underlying and unquestioned assumption being that the proletariat has been vested by an unknown providential immanence with a sacred historic mission, of which Marx and Engels were the interpreters. Transfigured into the hypostasis of the proletariat, Stalin had license to commit any conceivable act, no matter how grossly it violated the constitution of the state, the statutes of the party, and unwritten moral law; he acted behind a shield of doctrinal rationalization that neither Trotsky nor Bukharin nor any of their followers had the intellectual courage or political strength to call into question. "My Party, right or wrong," said Trotsky. "The Party is always right," Bukharin proclaimed in his own way. Both they and their followers vied in protesting their faithfulness to a faithless autocracy, thus simulating ideological disputes when the real issue, as Zinoviev and Kamenev confessed in 1926, was a struggle for power, a struggle in which Stalin acted without scruple or principle.[6] Absolute master of the party apparatus that had been superimposed on the government structure, Politburo representative on the ruling collegium of the GPU, where he necessarily had the last word, Stalin was able to annihilate and temporarily dishonor the oligarchy established by Lenin, and replace it with another that was abjectly obedient to his every whim.

These elements of Stalinism are nontransferable. They do not appear in any statement of doctrine. The official dogma disguises them as the orderly procedures of an authentic democracy. Holding a veritable monopoly over the information media, Stalin imposed on the country the fictions that served his political needs, and, what is even more amazing, gained credence abroad for myths that fly in the face of simple common sense. The entire Soviet population being in the service of the state or dependent on it, everyone felt himself at the mercy of the government, and the slightest resistance to the will or caprice of the tyrant meant some form of disfavor, if not death. The feeling of insecurity for oneself and those nearest one; the suppression of human rights and elementary judicial guarantees; the sundering of families by order of the police; the terrifying activities of the GPU; the dread inspired by blind repression; the mass deportations; the innumerable secret executions—none of these are acknowledged aspects of Stalinism. Instead, the writings of Stalin and his mouthpieces rely heavily on such fictions (the scholar's word for lies) as the importance of protecting the purity of Marxism-Leninism against perversions from left and right and against foreign influences; maintaining party unity against schismatics and dissidents; defending the conquests of the revolution against saboteurs, the remnant of the old exploiting classes, and the agents and spies of imperialism; vigilance by the organs of public safety, spurred by the holy anger of the working class in the face of internal and external threats.

The Bolsheviks made their first error in sincerely and blindly accepting and preaching the historic mission of the proletariat. Their next mistake was the transferral of that mission to their party, which they saw as the conscious instrument of world history. Then they lied to themselves, transforming a questionable hypothesis into a never-to-be-questioned thesis, which they put over by increasingly immoral methods of conquering without convincing. Finally, they knowingly and systematically lied to others, in order to consolidate their power at home and their influence abroad. In this irreversible perversion of Bolshevism, the responsibility, first of Lenin, then of his immediate successors, is such that Stalin's unique, personal contribution is impossible to discern. Stalin's originality lies in the combined use of trickery and violence, pushed to the furthest extreme, to attain his ends, and above all in his capacity for extending the imaginable limits of tyranny and all that tyranny can mean in terms of inhumanity and immorality.

Strictly speaking, Stalinism is forceful and distinctive not as a language, but as a series and chain of actions. To Stalin goes the credit of having established in the largest country in Europe and Asia a permanent regime of state terrorism unexampled in history; for having carried out, to this end, mass murders and deportations uncatalogued even now by any known statistic; for having conferred on his secret police the right of life and death over subject populations; for having massacred and uprooted peasant families by the million in order to collectivize agriculture; for having produced an artificial famine that took millions of lives. Stalin could boast of having dishonored, degraded, and put to death the entire upper echelons of the party, state, and army, selected by Lenin in his lifetime, through the institution of torture as a standard means of extracting false confessions from innocent men and of mock trials as a cover for his homicidal enterprise; of having, with cool deliberation, wiped out almost the entire generation of veteran socialists, of all shades of belief, after first dissolving their harmless associations, suspending their publications, and censoring their writings and memoirs, just as he had withdrawn from circulation the printed works of all of his victims, and even censored Marx and Lenin; of having suppressed the Marx-Engels Institute and its learned publications, *Annals of Marxism* and *Marx-Engels Archives*; of having deported its founder and director, D. Riazanov, and most of his staff; of having murdered his own wife, Nadezhda Alliluyeva, his brother-in-law, A. Svanidze, his closest childhood companions, A. Enukidze, S. Ordzhonikidze, and B. Mdivani, his "friend" and toady Sergei Kirov, whom he "avenged" by decimating the population of Leningrad. It was Stalin's special contribution to have made the pact with Hitler that unleashed the Second World War and its train of indescribable horrors, including the holocaust that took the lives of millions of Jews; to have conducted the war with such indifference to human life that Soviet losses were four times those of Germany (which had a population a third as large); to have deported entire ethnic groups from the Volga to the Caucasus, and to have wanted to liquidate the Jewish minority after the fashion of Hitler's "final solution"; in short, to have pushed Russian civilization and society back to the barbarous times of Ivan the Terrible.

This cursory listing of depravities, crimes, and atrocities can be taken as a rough outline of Stalin's biography. It does not, strictly speaking, define Stalinism, since any "ism" is assumed to have a more or less coherent underlying doctrine, based on some kind of principle, however uninspired. Stalin had no principle other than the cult of his own person (not having a real personality), in the service of which he brought into play all the techniques available to a modern state, boggling at no act of foulness or cruelty that would satisfy his *libido dominandi*. He dared to commit what we now call genocide, comparable in modern times only to the massacres of Armenians by Abdul Hamid and to the butchering of Jews by Hitler, his sometime ally; but Stalin's slaughters far exceeded those of the Turk and the German: at his death, if we collate the estimates of the best-qualified statisticians, the population deficit of the Soviet Union was considerably more than one hundred million people.[7] The concentration camps—created to swallow up the elites of all the Sovietized peoples, Russian and non-Russian, by wearing them down with penal drudgery until they died from exhaustion and disease—these death camps, although copied by Hitler, likewise surpassed in enormity anything in recorded history.

The reality that was Stalin's regime, or Stalinism in practice, appears only rarely in the official documents and literature of the period, and then under a camouflage that renders it unrecognizable. But a power claiming to adhere to Marxism-Leninism could not escape the need to speak in doctrinal language, if only to maintain the appearance of fidelity to the sources. In addition to the Marxist fiction of the dictatorship of the proletariat and the Leninist fiction of socialism in one country, Stalin borrowed from Lenin the need for "barbarous means to combat barbarity" (as if the end and the means could conflict),[8] and to "catch up with and surpass" at all costs the most economically advanced capitalist countries, a goal pre-revolutionary Russia was on its way to meeting by more humane methods than Soviet totalitarianism.[9] Where Stalin did take the initiative, however, was in finishing off the NEP, which Lenin had intended to continue "seriously and for a long time to come," which the right planned to carry on with, and which the left had never proposed to abolish. "Lenin did say that the NEP was introduced seriously and for a long time to come, but he did not say that it was to last forever," declared Stalin, for whom Lenin's name was a sufficient cloak, in 1929. In truth Lenin's pronouncement on the NEP reflected a carefully considered policy, which became more marked as it became evident that the European revolution that had fueled Bolshevik illusions in October and for the next five years was a chimera.

After suppressing the NEP, Stalin practiced a new kind of war com-

munism, this time civil-war communism, making what actually amounted to war on the peasants in collectivizing the country's agriculture by
brute force. Lenin had placed his hopes in voluntary cooperation, even
if he was not above exerting party pressure to drum into the villagers
the advantages of collectivism. As the new civil war in the countryside
intensified, the concentration camps multiplied and grew; soon recalcitrant peasants were joined by Communists expelled from the party,
workers dismissed from the factory and workyard, intellectuals driven
from the university, editors, engineers, clergymen. The economic dis-
order, food shortages, and scarcity of consumer goods caused a decline
in production, labor instability, and crises of every description, to which
Stalin replied with Draconian measures intended to instill iron discipline in the labor force and to curb negligence and pilfering. A series of
decrees made the death penalty an administrative measure to be imposed
as the "supreme measure of social defense."

Never had the death penalty been inflicted on working men and
women with such indiscriminate abandon, for such petty transgressions
as having broken rules, caused accidents, damaged state property, as
in this "workers' fatherland" governed by a "dictatorship of the proletariat," the country of which Stalin said in 1936, "The total victory of
the socialist system in all spheres of the national economy is now an
accomplished fact.... The first phase of communism, socialism, has
now been fully realized throughout our country."[10] This innovation of
Stalin's was a distinctive feature of Stalinism. The Bolsheviks, along with
all the Socialists of the International, had spoken out many times against
the death penalty, for political and nonpolitical crimes alike. They had
reintroduced it, abolished it, and brought it back again under Lenin,
keeping it in force long after the exceptional circumstances that supposedly had required if not justified it. But the abuses of the death penalty under Stalin have left a stamp of fantastic tragedy on the somberest
annals of Russian history. Though the magnitude of the slaughter was
reflected in the population curves of the general census of 1937, revised
in 1939, no statistic conveys the deadly effects of this legislation. The decrees promulgated from 1927 to 1934, signed by various high officials but
dictated by Stalin, delivered all Soviet subjects, who had no legal recourse, into the arbitrary hands of a government and police force un-
checked by law, acting in silence and in secret.

The "statute on counterrevolutionary crimes against the state and
crimes particularly dangerous to the established order," a catchall law
adopted in February 1927, contains twenty-seven sections, nineteen of
them providing for the death penalty. In the absence of any judicial or

legal protection, anyone could be condemned to death for anything, with no chance whatever of defending himself, of summoning witnesses, or of appealing to an unbiased judge, a lawyer, or public opinion. The decree of 1931 on discipline in the transport industry allowed capital punishment for the smallest on-the-job mistake. The decree of 1932—aimed primarily at railwaymen and seamen and indigent peasants and workers guilty of filching a little food—established the death penalty for simple theft. The decree of 1934, directed against those who were "betraying the fatherland," extended the death penalty to anyone attempting to leave the country, and codified the taking of hostages by sentencing all the adult relatives of the condemned person (who might well be innocent) to five to ten years in prison. Finally, the decree of 1935 went beyond all the earlier decrees, providing the death penalty for theft, breaches of labor discipline, and betrayal of the fatherland applicable to minors 12 years of age and older—a decree with no known precedent in any country, under any dictatorship.[11]

The decree of 1934, aimed at "betrayal of the fatherland," coincided with a cynical about-face by Stalin in the field of foreign policy, occasioned by Hitler's rise to power. For years the party's appointed thinkers had been prophesying an imminent imperialist war against the Soviet Union led by France and England. The only aggressor that neither Stalin nor Trotsky nor Bukharin ever anticipated was Germany. The German danger suddenly loomed up with the triumph of National Socialism, whereupon Stalin made hasty advances to imperialist France and England, unblushingly joined the League of Nations, which the day before he had called the League of Brigands, and proclaimed the necessity for a united front of Communists and socialists. All the while he stepped up his overtures to Hitler and Mussolini, indifferent to the treatment that the Nazis and Fascists were inflicting on the Communists of Germany and Italy. While the bloody repressions and chronic purges continued, one fixed aim was taking shape in his mind: to reach an understanding with his most formidable potential enemy—Hitler. This was one of the major reasons for his determination to kill off the traditional cadres of the party and state founded by Lenin: the "Old Bolsheviks," the military men, the diplomats, who had always pursued a foreign policy that was hostile to imperialism, yet related to democratic socialism, despite the opposition between Bolshevism and reformism. Indifferent to ideology, concerned exclusively with power alignments, Stalin patiently devoted himself to deflecting toward the West the hostilities that threatened, reckoning that the warring nations would exhaust themselves and leave him to jump in at the end with his large armies intact.[12] There is a striking contrast between Stalin's maneuvering for military advantage and Lenin's revolutionary defeatism.

One sees the roots of many features of Stalin's regime in the state of Soviet affairs created by Lenin, but this does not alter the fact that differences in degree grew into differences in kind. Furthermore, experience was leading Lenin away from the direction that Stalin took. Stalin did not invent the political system in which a single party takes the place of the proletariat and treats it like someone who has not come of age; in which a narrow circle of leaders takes over the functions of the ever-more-servile party, until finally a single man is the Law and the Prophets incarnate; in which the interests of the party and the interests of the state, interpreted by a permanently installed Party Secretary, become identical; in which all checks and balances, all separation of powers evaporate; in which a state of siege gradually becomes the normal condition of society; and in which the end and the means are so at odds that present generations must be sacrificed to the imaginary advantage of future generations. Stalin did not think up all by himself a democratic centralism devoid of any democracy, the doctrine of the infallibility of the self-appointing Central Committee, Politburo, and General Secretary, the use of terror as a permanent instrument of government, or the death penalty used without judicial control or restraint by the secret police. Before his rule, the ruling clique had arrogated to itself doctrinal omniscience and the exclusive right to define and condemn heresies from the left, deviations from the right, opportunism, inopportunism, revisionism, dogmatism. But while admitting this, and without resorting to the old Hegelian-Marxist cliché that quantity becomes quality, the impartial observer must conclude that what had existed under Lenin was carried by Stalin to such extremes that its very nature changed. A system that was evolving in a more humane and moral direction was brutally exaggerated into one of monstrous inhumanity and immorality, and this process makes legitimate a distinction between "Leninism" and "Stalinism."[13]

Certain personal traits that had degenerated into pathological behavior (excessive ambition and cruelty, complexes, persecution mania, delusions of grandeur) disappeared from Stalinism with Stalin's death, but the practices and theories he adopted over a quarter of a century have left a heritage that the heirs only partially renounce. The form of this residue has been condemned, but its content remains unchanged. Stalin completely revised Lenin's ideas about the state, socialism, and social classes. According to Stalin, the state must be not weakened but strengthened, even under communism, so long as there exists anything that can be interpreted as capitalist encirclement; Lenin, by contrast, had said, "the proletarian state begins to wither away immediately after its victory, for, in a society without class contradictions, the state is useless and impossible."[14] In 1932 the Seventeenth Party Congress claimed that the "bases" of socialism had been established; in 1936 Stalin celebrated "the total victory of the socialist system in every sector of the national economy" and the liquidation of "all the exploiter classes." Nonetheless, Stalinism, even without Stalin, still stands for the perpetuation of the state and of a magnified role for the party, and hence for continuation of the dictatorship of the proletariat, class struggle, and classes—which makes the establishment of socialism unattainable, at least if we accept the definition given in the outmoded teachings of Marx and Lenin. Long before Milovan Djilas, as early as 1923, Bukharin had a presentiment of the formation of a new privileged class in Soviet Russia: "Even a proletarian background, the most calloused hands, and other equally remarkable qualities are no guarantee against transformation of the privileged proletarian elements into a new class."[15] Stalinism, be it eponymic or epigonic, ignores the evidence that this has happened, and clings to a theory that flies in the face of reality.

Stalin also differed from Lenin in his pathological pretensions to absolute infallibility in everything, which resulted in what semipenitent Stalinists like to call, euphemistically, the "cult of personality," but which, more accurately, was the deification of the tyrant—with all the sinister consequences, past and present, that that implied. Lenin frequently admitted that there were many mistakes for which he was responsible; in his last speech before the Communist International he was not afraid to say, "We have committed an enormous number of stupidities, and shall commit more." His correspondence and the published minutes of Politburo and Central Committee meetings show him patiently treating his colleagues as equals, urging them to educate themselves and to do their own thinking. Stalin was the opposite, demanding extravagant praise from his terrorized entourage, who in turn were backed by a chorus of innumerable fawning underlings. In the end he became the incarnation of all knowledge, all wisdom, all talent, all virtue—the universal genius. Using selected puppets to nurture and manicure his own image, and even, in certain cases, interceding to contribute a few superlatives of his own, he turned in a truly unprecedented performance: he ordered first the history of the party, then the history of Russia, rewritten to his specifications, had encyclopedias, dictionaries, and textbooks retailored to fit his legend, and carried out a general purge of the libraries and reduced millions of books into pulp. Such an insane enterprise was unable to survive its founder, though it stamped a sinister imprint on Soviet life and international Communism; latter-day Stalinists continue the shameless practice of falsifying history and glorifying a single leader. One cannot imagine Lenin, with his devotion to "scientific socialism," tinkering with history to give himself greater stature than he had earned, or falsifying statistics, as his Marxist-Leninist disciples do now.

As he expelled from the party, and hence from government leadership, the representatives of the principles that had animated the socialism of the founding fathers, Stalin laboriously contrived a working variety of National Socialism—or, if one prefers, National Bolshevism—in which Soviet nationalism, artificially fanned into chauvinism, coexisted, but only on paper, with a vaguely anticipated socialist utopia, the ideological adornment of political atrocity. His absolute rule, camouflaged by "the most democratic Constitution in the world" (a pack of lies from end to end), was accompanied by a unique obscurantism that relied heavily on pedantic terminology. It convinced only a few ignorant young people, and was kept going by inquisitorial techniques that included, in addition to the death penalty, medieval tortures that were applied on any pretext—or on none. Stalin's National Socialism, in both its internal development and its foreign policy, became markedly similar to Hitler's system in its innate hostility to the bourgeois democracies. Like Hitler, Stalin discovered a "Jewish problem" that required a "final solution." Little by little Stalin's personal Judeophobia, which he had already given vent to in intraparty struggles, developed into systematic mass persecutions prefiguring a final pogrom, which was to have been touched off by the spurious plot of the Kremlin doctors, the "assassins in white." Death alone prevented Stalin from deporting the entire Jewish population to the extermination camps of polar Siberia. And on this score the aftermath of Nazism persists, in the discriminatory practices of present-day Stalinism.

Just as Soviet racism hides behind a constitutional façade of ethnic equality and religious freedom, most Communist realities hide behind theoretical and propaganda fictions. A catalogue of the fictions and realities would add up to a truthful history of the party, the Soviet Union, and the Communist International. This immense task is made no easier by the strict secrecy in which Moscow keeps the essential elements of that history: the telltale archives are not open; the records of the purge trials are a closed book; the writings of the victims are locked away in safes; even the papers of Lenin have been "screened." As for the papers of Stalin and his accomplices, there can be no question of letting anyone see them. Part of the truth was revealed by Khrushchev at the Twentieth Party Congress and by his collaborators and helpers at the Twenty-second Congress, but this is but a tiny fraction of the whole truth. Thirty years after the murder of Kirov we still await the results of the investigation announced by Khrushchev in 1956. In the memoirs of a Soviet general published in 1964, a Moscow review discreetly alluded, for the first time, to the brutal treatment that he endured under interrogation.[16] Innumerable examples can be cited showing the extent to which Stalinism in action is still unknown, underrated, and undocumented, notwithstanding so valuable a find as a fragment of the Smolensk archives. The attitude of Stalin's successors in this regard hardly disproves the persistence of Stalinism in a Marxism-Leninism that claims to return to the sources.

Printed or written references obviously are not needed to prove that Stalin broke with Leninism when he first domesticated, then dissolved, proprio motu, the Third International. Lenin's life and work adequately attest to the importance he attached to this creation of his. From 1914 onward he was wholly convinced that he had fulfilled his historic mission in splitting the Socialist Workers' International to form the Communist International. The part that he took in the four congresses of this young organization proved how close it was to his heart, and it would be to completely misconstrue his thinking to suppose him at odds with it over either domestic or foreign policy at any time.[17] Stalin purged the foreign Communist parties much as he had purged his own party, making them arms of the Soviet secret police; that there was less bloodshed was for reasons beyond his control. When he was ready, he abolished the Third International with one stroke of his pen, confident that its docile membership would continue to support his diplomatic and strategic maneuvers on the chessboard of international politics. Here too, Stalinism, which is still alive, conflicts flagrantly with Leninism.

Outwardly there is some continuity between Stalinism and Leninism in the matter of colonialism, if, with General de Gaulle, we believe that "the Soviet empire is the largest and last colonial power of this era."[18] Lenin, theoretician and champion of the right of peoples to run their own affairs "up to and including separatism," certainly violated his own principles and the promises he had made in October by using force of arms to put the disintegrating Russian empire together again. He did not, however, intend to subject non-Russian nations to Great Russian chauvinism, which he roundly condemned in his dispute with Stalin over Georgia.[19] He showed unmistakable intentions of allowing the nationalities comprising the Soviet federation to develop autonomously, and the example of the NEP entitles us to believe that his centralist pol-

icy was evolving in a relatively liberal direction. Whether under circumstances he could not have foreseen he would have ventured to reduce
neighboring countries to servitude by military occupation can only be
a matter of conjecture. As for Stalin, he flayed the downtrodden ethnic
minorities with fire and sword; he annexed territories with millions of
protesting inhabitants; he colonized the captive nations and made them
satellites—until it was indeed the case that "the Soviet empire is the
largest and last colonial power of this era." The building of such an
empire under the banner of anti-imperialism may be a plus or minus
for Stalinism, depending on one's point of view; but it was an impressive achievement which doctrine utterly fails to explain (except to bra-
zenly call it a process of free federation), and which Stalin's heirs refuse
to undo.

One gathers that "the peaceful coexistence of countries with differing
social systems," another of Stalin's fictions designed to assure the permanence of his conquests while he carried on the cold war, has not been
repudiated either. Stalin added nothing new to Communist tactics when
he talked about "peaceful cohabitation" and "peaceful coexistence"; he
merely enriched the vocabulary of propaganda and described what had
been a fact since Lenin's day.[20] At the same time he formulated a line
of conduct that President Kennedy decoded very well as meaning
"What's ours is ours, what's yours is negotiable." Understood thus,
peaceful coexistence—a synonym for cold war—means keeping all territorial acquisitions and every possible advantage, all the while exerting
maximum pressure from every side and continuing to maneuver, intrigue, infiltrate, corrupt, subvert, in order to prepare the ground for
new Communist advances at the first opportunity that does not risk precipitating nuclear war, which is equated with suicide. It must be admitted that this sort of foxiness is a direct legacy from Lenin, and that
it thus has a legitimate place in the Marxism-Leninism of his heirs.

In short, that incoherent mixture of handed-down theories and practical improvisations, the jumble of dogmatism and opportunism, complicated by doctrinal distortions and makeshift expedients, which constitutes Stalinism, can hardly be grasped except at its completion—incon-
clusive though it may be, for Stalin had not had his final word when
death surprised him in the midst of plans for new purges and genocide.
He did, however, leave a system of monolithic government and a set of
practical precepts which are extremely useful to his successors, and which
seem to stand the test of contemporary history in the absence of any organized resistance at home and all but the most harmless opposition
abroad. Still, the durability of such a regime does not prove its worth,

for it endures only by disavowing its original program and violating its current one, by invoking the name of socialism only to perpetuate its antithesis. Jaurès, then, showed remarkable foresight when at the beginning of the century he wrote to Péguy that "a class born of democracy, which instead of abiding by the law of democracy, prolonged its dictatorship beyond the first few days of the revolution, would soon be nothing more than a gang encamped on a country's territory, wasting its resources."[21] How much truer this is when it is not a class but a party that indefinitely prolongs its dictatorship, a party that stoops to serving a new oligarchy of profiteers whose specious ideology, be it Stalinism or Marxism-Leninism, masks an implacable exploitation of man by man—which is the very negation of classical socialism and communism.

# Khrushchevism

To understand Khrushchevism one must begin with Khrushchev the man, with what he was like in his days of power. Shrewd, earthy, endowed with boundless energy, a bouncing confidence, and a quick, if coarse, wit, he was the very epitome of the self-made man in any society. Like most self-made men, he believed profoundly that the social order which nurtured him and conferred its highest honors on him was a society whose virtues could not be impugned. When Spyros Skouras, the movie magnate, during a Hollywood luncheon for Khrushchev, cited his own rise from rags to riches as a symbol of the opportunities that America holds out for the lowly, Khrushchev replied: "Mr. Skouras said he had risen from the ranks.... Would you like to know what I was? I began working when I learned to walk. Till the age of 15 I tended calves, then sheep, and then the landlord's cows. I did all that before I was 15. Then I worked at a factory owned by Germans and later in coalpits owned by Frenchmen. I worked at Belgian-owned chemical plants, and now I am Prime Minister of the great Soviet State."[1]

In the course of his lifetime, Khrushchev saw Russia transformed from a relatively backward country into one of the world's leading industrial and military powers, and he was understandably proud of this rapid progress and his own role in it. He gave every evidence of believing that the Soviet Union not only embodies the most progressive and just social structure that mankind has attained, but that it is also blazing a trail into the future that people everywhere will enthusiastically follow. "I am convinced more than ever," he told reporters toward the end of his American trip, "that the holiest of holies, the best that man can create is socialist society, the Communist system."[2]

Nor can such remarks be dismissed as mere propaganda, the public pronouncements which a Soviet leader is duty-bound to make and which do not necessarily mirror his fundamental outlook. Difficult as it is to be certain that one has ever penetrated the inner recesses of a man's

character, the self-portrait that emerges from Khrushchev's countless im-
promptu remarks is fairly clear: he saw himself as a man of faith, believing that communism provides a key to the world's problems. He
was a propagandist in every fiber of his being, but propaganda in his
case was inseparable from his deepest convictions. In a characteristic
speech to the Fifth World Congress of Trade Unions in 1961, he observed: "It may be said that Khrushchev is again handing out propaganda. If you think so, you are not mistaken. Yes, I was, am, and always
shall be a propagandist. As long as the heart continues beating in my
breast I shall propagate the ideas of Marxism-Leninism, the ideas of communist construction!"[3]

A man of limited formal education, he found his teacher in the Party.
The Party provided him with a view of the world that confirmed his
own experience, and its simple tenets were endlessly reiterated in his
speeches. Capitalism is a system of exploitation whose days are numbered.
Communism represents the wave of the future because it is a superior
social and economic system that frees the masses from exploitation and
promotes the well-being and happiness of all mankind. The Communist
Party, which led the working class of old Russia to victory, provides a
pattern of organization and leadership which alone can guarantee the
triumph of Communism on a world scale. For Khrushchev these propositions were sacred and unassailable. As a worker in Tsarist Russia he
experienced exploitation. Recruited by the Party in 1918, he fought in
the ranks of the Red Army during the Civil War, helped drive the
Whites out of Russia, and shared the exhilaration of victory in the face
of apparently hopeless odds. His rapid rise in the party hierarchy during
the next decades only served to reinforce his faith in the Communist
cause.

As one of Stalin's lieutenants, he was chained to a jealous master who
demanded unquestioning obedience and obsequiousness from all who
served him. The evidence now at hand makes clear that Khrushchev
chafed under the restrictions, but at the time no one could match him
in fulsome tributes to his mentor, and no one was more zealous in defending Stalin's course. The purges that represented catastrophe for
countless of Khrushchev's colleagues spelled opportunity for him. With
every turn of the wheel, his fortunes prospered; on those rare occasions
when he suffered a temporary setback, he demonstrated a remarkable
resilience in bouncing back. Khrushchev obviously possessed the qualities
of toughness and ruthlessness that were required to maneuver one's way
to one of the top places in Stalin's entourage. Trained in the Stalin school
of falsification, he demonstrated an impressive capacity to meet the ex-

pectations of his master. Against the background of the Stalinist years it is tempting to dismiss Khrushchev as a cynical manipulator for whom ideology had at best an instrumental significance. It is a temptation that should be resisted. The evil that men do in order to survive and gather power may corrupt the ends they serve, but it does not necessarily lessen the need for a justifying vision. Indeed, in some cases, it may intensify it. For Khrushchev the justification was found in Stalin's construction program, in building the greatness of Soviet power and helping lay the foundations for Communist victory at home and abroad.

His administrative assignments under Stalin were largely confined within the party apparatus. Although Stalin heaped increasingly heavy responsibilities on him, they remained party-centered. His were the typical practical concerns of the party apparatchik, prodding and driving his subordinates to meet the ambitious targets of the Five-Year Plans. Already under Stalin he was the agitator par excellence, not content to direct proceedings from a remote office, but enjoying face-to-face contacts, constantly roaming his domain, and making frequent appearances at the construction sites and collective farms over which he exercised supervision.

His experience until Stalin's death was narrowly provincial. His secretarial duties within the party provided no opportunities for foreign travel and little in the way of foreign contacts. As a member of the Politburo from 1939 on, he was undoubtedly exposed to high-level discussions of foreign policy, but since they were largely marginal to his direct concerns and responsibilities, it is doubtful that he gave them his prime attention. The world outside the Soviet Union was terra incognita, to be comprehended largely in terms of Marxist-Leninist categories. His first view of the West did not come until he had passed his sixtieth birthday; it would have been remarkable indeed had he been able to free himself of the stereotypes he brought to the exposure.

Yet there were elements in Khrushchev's character that were responsive to fresh experience. He had a pragmatic bent for testing ideas by their workability. An avid learner in practical affairs and a man of wide-ranging technical curiosity, he was quite prepared to borrow techniques from the West when he thought they could advance his own purposes. Nor were his travels abroad without influence on his assessment of Western developments. "I have seen the slaves of capitalism—and they live well!" Khrushchev declared while visiting the farm of Rosswell Garst in Iowa in September 1959.[4] The significance of this spontaneous tribute was not diminished by the fact that it went unreported in the Soviet press.

At the same time his awareness of the superiority of Western living standards was matched by a conviction that capitalism is a dying system and that the Soviet Union would soon outstrip America in both productivity and welfare. Running through many of Khrushchev's speeches is a curious defensiveness, an extraordinary sensitivity to outside criticism of Soviet weaknesses, which is overcompensated by a boastful pride in Soviet achievements. Plans for the future tend to be presented as if they were actualities, and demagogic promises mask very real problems. But beneath the rhetoric one could also detect a growing conviction that the Soviet system would be judged by its results and that the competition with capitalism could not be won by words alone. "Now I ask you," he said in one of his more homely moods, "would it be bad if we spread our Marxist-Leninist teachings with a piece of butter? I say that with a good bread spread like that, Marxism-Leninism would be even more tasty. And with good housing, with a better and more abundant life, with good schools, we will win all the peoples for socialism and Communism."[5]

To understand Khrushchevism as it took shape after Stalin's death one must begin with the man, but one must also understand the situation in which he found himself and the necessities he was compelled to face. Stalin's legacy to his successors was replete with problems. His impressive achievements in forcing the pace of Soviet industrialization, in building military power, and in expanding his domain into Eastern and Central Europe were all purchased at a heavy price. Soviet agriculture remained backward and stagnant, and the food available to Soviet consumers was monotonous, scarce, and high-priced. Stalin's obsession with the development of heavy industry meant that light industry was ignored and underdeveloped, and shortages of consumer goods and housing were acute and widespread. The system of terror on which Stalin relied to protect his own security and to enforce his regime of deprivation and sacrifice had its debilitating effects. It bred a cowed and submissive populace for whom the regime was "they" and not "we." Frightened bureaucrats shrank from exercising initiative; there was a frozen and congealed quality about Soviet life that tended to rob it of all dynamism and revolutionary appeal. The East European satellites formed an extension of the Soviet prison house. Yugoslavia, to be sure, had broken away amid the curses and maledictions of the Cominform, and, in the East, Communist China presented a special case with its own independent power base. For the rest, the Communist bloc was managed by puppets utterly dependent on Stalin. The Soviet empire was in effect sealed off from the West, and as a result of the Korean War the Soviet Union and the United States were involved in a spiraling arms race that threatened the world with a nuclear holocaust. After the great burst of expansionism that followed the Second World War, bringing the East European satellites and mainland China into the Communist fold, the forward momentum of the Soviet bloc was arrested. The Marshall Plan and NATO brought a measure of stability to Western Europe. While Ho Chi Minh was able to press forward to victory in North Vietnam, the Communist-sponsored risings in India, Burma, Malaya, Indonesia, and the Philippines proved abortive, and left in their wake a suspicion of Soviet intentions toward the new nations that would not be easily allayed. In Korea the two sides were locked in stalemate.

This was the situation that confronted Stalin's successors. The choices open to them, as Communists, were not infinite. They could not be expected to preside over the liquidation of Stalin's empire. As party leaders, they might seek other means than Stalin's to promote Communist objectives; but they shared with him not merely a common experience but also a common commitment. What they also now shared with each other was a responsibility they could not escape: they had to make their own decisions.

Government by committee is never easy. It is rendered all the more difficult when each member of the group is engaged in a contest for ascendancy, and every position taken is weighed not merely for its contribution to the common weal but for its effect in the power struggle. It is not easy to disentangle Khrushchev's role in the period immediately after Stalin's death; such evidence as we have derives from him, and he is not an altogether unbiased witness.

The tone set by the new leadership in the months after Stalin's death was one of relaxation of tension at home and abroad. Amnesties, price cuts, and promises of more consumer goods and housing augured a new disposition to seek popular support. The ending of the Korean War contributed to ease relations with the West. So far as we know, Khrushchev participated in and approved of these actions, as he no doubt ratified the decision to suppress the East German rising in June 1953 and joined in the purge of Beria soon afterward.

At the September 1953 session of the Central Committee he was elected First Secretary. His report to the Central Committee on the agricultural situation, which was delivered on September 3, represented his first important independent pronouncement in the post-Stalinist period. It contained a blunt and even sensational acknowledgment of the seriousness of the agricultural crisis that the new leadership had inherited from Stalin. Although many of the reforms that Khrushchev advocated had been foreshadowed by earlier Malenkov proposals approved by the Supreme Soviet in August, there was a quality of frankness in Khrushchev's speech that was novel. In essence, he argued that Soviet agricultural productivity could not be raised unless additional incentives were offered to the collective farmers. In most other respects, the speech remained within a conventional framework: there were no proposals to modify the system of state and collective farming, and the thrust of his organizational proposals was in the direction of strengthening party controls and buttressing the role of the machine-tractor stations rather than dismantling them. His propensity for bold and daring ventures became more clearly manifest in early 1954, when he obtained the approval of the Central Committee for his virgin-lands program. Designed to obtain a vast increase in grain output with minimal capital investments, its success hinged on favorable weather in areas where drought and short growing seasons were endemic. Undeterred by obstacles and despite the skepticism displayed by Malenkov, Molotov, and Kaganovich, he pressed ahead and gambled his political future on harvests that might not materialize. Fortune favored him in the early years, and as his power and prestige mounted, the range of his interests broadened. He sought to learn at first hand about the problems with which he would have to deal. In 1954 he journeyed to Warsaw and Prague, and then to China. On the way back he toured the Soviet Far East and Siberia, solidifying party contacts and observing developments as he went.

During this period there were few signs of the de-Stalinizer to come. There was a settlement of accounts with various Beria henchmen, and a number of Stalin's victims were discreetly rehabilitated. But at the time Khrushchev claimed no special personal credit for these acts. Except for the innovations he sponsored in agriculture, his public pronouncements followed a conservative course. His militant speech at Prague, with its declaration that a nuclear war would spell the end of capitalism, contrasted sharply with Malenkov's earlier declaration that nuclear war would mean the destruction of world civilization. In an address on December 7, 1954, to an All-Union Conference of Builders, Khrushchev placed Stalin on a par with Lenin as an architect of Soviet industrialization and reasserted the priority of heavy industry for the future as well as the past. He clearly dissociated himself from Malenkov's consumer goods campaign. In a speech to the Central Committee of January 25, 1955, which was obviously aimed at Malenkov and provided the signal for demoting him from the chairmanship of the Council of Ministers, Khrushchev declared:

"In connection with the measures lately taken for increasing the output of consumer goods, some comrades have confused the question of the pace of development of heavy and light industry in our country. . . .

These pseudo-theoreticians try to claim that at some stage of socialist construction the development of heavy industry ceases to be the main task, and that light industry can and should overtake all other branches of industry. This is profoundly incorrect reasoning, alien to the spirit of Marxism-Leninism—nothing but slander of our Party. This is a belching of the rightist deviation, a regurgitation of views hostile to Leninism, views that Rykov, Bukharin, and their ilk once preached."[6]

It is not easy to determine whether the positions taken by Khrushchev at this time represented his deep convictions or whether they were influenced, in greater or lesser degree, by his desire to undercut such support as Malenkov enjoyed among the more conservative elements in the Presidium. What is clear is that Khrushchev subsequently adopted Malenkov's formulation on nuclear warfare, wavered on the issue of heavy industry versus light industry, and developed a new-found sensitivity to consumer claims.

With the downgrading of Malenkov, Khrushchev's field of maneuver widened, and he began to place his own personal stamp on foreign as well as domestic policy. The Khrushchevian style was characterized by boldness as well as opportunism; above all, it was masked by a willingness to experiment and strike out in new directions without necessarily calculating or anticipating costs and consequences. On the domestic front, primary attention was concentrated on agriculture. Hard on the heels of the virgin-lands program came another grandiose effort to solve the food problem—this time by massive extension of the crop acreage devoted to corn in order to provide a feed base for animal husbandry. Encouraged by the report of a high-level Soviet farm delegation that visited the corn lands of the United States and Canada, Khrushchev tirelessly preached the virtues of this magic crop, and, characteristically, pressed for its widespread adoption regardless of climatic hazards.

Khrushchev's most dramatic initiatives during this period were reserved for the field of foreign affairs. Of these none was more startling than his effort to woo Tito back into the Soviet bloc by flying to Belgrade and making Canossa-like confessions of past Soviet errors. The expedition, which was undertaken over the opposition of Molotov and eventually led to his dismissal as Foreign Minister, was apparently inspired by Khrushchev's faith that shared Communist ideological commitments would serve to transcend all past difficulties. While the visit did result in improved Soviet-Yugoslav relations—for which, incidentally, Khrushchev undertook to pay a not inconsiderable price in promises of substantial Soviet economic aid—Tito's insistence on maintaining his own independence in both domestic and international affairs hardly made it an unqualified victory for Khrushchev. The long-term consequences in terms of the hoped-for solidification of the Soviet bloc were to be even less happy. Khrushchev's recognition of Tito's special position set a pattern that other East European regimes could only envy, and that some were shortly to seek to emulate.

At the same time Khrushchev sought to create an image of himself as a man of peace, and he moved toward an easing of relations with the West. The conclusion of the Austrian State Treaty in May 1955, which put an end to the occupation regime in Austria and adopted a formula for neutralization of that country, marked the first significant withdrawal of Soviet power in Europe. Against this background of a negotiated settlement, Khrushchev met with Eisenhower at the summit meeting of July 1955 in Geneva. No agreements of substance emerged from the conference, but the very fact that the sessions took place in an atmosphere of relative cordiality raised the hopes for peace throughout the world. "The spirit of Geneva," as it came to be called, provided Khrushchev with a useful symbol of his peace-seeking proclivities.

Another major Khrushchevian initiative involved efforts to strengthen Soviet influence among the new nations of Asia and Africa. Turning his back on the earlier Stalinist line, which encouraged local Communists to try to seize power in these countries, Khrushchev now undertook to identify himself with their anti-colonial and anti-imperial grievances, wooed their nationalist leaders with offers of aid and trade, sought to weaken their ties with the West, and tried to influence them to adopt a policy of positive neutrality favorable to Soviet interests. Khrushchev's trip to India toward the end of 1955 marked the beginning of a major campaign to win new friends in the underdeveloped countries. Meanwhile, a more ominous note was struck with the conclusion of a large-scale Egyptian arms deal, which appeared deliberately designed to stir up trouble in the Middle East by aligning the Soviet Union with the anti-Israeli and anti-Western forces of Arab nationalism.

While the new dynamism thus introduced into Soviet foreign policy reflected the Khrushchevian touch, it remained for the Twentieth Party Congress, held in February 1956, to define the content of what has since come to be described as Khrushchevism. The high spot of the Congress was the "secret speech" in which Khrushchev combined a wide-ranging condemnation of Stalin's methods of rule with sensational disclosures of his terrorist crimes. What inspired Khrushchev to open this Pandora's box is still open to debate and may long remain so. The speech can be read as a bold maneuver in the struggle for the succession, as part of Khrushchev's efforts to dissociate himself from responsibility for Stalin's crimes by taking the initiative in denouncing them and by demonstrating that his Presidium rivals, Molotov, Malenkov, and Kaganovich, were intimately involved in all the Stalinist excesses. Khrushchev himself defended the speech as a necessary surgical operation to restore the health of the Party. In repudiating Stalin's terrorist practices, he in effect offered his personal guaranty that he would not repeat them. More positively, he held out a vision of a Soviet society in which citizens could breathe more freely, officialdom could exercise initiative without fearing the consequences, the bond between Party and people would be strengthened, and the authority of the regime would be built on the rational foundations of regularized procedures, concern with popular welfare, and confidence rather than fear.

The refurbished image that Khrushchev held out to his own people had its counterpart in a series of ideological innovations designed to make Communism more attractive and acceptable abroad. The doctrine that Lenin had formulated and Stalin reiterated—that war between the Soviet Union and the so-called imperialist states was inevitable—was now amended to read that war was not "fatalistically inevitable." In Khrushchev's words: "As long as imperialism exists, the economic base that gives rise to wars will also remain. That is why we must display the greatest vigilance. As long as capitalism survives in the world, reactionary forces that represent the interests of the capitalist monopolies will continue their drive toward military gambles and aggression and may try to unleash war. But war is not a fatalistic inevitability. Today there are mighty social and political forces possessing formidable means to prevent the imperialists from unleashing war, and, if they try to start it, to give a smashing rebuff to the aggressors and frustrate their adventurist plans. For this it is necessary for all anti-war forces to be vigilant and mobilized; they must act as a united front and not relax their efforts in the struggle for peace. The more actively the people defend peace, the greater the guaranty that there will be no war."[7]

The new formulation that "war is not fatalistically inevitable" laid the groundwork for a reaffirmation of the theory of peaceful coexistence, this time without the usual qualification as to its temporary character. But peaceful coexistence as proclaimed by Khrushchev did not imply a static acceptance of the existing correlation of forces between the camps of Communism and capitalism or a balance of power that was forever frozen. As he later elaborated in an interview with William Randolph Hearst, Jr., in 1957, "Society develops in accordance with its laws, and now the era has come when capitalism must make way for socialism as a higher social system than capitalism."[8] Nor did he envisage that these changes would take place everywhere peacefully. "Of course," he noted in his report to the Twentieth Congress, "in those countries where capitalism is still strong, where it possesses a tremendous military and police machine, serious resistance by reactionary forces is inevitable. The transition in these countries will take place amid sharp revolutionary class struggle."[9] While renouncing any intention of initiating an aggressive war, he made clear that the Soviet Union would extend support to "colonial peoples" struggling for independence. In an important speech on January 6, 1961, dealing, among other things, with so-called wars of national liberation, he elaborated the point: "What attitude do Marxists have toward such uprisings? The most favorable.... Communists fully and unreservedly support such just wars and march in the van of the peoples fighting wars of liberation." And in the same speech he proclaimed: "The struggle against imperialism can be successful only if the aggressive actions of imperialism are firmly resisted. Verbal denunciations will not restrain the imperialist adventurers. There is only one way to curb imperialism—by tirelessly strengthening the economic, political, and military might of the socialist states, by rallying and strengthening the world revolutionary movement in every way, and by mobilizing the broad masses for the struggle to ward off the danger of war."[10]

Khrushchev's effort to present Communism in a more attractive guise was particularly evident in the theses on the forms of transition to socialism in different countries that he presented to the Twentieth Congress.[11] Invoking the sacred authority of Lenin, he condemned Stalin for his insistence that foreign Communists slavishly imitate Soviet practice. He defended the proposition that there were different roads to socialism, described adjustment to "the peculiarities and specific features of each country," as "creative Marxism in action," and went so far as to include the Yugoslav administrative arrangements in his approved list of experiments. Even more startling was his bland statement that the parliamentary road to power was now open to the working class "in many capitalist countries," though he added the qualifications that victory would be possible only under Communist leadership and that the use or non-use of violence would depend on the resistance offered by "the exploiting class."

The de-Stalinization campaign and the ideological reformulations launched by Khrushchev at the Twentieth Party Congress were intended both to broaden the appeal of the Communist movement and to strengthen Khrushchev's own position within it. In the event, they came close to destroying Khrushchev, and they released divisive forces within the Communist world that have not yet run their full course. Within the Soviet Union, the ferment stirred up by Khrushchev's secret speech infected wide circles of the intelligentsia and student youth and inspired a protest literature that went beyond denunciations of Stalin to criticism of the Soviet system itself. The disarray within the bloc assumed proportions serious enough to threaten the Soviet hold over Eastern Europe. The gathering unrest came to a climax in October 1956, when large contingents of Soviet troops had to be rushed into Hungary to suppress a revolution in which native Communists were leading workers into battle against the Soviet Union. In Poland, direct Soviet military intervention was narrowly averted when a last-minute modus vivendi was worked out that recognized Gomulka, who had reassumed leadership in the Polish Party over Soviet objections. The bloody repression in Hungary and the reimposition of cultural curbs within the Soviet Union in reaction to the revolt served to tarnish the image of Khrushchev as the great liberalizer. In the aftermath of Hungary, Khrushchev's prestige declined sharply. His handling of Hungarian events contributed to exacerbate relations with Tito. The Chinese Party leadership gave him public support, but, as subsequent disclosures have made clear, they were privately highly critical of his de-Stalinization campaign, of his ideological initiatives, and above all of his failure to consult with them. Within the Soviet Party itself his Presidium opponents began to organize a cabal to unseat him, and, by dint of the additional support that they gathered in opposition to his industrial reorganization plans, by May 1957 they were able to mobilize a seven-to-four majority against him and to confront him with a demand for his resignation.

It is a measure both of the power concentrated in the office of the First Secretary and of Khrushchev's capacity to turn adverse developments to his own advantage that he was able to triumph even in these circumstances. By transferring the arena of the struggle to the Central Committee, where his followers were strongly installed, he turned the tables on his opponents and emerged from the encounter stronger than ever. In October of the same year he further consolidated his position by ousting his erstwhile supporter Marshal Zhukov from the Presidium and moving quickly to bring the armed forces under firm party control.

At this stage of Khrushchev's career, fortune seemed to be smiling on him. He had rid himself of his Presidium opponents, and his position as party leader appeared to be unassailable. He had surmounted the crisis in Eastern Europe, and, while restiveness was still evident, there were no threats of armed uprisings. The ferment among Soviet youth and intellectuals gave every outward appearance of having subsided; in any case, it presented no organized challenge to the regime's power.

Most important of all, the world was now treated to a startling demonstration of Soviet accomplishments in rocketry. On August 26, 1957, the Soviet government announced the successful firing of an intercontinental ballistic missile. On October 4 the Russians launched the first space satellite, Sputnik I, which was followed on November 3 by Sputnik II with the dog Laika aboard as passenger. These dramatic developments lifted Khrushchev's prestige to new heights. In the excitement that attended the launching of Sputnik I, the simultaneous dismissal of Marshal Zhukov was all but forgotten. National pride and respect for the regime's attainments were both sharply reinforced. Esteem for the achievements of Soviet science and technology was greatly enhanced throughout the world. The Soviet space exploits had obvious military implications, and Khrushchev was not slow to point out that they marked a significant shift in the balance of power that presaged Soviet ascendancy. He quickly initiated a major drive to translate Soviet rocket superiority into diplomatic gains, holding out the Soviet experience of rapid industrialization and scientific progress as a model to be imitated in the underdeveloped world and playing on a decline of confidence in American leadership to deepen fissures in the Western camp. In a militant speech to a Polish-Soviet Friendship Meeting in Moscow on November 10, 1958, he ignited the Berlin crisis with a demand for the liquidation of the occupation regime in West Berlin. This time Khrushchev overreached himself. The decision of the Western powers to stand firm exposed the emptiness of his ultimatums, bluster, and threats.

It is worth pausing at this point to sketch out the problems and choices that Khrushchev faced. Despite undoubted industrial progress and dramatic space achievements, there were limits to the pressure that Moscow could apply on the West. The United States was still a formidable thermonuclear power with larger resources than the Soviet Union, and any confrontation that imperiled vital American interests raised the danger of a thermonuclear holocaust with potentially disastrous consequences for both sides. As long as relations between the United States and the Soviet Union remained tense and difficult, the stage was set for the continuation of an expensive arms race that diverted resources from domestic development and spelled persisting hardships for the Soviet people. An easing of relations with the United States, by contrast, opened up tempting perspectives of more rapid improvement in the Soviet standard of living and accelerated economic development. A real détente with the West, however, could be achieved only at the price of accepting the status quo in world affairs and forgoing opportunities for revolutionary advance, at least for a defined period. However expedient such a course of action might appear from the Soviet point of view, it held out dangers for Soviet relations with its allies in the world Communist movement. It subordinated their interests to those of the Soviet Union. It implied, for example, that Communist China would not be able to count on Soviet assistance in pressing its campaign to regain Taiwan and that Chinese expansionist ambitions elsewhere would have to be curbed to serve Soviet national needs. It meant that Khrushchev might be forced to impose brakes on the revolutionary enthusiasm of Communist parties anxious to come to power, and might thus be maneuvered into a position where he could be accused of betraying the revolutionary cause.

It is unlikely that these sharply defined alternatives were either recognized or accepted by Khrushchev. Like leaders elsewhere who face multiple pressures and impulses, he sought to escape hard choices and found himself responding to events and pursuing policies with contradictory implications. Thus Khrushchev's professed and probably real desire to achieve a relaxation of tension with the United States, which would enable him to concentrate greater resources on internal development, was periodically negated by actions that placed a strain on the relationship. The Berlin ultimatums and the building of the wall between East and West Berlin, the Congo adventure, and the Cuban missile crisis were symptomatic of an unresolved dilemma in an area where doctrinal commitments and Realpolitik considerations clashed.

Equally difficult problems and choices confronted Khrushchev in working out his relations with his allies in the Communist bloc. In the armory of Khrushchevian theory there was no place for conflict among Communist powers. The axiom that all Communists share a common commitment to Marxism-Leninism was assumed to guarantee the unity of the Communist camp. But, as Khrushchev was soon to discover, the fact that conflicts go unacknowledged does not mean that they do not exist. The ideological bonds that unite Communist nations provide no automatic answers when leaders of these nations begin to interpret their interests in divergent terms.

The potential for conflict may be suggested by a series of questions. What obligations should the more powerful and highly developed Communist nations assume toward their less developed Communist associates? Should the gap between them be narrowed as rapidly as possible, or should priority be given to increasing the strength of the most advanced power on the theory that it carries the critical burden of defending and promoting the Communist cause? Should the development of the Communist bloc be planned as an integrated unit, and if so, under what scheme of control and on the basis of what regulating principles? Should existing divisions of labor between Communist nations supplying raw materials and Communist industrial nations be perpetuated, or should each nation be allowed to develop its own industrialization program and its own trading patterns? Under whose control and to what degree should military planning and strategy be integrated? Should the Soviet Union share its thermonuclear power and its most advanced weaponry with its allies, or should it reserve exclusive control over them? How should priorities in foreign policy be determined and differences reconciled? Should the Soviet Union exercise unquestioned leadership, or should there be mutual consultation on a commonwealth pattern, with each nation reserving freedom to pursue its own objectives? How much flexibility should be permitted in domestic affairs? Should each Communist nation strive for a uniform pattern modeled on Soviet experience, or should it feel free to work out its own special design?

To put these questions is not merely to emphasize the potential for conflict; each one became a source of controversy that Khrushchev found it more and more difficult to contain. In Khrushchev's eyes, the building of Soviet economic power was synonymous with bloc progress and Communist revolutionary advance; the discovery that leaders of other Communist states or parties looked on the relationships differently was not easy to absorb. This is not to say that Khrushchev was unaware of the pressures generated within the Communist camp to narrow the gap between the less and more developed Communist states. But his tendency was to deal with the problem at an agitprop level, giving promises of future rectification instead of immediate practical deeds. In a speech to Hungarian workers of the Csepel plant in 1958, he declared:

"It is out of the question that we, Communists and internationalists of the Soviet Union, the first to seize power and to engage in the great cause of Communist construction, should come to Communism alone, and, to use a figure of speech, should eat ham every day while the rest look on and lick their chops. That would be wrong.

"Where would the proletarian solidarity, the internationalism of that socialist country be then? The country with the more developed economy, capable of raising the living standard of its people still higher, must by all means help the other socialist countries to level out their standard of life. The scale of production in the countries of the world socialist system will doubtlessly level out with time. All the countries will rise to the level of the foremost ones, which are also not going to mark time. We must enter the Communist world all together."[12]

This relatively precise promise was subsequently reformulated to read that "the countries of the world socialist system" would enter Communism "in the same historical epoch." The ambiguity was not uncalculated. With Soviet resources already overstrained by ambitious internal investment programs and military demands, the real significance of the revised statement was to reassert the primacy of domestic development.

Khrushchev's tendency to put Soviet interests in the forefront was manifest in many aspects of intra-bloc relations. It became most sharply evident as the Sino-Soviet dispute developed. Faced with a choice between providing massive economic and military assistance to the Chinese Communist regime or concentrating primary resources on the development of the homeland, he unhesitatingly opted for the latter. Fearing that the Chinese Communist leaders might embroil him in an undesired war with the West, he denied them nuclear weapons and gave them only token support in their campaign to win Taiwan. Concerned to maintain good relations with the neutral nonaligned nations, he refused to back the Chinese in their border conflict with India, called for a cessation of fighting, and continued to provide India with economic and even some military assistance. Determined to bring the Chinese to heel and apparently persuaded that their dependence on the Soviet Union was absolute, he imposed more and more severe sanctions on them, cutting down trade and military and technical assistance, withdrawing specialists, demanding the repayment of debts, and exerting pressure on the East European members of the bloc to take corresponding measures. Faced with defiance by the Chinese and their not unsuccessful efforts to mobilize support within the international Communist movement, Khrushchev sought vainly to persuade them to desist from attacks on the Soviet leadership. When that failed, he moved to solidify his own ranks and excommunicate the Chinese and their allies as heretics who had broken away from the true faith.

At the root of the Sino-Soviet dispute lay the fact that Communism had become intertwined with the destinies of two great nations. Each had its own defined set of interests, in part inherited from the past and in part projected into the future, and both had very different conceptions of how those interests could best be promoted. For Khrushchev, Russian national interests and Soviet Communist objectives were indistinguishable, and despite lip service to the conception of a Communist commonwealth of nations, Soviet leadership of the world Communist movement was axiomatic. Charged with safeguarding Soviet interests and promoting the Communist cause in a thermonuclear age, Khrushchev saw his main tasks as those of building up Soviet power, minimizing the risks of thermonuclear war, demonstrating the superiority of the Soviet system, and exploiting the weaknesses of the non-Communist world in order to win opportunities for Communist advance within the framework of a nuclear stalemate. The Chinese leaders saw their problems in different and more urgent terms. Inheriting the imperial ambitions of their predecessors, hemmed in by American military power, subject to the humiliation of Russian patronage, and conscious of their economic weakness and of the need to overcome it rapidly, they were possessed by a drive to break out of their backwardness and to assume a role worthy of a great Communist power. The liquidation of the Chinese Nationalist regime in Taiwan was a prime objective, but involved with this, and going well beyond it, was the pressing need to eliminate the American presence in Asia in order to expand Communist Chinese influence and power in the area.

From the Chinese point of view, the policies espoused by Khrushchev held out little hope of resolving their problems. Indeed, in many respects they appeared counter-productive. His denial of large-scale military and economic assistance imposed a sharp brake on the growth of Chinese power and limited the Chinese capacity for bold, independent initiative. The substantial economic aid that the Soviet Union extended to India had the effect, in Chinese eyes, of shoring up a non-Communist regime that constituted one of China's prime competitors in Asia. Above all, Khrushchev's caution in challenging American power implied a prolonged stalemate, during which Communist China might be condemned to frustration in Asia.

Despite many assertions to the contrary, the Chinese Communist leaders did not call on the Soviet Union to launch a thermonuclear war against the West. While they apparently believed that they had less to fear and more to gain should it occur, their quarrel with Khrushchev was simply that he was too timid in asserting his power. Operating on the assumption that the American will to resist would crumble like a paper tiger in the face of Soviet pressure and thermonuclear threats, they urged a far more militant and aggressive Soviet stance that would put revolutionary activity in the forefront, particularly in the underdeveloped areas. Faced with formidable internal problems and unrealized external ambitions, the Chinese leadership saw its salvation in accelerating the timetable of world Communist triumph.

Khrushchev's dilemmas took a different form. His credentials as a revolutionary leader of world Communism were placed in jeopardy by constant Chinese attacks on his caution and timidity and animadversions to the effect that he was sacrificing the revolutionary prospects of

Communist parties abroad on the altar of Soviet economic development. Failure to respond effectively to these criticisms raised the danger of a growing loss of Soviet influence in the more militant circles of the international Communist movement and more especially in the Asian parties, which looked to the Chinese revolution as their model. Yet the strategy to which he was committed in the underdeveloped areas offered little in the way of comfort to impatient revolutionaries eager to come to power. To be told that their day would dawn but that it was not there yet could only antagonize Communist militants who saw their associates jailed by the very Nassers and Nehrus whom Khrushchev extolled and buttressed with aid and trade. Nor were they made any happier by the reflection that Soviet prestige among the non-Communist leaders of the new nations was being purchased at their expense.

The alternative of responding to Chinese demands for increased militancy opened up a different order of risks. In the underdeveloped areas it meant breaking the links with the neutralist leaders of the new nations that Soviet foreign policy had so carefully forged. In relations with the West it meant risking a sharp increase in the danger of thermonuclear war and intensifying the arms race. In domestic terms it meant slowing down the Soviet growth rate and negating Khrushchev's vision of welfare Communism, which was designed to magnify the Soviet appeal both at home and abroad.

Faced with these alternatives, Khrushchev chose to stand firm on the policy lines to which he was committed. Indeed, as the bitterness and virulence of the Sino-Soviet dispute mounted and prospects of reconciliation faded, the positions of both sides hardened. In the wake of the Cuban missile crisis of 1962, with its sobering reminder of how close the world had come to thermonuclear extinction, Khrushchev demonstrated a renewed eagerness to improve his relations with the United States and the West. He turned his back on Communist China to sign a nuclear test ban treaty with the United States and Britain, joined in establishing the so-called hot line between Washington and Moscow, undertook in cooperation with the United States to ban missiles in orbit and to cut back the production of fissionable material, negotiated a consular convention with the United States as well as a number of agreements on cultural exchanges, pressed restraint on Castro, and relaxed tension over Berlin. All these efforts to "normalize" relations with the West were greeted by Peking as additional confirmation of Khrushchev's apostasy from true Marxism-Leninism. They served to deepen a split that was rapidly becoming unbridgeable.

Khrushchev's decision to seize the "peace issue" even at the cost of further alienation of Peking was not without its positive advantages. To the extent that Khrushchev could make good his indictment of the Chinese leaders as "madmen" and "adventurers" who were prepared to risk world destruction in order to realize their ambitions, he could count on widespread support, not only in the Soviet Union, but among all people, Communist as well as non-Communist, who feared nuclear war. The strength Khrushchev derived from his identification with peaceful coexistence was perhaps best measured by the labored and defensive efforts of Peking's leaders to demonstrate that they, not Khrushchev, were the true architects of disarmament proposals that would bring lasting peace to the world.*

Perhaps the most compelling reasons for Khrushchev to seek a détente with the West had their origins in domestic strains and difficulties. The decision of the post-Stalinist leadership to provide more food, consumer goods, and housing whetted the appetite of the Soviet populace but did not satisfy it. The widespread yearning of Soviet consumers for a rapid improvement in their standard of living, an aspiration that Khrushchev sharpened by his promises of plenty, could not be met without a diversion of investment from armaments and heavy industry to light industry and agriculture. The situation in agriculture was particularly troublesome. The banner harvest of 1958, which was largely attributable to uniformly favorable weather, was followed by a series of mediocre harvests. Disaster struck in 1963, when bad weather and widespread drought sharply curtailed output and compelled the purchase abroad of approximately 12,000,000 tons of grain to meet minimal consumer needs. While the causes of the decline in agricultural output reached out in many directions, one of the chief among them was the failure to pour adequate capital into the land. In a belated effort to face up to the problem, Khrushchev launched a large-scale program for the expansion of the chemical industry, the building and importation of many new fertilizer plants, the increased output of agricultural machinery, the construction of irrigation facilities, and other measures that required substantial new capital input. With resources already overstrained, the reallocation of the limited capital available meant cuts in such branches of heavy industry as iron and steel as well as reduced investments in other sectors, including the military.

Nor were Khrushchev's problems limited to agriculture. While the Soviet industrial growth rate remained high, Soviet statistics made clear

---

* The first nuclear explosion by China in October 1964 was quickly followed by its proposal for a summit conference for complete disarmament and universal destruction of nuclear weapons.

that it was declining, despite desperate measures to maintain and increase it. Its drop and the sharp fall in agricultural output combined to produce a dramatic decline in the overall 1962–63 growth rate, a development that hardly conduced to enhance Khrushchev's prestige, even though a recovery in agriculture from the 1963 low point appeared highly likely.

Meanwhile, the difficulties on the domestic front engaged a large share of Khrushchev's attention and offered no temptations to foreign adventure. While there were few clear indications at the time that his position as leader of the party and government was in peril, the image of success and assertiveness that he had previously radiated appeared tarnished. The promises of rapid improvement in living standards that he had made to his own people were belied by food shortages and an apparent inability to master the agricultural problem. The enthusiasm and initiative he had hoped to evoke by his de-Stalinization measures and his efforts to revitalize the party were strangely absent. Instead, the prevailing mood was one of uncertainty, shaken confidence, and lack of a sense of direction. Ideological appeals and promises of future plenty were increasingly ineffective in spurring intensified effort. At almost every level of Soviet society there was a demand for more amenities and improved incentives. The dynamism that Khrushchev had initially generated showed signs of slackening. Established routines and traditional attachments resisted dislodgement. The continuing debate on allocation policy that was cautiously aired in Soviet journals revealed the usual array of bureaucratic vested interests each seeking to defend its special position. Despite Khrushchev's efforts to resolve intractable economic problems by periodic reorganizations of the state and party machinery and his calls for innovation and sacrifice, the Soviet Union was beginning to display many of the signs of a mature and immobile society, not easily moved from the grooves into which it was settling.

Yet there were also long-term forces at work that promised to reshape it. As the Soviet Union became a more and more highly industrialized society, dependent on its scientists, engineers, and managers to maintain its technological momentum, some redefinition of influence within the society appeared inevitable. The authority of scientific knowledge could not be denied without doing damage to the society's prospects. This did not necessarily challenge the Party's monopoly of political power. It did mean that Party functionaries would have to acquire an increasing degree of scientific and technical knowledge if they were to exercise their leadership role intelligently. It also meant that the scientific and technological community would exert an increasing influence over decision making in specialized areas where a high level of sophisticated knowledge was decisive. More important, it opened up the prospect of the gradual erosion, adaptation, and even outright rejection of ideological dogmas that operated as barriers to technical progress. A party that saw forced-draft industrialization as a key to its salvation promised to be transformed by the very burdens it had assumed. Not the least of Khrushchev's achievements was his recognition of the Party's need to come to terms with the scientific community, even though his curious attachment to the charlatanry of Lysenko suggested a residual ambivalence.*

While Khrushchev could readily understand the practical importance of scientific pioneering and experiment in promoting the growth of Soviet power, he was far less sympathetic to innovations in the arts and literature that were stimulated by his own de-Stalinization program. Implicit in the post-Stalinist cultural thaw, with all its ups and downs in alternating periods of liberalization and restriction, was the regime's recognition of a widespread yearning among the better writers and artists for greater freedom of expression. Most operated within a framework of loyalty to the Soviet system and the Party, but within that framework they claimed the right to speak the truth without embellishment, to criticize aspects of Soviet life that they believed merited criticism, to address themselves to personal as well as social problems, and to engage in stylistic experimentation. Even in the post-Stalinist context, these far from revolutionary demands were blown up by their critics to semi-revolutionary proportions. While Khrushchev's own position wavered at various stages of the continuing cultural debates, it was fundamentally shaped by a combination of practical party considerations and simple, conservative literary and artistic tastes. Khrushchev's prime concern was to enlist the energies of talented writers and artists in the party cause. But his conception of how so-called cultural workers could best serve the party cause differed significantly from the views of some whose talents he sought to mobilize. He, too, called for truth and condemned embellishment, but the "truth" that he demanded required a positive affirmation of the virtues of the Soviet system, rather than naturalistic portrayals of dark spots on the landscape that might induce pessimism and cynicism. He, too, defended the right to criticize aspects of Soviet reality, but he also insisted that the criticism be constructive and reinforce loyalty to the Party.

* Lysenko's theory, that environment can change hereditary traits of an organism and that these changes can be traced in future generations, flies in the face of the findings of modern genetics. Since Khrushchev's removal a campaign has been initiated to discredit him and to break his control of Soviet agricultural research.

What Khrushchev could not accept in any form was the antithesis between personal and social problems. The literary escape from the political into personal and family concerns could only be condemned as a flight from social obligations. His hostility to artistic innovation and experiment was deep-seated and personal. Abstract art, atonal music, obscure poetry, and symbol-ridden prose baffled and angered him. A man of plebeian tastes, he believed that art should minister to the needs of the masses, that paintings and sculpture should be representational, that poetry should be easily understood, and that literature should carry a social message. Given these predilections, it was perhaps inevitable that Khrushchev should find himself increasingly out of tune with the bolder and more daring spirits who found his cultural outlook oppressive. While the power that Khrushchev wielded drove them into a show of conformity, it also sharpened their frustration. The paradoxical result of Khrushchev's experiments in controlled relaxation was to intensify dissatisfaction among those who had most eagerly welcomed his reforms.

In Khrushchev's vision of Soviet society there was no place for the heretic, the rebel, or the skeptic. As he put it in one of his more important cultural pronouncements: "The press and radio, literature, painting, music, the cinema, and the theater are a sharp ideological weapon of our Party. The Party is concerned that its weapon be always in battle readiness and that it hit the enemy accurately. The Party will allow no one to blunt its edge, to weaken its effects. In questions of creative art the Party Central Committee will seek to obtain from all—from the most honored and best-known writer or artist and from the young fledgling creative worker—unswerving execution of the party line."[13] His henchman L. F. Ilichev, the chairman of the Central Committee's Ideological Commission, reinforced Khrushchev's point. "The question of creative freedom," Ilichev insisted, "must be fully clarified.... We have full freedom to fight for Communism. We do not and cannot have freedom to fight against Communism."[14]

Despite Khrushchev's repudiation of the Stalinist legacy of terror, the model he held out for Soviet society was no Liberty Hall where individualism would run rampant. Even when communism was fully realized, he reminded his countrymen, the Soviet Union would remain a highly organized, ordered, planned, and disciplined society, in which the Party would retain its leading role. In Khrushchev's words, "Each person must, like a bee in a hive, make his own contribution to increasing the material and spiritual wealth of society. The Party's policy expresses the interests of society as a whole and consequently of each separate individual as well. . . . As an orchestra conductor sees to it that all the instruments sound harmonious and in proportion, so in social and political life does the Party direct the efforts of all people toward the achievement of a single goal."[15]

The beehive analogy, to which Khrushchev reverted on several occasions, offers a striking insight into his conception of society as a productive enterprise to which all other purposes must be made subordinate. In Khrushchev's social order there was no place for drones. Anyone who refused to work must be expelled from the working community as a parasitic element that may infect it. In exile, he must be made to work so that he carries his full share of the common burden. But Khrushchev's obvious preference was for willing workers, bee-like in their instinctual love of work, profoundly believing in the cause to which they devote their efforts.

For Khrushchev the key to mass freedom was conscious, self-imposed discipline, a populace that willingly accepts the regimen of the party leadership because it recognizes that the Party is the supreme guardian of the interests of the people and is selflessly dedicated to promoting their welfare. What most sharply distinguished Khrushchev from Stalin was his apparently sincere faith that a society of the Soviet type could be governed without reliance on large-scale repression. This populist bias, if it can be so termed, expressed itself in many directions. It was implicit in his constant reaching out for grass-roots support and in the obvious satisfaction he derived from contact with people in his frequent peregrinations through the Soviet hinterland. It was manifest in the "popular" trappings in which he invested his authority—in his repeated calls for the recruitment of "leading" workers and collective farmers into the Party, in his injection of the principle of rotation into state and party office holding, in his revival of comrades' courts to improve workers' discipline, in his use of people's guards (*druzhiny*) to enforce public order, and in his reliance on neighborhood assemblies to mete out punishment to deviants and parasites. It is strikingly evident in a number of the theoretical formulations that he devised to mark the Soviet entry into the stage of building communism. Thus, the theory of the dictatorship of the proletariat was replaced by the concept of an all-people's state, while the party of the proletariat became the party of the whole people. The 1961 party program promised that as the state withered away agencies of public self-government would gradually replace state organs. It pointed to already announced transfers of authority to trade unions, sports societies, the Komsomol, and soviets as marking the pathway of future development.

While Khrushchev obviously envisaged wider mass participation in the exercise of administrative functions, he also made clear that such participation would be subject to strong party guidance. The Party will not wither away in the communist stage; indeed, Khrushchev said, it will become stronger than ever, performing the indispensable role of directing, guiding, and controlling society, including "the organs of public self-government." Given this overriding commitment, such apparently bold Khrushchevian theoretical initiatives as the substitution of the all-people's state for proletarian dictatorship and the enhancement of the role of organs of public self-government dwindle in significance. Designed to provide a more attractive gloss on party rule, they risk dismissal as rather clumsy exercises in semantic manipulation. As long as the political monopoly of the Party continues undisturbed and power remains concentrated in the hands of its top leaders, the effort to obscure the elite character of the Party by calling it the party of the whole people only emphasizes the gap between reality and profession.

Khrushchev's attempt to square the political circle took the form of combining the appearance of popular control with the reality of party rule. The thrust of his major institutional reforms was to strengthen party direction in every walk of Soviet life. While relying on the Party to provide the unifying discipline to force the Soviet populace to march in step, he sought at the same time to enlist mass energy and initiative in support of party-determined objectives. He widened the opportunities for popular participation in low-level public activities, but since these activities are always party-guided and -directed, they have tended to degenerate into mass mobilizations of party-oriented activists that provide little scope for independent citizen action or control from below. The policies that determine the destinies of the rank-and-file Soviet worker and collective farmer come down as directives from above; at best they are only remotely and indirectly influenced by the wishes of the citizenry.

Yet one of the keys to an understanding of the Khrushchevian era lies in Khrushchev's conclusion that these aspirations could not be ignored. Unwilling as he was to part with substantive authority, he recognized that there were grievances to be repaired. His decisions to mitigate Stalin's terror and to provide greater welfare benefits for the Soviet people represented an effort to establish his regime on a more rational, efficient, and popular basis. One of the questions still to be answered is whether this formula of "popular" or "welfare" totalitarianism, which constituted the domestic essence of Khrushchevism, will prove viable, whether the aspirations to which he partially responded and helped

activate will acquire a momentum of their own which will transform
Soviet society in directions that his successors cannot fully anticipate or
control.

It is still too early to attempt more than a provisional assessment of
Khrushchevism. The announcement in the Soviet press on October 16,
1964, that the Central Committee of the Party had met two days earlier
and "granted" Khrushchev's request that "he be released" from his
responsibilities "in view of his advanced age and deterioration in the
state of his health" obviously could not be taken at face value. The first
indictment of Khrushchev, which appeared in *Pravda* on October 17,
1964, listed among his "sins" (without using his name): "harebrained
schemes; half-baked conclusions and hasty decisions and actions divorced
from reality; bragging and bluster; attraction to rule by fiat; unwillingness to take into account what science and practical experience have
already discovered." During the next weeks his successors poured specific
content into these general charges. Public polemics with Peking ceased.
Khrushchev's drastic reorganization of the party and governmental
structure into parallel industrial and agricultural hierarchies was can-
celed. A campaign was initiated to free Soviet agricultural research of
Lysenko's baneful influence. The new leaders announced the removal
of "unwarranted limitations" on the size of private plots of land and on
private livestock holdings. In industry the way was opened for reforms
in the incentive system designed to provide increased rewards for managerial efficiency in the use of resources.

The direction of these reforms pointed up the sources of dissatisfaction
with Khrushchev's performance. Yet it would be less than fair to rest
an appraisal of the Khrushchev era on the latter-day criticisms of his
successors. What can be said is that Khrushchev's record at home was not
without its achievements, though it was far from a series of unbroken
successes. The apogee of his prestige was reached with the space triumphs
for which his regime took credit, but the drain on domestic resources
that these entailed and his inability to translate them into concrete
foreign policy gains created its own complex of problems. Under his
aegis, the Soviet Union continued for a time to make rapid industrial
progress and to narrow the gap separating it from the United States,
but there were also disturbing indications toward the end of his reign
that the industrial growth rate was slowing and that planning and
managerial problems were becoming increasingly complex and difficult. Agriculture, with which Khrushchev was most closely identified,
was also the area in which least progress was registered.

At the same time, reduction in working hours, larger social security benefits, and the increased availability of consumer goods and housing gave content to Khrushchev's blueprint of welfare Communism. These were gratefully welcomed by the beneficiaries, but they still fell far short of the need and simply sharpened the demand for more. Khrushchev's de-Stalinization program evoked widespread popular support, but it, too, posed its problems, of which one of the most delicate was Khrushchev's own involvement in Stalin's crimes. The flood of disillusionment, criticism, and airing of grievances that de-Stalinization released threatened for a time to pass out of control. Though Khrushchev managed to contain its domestic manifestations, the restrictions that he imposed on creative freedom and the repressive measures he invoked to enforce them alienated some of the most talented voices in the younger generation and left a residue of smoldering resentment that he was powerless to stamp out. In domestic affairs Khrushchev suffered the fate of many essentially conservative transitional figures who undertake to build a bridge from the old to the new. As the limits within which he was prepared to tolerate change became apparent, his reputation as an innovator dimmed. His early accomplishments and bold initiatives tended to be taken for granted and forgotten, while he found himself increasingly measured by the expectations that he had aroused and failed to fulfill.

Khrushchev's record was least impressive in the foreign policy field. Whereas Stalin could point to a vast expansion of the Communist empire in Europe and Asia achieved in a period when the Soviet Union was in a much weaker position vis-à-vis the United States, Khrushchev, with much greater power at his command, was unable to register any large-scale gains. The accessions of North Vietnam and Cuba to the Communist camp were not insignificant victories, but taken together they hardly began to match Stalin's triumphs. In Europe Khrushchev was unable to break out of the stalemate inherited from Stalin; his unsuccessful efforts to dislodge the Western powers from West Berlin brought a major loss of face. The rebuff he received during the Cuban missile crisis further tarnished the myth of Soviet invincibility and revealed Khrushchev as an adventurer whose bluff could be called.

Fortunately for the world, Khrushchev's determination to test the resolution of his antagonists was combined with a vivid appreciation of the dangers of thermonuclear warfare. In contrast to Stalin, Khrushchev operated under a compelling necessity to adjust the strategy and tactics of Soviet foreign policy to the realities of the thermonuclear age. These realities not only brought to the fore his common interest with Western leaders in avoiding mutual destruction, they also impelled him to seek ways to advance the Communist cause that would minimize the risk of thermonuclear holocaust. Khrushchevian policies in the underdeveloped world fitted into this pattern. Trade, military and economic aid, technical assistance, and cultural penetration were the prime levers by which the Soviet Union sought to heighten its influence in these areas. In the interest of cementing relations with the nationalist leaders of these states, Khrushchev discouraged premature revolutionary bids for power by local Communists, though he tried when he could to insure that they would have a free field to organize, and he promised that the day would come when they would lead their nations into the Communist camp. Meanwhile, Khrushchev could point to few concrete gains in Communist power in the developing countries that were directly attributable to his policies. From the point of view of local Communists anxious to strike out for power, Khrushchevism was all brakes and no forward thrust. However valid Khrushchev's long-term prognosis for the underdeveloped world may turn out to be, it was ill-suited to a mood of revolutionary impatience, and it only provided fuel for the Chinese charge that Khrushchevism represented a betrayal of the world revolution.

Whatever Khrushchev's claims to greatness, his contributions to the unity of world Communism are not likely to be listed among them. In the eyes of his Chinese antagonists and their allies in the international Communist movement, Khrushchevism became a term of contempt, the symbol of a peculiarly degenerate form of revisionism that sacrifices the revolutionary élan of Leninism to serve the bourgeoisified interests of a chauvinist great power masquerading as a Communist state. However much Khrushchev may have thought of himself as actively promoting the Communist cause by creatively adapting Leninism to the facts of a thermonuclear world, he found himself disowned and repudiated by those who, in Leninist terms, should have been his dearest friends. His most poignant legacy to his successors may well be the recognition that a common ideological heritage provides no guaranty of political unity among Communist powers and that imperial conflict is no monopoly of the capitalist world. It should, perhaps, come as no great surprise that so powerful a force as nationalism should reappear in a Communist guise, but for those who have taken professions of brotherhood among Communist nations at face value, it has nevertheless come as a profound shock.

That Khrushchev should have contributed to the disintegration of the Communist world empire is a phenomenon inviting explanation. But it would be superficial to attribute the development solely to Khrushchev's personal idiosyncrasies. However much clashes of personality may have served to exacerbate relations between Khrushchev and Mao, the causes of their differences were more deep-seated, with roots in the very different array of domestic and foreign problems that they felt impelled to resolve. When a Communist regime sinks roots in national soil, its perception of its needs cannot avoid being colored by the environment in which it functions and the pressures under which it operates. Insofar as Khrushchevism was something more than Khrushchev, it must be seen as an ideological expression of a stage of development in Soviet history. The Soviet regime had come under strong pressure to raise the living standards of its own people after decades of deprivation and sacrifice under Stalin, and it was understandably reluctant to make further sacrifices to lift the level of poorer Communist countries up to its own. A relatively advanced industrial power with a vested interest in preserving hard-won gains, it was not prepared to support a reckless and adventurous revolutionary strategy that would pose risks of thermonuclear extinction. As the historic leader and most powerful nation in the Communist camp, it was anything but eager to build up rivals who would challenge its mandate to direct Communist tactics everywhere. As a residuary legatee of Russian national interests, it tended to see China as a threat, in national as well as in Communist terms. In all these senses, Khrushchevism served to articulate the conservative interests of a mature Communist power with a relatively high stake in the preservation of the status quo.

If these be the parameters that gave Khrushchevism form, it is not difficult to see how they led to conflict and disunity within the Communist camp. For followers of Mao they were suspect on almost every count, and at best offered only meager and grudging support for China's industrial development. They provided no real assistance to China in breaking out of American encirclement. They put a damper on the prospects of Communist revolution in the underdeveloped countries. And, perhaps worst of all, they suggested that the Soviet leaders saw Communist China not merely as a rival for supremacy in the Communist camp but as a potential national enemy. Maoism may be viewed as a reaction to Khrushchevism. It registers the plight of an underdeveloped and ambitious Communist country which is motivated by an urgent desire to achieve great power status quickly and which sees the key to future strength in assuming the leadership of the world revolutionary movement and in forcing the pace of revolutionary change wherever it can find pliable instruments.

If Khrushchevism bred its polar opposite in Maoism, both unwittingly conspired to create a situation in which even such a previously abject

Soviet satellite as Rumania was emboldened to proclaim its economic independence and every Communist regime or party is now tempted to place its own interests in the forefront whenever and wherever it can. The confrontation of Khrushchevism and Maoism became more than a contest for world Communist leadership; it set the stage for the emergence of Communist forces that sought to escape the discipline of both. The ultimate irony of Khrushchevism was the belated discovery that a Communist world empire could not be built on Soviet interests alone.

Adam B. Ulam

# Titoism

It is perhaps insufficiently realized how the movement that received its first organizational expression one hundred years ago has colored our political and sociological concepts and our terminology. Our grandchildren may not live under Communism, but the grandchildren of our political scientists and sociologists, if they should follow the professions of their grandfathers, will most certainly discourse about "revisionism," "Titoism," "Maxism," and all the other "isms" that Communist practice has almost hypnotically induced us to use. We know that there is no such thing as "Bismarckism" or "Disraelism," and that the term "Gladstonian liberalism" represents a more meaningful and somehow more dignified description of an ideology than the various "isms," many of which have simply been taken over from the pejorative terms of Communist propaganda.

As one who has succumbed to the fashion and used "Titoism" in the title of a book, I cannot now dissociate myself from this wretched practice. But we should remember that an uncritical acceptance of a term very often forms an initial barrier to our understanding of the phenomenon under discussion. To digress, one may nevertheless say that to talk about Titoism is certainly not as misleading as to refer to certain phenomena in the contemporary Communist world as "revisionism" or "neo-revisionism." Certainly Eduard Bernstein, that most humane and democratic man, would turn over in his grave were he to realize that he is being lumped together with, or somehow thought related to, a motley company including Marshal Tito, various dissident Polish and Hungarian Communists, and so forth. He would not be pleased, I think, even with the attempts to connect him with various theories and practices of avant-garde art and literature that arouse the ire of Communist bureaucrats. Let us then protect the reputation of revisionism for what it was—an attempt to rethink Marx and bring him up to date in terms of social and economic facts of the 1890's—and let us guard this definition like the apple of our eye.

Turning now to Titoism, I would submit that the term, if used at all, properly describes certain phenomena in the Communist world centered around the Communist Party of Yugoslavia between roughly the years 1947 and 1953. What happened both before and after in Eastern Europe, although organically connected with the resistance of the Yugoslav Communists to Moscow, is still of a somewhat different character. In brief, Titoism is perhaps a proper name for a *historical moment,* but not for an ideology or a deviation. For one thing, it is impossible to imagine Titoism without Stalinism, or again, to be pedantic, to imagine Tito's rebellion without Stalin as its target.

But the subject of Titoism, as it is usually thought of, obviously has a broader connotation. This broader meaning might best be translated as resistance on the part of a Communist party to the domination of the Russian Communists. Another expression, "national Communism," will not do for reasons that will be spelled out later.

Taking Titoism in this broader meaning we shall see that it has a long and distinguished ancestry. The very foundation of the movement that was to give birth to Communism, the Second Congress of the Russian Social Democratic Party in 1903, witnessed a "Titoist" episode. The representatives of the Bund demanded and failed to obtain a wide organizational autonomy within Russian Social Democracy. That Lenin later chastised those like Rosa Luxemburg who held that the plea for national independence has no place in a socialist program, was to make the future national dilemma of Communism only sharper. When the political and ideological centralism inherent in Communism was combined with the plea for the fullest state and national independence, it became obvious that the two could not coexist without clashes. Eventually one of the principles had to come to express the political reality, while the other one had to atrophy into a mere window dressing and propaganda point.

This paradox was concealed, as were so many during the earlier period of Soviet Communism, by the personality and policies of Lenin. It was also minimized and obscured by the victory of Communism in only one country. Had the Soviets triumphed in 1920 in Poland, or especially in Germany, infant Communism would have been faced with such a Titoist dilemma that its chances for survival as an international movement might well have been fatally damaged. It was well for Communism that the U.S.S.R. was allowed to grow powerful without any other Communist state being in existence to disrupt this illusion of the compatibility of the doctrine with national independence.

To be sure, even within Russian Communism this issue soon manifested itself. With Lenin on his deathbed the problem of the domination of Moscow over the affairs of the Communist Parties of the Ukraine and Georgia was raised at the Twelfth Congress of the Russian Communist Party in 1923.

This Congress is instructive on two counts connected with our subject. First, it demonstrated the inherent impossibility of solving the conflict of sovereignty between Communism and the individual state within the framework of Communist doctrine as formulated by Lenin. In the second place, it furnished ample proof that "Titoism" cannot be described simply as national Communism. It was not quite that and at the same time much more than that.

On the first count, among many complaints heard about the domination by Moscow and the Great Russians (and that was in 1923!), not a single one was accompanied by an idea for a solution. They all dwelt on such phenomena as the presence of too many Russian officials in the other republics, the rude behavior of the Moscow authorities, and so forth. The boldest critic, Rakovski, demanded that nine-tenths of the proposed powers of the federal commissariats (the U.S.S.R. was not officially proclaimed until the next year) be taken away from them and given to the constituent republics. But how could it have helped? The basic policies and the ideology *had* to be the same, and nobody could question that without ceasing to be a Communist. All the federal commissariats could be abolished but the "correct" policies toward the peasants, industry, civic freedom, etc., still had to be formulated in Moscow.

In the second place, though the pleas were being uttered on behalf of the Ukrainians, Georgians, and all the rest, it is difficult to see in them any pure and simple nationalism (and perhaps there is no such thing). Rakovski became a Ukrainian by assuming the Chairmanship of the Council of Commissars of the Ukrainian Soviet Republic. Mdivani and Makharadze, the Georgian dissidents, had worked for and greeted the Russian Soviet Army, which had then destroyed the short-lived independence of their country. Their opposition to Great Russian domination fed upon being dismissed, demoted, or reduced in the extent of their own powers. To be sure, by a simple psychological process, they soon became not only disappointed or threatened power seekers, but also spokesmen for some of their constituents' national grievances. Still, their position was really logically untenable, and that as well as the strength of the party leadership made their defeat inevitable.

The existence of the Comintern in the period 1919–39 provides further proof that there was this complete incompatibility between Communism as fashioned in the Bolshevik Revolution and non-Russian nationalism. Who can cite a single case of major defection from the Communist ranks in those years based on the rebel's argument that the national interests of his country were being sacrificed for those of the U.S.S.R.? There were many discussions within the individual parties, notably in countries with a heterogeneous population, as to the most desirable nationality policy to be followed. There were defections based on or alleged to be based on Trotskyism, Bukharinism, ultra-leftism, and so on. But no Comintern Congress since the Second, held in 1920, had ever considered the problem of the clash of nationalism with Communism. There were no protests heard when at the Third Congress Lenin, in a roundabout and somewhat embarrassed way, suggested that one of the good works the foreign Communists might do would be to follow the activities of the Russian émigrés abroad, something that his "excellent Cheka," as he used to call it, was still not fully prepared to do. The notion of the supranational character of the Third International was already very frail by 1922. When a group of Russian Communists chose to complain to the Executive of the Comintern about the conditions in their own party and cited ample and frightening evidence of the police methods already in use against the opposition, their complaints were brushed aside. They were told that in effect they were helping the Mensheviks and the White Guardists by spreading such slanders about the Russian Communist Party and its leaders.

Internationalism and Communism could not coexist. Soon all Communist parties, whether in France or Iceland, became part of what Léon Blum called "a Russian Nationalist Party." Nor can we associate this fact exclusively with Stalinism. Many things would have been different had Trotsky, or, say, Bukharin emerged as the supreme leader, but no Communist party would have been less subservient to the interests of the Russian state. Only the appearance of Communism in power in *a major state* could have challenged this organic connection between Communism and Russian nationalism.

How deep this connection became is well illustrated by what happened at the height of Stalinism, in the thirties. The disgraced and then liquidated leaders Trotsky, Bukharin, and Zinoviev had all been men with enormous followings among foreign Communists, men for whom Stalin was an upstart provincial who knew neither French nor German and was certainly unfit for the leadership of an international movement. Yet at this very time the worship of Stalin among foreign Communists surpassed any previous apotheosis of Lenin. Trotsky, for all his romantic appeal, managed to create only a puny movement, and his own unwillingness to speak more harshly of the Soviet regime, as distinguished from Stalin, must be also attributed to his realization that he would have *no* attraction for foreign Communists were he to attack Russia. Yet before 1914 few Russian Marxists hesitated to condemn some national characteristics of their countrymen, or to wish a military defeat of their country, since it would lead to a political liberation. The purges of the foreign parties in the thirties do not affect this general picture. They bore a sympathetic character to the same phenomena within the U.S.S.R., and again it is difficult to find a genuine case of opposition to the *Russian* character of Communism being given as the reason for a purge of an individual or a group.*

It is well to point out that this character of foreign Communism, and the emotional Russophilia that became ingrained in every Communist, bore with it a corresponding danger for the future. A less emotionally charged relationship would have prevented some of the violence of the future reactions of disillusionment and betrayal. And in the case of Yugoslavia this emotional nexus was to play a vital role.

It might be asked how aware the Russians were of the danger that was paradoxically inherent in the spread of Communism to other countries. Certainly the limitations of their own dogma did not allow them to ponder the problem, and even now they do not realize the full extent of the dilemma. But as one follows Stalin's policy during and immediately after the war, one may detect some apprehension in the back of his mind as to the possible effects of too rapid a spread of Communism. At one point during the war the Russians evidently considered the possibility of what might be called the Finnish solution for many of their future satellites. Their governments would be bound to Russia in questions of foreign policy, they would ban the anti-Russian elements from their political life, but the regimes would not be completely or even largely Communist in character. How long this phase was to last is not clear. In any case, after the Soviet conquest of Eastern Europe, and the lack of any serious opposition by the West to its sovietization, those plans were shelved in favor of using People's Democracies—that is, of imposing Communist rule with or without the pretense of a coalition with other "progressive" parties. In this connec-

---

* The Russo-German Pact of 1939 requires no commentary in this connection. It disillusioned many people sympathetic to Communism, and some especially sensitive individual Party members, but it led to no major defections.

tion the Soviets also had to deal with the feverish anticipation of power on the part of local Communists, who were extremely unwilling to be sensible and take a long-range point of view. In one case, that of Greece, a satellite manqué, there seems to have been a definite attempt to suppress the more impatient wing of the Greek Communist Party. But though Stalin could do almost everything with the foreign Communists, to persuade them to slow down in demonstrating their loyalty to Russia by taking over power in their own countries was beyond even his powers. In Eastern Europe, the complexities anticipated from the emergence of several Communist states could not have been too great. None of the countries were large enough to offer rivalry to Russia, and none of the Communist parties—except possibly those of Yugoslavia and Czechoslovakia, and the latter did not prove an exception after all—were strong enough to seize power and rule over their countrymen without the presence or the threat of Soviet bayonets.

One wonders in this connection about France and Italy, whose Communist parties were to be accused in 1947, at the founding meeting of the Cominform, of not cashing in on the opportunities that were within their grasp following the Liberation. A great deal of research remains to be done in order to determine whether the national and coalition posture of those two parties, which persisted well beyond 1945, was due mainly to the nationalistic impetus they had imbibed during the war, to an expectation of coming to power through the electoral process, or to promptings by the Russians, who, still incredulous over the ease with which things were going their way in the East, may not have wanted to exhaust Western patience by a too-militant threat of Communism in France or Italy.

There was a period in post-1948 Yugoslavia when the government publicists speculated on and regretted the failure of French and Italian Communists to seize power. It was even suggested that this would have been a deadly blow to Stalinism, and that Messrs. Thorez and Togliatti would certainly have proved as tenacious in defending their nations' independence and honor as Tito was. This thesis must remain one of the great problems of recent history. Certainly one can speculate that Communist France would not have surrendered her empire but would have transformed it into a free federation of nations on the Soviet model, and that M. Thorez would have proved a less obstreperous partner for the United States than General de Gaulle. But French cooking would have suffered, Picasso would be painting big glaring canvases, and Mmes. de Beauvoir and Sagan could not have written their charming novels. One cannot have it both ways.

Another question, this one having been studied but not exhausted, is how deep the seeds of Titoism lie in relations between the U.S.S.R. and Yugoslav Communism in the years 1941–44. Certainly in Communist politics, as in marriage, there is a great tendency, after the breach has occurred, to go back and maximize the importance of early and trivial dissonances, to which nobody attached much importance in the happy days but which now are clearly seen as the first signs of eventual treachery and collision. I have touched upon this problem in an earlier book* but it certainly requires a more thorough investigation. Following the break, especially between 1949 and 1952, the Yugoslavs published copious memoirs, pamphlets, diaries, etc., the gist of which was that they had grown disenchanted during the war with the extent of Soviet help, that the Russians had disregarded their valiant struggles and were asking them to subdue their Communist fervor, and so on. They manage to convey the impression that the Yugoslavs were evidently displeased by the Russians' sins of commission, and especially of omission, in regard to themselves. But in their then flamboyant frame of mind, it appears that nothing short of Stalin's personal appearance in Marshal Tito's headquarters would have reassured the Partisans that the epochal and decisive nature of their struggles was being fully appreciated in Moscow. The echoes of the Russian irritation with the posturings of Tito and his group are found in the famous correspondence of the two Central Committees in 1948. There the Russians, with considerable justification but with terrible psychology, ridicule the Yugoslavs' claims that they had invented Partisan warfare, that their struggle was a major contribution to the Allied victory, and more. Such early discord did not indicate any thought on either side of the slightest possibility of a future split. It is enough to read Dedijer's diary of Djilas' record of his first visit to Moscow to conclude that in addition to their ideological tie and loyalty to the U.S.S.R. the Yugoslav Communists had what can only be described as a "crush" on the Russians, and on Stalin in particular. To write "Long Live Stalin" on the walls of the captured towns meant compromising the allegedly non-Party character of the Partisan movement at a time when Tito was seeking recognition and support from the Western Allies. But the emotional involvement of Yugoslav Communists was too strong to allow them to be fully statesmanlike. There was the business of the red star, hammer and sickle insignia on some of the Partisan units' uniforms, which even the Russians believed went too far. As Tito said in his report at

* *Titoism and the Cominform* (Cambridge, Mass., 1952), pp. 29–38.

the historic Fifth Congress of the CPY: "Our Party did not carry out its role of leader in the Liberation War...illegally in disguise."*

This brings us to another point, which is extremely important in analyzing Titoism's earliest phase. The high command of the CPY was with few exceptions extremely young and cohesive in character. If we exclude such few relative oldsters as Moša Pijade, the previous purges and splits had done their work only too well, which later must have led to some rueful comments in Moscow. Thus there was no real barrier to building a cult of Tito's personality within Partisan ranks. There were no ancient workhorses of the Comintern who could successfully dispute the leadership of Yugoslavs who had been there during the armed struggle. Compare it with the postwar situation, say in Bulgaria or Czechoslovakia, or even with a Communist party like the Polish one, whose leadership prior to 1939 had been decimated even more thoroughly than that of the Yugoslav Party. In each case there were Moscow men available who could be sent in, but they would feel scant solidarity or companionship at arms with the men who had been in their countries during the war. The solidarity of the Yugoslav Communist leadership over the years has been truly amazing. After the elimination of the relatively few "Stalinists" among them in 1948-49, practically the same men have ruled Yugoslavia as a team for sixteen years. From young Partisan fighters they have now grown into middle-aged bureaucrats, without engaging in one of those bloody and criminal rivalries of power which have characterized the life of practically every Communist party in power. Even the obvious exception, the case of Djilas, underlines this uniqueness of the Yugoslav Party. For Djilas is the rarest of Communist birds, a man who challenged the ruling faction because of ideological and temperamental differences, and not because he craved the top position for himself, and who only then proceeded to erect an ideology.

Of the Eastern Communist parties after the war, the Yugoslav one must have been regarded by the Russians as the most promising, and at the same time the most likely to prove troublesome. Religious enthusiasm, as many churches have recognized, can often be a dangerous thing. It tends to interfere with the quiet and prudent worship that is a greater safeguard for remaining within the communion than flights of ecstasy and excitement. And Tito's Communists were especially prone to exhibit unreasoning fanaticism and enthusiasm. Their attitude on the Trieste issue threatened a premature clash with the Western

* *The Fifth Congress of the CPY* (Belgrade, 1948), p. 105.

Allies. Their abrupt and rapid sovietization of their country complicated the tasks of Soviet policy in the Balkans. One cannot credit the
Soviet charge that the Yugoslav Communists wanted them to go to war
on the issue of Trieste, but obviously Yugoslav intransigence and haste
were jeopardizing the whole cautious timetable of Soviet policy.

We pass now to the more substantive issues of the Russo-Yugoslav
disagreements that culminated in the break. For all the voluminous
writing on the subject, it is difficult to determine which was the straw
that broke the camel's back. Grievances on the Yugoslav side and suspicions on the Russian side had been accumulating since the end of the
war. The disorderly behavior of Russian troops in Yugoslavia provoked
Djilas' tactless remarks, which were conveyed to Moscow. The inadequate Russian support on the Trieste problem led to Tito's speech in
Ljubljana on May 28, 1945, which the Russians somewhat morbidly
interpreted as an attack on them.* A careful reading of the speech leads
one to believe that Tito's main purpose was to state that the Russians
were not supporting him strongly enough, or were acquiescing in Britain's influence in the Balkans, rather than to make any declaration of
independence from the U.S.S.R. He merely wanted a Soviet reassur-
ance that Yugoslavia was still the U.S.S.R.'s favorite in the Balkans.
But the Russians replied with a strong diplomatic protest, the tenor of
which must have astounded the Yugoslav officials: their complaint that
they were not being loved enough by the Russians was being interpreted as an "attack on the Soviet Union." Kardelj, according to the
Russian version, soothed their ambassador by assuring him that the
Yugoslav Communists were envisaging their country as a future member of the U.S.S.R. By 1945 such views were quite anachronistic, and if
Kardelj in fact made this remark, it must have only increased the Russians' suspicions.

The involved subject of the Yugoslavs' economic plans was also leading to mutual recriminations. Just as in foreign policy so in industrialization the Yugoslav Communists set their goals unrealistically high.
The Russians offered them some good advice on the subject, which
again was taken with a lover's hurt feelings. The Russian comrades did
not believe that Communist enthusiasm was enough to industrialize a
country or introduce collectivization in a hurry. But the Russians' advice was given out of more than solicitude; they anticipated and acknowledged the Yugoslavs' demands for economic help. In those days
the only "help" Russia was willing to give to her satellites came in the

---

* George W. Hoffman and Fred W. Neal, *Yugoslavia and the New Communism* (New
York, 1962), p. 114.

form of the famous joint companies, which meant that a country's natural resources would be exploited for the dubious return of Soviet expert help and some negligible provisions of capital goods by the U.S.S.R. Great though the love of Stalin and Russia was in the hearts of the Yugoslav Communists, their conviction that a self-respecting socialist country must industrialize at a rapid pace was equally strong. The tangible proof of Russian selfishness and duplicity in the matter must have been the hardest blow up to that time.

Is it reasonable, one might ask, to use terms like love and betrayal when dealing with political systems, and with seasoned politicians? Even if most of Tito's subordinates were young and naïve, was not Tito himself a veteran Communist, one who had survived and advanced while foreign Communists were being liquidated wholesale in the Russian purges? An analysis of mine couched in such terms was once criticized for not attaching enough importance, indeed for not taking seriously, the "real" ideological issues and differences that produced the conflict. Communists, it was argued, do not quarrel because of hurt vanity, unreasonable suspicions, or even considerations of power; an interpretation couched in such terms descends to the level of sensationalism. There *must* have been some ideological grounds for the Russians' suspicions of Tito's regime, some basic disagreement with his economic policies.

I think that although the use of personal and emotional explanations of the conflict can be overdone, it is still true that one cannot understand the conflict without taking them into account. And in a sense they also spill over into the realm of ideology. The Yugoslavs' passion for industrialization and their eagerness to communize the Balkans were ambitions and passions bred by ideology. So, too, was their belief in the omnipotence of the Soviet Union as the representative of the wave of the future, and their consequent inability to understand why the Russians could "deny" them Trieste. All those things were undoubtedly combined, at least on the part of the more experienced Yugoslav leaders—Tito himself, Pijade, and Kardelj—with a prudent consideration for their own and their country's position. Unlike young hotheads like Djilas, they were probably under no illusion that it was enough to be a good Communist and to love Russia in order to remain in Marshal Stalin's good graces. They initiated plans, evidently with the agreement of some Bulgarian Communist leaders, to provide for a closer collaboration of the two countries and an eventual federation. Tito's diplomatic tours of various East European capitals were apparently intended to broaden this pattern. There was nothing inherently disloyal in these policies and trips; the Balkan Federation had a prior Soviet blessing and so did Yugoslavia's de facto protectorate over Albania. But sooner or later Yugoslavia's strenuous politicking among satellites was bound to arouse the Soviet Union's disapproval. That it did not find a drastic expression earlier than it did was probably because the Soviets saw a more urgent task in Eastern Europe, the final reduction of Poland and Czechoslovakia to satellite status.

To deal with a multiplicity of problems, among them the Yugoslav one, the Soviet Union embarked on the creation of a formal instrument of Communist cooperation—the Cominform. The experiment was abortive. Few international institutions of a comparable kind have had such a brief and disastrous history. It failed utterly in its main objective, which was to create an international veneer for the Soviet domination of foreign Communism. It could not cope with the first and only crisis it was supposed to solve, the Yugoslav defection. It lingered on as a newspaper and a fifth wheel for a few years, its expiration in the back-washes of Stalinism almost unnoticed.

Yet its original concept and functions are certainly interesting and instructive. Its failure illustrates how difficult it was in 1947–48 for Communism to assume even the appearance of genuine internationalism. After the Tito affair the Cominform died, one might say, of a surfeit of unanimity and sameness. You could not then create an international Communist body because the Communists agreed too much. You cannot create one now, as Khrushchev and his subordinates discovered, because they now disagree too violently. Here is the pathos of Communist history in the last two decades.

Membership in the Cominform was limited to the prize pupils: the two large Western parties and the parties in power in Eastern Europe. Albania was excluded, probably because of its status as a sub-satellite. In China the Communists were still struggling for power, and anyway the Chinese were even then assumed to present a special problem, though it was not realized how much of a problem they would turn out to be. Special reasons accounted for the exclusion of the German Communists. The Finnish Party must have felt hurt at its exclusion; few people at the time did not see Finland as eventually sharing the fate of Poland, or indeed of Latvia or Estonia. The Russian officials who devised the Cominform were faced with a serious problem: What was to be the ostensible purpose of the new organization? They came up with the humorous notion that the participating parties were to exchange information. You don't pay enough attention to agitation, the Poles might say to the Hungarians, and you to propaganda, the Hungarians would presumably reply; and so both could cheerfully say, Well, let us see how the Russian comrades have solved the problem!

The Yugoslavs' performance at the founding meeting was thoroughly in their pre-1948 style; they threw their weight around and sulked at being put in the same class with such inept pupils as the Poles and Rumanians. On the Russian side, it was probably thought the height of generosity and subtle flattery to ordain that the misbegotten institution should have its seat in Belgrade. Somebody must have remembered how in the earliest and most innocent days of the Comintern there were objections to having its seat in Moscow. Won't some people draw the wrong conclusion, they thought, from the fact that the capital of the movement should coincide with that of Soviet Russia?

But the Russo-Yugoslav conflict could not be warded off by such contrivances. One might mention some of its major elements as it ripened in 1948. There was the Soviet veto of the Balkan Federation. There was an anti-Tito intrigue within the Communist Party of Yugoslavia that led to the dismissal and then the imprisonment of two Yugoslav Communists, presumably groomed by the Russians as opponents of Tito and intended to be his possible successors: Andrija Hebrang and Sreten Zhujovich. There were open clashes between Soviet advisers and Yugoslav officials. But we need not go into the details, which have been covered in many books. Titoism was finally born in the spring of 1948.

It may be useful at this point to recall some of the contemporary explanations for it. There was the usual simplistic one: this was only a put-up job between two scheming Communist countries, a devious attempt to suck in American money and throw Western statesmen off the track. More seriously, many in the West pondered what ideological deviation the Yugoslav Communists were guilty of. Since many people still believe that the roots of the Sino-Soviet dispute lie in the fact that the Chinese won power by concentrating on winning over the countryside, against Soviet instructions to concentrate on winning over the urban workers, it is not surprising that in 1948 Titoism was being examined in the light of its possible relationship with Bukharinism or Trotskyism. The Russians, it was argued, were displeased with their Yugoslav colleagues because they were not collectivizing fast enough— or, to the contrary, because they were bent upon industrializing too rapidly.

More interesting are the interpretations that were probably made by the two parties to the dispute. The Soviet assumption must have been that Tito's Communists would seek Moscow's pardon. Were they to do so, their position would be compromised and the next step would be a leisurely liquidation of the current leadership of the CPY and its replacement by persons more amenable to Soviet direction. Whether Stalin said, as Khrushchev later claimed, that he could crook his little finger and there would be no Tito, is at least doubtful; Stalin, for all of his vast vanity, was an astute politician. But it was difficult to see how the Yugoslavs could in fact resist the Russian proposals to lay the whole issue before the Cominform and abide by its impartial judgment. Without Russia, Yugoslavia was isolated. The Western powers had not intervened to save the remnants of democracy in Czechoslovakia; were they going to protect one Communist dictator against another? The economic considerations in themselves were pressing enough to force the Yugoslavs to a compromise. Their foolhardy policies would sooner or later involve the country in a disaster, and the CPY could not hope to soften it without outside help. The harsh and peremptory tone of the Soviet messages to the Yugoslav Central Committee was undoubtedly meant to dispel any hopes that the Tito regime could maintain its posture and still count on the U.S.S.R. to save it from a disaster.

On the Yugoslav side, the attitude that the Russians would realize their hastiness and the unfounded character of their charges must have alternated with a less naïve political calculation. An admission of their "errors," which was all that the Russians demanded in the first instance, would have been only a first downward step toward the eventual destruction of the leadership of the CPY. There have been misunderstandings since 1945 at least, and they have been cleared up. There was no reason to believe that once the Russians saw the justice of their cause they would not desist.

Thus the period of Titoism, 1948 to 1954, can be divided into two sub-periods. The first, which extends to 1950, might be called the phase of innocence. The second one is that of classical Titoism—a posture of open defiance of the U.S.S.R. and the creation of an ideology to give it a rationale. During the first phase the Yugoslav leadership faced, reluctantly and incredulously, the prospect of a final break. After all, even at the Fifth Party Congress, in July 1948, they chanted slogans honoring Stalin. Then, painfully and slowly, Yugoslavia's foreign policy began to diverge from Russia's. The attitude of suspicion and hostility toward the only quarter from which they could now expect help, the West, gave way—but again, gradually and reluctantly. The doctrinaire economic policies were for the most part unchanged.

The ideological distress that the Yugoslavs experienced during that period was best expressed in the writings of their chief ideologue of the time, Milovan Djilas. Gradually his viewpoint shifted to a condemnation of Stalin's personal dictatorship and his ascendance within world Communism. It was then easy to take the next step and to consider Russian Communism as warped, although not hopelessly so, by bureaucratism and chauvinism. Along with other Communist heresies, Titoism embraced the myth that there had once been an innocent and perfect type of Communism, which had been corrupted by the men in power in the Soviet Union and by certain basic defects in the Soviet Union's governmental structure. Thus the remedy would lie in a return to the original concept, to Communism unspoiled by great-power chauvinism, and by bureaucratism. The term "cult of personality" was not yet being used.* By 1950 the Yugoslav Communists were passing from an enchantment with Stalin to an attitude in which they were ready to see in him the prime source of political evil.

The same period, from 1948 to 1950, was one of what might be called wishful polycentrism. The victories of Chinese Communism were reported in the Yugoslav press with a satisfaction that went beyond mere happiness with the success of their coreligionists. It was argued explicitly that the victory of Communism in a country so vast as China was bound to change the whole picture of world Communism, so that the Russians would no longer be capable of lording it over the other parties. All of which shows that our wishes and fantasies often come true, but sometimes in a strange and unexpected form.

In 1950 Titoism became a self-conscious ideology. There is now little left of the early hopes that the Russian Communists would reform. Stalin's tyranny was clearly recognized, but the attacks began to be more general, directed against the whole Soviet system and considerable portions of the Communist doctrine. Much of the earlier illusion about the spread of Communism automatically curing its own defects disappeared. Shortly after the beginning of the Korean War, there was an agonizing reappraisal of the Chinese and a discarding of the earlier hopes for them. Then there came a definite rapprochement, a virtual alliance, with the West. Finally, an end was put to the ruinous economic policies. Titoism came of age.

### The Heyday of Titoism

What then was this newly fledged system, this curiosity, a Communist country separate from the Soviet bloc? In many ways the Yugoslavs simply lopped off the pathological parts of Stalinism from their

---

* One of the earliest relevant references to the term is in a little-known article on Lenin by his old friend Mikhail Stepanovich Olminsky, written in 1920.

theories and practice. Stalin's famous dictum—the closer one gets to socialism the sharper becomes the character of the class struggle—was repudiated by the Yugoslav Communists well in advance of Khrushchev's denunciation of 1956. Terrorism was largely abolished, and Yugoslavia moved closer to the traditional practices of Eastern European police states and away from its fantastic Communist perversion. In many ways the regime could well afford this relaxation, since its struggle for independence endowed it with dignity and popularity even in the eyes of opponents of Titoism and its brand of Communism. The repression of Stalinism did not have to be very extensive. There were few bona-fide believers in the old communion with the Soviet Union. Many people purged or arrested for Stalinism were in all likelihood victims of personal rivalries, or ancient animosities, which even in the most reasonable Communist dictatorships find their expression in ideological denunciations. Those sharp edges of the struggle against religion, and against the Catholic Church in particular, were dulled. The average citizen's life became easier.

In foreign policy, Yugoslavia veered toward the theory of coexistence. This was, in fact, the only policy the Communists in Yugoslavia could, or can, adhere to: coexistence of the two blocs is the only guarantee of the continued existence of their own regime. Were the Soviet bloc to disappear, Yugoslavia obviously could not survive as a Communist state. Were the Western powers still further reduced in their sphere of influence, the Soviet Union, even under the post-Stalinist leadership, would have few reasons not to liquidate the inconvenience that Tito's Yugoslavia represents.

Between 1950 and 1954 the Yugoslavs began looking around for an ideological anchor. What makes a Communist system, even at its mildest, a source of perturbance both to its own citizens and to other states is its inability to stand still. The Communist is a classical illustration of Pascal's dictum about the tragedy of human existence. The Yugoslav Communists were not content to do away with the major abuses of the doctrine; they needed an ideology of their own. In this period they made a frantic search in many directions. At one time the doctrines of the left wing of the British Labour Party were examined and found wanting. Efforts were made to study the esoteric doctrines and practices of Oriental left-wing movements. To find a meaning for Titoism, its originators engaged in modest missionary activity among the largely formless socialist and left-wing movements in Asia.

The failure of this effort deserves some comment, for it sheds some light on Titoism in the broader meaning of the term—that is, as an attempt to find a form of Communism divorced from the Russian pattern and not subordinate to Moscow. It became evident to the Yugoslav policy makers, though they would return to a similar enterprise later on, that a country of the size of Yugoslavia was simply not capable of successful ideological proselytizing. For all the sympathy that the Yugoslav stance aroused in countries such as India and Burma, there was little relevance for those countries in the Titoist experiment. Their local Communists, like all Communists out of power, were bound to look to a great Communist country for leadership and inspiration. Their left-wing non-Communist movements could likewise find little in the Yugoslav example. Stalinism has become so firmly imprinted on Communist dogma and practice that if it were to be rubbed off completely there would be precious little of Communism left.

The truth of this statement must have struck the Yugoslav leadership in 1952–53, when they began a major structural alteration in their system, which they hoped would give a concrete meaning to Titoism. The changes began—this is an old technique of Communism—with the application of new names. The Communist Party became the League of Communists, the People's Front the Socialist Alliance. Other name changes were designed to increase the difference between Yugoslav terminology and that of the U.S.S.R. and the satellites. An elaborate constitutional scheme was designed in 1953. In their frenzied search for innovations that would set them as far apart as possible from the Soviet model, the Yugoslav Communist leaders came up with some devices that bring to mind, ironically enough, the representative schemes of Mussolini's Italy. A discussion of those provisions, and of the further alterations of the system in 1962, is beyond the scope of this essay; but it can be said that were Yugoslavia not a one-party state, its constitutional and administrative structure would lead to a most appalling political chaos.

The same observation can be extended to the elaborate system of local government based on the Yugoslavs' devices of the communes and the workers' councils. It would be most unfair to dismiss these as window dressing. They represent an honest attempt to establish what might be called grass-roots Communism, to really enlist the masses in the task of government, and to exercise a real check on the bureaucracy's powers and privileges. But the tragedy and paradox of all Communist attempts in this direction, from Lenin's time to Tito's and Khrushchev's, is that in a sense they only make more essential the ubiquitous grip of the Party on all spheres of political, economic, and social life. The more economic and administrative decentralization you have, the more necessary it will become to assure the unity of political centralization. There are periods when the truth of this is not obvious; but there always comes the moment of reckoning when it is seen that the workers' councils, just like Khrushchev's *sovnarkhozy,* can lead to economic anarchy or disorganization, and that the structure must therefore be tightened up.* It is difficult enough nowadays to secure or preserve a meaningful degree of economic or social pluralism in a democratic country. In a Communist one it is impossible without giving up the basic tenet of the creed.

What then is the essence of Titoism in internal politics? It is really an attempt at *depoliticization* (horrible word) of the average citizen's life. In the classical Communist pattern, which was Stalin's Russia, and to a lesser extent Khrushchev's, the average citizen is made aware of the political importance of every social act. Whether he works, goes to an exhibition, votes, etc., each of those acts is assumed to have a political meaning. There is no "neutral" picture, no casual attitude toward work, no element of personal or frivolous choice in electing an official. In Tito's Yugoslavia, on the contrary, there is a very elaborate set of devices and institutions designed to persuade the citizen that most of his activities are not connected with politics. In theory, the whole constitutional scheme floats apart from the strictures of Marx and Lenin. In his activities as a producer or as a member of the commune, the citizen is allegedly performing objective economic and administrative tasks, not fulfilling a set of directives laid down by an oppressive political authority. Politics is the business of the League of Communists, and the average citizen is relieved of the presence and pressure of Big Brother; indeed, he is asked not to notice that Big Brother exists. The Party officials have become obscured in their state and constitutional roles. The Secretary General of the Yugoslav Communist Party has presumably been swallowed up by the President of the federal republic.

This scheme cannot be dismissed as meaningless. Viewed from the pre-1950 perspective it implies a considerable broadening of the average Yugoslav's freedom, a considerable release from the tensions that accumulate under a more "activist" Communist regime. The citizen is not compelled to be "alert," "vigilant," and "on guard" against the enemies, be they Mensheviks, Stalinists, revisionists, or dogmatists. He is asked to be a good producer, and a man solicitous about the affairs

---

* The difficulty of trying to combine decentralization and Leninism was most recently borne out at the Eighth Congress of the CPY, in December 1964.

of his own community, and a good Yugoslav as well as a good Serb or Croat.

The trouble with this scheme from the Communist point of view is that if it succeeds too well it will present a threat to the regime as such. It is impossible to run a Communist state without a nucleus of devoted and ideologically minded people. Bureaucratized as most Communist regimes have become, it is still necessary to have a periodic influx of indoctrinated and politicized people. Without them, and without intermittent ideological mobilization, a Communist regime would inevitably tend in the direction of an old-fashioned authoritarian state à la Salazar or Franco, in which the original ideology has atrophied and the government expects and receives the tolerant apathy of its subjects but in turn sacrifices its original political and economic dynamism.

Nor can a Communist regime use the current Afro-Asian substitute for an ideology—anti-imperialism. With the direct threat of Russian intervention receding, Titoism has not been able to capitalize on nationalism to the same extent as during the heroic days of 1948–50. Along with the emotional impetus of anti-imperialism it was deprived of the possibility of indulging in its own brand of expansionism. The harsh realities of the international situation of 1950–57 turned Yugoslavia into an exemplary neighbor of Greece and Italy. The previous designs on Albania and Bulgaria also gave way to a sober reassessment. It was a depressing prospect of a quiet life that faced the Yugoslav Communist leaders in 1953–54. The madcap scheme of collectivization was given up. Helped by massive American aid, Yugoslavia's economy was showing gains, thus vindicating the concept of socialist planning. As early as 1921–22, Lenin had had the insight that socialism in one country could succeed, even without purges, mass resettlements, and a lowering of the standard of living—if the capitalists would help. Now, what he had not dared to dream about Russia in 1921—that the capitalists would help without exacting concessions in return—was coming true in Yugoslavia. Titoism represented the only concrete success of the West in Eastern Europe; it was not a success of its own making, but it was one which has rendered additional dividends in helping preserve Greece from Communism.*

But from the point of view of the leadership of the Yugoslav Party

---

* In foreign policy we are often victims of our own successes. Who would have dreamed that the splendid achievements of the Marshall Plan would result in de Gaulle, or that a Greece freed from the Communist threat would complicate our lives by her position on Cyprus? These bitter fruits of our successes correspond to those of Russia in helping to communize China.

all the advantages of her position in 1953–54, which undoubtedly were secretly envied by every Communist leader in Eastern Europe, added up to trouble within the Party. In the population at large the modest concessions were bound to produce more ambitious aspirations for greater freedom. Capitalism in our day cannot withstand long depressions. The whole rationale of Communism is in turn jeopardized by a long period of ascending prosperity.

The most tangible symptom of the restlessness within the CPY was the Djilas affair. It was entirely logical that this erstwhile fanatical Communist and Stalinist should now have become the most severe critic of the remnants of Stalinism in the CPY, and that he should begin the evolution which within a few years would lead him to become an exponent of democratic socialism and the multiparty system. One is reminded of G. I. Myasnikov, a ferocious Communist terrorist in the Russian Civil War. After the war he kept petitioning the Communist Party to restore freedom of the press "from the monarchist to anarchist press." After disregarding Lenin's fatherly strictures Myasnikov had to be expelled from the party, then jailed, and finally sent out of Russia. Djilas, obviously a man of much broader intellectual horizons, chose imprisonment.

With the eruption of the Djilas affair in 1953–54, the CPY took steps to tighten up party discipline and to curtail baneful Western influences. The regime realized the danger of completely losing support among the younger generation. Insofar as the young were concerned, the Party ran the danger of falling between two stools: some were bound to regret the good old bad days when there was a sense of purpose in being a Communist, and when a young Party member could shock and terrorize his elders. Others would turn to the new gods, imbibe the teachings of Djilas, and admire such inappropriate heroes for a Communist as Aneurin Bevan. A movement that exists largely on the basis of its appeal to the young—and the CPY was a classic case in point—cannot afford a sensible eschewing of radicalism of one kind or another.

It was fortunate for the Yugoslav Communists that their dilemma became apparent just as a great change was coming over Russian Communism. 1954–56 witnessed the first phase, as yet prudent and unpublicized, of de-Stalinization. For all its behind-the-scenes character, and its lack of the kind of sensational revelations with which Khrushchev later regaled the world, the period must be characterized as substantively the most "liberal" one in post-Stalin Russian politics. It represented, one can assume, a reasoned consensus of the Soviet leadership as a whole (including, one dares to conjecture, Beria and those other alleged Stalinists whom Khrushchev began throwing to the wolves, in hopes of obliterating his own tracks) that the despot's policies had been not only criminal but also mistaken. Insofar as foreign relations are concerned, the 1954–56 view of the Soviet leadership evidently held that the perpetuation of Stalin's policies would place an intolerable strain on the solidarity of the Communist world, and that more flexibility and a greater autonomy for other Communist countries was also needed from the Russian point of view. It was a period of a genuine, or almost genuine, search for an international formula that would assure the Communist bloc of a united position on basic issues and yet relieve the Russians of constant and troublesome vigilance over the day-to-day activities of their satellites. It is understandable that the satellite leaders greeted this shift with some apprehension; they could not be sure that the Russians really meant that they should quietly do away with the Stalinist relics in their policies and personnel, and that they should substitute a search for popularity among their peoples for sheer terror and compulsion.

The Russian gestures toward Yugoslavia, at first coy and then brazen in their cordiality, as when Khrushchev and Bulganin invited themselves to Belgrade, were a key *motif* in this policy. And they enabled Tito and his Party, after the initial bewilderment and reluctance to embrace the Russians again, to retrieve a sense of mission and self-importance. Tito was now seen as a pioneer of de-Stalinization, the man who wisely though perhaps prematurely tried to establish the right pattern of relations among the Communist states. Much as he became excessively entangled with the West, he also pioneered the concept of "separate roads" to socialism, thus avoiding those disastrous errors which marked the satellites' policies and which earned them unnecessary troubles with their populations (such as the Berlin uprising). Be *almost* like Tito—this seemed to be the lesson that Khrushchev and his colleagues were imparting to their satellite lieutenants in their travels (collective leadership in those days implied collective traveling).

For their part, by 1956 the Yugoslavs had thrown themselves wholeheartedly into the game. The Russian advances marked for them a welcome break in the ideological isolation that had bred such confusion within the Party. Once again, they could claim a degree of primacy within Eastern Europe, and assuage their own Communist zealots by pointing out that Yugoslavia was an object of emulation by Hungary and Poland. Marshal Tito resumed his trips.

The Polish and Hungarian developments of 1956 brought a quick and definite end to this phase. It is very important to differentiate between those two events not only in terms of their results but also in terms of their histories. Both marked an end, at least a temporary one, to the Soviet hope that de-Stalinization of the satellites could be carried out in an orderly and safe way without endangering the very bases of Soviet influence.

In the case of Poland, the Russians obviously expected that Gomulka and his group would be released, given honorable and minor jobs, that the pre-1956 Communist leaders could be sacrificed to the popular wrath as the tools of Stalin and Beria, and that another group of leaders could be put in charge. This scheme was defeated, among other things by the foresight of the Polish "Stalinists"; realizing what was in store for them, they became overnight fervent nationalists and forced Gomulka's election not as a director of a museum or a library, as the Russians had hoped, but as First Secretary of the Party. How their guile paid off can be best illustrated by the case of Edward Ochab. Head of the Party following Bierut's death, Ochab was instrumental in having Gomulka supplant him in that position. He remained within the inner circle and is today the official head of the Polish state: certainly a better fate than befell Rakosi, Farkas, or Chervenkov, three others who were politically liquidated. The Polish October was greeted by the Russians without great enthusiasm, to put it mildly. But they were later to discover that in fact they had unwittingly obtained in Poland what they had been clumsily trying to get all along: a Communist regime adhering strictly to Russian foreign policy and yet enjoying a large measure of popular acceptance, and in the first months a good deal more than that. From an "imperialist and Zionist agent" Gomulka became Khrushchev's favorite companion and adviser. Just as Khrushchev persuaded himself that in the old days he had fearlessly protected the Ukrainians from Stalin's wrath, so later he undoubtedly credited his own policy with the elevation of Gomulka.

The Hungarian sequel to the Polish events, however, posed a much more basic threat not only to the Soviet position but also to Tito's own position, as he was to realize after his initial doubts. From an intraparty crisis the events turned into a national uprising. An Italian patriot said in the nineteenth century, "We don't want Austria to become more tolerant, we want Austria to go away," and the people of Budapest said the same thing about Russia and Communism. Had the Russians not intervened with force (and the train of events suggests strongly that this decision was not reached without hesitations), the whole Soviet and Communist position in Eastern Europe would have been undermined. The repercussions would have extended in due course to Yugoslavia and

Poland, and would have threatened Communism there, "national Communism" though it was.

It is clear, then, why Tito—after some schoolmasterish remarks about how the Hungarian situation had been botched both by the local Communists and by the Russians and that it would not have occurred had everybody listened to *his* advice—accepted the suppression of Hungary, at first with secret, then with public, relief.

But the events of the fall of 1956 had to lead to a reappraisal on both sides of Russo-Yugoslav relations. The pattern that had been set just before the Hungarian-Polish explosion could not endure. Yugoslavia was now seen as a demoralizing example for the satellite bloc. Her attempt to rejoin the bloc while preserving a special relationship with the West was held to be one of the indirect causes of the whole sequence of events that had led to Budapest. On the Russian side, the struggle for leadership within the Communist Party of the U.S.S.R., which lasted throughout 1957 with Khrushchev's stock dipping and then rising again, postponed any re-evaluation of the Yugoslav problem. On Tito's side, there was no reason to take the initiative in redefining the relationship. The Yugoslav Party had every reason to hope for a perpetuation of the pre-Budapest pattern. At the same time, facing the danger of an abrupt return by Moscow to the methods that were employed before Stalin's death, they felt called upon to re-emphasize their independence in foreign policy.

In 1958 the Yugoslav Communists became "revisionists"; hints of this had been dropped earlier, in 1957. Actually, their party program and the speeches at the Seventh Congress contained nothing new or startling. They were in the spirit of the working agreement that they had had with the Russians in 1956. The condemnation of both the Warsaw Pact and NATO was perhaps a bit strong, and so had been their refusal to sign a Soviet-sponsored declaration endorsing the U.S.S.R.'s position in the cold war on the fortieth anniversary of Great October. Yet in both cases the U.S.S.R. in her post-1956 posture felt compelled to indicate that Yugoslavia's behavior was not ideologically correct. Titoism had now appeared, according to the dicta of the Moscow fashion-makers, in a new dress: it was no longer an outpost of imperialism and treachery as in the Stalin era, nor a prodigal son returning to the bosom of the socialist family of the 1955–56 period, but a deviation. The Yugoslav Communists, with the assistance of the satellites and of the Chinese, whose attacks surpassed even the Russians' in vituperation, were confined to this convenient purgatory of Communist terminology. There they still are, in the purgatory of revisionism—which has in recent years become a rather comfortable place compared with the hell peopled exclusively by the dogmatists.

In their continuing effort to be different, the Yugoslavs in 1957 found a new gambit. The underdeveloped nations of the world have been losing their chains and gaining substantial credits from the two super-powers. It was only fitting that Yugoslavia should make a bid for a spiritual leadership of that vast conglomeration of states ranging from the undoubted but threatened democracy of India, through such term-defying structures as Indonesia and Ethiopia, to what the American po-litical scientists call by the shameful euphemism of "one-party democra-cies" of Africa. (The latter term—and why not call a spade a spade?—is one that the Yugoslavs probably regret not having invented to describe their own system.)

The basis of the new "bloc" was certainly found in some identity of interests. All of its members have a vested interest in preventing a violent aggravation of Russo-American relations, and by the same token a vio-lent improvement. The first may lead to war, the second to a consider-able reduction, if not elimination, of the economic help that is poured in by the two colossi. All members of this third force, the neutral or uncommitted bloc, whatever it is called, proudly reject capitalism and certain rather unspecified items of the Soviet ideology. They join in the condemnation of imperialism and neo-colonialism. Since sharp dis-approval of the Soviet system is liable to have more drastic repercussions than criticism of the West, the uncommitted nations gravitate ideologi-cally toward a vague form of Marxism, which of course makes Yugo-slavia their logical leader.

But this new attempt to exercise leadership, and to find some firm ideological ground under their feet, has not served the Yugoslavs very well either. The underdeveloped third force is too underdeveloped, and too formless to be a real force in international affairs. In moments of real stress and danger, its members (witness India) have to forget their strictures about the sinfulness of both sides and the evil of great-power politics. The moral critic appears then in the garb of a humble petitioner for help. Thus an attempt to export Titoism is once more checkmated by the inexorable realities of international politics, and also by the material weakness of Yugoslavia. Barred from expansionism in the Balkans, shut out of the satellite countries, the Yugoslavs do not find themselves in a much firmer position in trying to exercise political leadership on a wider scale. That their example has been of some influence there is no doubt. They have navigated skillfully between the East and West, and they have preserved their independence from either of the two major blocs (or perhaps we should already say three major blocs). In that sense, the lesson of Yugoslavia is worthy of study by each of the new countries. But the Yugoslav Communists cannot provide them with any concrete help in achieving their economic or political objectives. And insofar as the ideology is concerned, what lessons can Titoism impart to the Moslem socialism of Nasser or the Pan-Africanism of Nkrumah? Ideologies in our own day have become subservient and secondary to the realities of world politics. Capitalist Finland exists within the Russian sphere of influence, and Communist Albania exists in defiance of all her neighbors, both Communist and non-Communist.

## The Lesson of Titoism

After the passage of sixteen years, it is possible to reach certain conclusions about the lessons of the Yugoslav experiment. As an ideology, Titoism, one must conclude sadly, is an optical illusion. A man saying "I am a Marxist" gives a definite indication of his philosophy, the laws of history in which he believes, his belief in the superiority of social over private ownership of the means of production, and so forth. But what, in that context, is the meaning of the statement "I am a Titoist"? Or, taking the same problem from a different angle, a man declaring himself to be a Communist can, or could until very recently, identify himself with a world movement, and the conviction that the socioeconomic system of Soviet Russia will spread over all the earth. Here again a self-professed Titoist would be at a loss about how to state his hopes and expectations. In its essence, Titoism is an amalgam of nationalism and socialism. Here it differs quantitatively from the examples of the same combination that we encounter in Egypt, Indonesia, or Cuba. The link with Marxism and Communism still persists, and so does the attempt to find some institutional expression of those creeds. But the essence of an ideology must be reflected in some quality that transcends national boundaries. And we have not yet and probably never will see an inhabitant of Africa, Asia, or America saying "I am a Titoist," although there are beginning to be specimens in those areas, including Mattapan, Massachusetts, ready to say "I am a Maoist."

Turning to the other dimension of Titoism, however, we find that its importance has been truly historic. This is its significance as a movement of revolt against Stalinism and Moscow domination. It has unmasked the essentially Russian character of Leninism as practiced since the October Revolution. It has broken the connection that many began to believe was an organic one between Russian nationalism and Communism. To reconstruct Communism as an international movement has become increasingly difficult since 1948. Those dogmas of pre-1948 Communism that were unchallenged even by Trotskyism—namely, that Communism implies the support of the Soviet Union and that the Soviet pattern for all its perversions must still remain the example for the rest of the world —now lie shattered, and it was small Yugoslavia that first directed a blow at the myth.

The consequences of this unmasking may very well have a profound influence on the development of Communism in Russia. For with Yugoslavia's defections there must have been sown the first seeds of doubt as to whether Communist imperialism is worthwhile, and whether there is in fact the identity of interests between world Communism and Russia or Soviet nationalism that has always been assumed. To be sure, this lesson has not as yet sunk in. The Russian Communists have gone on propagating their creed, as if the victory of Communism in Algeria or Ghana would still necessarily mean a tangible increase in Soviet power. To men of Khrushchev's generation it must be extremely difficult to rethink the whole problem of Communism as a world movement, and the same is true of his present successors, aged 60 and 58. The current difficulties and dissonances must appear to be temporary in their nature, ready to be resolved by some new institution or a joint declaration. But it is difficult to see how the problem is susceptible of a really long-range solution. The Chinese are now in effect accusing the Russians of being Titoists, of giving only lukewarm support to the spread of the doctrine and being uninterested in the promotion of Communism; and this may in time prove true.

The loss of the messianic and missionary impulse of the Communist Party of the U.S.S.R. would in turn have profound effects on Soviet society. The rationale of a totalitarian system demands an external threat or promise of expansion, or both. With the loss of external dynamism, Russian Communism would find it difficult to cope with its own society. It is the awareness of this dilemma that makes the Communist leaders push out of their minds the thought of the incompatibility between Communist expansion and the real interests of the Soviet Union. It also provokes them to take the sort of desperate gambles, on the order of the Cuban missile sites, that had been eschewed by Stalin.

What are the present prospects of Titoism both in its narrower and in its wider meanings? On the first count, there seems little doubt that the present system in Yugoslavia will continue, and that even the disappearance of Marshal Tito is not likely to bring about drastic changes in the regime. Yugoslavia's path is determined by the realities of present-day politics. No regime in the immediate future is likely to be doctrinaire enough to cut off its ties to the West, or to become pragmatic to the point of discarding the veneer of Communism in its nationalist, Titoist form. Yugoslavia's main stake lies in the preservation of the present uneasy equilibrium in Russo-American relations. To the best of their abilities the Yugoslav Communists will also attempt to continue in their self-proclaimed role as the champion conciliator and teacher of the Afro-Asian nations. Tito's disappearance from the scene is likely to lead to some contention for power, and quite possibly the factions will range themselves on the issue of more versus less pro-Soviet attitude, but whichever one prevails it is very likely to continue the traditional (since 1958) Titoist policy in international relations.

In its broader sense, the issue of Titoism has become submerged in the present Sino-Soviet dispute. Chinese Titoism, once a dissident voice, has become what its Yugoslav counterpart never could be: a challenge for the leadership of the Communist movement as a whole. At present this attempt is expressed by pressure on the Soviet Union to assume a more militant and expansionist attitude. In due time it would undoubtedly take the form of Communist China's trying to replace the Soviet Union as the leader of world Communism.

The present phase of the conflict is reminiscent in some ways of the old struggles of the Bolsheviks and the Mensheviks. It was Lenin's tactic to accuse the Mensheviks of shameful moderation, of being "liquidators," etc., and thus achieve the double aim of shaming them into intermittent militancy while at the same time branding them as the betrayers of the working class. The current Chinese effort runs on parallel lines: the Soviet Union is to be shamed out of any possible accommodation with the United States, and at the same time any Soviet act of militancy is branded as insufficient. Thus the Chinese Communists may well expect to expand their clientele not only among other Asian Communist parties but also among militant and impatient Communists everywhere. It takes little imagination to see why a Communist in New Zealand or Norway would look with favor on a more militant policy by the great Communist powers while those Communists who rule their countries have a more sober attitude on the subject. The racial undertones of the Chinese propaganda are also likely to prove a barrier to its acceptance among such large parties as the Italian and French ones. But the Chinese viewpoint may well become the dominant one among the "underprivileged" Communists (that is, the non-white ones) and those who compose only tiny groups in their own countries and who cannot conceivably dream of power without a decisive defeat of Western influence throughout the world.

The most recent phase of the Sino-Soviet relations brought forth an interesting development on the part of the satellite regimes and Yugoslavia. They have all of course lined up on the Russian side of the dispute, and the Yugoslav Communists have been the objective of particularly violent vituperation by the Chinese. The Chinese see Yugoslavia, and with great justification, as a terrible preview of what Soviet Russia *might* become: a Communist regime which has lost its ideological and missionary fervor, retaining the ideology because there is nothing else to take its place but attending mainly and prudently to its own national interest. This "secularization" of Yugoslavia and her sensible relations with the West are seen by the Chinese as a threat to Communism everywhere.

Yet paradoxically we have recently observed the Yugoslavs and some other satellite regimes trying to exert their influence to prevent the Sino-Soviet split from becoming sharper and more definite. The reasons for it are not hard to find. Just as the Yugoslavs have a vested interest in the precarious balance of power between the Soviet and Western blocs, for a definite victory of either would threaten them with disaster, so they have come to appreciate that they have a similar interest in a moderate degree of hostility and a precarious balance of power *within* the Communist world. A definite split between the two Communist giants or military action (which can no longer be ruled out) would make a complete shambles of Communism as an international movement. It might lead Soviet Russia to assume "isolationism," to lose interest in the preservation of the Eastern European outposts of Communism. A "secularization" of Soviet society is now seen as a threat not only in Peking, but in a different way also in Belgrade and Bucharest. Where would the Communist regimes in Eastern Europe be if Soviet Russia decided that her interests might be better served by a real accommodation with the West, and by a policy of spheres of influence that would not necessarily demand ideological as well as political subservience. In the last resort, every Communist regime in Eastern Europe is maintained by the fear of Soviet intervention and the memories of Budapest, and the situation in Communist Yugoslavia is not materially different. It does not rely on Soviet bayonets, but on the conviction of the majority of the population of the Federal Republic that *under present international conditions* the only alternative to Titoism is a return to outright satellite status. If that conviction disappears, voices like those of Djilas will not remain isolated and eccentric.

The present turn of events in the Communist world brings Titoism once more into sharper focus. In its broader sense it can be seen as an organic and inevitable disease of non-Russian Communism when in power. Ironically, many of the theses of Marxism-Leninism that were intended to describe inevitable tendencies within the capitalist world have proved to be true of the Communist one. Imperialistic rivalry, for instance, is really the highest stage of *Communism*. This rivalry in turn enables the satellites and ex-satellites like Yugoslavia and Albania to play an independent if apprehensive role in world politics. It is still an open question whether a formula can be found which could appease their fears and ambitions, which would preserve a *formal* unity of the Communist world without leading again to its domination by a single power, and which would leave the doctrine with some of its meaning and dynamism without increasing the danger of a world holocaust.

It is difficult to see how the Communist world could really become polycentric. Certainly the history of Communism is not encouraging in this respect. Old Russian Social Democracy was polycentric in the sense that a variety of approaches and tactics were advocated within the party. But the essence of Bolshevism from the beginning was that there was only one correct ideology, one correct road to power, and only one center of power and ideological arbiter. The only departures from this pattern were the result of struggles for succession or drastic external threats. It may very well be that the rulers of Yugoslavia, if their ability to improvise a way out of an ideological cul-de-sac is not exhausted, may attempt yet another ingenious solution to the intolerable dilemmas facing world Communism. But the success or failure of such an effort will depend on factors that are not within their power to determine.

Arthur A. Cohen

# Maoism

Crucial to an understanding of the thought of Mao Tse-tung is the view one takes of the practical application of that thought. Maoism can be viewed abstractly, without reference to policies—that is, in such terms as "nationalism implementing Marxism through history"—or it can be viewed concretely. Abstractions are best rejected as unrewarding, inasmuch as they impede a precise understanding of the operative political concepts and methods of Mao's career. Abstractions about China evade discussion of the specific policies Mao has imposed on the Chinese. Further, no practical purpose is served by insisting that Mao is basically a nationalist, inasmuch as all national leaders in this world are, or that he does not take his Communism seriously, inasmuch as he frequently does. Moreover, to say that Mao's concepts are specifically "Chinese" and "Asian" because he is, is to evade the problem of delineating Maoism. The simplest statement would seem to be: Mao's thought draws its uniqueness from his revision, improvement, or even complete abandonment of various aspects of Communist doctrine and Soviet practice. It is on this statement that the following discussion will focus.

## Early Views

Prior to 1911, Mao's political views (according to his statements to Edgar Snow) were primarily those set forth by the Western-influenced, Neo-Confucian reformers K'ang Yu-wei and Liang Ch'i-ch'ao.[1] In this period he first came upon the concept of socialism, and dipped lightly into the works of Smith, Darwin, Mill, Rousseau, and Spencer. He acquired only a small understanding of Western ethical and political thought, warming to discussions "only of large matters—the nature of man, human society, of China, the world, and the universe." A totalistic concept of society began to displace individualism in his thinking as he turned away from ideas of gradual, piecemeal reform. During his years as a student at Changsha, from 1912–1918, Mao's political ideas began to take shape, and he had his first taste of "social action," organizing a radical group—not completely, or even predominantly, Marxist—resembling groups organized by students in other mainland cities. By the end of the First World War, Mao had discarded the Neo-Confucian reformers and had been drawn toward the ideas of social revolutionaries, accepting many anarchist as well as Communist concepts. When he became a Marxist in the summer of 1920, under Ch'en Tu-hsiu and Li Ta-chao, Mao completely rejected gradualist methods of rectifying social evils and accepted the doctrine of class warfare. He emphasized the point in November by attacking Bertrand Russell, who was lecturing in China and who had made the idealist's mistake of proposing education, rather than destruction, of capitalists. At the same time, Mao was confirmed in his conviction that only mass political power, secured by mass action, would open the way to social justice.

He soon thereafter became a Leninist, accepting the view that an elitist political party embodying the will of the masses was the only instrument that could destroy the old order. From this crucial decision, he went on to participate in the founding meeting of the Chinese Communist Party (CCP) in 1921 and then to organize workers.[2] Mao persisted in this course until the summer of 1925, when he went out to the Hunan countryside to organize the miserable peasants, work in which he was to excel.[3] His dedication to mass revolutionary violence was made clear in the most striking piece he ever wrote—the report of March 1927 on peasant insurrections in Hunan. Confucian moderation was explicitly disparaged, revolutionary excesses were exalted, and at several points the peasants were encouraged to trample the landlords underfoot after bringing them down.

Mao reported on the peasants' ruthlessness in struggle as a member of two parties—the CCP and the Kuomintang (KMT)—that had been organized on elitist disciplinary lines. The Chinese Communists had been compelled by the Comintern in August 1922 to go beyond a mere alliance with the KMT and to form a bloc *within* it, and for their grudging acceptance of this tactical subordination to Sun Yat-sen's bourgeois national party, they were scolded like small boys by Radek at the Fourth Comintern Congress in Moscow in November 1922. Because of its subordination to the KMT, the CCP adopted a policy that went against the grain of Mao's thought: the curbing of peasant excesses against the gentry. This new line was intended to ensure a smooth working relationship with the KMT.

However, the policy of subordination facilitated the destruction in

April 1927 of many Communists in Shanghai and Nanking who were not alert to the prospect that Chiang Kai-shek, a revolutionary colleague, would turn on them with the fury of the enemy. When the Comintern had directed the CCP to enter the KMT Wuhan government in December 1926, Stalin had not perceived that the elitist and highly disciplined KMT organization was tough to crack from within. Further, Chiang's training in Moscow had not reduced his personal independence, ambition, and dedication to the removal of political competitors. Faced with total destruction, the CCP gathered its depleted forces and, with a degree of Comintern guidance at the August 1927 emergency conference, prepared for opposition to the KMT and violent revolution.

The program of the emergency conference provided Mao with his first opportunity to combine the ideas of peasant insurrection and regular military operations, since it called for the scattered armed units of peasants and workers to be rebuilt, on a uniform plan, into a "well-organized, solid force." Mao went back to Hunan to organize peasant uprisings in accordance with this program—and failed. He was rebuked by the CCP leadership in November 1927, reportedly on the grounds that sufficient numbers of peasants had not been enlisted to support the military effort. Justified or not, the criticism stressed a point that had already become a basic principle of Mao's thinking: organize the peasants. The real issue was how to enlist peasant support in a rural war and how to make that war a revolutionary success. Chu Teh, who joined Mao in May 1928 in the mountain stronghold of Chingkangshan, brought considerable experience to the problem of changing the peasant into a revolutionary guerrilla. This veteran of earlier revolutionary battles collaborated with Mao in gradually hammering out an important and unique program of Communist guerrilla warfare waged from an independent rural base-area. Chu and Mao sustained their forces by a heroic display of personal perseverance and pugnacity, combined with a willingness to die in the Communist cause, that remained the hallmark of their guerrilla units during even the most barren struggles against superior KMT forces.

It is now clear that Mao assigned the peasants a rather greater role in revolution than did Lenin, but he did not change the basic tenet that even a peasant revolution must be led by the proletariat—that is, by the Communist Party. Beyond that, Mao developed the concept of a "long war," which was Chu Teh's and his own pragmatic generalization from the military and geographical position they were driven to accept. That is, they drew on Lenin's dictum of party leadership, but made significant innovations on the matter of guerrilla warfare, tactics, and strategy. The treatises Mao wrote both before and after 1927 emphasize first a doctrine of revolutionary advance and then a strategy of retreat, which became the strategy of the long war. They are not marked by doctrinal erudition or facility. They center on practical guidelines on how to fight, how to stay alive, and how to gain peasant support. His personal insights into the practical requirements of the anti-KMT struggle seem to be free of doctrinaire blind spots; he is plainly a tactician rather than a theoretician. This emerges so clearly from a reading of his works of the 1920's that Party propagandists were later directed to warn cadres against any open expression of such an appraisal. Theorist Li Ch'i stated in the theoretical journal of the CCP, *Hsüeh-hsi,* on March 1, 1952: "There are a few infants (if not infants, then persons with ulterior motives) who say that in the period of the First Revolutionary War [1924–27], the CCP had not yet acquired Marxist-Leninist theory and that at the time Comrade Mao Tse-tung was not yet a well-versed Marxist-Leninist theorist. It is easily seen that such prattling talk is completely at odds with historical fact and, therefore, entirely mistaken. Criticism should be leveled against it."

## Guerrilla Revolutionary

Mao radically changed the traditional Communist view of the road to revolutionary power as a city-centered uprising. Reversing the Soviet precedent, he swept from the countryside to the cities in a protracted war, using rural base-areas for his power centers. As early as 1928, he was explicit in pointing to the uniqueness of his rural base-area concept;* eight years later he was depicting his road as the future "example for the people in many colonial countries."[4]

There had been no precedent in Lenin's and Stalin's experience for creating a self-sustaining rural base-area and making a national revolution with a guerrilla army. In one work—*Partisan Warfare* of October 1906—Lenin came close to saying that partisan warfare could become the way to power, but he did not develop the thought. He used the term partisan warfare to mean isolated acts of terrorism, such as holdups of banks and customs houses; this type of banditry was intended to in-

---

* In *Why Can China's Red Political Power Exist?* (October 1928), Mao stated: "The phenomenon that within a country one or several small areas under Red political power should exist for a long time amid the encirclement of White political power is one that has never been found elsewhere in the world." Also relevant is Mao's claim in *A Single Spark Can Start a Prairie Fire* (January 1930) that, "The tactics we have derived from the struggle of the past three years are indeed different from any other tactics, ancient or modern, Chinese or foreign."

crease revolutionary funds. It was not warfare conducted by an army, but small-scale terror directed against secondary targets. However, *Partisan Warfare* went on to say that "Marxism does not tie the movement to any particular combat method"—a formulation that opened the door to any tactic which might lead to success.

As he built his army, Mao and the Communist military men around him began to arrive at a theory of war that, in the 1930's, he developed into a doctrine. Mao, Chu Teh, P'eng Te-huai, Lin Piao, and other leaders contributed to this doctrine, whose evolution Mao described in December 1936, in *Strategic Problems of China's Revolutionary War*: "By May 1928, basic principles of guerrilla warfare, simple in nature and suited to the conditions of the time, had already been evolved, that is, the 16-character formula: 'The enemy advances, we retreat; the enemy camps, we harass; the enemy tires, we attack; the enemy retreats, we pursue.' ... Later, our operational principles were developed a step further.... [In 1930] the principle of 'luring the enemy in deep' was put forward and, moreover, successfully applied.... [By 1931] a complete set of operational principles for the Red Army had taken shape." After these and other principles had been established, Mao in the mid-1930's turned to systematizing them, and only in this later period did he cite various historic battles and the statements of Sun Wu-tzu, a Chinese military strategist of the fifth century B.C., to "illustrate" (Mao's word) his meaning.[5]

The central feature of Mao's code was his stress on the long war. When, in December 1936, Mao said that "to wage a revolutionary war for ten years, as we have done, might be surprising in other countries," he was rejecting modern Western and Soviet military doctrine on quick-decision ("impatient") war, and supplying Chinese Communist military thought with one of its most valuable concepts. It meshes well with his other concept of the period: "Absolute superiority exists only at the end of a war or campaign. It rarely exists at the outset." (These ideas have been, and are, key elements in the Vietnamese Communists' military thinking.) Mao's strategy called for expanding the self-sustaining bases as opportunity permitted, retreating when necessary in the hope that the advancing enemy would be worn down or overextend himself, or both. In offensive operations, the most important principles were careful planning, concentration of superior forces—Mao's proportion is ten to one—and surprise. In both defensive and offensive operations, the army was to fight decisive engagements only when confident of victory, and it was to avoid "absolutely" a decisive engagement on which the fate of the nation would be at stake. In extension of the second point, Mao said in May 1938: "Even a gambler needs money to gamble with, and if he stakes all he has on a single throw of the dice and loses it through bad luck, he will not be able to gamble again."

The political aspect of Mao's strategy reflects his view of revolutionary war as total war. That is, the CCP acted to organize most segments of the population and the economic potential of an area, its first aim being not annihilation of the enemy's armed forces—a future goal—but control of the population in whose midst war was being waged. Control was secured by eliminating landlords and other political opponents and then, on the basis of this display of power, organizing the peasants to resist KMT and Japanese forces. CCP organizers were significantly aided by the circumstance of Japan's invasion of China in 1937: "It is no accident that the CCP, after being dislodged from the mountains of South China, made its comeback in the Northwest in war-time. While the destructive aggression of Japan smashed the modern façade of Nationalist China and forced the Kuomintang onto the defensive in the backward regions of the Southwest, the war of resistance gave Chinese Communism a new sanction for its revolutionary effort. Patriotic mobilization and sacrifice for war against Japan had an appeal for young China which the anti-landlord crusade of the Chinese Soviet Republic in Kiangsi never had. As in other parts of Asia, the presence of an aggressor gave the Communists a golden opportunity to link their domestic revolution with national survival. Thus the political crises of the times, in the two decades since Japan's aggression began in 1931, have provided abundant opportunity for political organizers. Refugee migrations brought the intellectuals directly into the peasant villages of the interior, after 1937, and the juxtaposition of these key elements produced a natural chain reaction which could be guided and fostered by a party organization."[6]

Recruits to the guerrilla forces were indoctrinated by Mao's very original thought-reform and group-struggle techniques, requiring participation in small study groups and the rote memorization of the political rules of the army and CCP. The intensity of this indoctrination was a distinctive Maoist feature that went far beyond Soviet methods. It is a Maoist feature of all indoctrination in China today, whether in the army, Party, or university.

After the Long March of 1934-35, when Chu Teh's light burned brightly,[7] and the defeat of Japan in 1945, the issue between the CCP and the KMT was gradually transformed from political revolution to military showdown, particularly from 1947 to 1949. Many crucial battles were decided by tactical ingenuity and by the spectacular mobility of the forces directed by Mao's brilliant generals, including Lin Piao, Liu Po-ch'eng, P'eng Te-huai, and Ch'en Yi. And when these forces swept down from the North China plain across the Yangtze, many millions supported Mao for having destroyed the legitimacy of Chiang and the warlords. Eyewitnesses noted in particular the fervor of the intellectuals in defending Mao against doubters as People's Liberation Army units (PLA) entered the major cities. Mao's guerrilla warfare strategy now forms the basis for the CCP claim that the Chinese revolution—"the road of Mao Tse-tung" in Chinese usage—is a new model for Communist seizure of power. This model is being applied in detail by the Vietnamese Communists and Communists in other underdeveloped countries, who accept it as the new classical doctrine for revolution.* The adaptation of guerrilla warfare extends the practical influence of Mao's clearest departure from the precedent of Lenin's October Revolution to countries in which Peking's influence is otherwise insignificant.

*Philosopher*

As political organizer and guerrilla leader, Mao was a genius, but in December 1950 the CCP began to claim that he was a philosopher genius as well. The publication in that month of *On Practice* in both the Soviet Union and China marked a new stage in Mao's effort to be recognized as a senior leader in the world Communist movement. His first major piece on philosophy, written in 1940, *Dialectical Materialism,* was a conceptual potpourri, reflecting ignorance of many of Engels' and Lenin's views on the subject. His own lieutenants found it "full of errors," and within several years it was proscribed.[8] By contrast, his *On Practice* of 1950 and *On Contradiction* of 1952 were logically clear in most respects and doctrinally correct. Unlike the 1940 fragment, they emphasize the distinction made by Marx and Engels between sensation (the first stage) and conception (the second) in the process of attaining knowledge. Further, they posit two views of dialectics that seem to have been unknown to Mao in 1940: (1) matter is self-motivated, and (2) contradiction is

* Appraising various aspects of Mao's road, a North Vietnamese Party propagandist stated: "This vital experience on the proper revolutionary line, revolutionary forces, and revolutionary method has blazed a new path that suits many countries." (*Tuyen Huan,* April 1964.) Use of the qualifier "proper" was intended as an implicit rejection of Khrushchevian views and of the earlier Soviet model. More and more, however, the Vietnamese Communists have declared that their own road—as applied to a colonial rather than a semi-colonial country "like China"—also has provided an internationally significant model: "Our Party's military line ... is a great contribution to the national liberation revolution in Asia, Africa, and Latin America." (Senior General Vo Nguyen Giap in the Hanoi *Quan Doi Nhan Dan,* December 22, 1964.) In his article Giap described the Viet Cong's strategy in South Vietnam as the "partial revolt." Giap concluded by warning army cadres against applying the military techniques of other Communist countries "mechanically and dogmatically"—an allusion to both the USSR and China.

dominant in things and unity subordinate to it. Ever since 1950, CCP theorists have claimed that *On Practice* and *On Contradiction* were "written" in essentially their present form in 1937, that is, before the jumbled fragment on dialectics, a claim it is hard to credit. Inasmuch as *Dialectical Materialism*, written in 1940, is "full of errors," it seems reasonable to assume that any lectures Mao may have given in 1937 on Marxist philosophy were equally primitive and erroneous.[9] The fairest conclusion would seem to be that Mao's revisions of his earlier lectures are so drastic that the more recent versions are altogether different from them. The one original feature of *On Contradiction* was a new gloss on the Engels-Lenin doctrine of qualitative change in things; aside from this, the essay makes profundities out of platitudes. For example, in his discussion of the transformation of opposites, Mao states that the First World War was "transformed" into postwar peace.

Mao's February 1957 statement that in a "socialist society, certain contradictions do exist between the leaders and the led," was unprecedented in Communist literature. The statement was objectionable to Khrushchev at the time not because it was false, which obviously it was not, but because Mao had broken new ground in applying his concept to all bloc countries and had once again disregarded Moscow's claim to be the only source of doctrine in the world movement. As for the intellectual merit of Mao's statement, it was a lesson in the obvious. Mao said nothing new on the knowing process in his latest piece (May 1963) on the subject.[10] As one might expect of a Marxist-Leninist, he emphasizes that knowledge is primarily a generalization from practice and only secondarily a reflection of personal insights: "Where do man's correct ideas come from? Do they drop from the sky? No. Are they inherent in one's head? No. Man's correct ideas can come only from social practice, from the three kinds of social practice—production struggle, class struggle, and scientific experiment." Mao's stress in this piece on the necessity of a careful, rational mental process for reaching correct policies is one reflection (there are many more) of his effort since late 1958 to prove that he had not been personally responsible for the economic irrationality of the Great Leap Forward and the communes. Whether the rationality he argues for will in fact prevail in Chinese Communist domestic policies depends on the degree that he, rather than Party cadres, has been sobered by the failures of 1958 and 1959.

## View of Stalin

Of all the conflicts that eventually led to the Sino-Soviet dispute, two fundamental ones existed for many years: the independence from Soviet control of the CCP's apparatus and Mao's insistence on his own policies for the party. Relations between Stalin and Mao had never been smooth. Unlike other Chinese, Mao had never served as a mere instrument of the Soviet Union's (i.e., Stalin's) foreign policy, although in the early years he aligned himself with this policy in all its twists. Mao did not bear lightly the thought that from 1926 to 1935 Stalin's favor had been given primarily not to him but to other Chinese leaders, and that his rise to CCP power was accepted only after it was an accomplished fact, that is, only after he had dislodged the then dominant leaders in 1935. Nevertheless, he studied Stalin's works and in some respects adopted his political style.* The relationship improved in 1949, when Mao did what Stalin believed he never could do—namely, completely defeated Chiang's forces. It became still warmer in 1950, when Stalin acted to gain Mao's goodwill by concluding the Moscow–Peking treaty of alliance (February) and by directing his propagandists to praise the newly published *On Practice* as creative (December).

In the earlier years of his party career, Mao had been associated only with certain parts of the complex and often confused program that Stalin was endorsing and supporting in China. He was fully aware—as later evidence proves—of the seriousness of Stalin's blunder in directing the CCP to work within the KMT in 1927. However, while Stalin lived, Mao was careful to criticize Trotsky and those Chinese leaders who had followed the Comintern line prior to 1935, particularly the chief scapegoat, Ch'en Tu-hsiu; when the Soviet leader died in 1953, Mao's eulogy reflected a genuine feeling of loss. After Khrushchev, with his "secret speech" of February 1956, acted to shock the CPSU into turning away from Stalin's course, Mao apparently protested to Soviet officials, insisting, in April, October, and November, that the criticism had been unbalanced and that Stalin's merits outweighed his faults. The degree of Mao's outrage is unknown. It is not clear whether he objected more to the substance of Khrushchev's accusations or to his right to diminish Stalin's stature without consulting the CCP.† In any case, by the time he made his liberalization speech in February 1957, Mao was not averse to disparaging some aspects of Stalin's leadership, primarily, as Mao put it, "rule of terror and liquidation of thousands of Communists."[11] Mao also

---

* Mao's chief Chinese eulogist, Ch'en Po-ta, has written that during the 1930's, Mao "had the opportunity to read Stalin's works extensively. He read and pondered with the greatest enthusiasm all the available works of Stalin." *Sino-Soviet Friendship*, December 15, 1949. The current effort in Peking to portray Mao as closer in political views to Lenin than to Stalin is a reversal of the effort in the early 1950's to depict Mao as primarily Stalin's disciple.
† When Khrushchev attacked Stalin, "he failed to consult the fraternal parties in advance on this question of principle, which involves the entire international Communist movement, and afterward tried to impose a *fait accompli* on them." Joint article, *People's Daily* and *Red Flag*, September 13, 1963.

implied that he (Mao) was incapable of such brutality and that personal modesty had prevented the development of a personality cult in China. Further, when Mao's propagandists defended Stalin's name during polemics with Khrushchev's writers in September 1963, Stalin's blunders on China policy were exploited more fully than ever before in published CCP materials. It was Mao's purpose to establish his own infallibility on policy and that of his chief lieutenant, Liu Shao-ch'i.*

Mao did not completely discard the legacy of Stalin. The CCP's defense of Stalin was constructed to fix the late Soviet leader in the history of the Communist movement as a great but imperfect "eagle"; Khrushchev as a mere "hen in the backyard of the working-class movement, among the dungheaps"; and Mao as a beneficent—almost cosmic—confessor, who appraised the fallen eagle's faults as "secondary," but nonetheless as faults.[12] The Maoist public position depicts Stalin as a good revolutionary who cannot be praised as perfect since his record includes error and illusion. On the question of a personality cult in China itself, the position is simply that it does not exist because "at Comrade Mao's suggestion," the CCP forbade public celebrations of party leaders' birthdays and the naming of places after them.[13] In this way, Mao absorbed Khrushchev's simultaneous criticism of Stalin's and Mao's personality cults, and used the downgrading of Stalin as the occasion to take a big step forward in international prestige.

Stalin left his mark on Mao's view of internal policies. Stalin went further than Lenin in imposing total control of the Russian people's lives, effectively destroying the pre-Soviet political, economic, military, and social institutions. Stalin's legacy helped Mao transform the CCP into an instrument of political power that was closely knit by a rigid discipline of dedication and obedience; Lenin had not worked out in detail the extensive bureaucratic controls within the party that Stalin established. Particularly in the 1930's, Mao began to read Stalin's works. But by improvising—i.e., by using his own thought-reform techniques—Mao attained a control over the mental environment and personal commitment of the Chinese Communists that went even deeper than Stalin's

---

* "Long ago, the Chinese Communists had first-hand experience of some of his mistakes. Of the erroneous 'left' and 'right' opportunist lines which emerged in the CCP at one time or another, some arose under the influence of certain mistakes of Stalin's, insofar as their international sources were concerned. In the late 1920's, the 1930's, and the early and middle 1940's, the Chinese Marxists-Leninists represented by Comrades Mao Tse-tung and Liu Shao-ch'i resisted the influence of Stalin's mistakes. They gradually overcame the erroneous lines of 'left' and 'right' opportunism, and finally led the Chinese revolution to victory." Joint article, People's Daily and Red Flag, September 13, 1963. Mao and Liu resisted more than the influence of Stalin's mistakes; they were constantly compelled to guard against his effort to support an anti-Maoist leadership.

control over members of the CPSU. Mao adopted Stalin's policy of periodic purge and the extraction of confession—the party "rectification" campaign—to stifle opposition and increase intraparty cohesion. Mao also imposed on the army a vast, Stalinist political apparatus, with its own pyramidal structure, directly responsive to the CCP Politburo and to Mao. Mao and his lieutenants derived from Stalin the concept of long-term, high-speed industrialization by a "shock-brigade" effort—a concept that went beyond Lenin's idea of a relatively short-term attempt to attain full communism by adding "electrification" to Soviet power. Since 1958, when Mao considered the advent of full communism only several years in the future, he has made the period of socialist labor and austerity even more prolonged than Stalin—a matter of "from five to ten generations."[14] Finally, Mao adopted from Stalin, not Lenin, the policy and method of the forced-labor camps. One may legitimately ask whether the Maoist method of "reforming" camp prisoners was put into effect, like the Stalinist method of "reforging" them, primarily to justify the severity of the policy.

Mao did, however, reject the most extreme form of the Stalinist intraparty purge. Although Mao had physically eliminated opposition military leaders in December 1930, he acted against real rather than imagined conspirators and avoided the appearance of a capricious blood-purge. His chief aide, Liu Shao-ch'i, explicitly quoting Stalin's words on intraparty discipline and implicitly attacking Stalin's practice, made this statement in 1941: "Bolshevik criticism has its Bolshevik toleration. Excessive criticism, the exaggeration of the mistakes of others, and baseless accusations are all wrong. It is not true that the fiercer the intraparty struggle the better. It should have appropriate limits and seek a suitable level."[15] Liu went on to discuss unacceptable ways of handling disagreements between party members, and rejected "aggressively unreasonable and irrational" methods of criticism. However, the attempt of Mao and Liu in the 1940's to erect safeguards against capricious purges in the CCP did not mean that they rejected the techniques of psychological terror. Mao made it clear in 1942 that in "helping" comrades, a scare device must be used to attain political obedience and reestablish devotion to the party's policies: "The first method is to administer a powerful shock to the patients; yell at them 'you're sick!' so that they are frightened and break out all over into a sweat. Then we tell them to take the [thought-reform] treatment."[16]

The same device is directed not only at party members who are to be retained, but also at those who are to be expelled from the ranks. The criterion for rehabilitation and retention in the party is not the willingness to confess to opposition, as confession is extracted even from members who are discarded. The criterion would seem to depend on the CCP leaders' appraisal of the individual's potential for reviving opposition to Maoist policies. A major opponent of the 1930's, Li Li-san, was kept in the party because he was no longer a threat to Mao's dominance of the CCP apparatus and because he provides "proof" that Mao is more lenient with former opponents than Stalin.

Partly because personal relationships were smooth and partly because Mao rejected Stalin's policy of purging imagined opponents, the CCP leaders remained united from 1935 to 1954, the notable exception being the defection of Chang Kuo-t'ao. However, major purges of top-level leaders in 1954 and 1959, stemming from maneuvers for power and sharp policy disputes, have made it clear that the CCP Politburo is not a harmonious monolith. Moreover, important factions have developed, the most recent having arisen in the period of the Great Leap Forward. Throughout the Leap, in 1958–59, the Chinese press made frequent references to the existence of a persistent group, apparently in the party, that shied away from the economic hazards involved in the drive. This "gloomy clique" was depicted in mid-1958 as feeling that the final statistics of 1958 would bear out its misgivings. T'an Chen-lin, a leading propagandist for the Leap, stated in February 1959 that there was still a group of doubters who asked, "Why is there no flour if there was a bumper wheat crop?" T'an commented darkly, "If the ideological problems of these comrades are not solved quickly, damage will be done to this year's Leap." The downgrading of Politburo member Ch'en Yün in 1959 suggests that this leading economist was among the doubters in the "gloomy clique." The provincial-level party cadres who were purged in October 1958 formed yet another "faction" (the CCP's word) in Liaoning; other provincial-level cadres in various provinces were removed from their posts. By far the most important, politically, was the group formed around the famous former Minister of Defense P'eng Te-huai. The existence of such a group was confirmed in captured Chinese Communist documents—the *Work Bulletin (Kung-tso T'ung-hsün)* of January 3, 1961—in which reference was made to the "P'eng-Huang anti-party group." Huang K'o-ch'eng was one of several men brought down with P'eng Te-huai in 1959 at the Lushan Plenum of the Central Committee. Among other things, they apparently had solicited support from Khrushchev to change basic Maoist policies.*

---

* Khrushchev later defended them in October 1961: "In talks with the CCP delegation, Khrushchev flatly turned down our criticism and advice and even expressed undisguised support for anti-party elements in the CCP." Joint article, *People's Daily* and *Red Flag*, September 6, 1963.

*Approach to Domestic Policy*

A measure of Mao's ability was his complete defeat of Chiang Kai-shek in the art supposed to have been the latter's chief strength, the art of war. The contrast between the two men is made even sharper by Mao's superior ability to handle the problem of single-party rule in China. The PLA and the CCP were, in 1949, more closely knit and dedicated organizations of power than those which Chiang had established. They provided Mao with the essential instruments for rooting out opposition to his policies, for destroying traditional institutions and views, and for imposing new institutions and views. Three major mass campaigns were used to destroy the chief sources of resistance. These Maoist drives involved much larger segments of the populace than the CPSU campaigns in Stalin's lifetime: however, they were as controlled and deliberate as Stalin's had been and provided the people with an equally clear demonstration of the power of the Communist Party.

In the first major campaign after the Communists came to power, CCP control was consolidated in the countryside in 1950–52 by several Maoist policies, the most effective being the vigorous application of the Agrarian Reform Law. "Reform" was a euphemism. After the peasants were promised the landlords' fields and enlisted in the cause of redistribution, CCP cadres insisted that class hatred of the gentry must be intense and uninterrupted, mass public trials must "release anger," and public executions must take place even in the villages where the need did not exist.[17] In the second major campaign—the Five Anti's of 1952—Mao mobilized the CCP and the masses for class war against even the smallest merchants, who were forced to exhaust their savings and liquidate all concealed assets. Psychological terror reportedly compelled several thousand in Shanghai alone to commit suicide, and those who escaped with their lives saved nothing but a small share of their own businesses. The campaign continued until the CCP attained substantial amounts of money, some of which was earmarked for military use during the Korean War, and until the capitalists had been given a stern lesson in political power. This softening-up campaign was absolutely essential for the Maoist policy of gradually taking over private enterprises between 1953 and 1956, that is, for the "peaceful" transformation of private industry and commerce.

In the third mass drive of the early period, the Three Anti's in the first half of 1952, Mao mobilized the party against its own "corrupt" members—men accused of taking bribes or retaining confiscated property. As in the other campaigns, the "sharp spearhead of mass struggle" as "mass investigation," uniquely Maoist in intensity and extent, was used to compel party cadres to "confess guilt."[18] Several hundred thousand party cadres apparently were expelled, including high provincial officials; the influx, thereafter, of large numbers of new cadres indicated the extensiveness of the purge. Mao's formula of "unity-criticism-unity," that is, criticism of party members in order to retain them in a purer form, was in practice merely a locution for the view that the CCP must work with those cadres the leadership had decided not to expel. A sizable number of "big culprits" (Mao's phrase) who escaped with their lives are now in the forced-labor camps.

The hard core of actual and potential political opponents—the KMT officials who had been permitted to hold minor posts, and those Chinese who qualified their support for the CCP—were eliminated in the course of a more basic and continuous drive. The "suppression of counterrevolutionaries" drive, which was sustained with varying rigor from 1949 to 1955, took a toll in human life well beyond Mao's February 1957 figure of 800,000. Clear evidence that many innocent Chinese were swept away as "counterrevolutionary" appeared, among other places, in the statements of Liaoning Province party officials, who insisted that the drive's main feature was a series of "mistakes" rather than "achievements."[19] Party officials were clearly aware that many imagined rather than real opponents of the regime had been eliminated. The process was facilitated by the destruction of all "bourgeois" concepts of legal protection and by the establishment, whenever necessary, of ad-hoc people's tribunals to administer the judicial phase of the drives. In the June 1957 version of his liberalization speech, Mao admitted that, "In the suppression of the counterrevolution, good people were sometimes mistaken for bad." But he did not call for the establishment of an effective judicial system; he merely issued the ambiguous warning that cadres should "draw a sharp line between our own people and our enemies." In short, Mao's rule is as arbitrary as Stalin's, and, in the view of several Parties within the Communist bloc, even more rigorous in its control of dissent.

Destruction of the major sources of resistance eased the way for two far-reaching CCP successes in 1955 and 1956. (1) Transformation of agricultural units from mutual-aid teams to cooperatives collectivized hundreds of millions of peasants without large-scale bloodshed. This was only possible because most of the destruction of landlords had taken place in the initial land reform of 1950–52. (2) As a result of the complete transformation of small capitalist enterprises and the introduction of a new form of "buying out"—guaranteeing a percentage of the capital invested in mixed enterprises—all privately owned means of production were converted into joint enterprises. The administration of these enterprises was smoothly transferred into Party hands. These two achievements, hailed in Peking as new developments in Marxist-Leninist doctrine and improvements on Soviet practice, increased the prestige of the CCP among non-Soviet Parties in the bloc and in the world Communist movement. But the failure of the Hundred Flowers campaign in mid-1957 reduced this prestige and, from all the evidence, apparently convinced Mao that de-Stalinization and a gradual loosening of the controls on intellectuals was the wrong course for any Communist regime. This conviction developed into a pervasive drive for revolutionary militancy in domestic and foreign policy and a deeply anti-Khrushchevian attitude.

By May 1958, when Mao's lieutenants implicitly attacked the basis of peaceful coexistence and détente with the United States as set forth by Khrushchev, economic rationalization within the Soviet Union and Soviet economic programs were rejected as models for China. Mao's Great Leap Forward and the People's Commune program of 1958–59 were implemented in the teeth of Soviet warnings.* The major domestic warnings came from the "gloomy clique" of economic specialists. To understand the reasoning behind the economic irrationality of the programs one must recognize the doctrinal compulsion at work among the CCP leaders, including Mao. Mao believed, as many CCP materials indicate, that he had found a better way to industrialize the country and that his program would be closer to early Marxist dictums than to the programs of Khrushchev and Stalin. The degree of Mao's dedication to Communist doctrine may be gauged from his disregard for the pragmatic advice of specialists and his application, in the face of their warnings, throughout rural China of a Marxist program which, in conception and magnitude, was later described by CCP leaders themselves as utopian. (Chu Teh used the term in November 1958.)

The communes took over privately held plots, orchards, and some domestic animals. They adopted a "wage-plus-supply" system, under which members were provided, in addition to a wage, with "free" staples such as rice or wheat, and other necessities such as clothing. "Supply" was supposed to be determined in accordance with the Marxist principle "to each according to his needs." The CCP intensified indoctrination on behalf of putting the interests of the state first. Mao apparently calculated that insofar as production was increased and consumption reduced, the rate of capital formation would be stepped up. Large labor armies would make it possible to shift workers more freely between agriculture and

---

* Khrushchev later stated that he had warned Mao in Peking in the summer of 1958, that the commune program would not work, but at the time, Mao "was not asking me, he was telling me." (Speech of April 15, 1964.)

industry, and communal mess halls would restrict "excess" consumption. (His reasoning included the belief that speeding up the eating process would give workers more time on the job.) In short, Mao asked more of the human material than it could stand, and more of economic processes than rationality would permit. The commune penalized the more efficient producer by taking all but a bare minimum away from him. Entire villages or cooperatives had to sustain the less efficient ones under the super-amalgamation scheme. By thus penalizing the better farmer, Mao destroyed his incentive to excel. By fall 1958, there was increasing grumbling because of (1) the loss of private plots, orchards, livestock, fowl, and other holdings; (2) the degrading of the peasant's status from that of part-owner to hired hand; and (3) the introduction of an almost monastic way of life, with hard work, little food, strict military discipline, and only two days off a month. And this, the CCP had proclaimed for several months to the Communist bloc, is what life under Communism will be like.

No distinctive aspect of the commune program was traditionally Chinese. The policies diverged from tradition as sharply as the policies of the early 1950's, which were in part directed at the vestiges of Confucian and Western liberal thought. They indicated decisively that Chinese Communist theory—that is, the thought of Mao Tse-tung—is not concerned with tradition as such, unless tradition is held to mean primarily patriotism and national pride.

One of Mao's greatest gambles became the greatest failure of his career. Mao retreated in 1959–60 on his boldest doctrinal advances in 1958: supercollectivity, communal eating, and even claims to have approached full communism. Severe economic dislocation and physical deprivation were compounded by drought and flood, and by 1961 signs of deep disillusionment spread beyond the rural populace to the CCP for the first time since Mao came to power. When the Chinese leaders attempted to combat this rural discontent and deterioration of party morale in 1961, some of their methods revealed an extreme callousness. Cadres in rural areas complained in 1961 that party authorities had encouraged rebellious and hungry peasants to beat them—a scapegoat procedure intended to deflect local resentment from party leaders. To further appease the peasants, party secretaries were executed in Kwangtung after public trials, on the charge of "brutality to farmers and mismanagement of communes."[20] This deliberate policy probably was applied to basic-level *hsien* (county) cadres in other provinces. Another complaint frequently raised by cadres was against long-term austerity.[21]

Throughout the period of retreat (1959–62), the Chinese leaders brushed aside suggestions that the "revolutionary blindness" which always appears in implementing the Maoist "mass line" should be modified. The mass line was reaffirmed as an important device for imposing CCP policy on the populace. The sharp difference between the theoretical formulation of policy by the masses and the practical application of policy by the Party was revealed in the following statement of T'ao Chu, the rising First Secretary of the CCP's Central-South Bureau:

"Party policies come from the masses and represent the interests of the masses, and have to go through a certain process before they can be accepted by the masses. When party policies are implemented, the broad masses who still follow old ideas and traditions need education so that their consciousness can be raised to a level sufficiently high to meet the demands of these policies....

"In disseminating party policies, our newspapers must have the following attitude: I will persist in saying this whether you believe it or not, whether you are abusive or shout and applaud. By adopting such an attitude of unbending firmness in disseminating policies of the party, we can make the masses accept the policies sooner. Can this be called to go it blind? No. I would call it revolutionary firmness."[22]

The view that "some party lines, however, emanate from the people, though others are clearly conceived by the party leaders first and then transmitted to the non-party Chinese," is not supported by the facts.[23] Policy failures of the Politburo, however, have been attributed to the masses, and discarded policies have been attributed to others after the fact.[24] On December 26, 1964, in reports to the National People's Congress by senior "legal" officials, the Procurator General, Chang Ting-ch'eng, stated: "Some criminal elements, who had put up an outside resistance and refused to plead guilty after repeated investigations and trials by the government and legal departments, could but bow their heads and plead guilty when the masses rose to wage a face-to-face struggle with them." Students of Soviet internal policies during Stalin's lifetime are aware of the striking similarity between this Maoist technique and the Stalinist technique of public extraction of confession. It would seem to be an improvement on the Soviet precedent only in matters of minor detail.[25]

The Tenth Plenum of the Central Committee (September 1962) ended the period of retreat and set forth a series of policies intended to tighten up the CCP ranks and increase the Party's control in all areas of work. The Ninth Plenum (January 1961) had already adopted certain key organizational changes in an effort to restore centralized control after the decentralization of 1958–59, but these proved inadequate to remedy the situation.[26] One of the Tenth Plenum's most important decisions was "to strengthen the work of the Party Control Commissions at all levels," and to elect additional members to the top-level Central Control Commission. In practice, this decision indicated that the records and actions of all party members would henceforth be subjected to much closer scrutiny, with a view to ferreting out incompetents or critics of Politburo policies, particularly on economic matters. The top leaders' intention to tighten their grip on the implementation of Politburo policies was also indicated by the Tenth Plenum's election to the Central Committee Secretariat of three new members, all of whom have long reputations for revolutionary purity and loyalty to Mao. They were Lu Ting-yi, who has had a major role in every CCP rectification campaign since 1942; K'ang Sheng, who has a considerable background of secret police work; and Senior General Lo Jui-ch'ing, formerly Minister of Public Security and now Chief of Staff of the PLA.[27] Throughout 1963 there were indications that this tightening-up of party control would be extended to various non-party sectors of Chinese society, that is, to the workers, peasants, intellectuals, and the military ranks. By early 1964, CCP materials began to indicate that a discipline roughly as rigorous as military discipline was precisely the goal Mao was determined to attain, particularly in economic work.*

Political units modeled on PLA political departments were established in economic organizations, in a move intended to comply with a directive attributed to Mao: "All our economic, industrial, agricultural, and commercial departments must study the methods of the PLA, must establish and strengthen political work, and then, in this way, we can stimulate the revolutionary spirit of the millions and tens of millions of cadres and the masses of the entire economic front."[28] There are two primary purposes behind this militarization of economic units. First, incentives are to be mainly spiritual, and secondarily material, as in the PLA. Second, Communist cadres must learn from army cadres "to carry out orders firmly, rapidly, and strictly, without arguing ... to do that which is ordered.[29]

Further, "the whole country must learn from the PLA," acquiring its dedication to state rather than personal interest, its discipline, and its

---

* For a different conclusion, see Franz Schurmann, "China's 'New Economic Policy'—Transition or Beginning?" *The China Quarterly,* January–March 1964, p. 88: "The situation in China appears to be the opposite of that in the USSR, where since the death of Stalin, there has been a consistent effort to make the Party into an active organizational instrument and give it greater power for making economic decisions at all levels of the system."

austerity.[30] This extreme tightening-up effort reflects Mao's wish to eliminate opposition to future harsh and doctrinally motivated economic programs at the very place in which it had been most bothersome in 1958–60 —in the economic machinery. Mao's domestic policies are now more militarized—that is, more explicitly based on the assumption that cadres and populace must respond like unquestioning soldiers—than they had been since 1949. Some observers believe that these policies are now more militarized than those of Stalin. Moreover, Mao's theorists now claim that to set up political departments like those of the PLA in economic organizations is "a new creation in the construction and management of modernized enterprises."[31] Primarily because this Politburo policy is now being applied, the claim is valid.

Sharply intensified control was set in motion in this and other sectors by the far-reaching "set of theories and policies" Mao handed down in a body in spring 1963.[32] Mao stressed the participation of party cadres in "collective productive labor" and the weeding-out of corrupt, impure, or incompetent members. Mao also ordered repeated, "extensive socialist education movements" in both the city and the countryside, and "a sharp tit-for-tat struggle" against regime opponents "in order to smash their attacks."[33] In practice, this group of Maoist directives has meant that the youth, the intellectuals, the peasants, and the workers, as well as CCP cadres, have been caught up in a gigantic purification drive ever since fall 1963. The degree of its harshness can be gauged from CCP published materials.

(1) Regarding Moscow's small concession in recent years to "humanism"—i.e., respect for individual dignity—Chou Yang, Deputy Director of the CCP Propaganda Department, declared: "Revisionist ... humanism sets personal dignity and personal happiness as the highest aim in life.... Revisionists ... in advocating the return of man to himself are actually advocating absolute individual freedom."[34] The attacks on "humanism" in CCP materials reflect Mao's determination to prevent any future mellowing of his struggle-directed world view when applied to China. He has had his propagandists insist on the rejection of Confucian and bourgeois harmony as a social concept relating to personal and family relations,[35] on the continuation of class struggle,[36] and on the unlimited applicability of class analysis.[37]

(2) Reports of the Young Communist League (YCL) Congress, which met in secret session in June 1964, indicated Mao's intention to regularize the indoctrination of youth and to close young people off from any moderating Soviet influence. Congress materials reveal that as early as the Tenth Plenum in September 1962, Mao had directed that "class

education for youth must be strengthened to ensure that our nation will remain revolutionary and incorruptible for generations and forever."[38] Mao is also perturbed by the thought that young people without the combat zeal of soldiers will never make good Communists. Talking to a few select dinner guests in late 1964, "Mao grumbled contemptuously that the youth were soft. They were untried by war and revolution, and only knew what they had learned parrot-fashion from books."[39]

(3) The intellectuals have been hit harder than most other groups by the "socialist education" drive, primarily because of Mao's contempt for their independence of mind, for their reluctance to accept completely his doctrinaire pronouncements. Scientists and technical workers are the last group of intellectuals to be caught up in the current drive, a reversal of the 1961 policy of easing off on their political education. A key article in fall 1964 defended the major Maoist policies toward intellectuals since 1949 and insisted on a close tie between science and the thought of Mao Tse-tung.[40] It may be conjectured, however, that the relatively small group engaged in Communist China's nuclear energy and missile programs have not been, and will not be, subjected to rigorous thought-reform struggles. The extent to which intellectuals in China are intimidated is suggested by the fact that the major scapegoats now under attack are accused more for what they had said in the distant past than in recent years. Few have stepped out of line since mid-1957, and proof of real deviation has become more difficult to uncover.

(4) Many rural cadres and peasants are being depicted as unreliable, and they are now the target of rural purification drives intended to further bolster central control. Reliable elements among the cadres have been directed to use Mao's mass-struggle technique to ferret out certain categories of opponents. These cadres have been told not to take halfway measures out of fear that they might choose innocent people or strike too hard:

"Some kindhearted people always have many worries about the revolutionary mass movements and insist on setting up many new restrictions for them, prohibiting the masses from doing this and that. They are afraid that mistakes may arise from the movements. Of course, mass movements are not as delicate a matter as doing embroidery.... It is absolutely wrong to refrain from fully mobilizing the masses for fear of mistakes that may arise from mass movements.... Against reactionaries in rural areas, it is sometimes necessary to repeat the struggle several times; and sometimes the struggle can be ferocious."[41] The Maoist elements in this policy are the emphasis on the use of the masses against CCP targets to create in the countryside an atmosphere and environment of fear, and the emphasis on the need to repeat the struggle several times, to reduce the chances that target-individuals will escape censure. Mao and his lieutenants seem to feel that in order to ensure whole-hearted responsiveness to the next economic stride forward in 1966, the mass-struggle drives must be sustained throughout 1965 and intensified periodically.

To sum up, the legacy of Stalin looms large in many aspects of the thought of Mao Tse-tung. The traditional Confucian, Neo-Confucian, and short-lived Western liberal pragmatic legacy is constantly under attack. Further, since fall 1962 (if not earlier), the post-Stalin Soviet programs have been explicitly disparaged for being too moderate and revisionist, for leading away from the dictatorial, revolutionary conceptions of Lenin and Stalin. The uniquely Maoist aspects of domestic policy seem to be more complete and more total and, therefore, more effective in manipulating the populace to accept Politburo policies than the Stalinist precedents on which they had been modeled.

## Approach to Foreign Policy

Mao's foreign policy is based on "struggle," and is even more distinctively centered around opposition to the United States than Stalin's. Stalin knew the meaning of international compromise with the United States, but Mao does not believe a Peking-Washington compromise possible in his lifetime. More than Stalin, Mao has had to reconcile strong revolutionary ambitions with outward containment. During the Korean War, it was imperative for him to demonstrate—despite hundreds of thousands of casualties among crack PLA troops—that the prestige of New China could not be diminished by American action. At present, it is for the same basic reason necessary to deny the United States the renunciation of force it seeks in the Taiwan Strait area.[42] Mao is dedicated to nothing less than the destruction of Nationalist China as a political unit, and revolutionary animosity against the Nationalists requires the same kind of animosity against their defenders, the Americans.

Mao's effort to break through military and political containment is as much a strategy for revolution as it is a policy for foreign relations, a policy apparently conceived in terms of combating the enemy rather than adjusting relations with him by negotiations. Revolutionary wars against his positions are encouraged and supported, and any compromise or concession is viewed as military surrender. Mao's strategy is pointed toward the goal of forcing an American withdrawal from the Taiwan Strait. He tried to attain this goal in 1954–55, and again in 1958, by direct pressure on Nationalist positions. Failure to reduce the American commitment to Taipei compelled Mao to shift his strategy to a more indirect one requiring pressures on American positions elsewhere in the world. On September 8, 1958, Mao called for others to drive the Americans out of military bases abroad at a time when the off-shore island venture indicated that Peking did not have the military capability to do the same thing on its own periphery. His linking of revolutionary wars and American withdrawal is similar to Castro's view of the need for pressure on the United States.* Castro's statement of January 2, 1965, that the United States may not meet his terms until forced to deal with several *other* revolutionary regimes is strikingly similar to the Maoist view that China cannot do the job alone now or in the near future.

The Chinese and other Asian Communists had tried the strategy of rural-area armed struggle in the Far East in the late 1940's and early 1950's, and had failed to make headway anywhere but in Vietnam. They took a new ("soft") approach in 1954–55, but various developments in 1957–58 prompted a return to the earlier policy. The encouragement of armed struggle against American positions became the key element in Mao's strategy by April 1960, as witness Peking's insistence then that the heart of Leninism was recognition of the inevitability of small wars. But this time the strategy was not confined to the Far East; it was extended to all emergent nations. The concept of a broad international front to "drive American imperialism from Asia, Africa, and Latin America"[43] reflects Mao's view that significant revolutionary pressures can be generated only among emergent countries, and that even if revolutionary opportunities did exist in major capitalist countries, chances of a power seizure would be slight. Revolutionary pressures must be real—that is, military—and their net effect should be to reduce the disparity in modern military strength between Peking and Washington. In Mao's view, revolutionary small wars not only are the most effective means of tying down and then eliminating American influence in emergent countries, they also provide the best way to ensure the consolidation of power after a takeover.

Mao's idea of armed struggle has now become a law of the process of revolution: "State power, independence, freedom, and equality can be

---

* Chou En-lai told Edgar Snow that "even if the United States does not withdraw from the Taiwan region and no breakthrough occurs there, breakthroughs will occur elsewhere. ... It is only a matter of time. As to where the breakthrough occurs first, this depends on the development of the struggle." *Look*, January 31, 1961. This concept of small "breakthroughs" against American positions abroad is at the heart of the Maoist encouragement of revolutionary wars.

won by armed force and armed force alone, and safeguarded by armed force and armed force alone. This has been and is the universal law of class struggle."[44] This is not the world view of a cultured scholar, humanist, or romantic—all aspects of Mao's popular image among certain Western observers—but of a guerrilla revolutionary. Emphasis on the small war is also intended to increase Mao's prestige as the guerrilla leader and Communist who creatively developed Leninist doctrine. He is said by his eulogists to have made a major contribution to theory by "placing a very high value" on "liberation struggle," and making underdeveloped areas the focus of the assault against imperialism.[45] And indeed there is some justification for this claim.

Mao is willing enough to forget class lines in appraising a bourgeois or an aristocrat as a national revolutionary leader, provided he advances the cause of the anti-American small war.[46] Peking has openly supported the Tutsis—notorious feudal aristocrats—against the Hutu peasant government in Rwanda. Despite the public Maoist position that Communists must take over leadership of a small war from the start, and must push for a socialist revolution "to the end," and that there is no place for the half-way, Soviet-sponsored "national democracy," Mao's real view is closer to that of the Soviet leaders. The CCP has told PLA officers that: "To oppose feudalism is not the most important thing, and to carry out a socialist revolution is even less important...in Africa."[47] Nevertheless, there is a difference precisely in the emphasis on inciting a small war (or vigorously supporting one already underway), and in the insistence that "Lenin said the peaceful development of revolution is an opportunity 'very seldom to be met with in the history of revolution.' "[48] Like Lenin, Mao stresses world revolution; but unlike Lenin, his stress is almost entirely on underdeveloped areas. Like Stalin, however, Mao's views are precisely consonant with national interest.

Mao's differences with the Russians over the years have arisen basically from his dedication to his own road to revolutionary power, as well as from his nationalistic impulse to create his own party apparatus, untouched by foreign influence. While Stalin lived, Mao did not challenge his personal leadership of the world Communist movement, even as he retained the right to revise doctrine and to depart from Soviet precedents. When Stalin died, however, Mao made it clear that he felt that by degrees he and his Party should attain at least an equal voice in devising strategy for the bloc. Khrushchev's attempt in 1954–55 to de-Stalinize Sino-Soviet relations was short-lived mainly because of the continuing undercurrent of rivalry for leadership of the movement. This rivalry

was deepened in 1956 as Mao and his Politburo comrades skillfully exploited the first great loss of CPSU prestige, caused by events in Poland
and Hungary, to increase that of the CCP.

The Chinese Communist leaders provided Khrushchev with some lee-
way as they pressed for nuclear weapons (from October 1957 to June
1959), and for more active Soviet assistance in forcing an American
withdrawal from the Far East (August 1958 to October 1959). However,
Khrushchev's refusal, in June 1959, to provide the Chinese leaders with
even "a sample atomic bomb," and his suggestion to Mao, in October
1959, after his visit to the United States, that Peking accept a peaceful
solution to the Taiwan issue, was sufficient cause for further intensifica-
tion of the Sino-Soviet dispute.[49] By April 1960, the Chinese were attacking Khrushchev's policy toward the United States, but obscured the
object of their attack with doctrinal trappings. When Soviet technicians
were withdrawn that summer, the total political defeat of the Soviet
leader became their goal. The chauvinistic aspects of their assaults on
Khrushchev's policies did not become apparent until July 1963, when foreign Communists were provided with first, Soviet charges of Chinese
special interests in the CPSU "Open Letter" and second, the nationalistic
Chinese reaction to the tripartite test ban treaty. Chinese special interests and "internationalist" doctrine pretensions were so expertly stripped
away by the Soviet Government Statement of September 21, 1963, that
it is the only major anti-CCP Soviet statement which has not been reprinted in the Chinese press. In short, under constant pressure from the
Chinese, the Soviet leader made his strongest defense against Mao when
his writers cut through the doctrinal shield to the real issues.[50]

Mao reversed his position on bloc unity as the conflict over bloc strategy
intensified. In 1957, Mao appealed to the others in the camp to unite
around Moscow on doctrinal grounds.* In 1964, he demanded a split with
Moscow again on doctrinal grounds.[51] He and his lieutenants showed
considerable tactical skill in compelling Khrushchev to adjust reluctantly
to each new CCP initiative. Khrushchev's respite in summer and fall
1963 was temporary, and the Chinese today are prepared to drive his
successors back to new retreat positions. Despite the appeals of Brezhnev
and Kosygin for a halt to polemics, the Chinese leaders insist that the

---

* In the course of a doctrinal discussion on the need for unity, the Chinese stated: "Imperialist forces do not fear one Poland, one Hungary, or one China. What they fear is the
unity of the socialist camp headed by the Soviet Union." *Hsüeh-hsi*, January 3, 1957. By
insisting on Soviet leadership, the Chinese also intended to sustain Soviet commitments to
assist any member of the bloc fully. However, the CCP in fact did not accept Soviet leadership even in 1957.

Sino-Soviet "debate...will never end" so long as the Soviets do not capitulate on the matter of bloc leadership and strategy.[52]

Mao's commitment to the "debate" is so unqualified that his propagandists have justified it, in doctrinal terms, as "inevitable." They have also attempted to explain the matter to the doubters in the CCP, who may not see the long-range wisdom of Mao's course. In his speech of October 26, 1963, CCP propagandist Chou Yang argued that "Engels said, 'Unity is quite a good thing so long as it is possible, but there are things that stand above unity.... One cannot be greatly grieved that the inevitable struggle has broken out.'" Chou then pointed out that Lenin, too, had denounced opportunists in his day as the CCP is doing now, so "What is there to feel strange about?" Finally, Chou predicted that skeptics would be proven wrong and that the Russians' prestige would be reduced. In the most striking statement of his speech, Chou placed Mao at the head of the world Communist movement, and justified his right, as the legitimate heir of the classical leaders, to attack CPSU policies: "Marx's theories...are revolutionary and critical because he had the courage not only to make a thorough criticism of the old world but also to assimilate critically the whole range of human knowledge... thus enriching and fortifying his theories.... The same is true of Lenin himself, of Engels, and of Stalin. It is also true of Comrade Mao Tsetung."[53] Mao's view of himself as the senior leader in the world movement, and of the CCP as the party destined to lead it, will continue to be the main irritant in the dispute.[54] The present Soviet leaders cannot placate him by tactical concessions that fall short of a surrender of leadership.

Peking will continue to support any regime antagonistic to the United States, the Soviet Union, and India, and in proportion to the extent of their antagonism. Particularly striking was Mao's move toward Pakistan, a socially "reactionary" country and a military ally of the United States, and away from India, a socially "progressive" country, and for many years a nonaligned one. In January 1964, the Chinese leaders also took the first steps toward a doctrinally coherent rationale for their policy of flexibility toward certain capitalist countries, particularly France. Ever since fall 1963, the Chinese leaders had been casting about for a common Sino-French goal or grievance. How could a capitalist country suddenly develop a benevolent aspect?

The question was finally answered in the *People's Daily* editorial of January 21, 1964. Because leaders of capitalist countries allied with the United States want to free themselves from American control, "They therefore have something in common with the socialist countries and the various peoples." The editorial went on to argue the doctrinal position that rulers in these countries have a "dual character," i.e., they are on the one hand exploiters, but on the other hand opponents of the United States.[55] "There is not a single country or people in the world today that is not subjected to the aggression and threats of American imperialism." This statement was deliberately categorical; it was intended to serve as "the objective basis for the establishment of the broadest possible united front against American imperialism." It was also intended to provide room for any anti-American government in the major capitalist countries, notably, of course, France.

This CCP policy required a minor modification of Mao's 1946 concept of a world "intermediate zone." This concept, advanced by Mao in August 1946 to Anna Louise Strong, already had been refined, in the March 4, 1963, *Red Flag* article, to include not just "many" but "all" capitalist countries in a large front against the United States. The January 21, 1964, *People's Daily* editorial, however, stated that there really are *two* intermediate zones, not one. The first is comprised of the countries of Asia, Africa, and Latin America, and the second "the whole of Western Europe, Australia, Canada, and other capitalist countries" (except the United States). This division apparently was intended both to focus on the key area of Chinese anti-American activity, the underdeveloped countries, and to preserve doctrinal continuity. The Chinese are anxious to appear doctrinally correct by distinguishing between leaders in underdeveloped areas (zone one), who are not exploiters, and leaders in capitalist countries (zone two), who are exploiters by classical definition. The loose dialectical formulation of January 21 on the "dual character" of leaders in the major capitalist countries is a more radical revision of doctrine than Khrushchev's description of some of these men as "sober-minded." Mao is not the first Communist leader whose revisions of doctrine are called "further developments" of Marxism by his own Party, which nevertheless depicts the revisions of other leaders as "right opportunist deviations."

*The Prospect*

Throughout his revolutionary career, Mao has displayed a disposition to project certain goals far into the future and a tenacity of purpose in pursuing these goals. He is now projecting small wars in underdeveloped areas for "ten years" if necessary; the dispute with Moscow for "twenty-five years, as a paper war"; the Sino-American stalemate for "thirty years regarding Taiwan"; and the duration of China's socialist stage before full communism for "from five to ten generations." Similarly, the

North Vietnamese leaders now declare that the Viet Cong will defeat the Americans "within ten or twenty years."[56] The long view has also been absorbed by Mao's lieutenants in the CCP, who have declared in recent years that they will not permit party members and party policies to evolve in a revisionist—i.e., more moderate—direction. Mao himself is said to have rejected the notion that a more tolerant group of party leaders will emerge in the next generation.[57] So long as his immediate successors remain dedicated to the legacy of Mao in domestic and foreign policy—and there is every indication that the leaders now in their 50's and 60's will remain so dedicated—the next decade is unlikely to bring any significant mellowing of this version of Communist doctrine and practice.

Theodore Draper

# Castroism

The question "What is Castroism?" inevitably leads to the question "What is the relationship between Castroism and Communism?" We must get to it sooner or later, and perhaps the sooner the better. The answer is a relatively simple one for two totally opposed schools of thought. One maintains that Fidel Castro is and always was a Communist; the other insists that he is not and could never be a Communist. The problem is far more complex for those who, like myself, think that Castro was not a Communist for all practical purposes before he took power but decided to cast in his lot with the Communists some time afterward.

Whatever position one may hold, however, the relationship between Castroism and Communism remains a problem. The first school must explain the open disagreements and bitter rivalries between Castro and the Communists until well into 1959; the second, why Castro and his closest associates now call themselves Communists and regard themselves as an integral part of the world Communist movement; and the third, why they were different in their origins and how their paths came together. Indeed the fact that we can intelligibly ask whether or how Castroism is related to Communism already presupposes some distinction between the two, if only the distinction between a species and a genus.

For the immediate purpose of defining Castroism, and its relationship with Communism, the history of Castroism may be distinguished from the history of Fidel Castro. The movement could not exist without the man, but neither can it be reduced to the man. It exists, in varying degrees and forms, in Latin America as a whole, and its influence has even been felt in Europe, Africa, and elsewhere. Fidel Castro was born about a quarter of a century before Castroism came into existence, and therefore he is older and in some ways more complex than his movement. In this essay, we are primarily interested in Castroism as a political phenomenon, and in Castro himself insofar as he is necessary to understand it, rather than in his personal history as a whole.

## The "26th of July Movement"

Historically, Castroism did not exist before July 26, 1953, the date of the unsuccessful attack on the Moncada army post in Santiago de Cuba, seventeen months after Batista's seizure of power. The attack enabled Castro to emerge for the first time as an independent political figure with his own personal following. The "26th of July Movement" owed its raison d'être as well as its name to it.

The conception of the movement appears to have been worked out concretely during Castro's imprisonment in the Isle of Pines from October 1953 to May 1955. It was in this period that he actually wrote, in its present form, the *History Will Absolve Me!* speech, originally delivered at his trial in October 1953. According to Melba Hernández, Castro asked her and Haydée Santamaría, the two women who participated in the Moncada attack, to take the first steps to organize the new movement. As a basis for this task, they asked him to provide them with a "program of action."[1] Castro, it seems, had already conceived of dramatically casting such a "program" in the form of his defense speech at the trial. He wrote a letter to Melba Hernández in April 1954 in which he mentioned "a pamphlet of decisive importance for its ideological contents and its tremendous accusations"; it was clandestinely published in June 1954.[2] There is, therefore, reason to believe that the pamphlet was far more "programmatic" than the speech, which had not been delivered with the same purpose or audience in mind.[3]

Politically, the pamphlet promised restoration of the 1940 Constitution and a "government of popular election," though not without a disturbing proviso for the immediate post-revolutionary period. In agriculture, it mainly advocated a land reform to restrict large holdings and increase the number of smaller ones. It made only marginal reference to the encouragement of "agricultural cooperatives," by which it clearly meant service organizations for independent landowners rather than organs of state control. The most radical note in the speech—but not to Cuban ears—was perhaps a brief reference to the "nationalization" of the U.S.-owned electric and telephone companies. None of these points were new or startling. The pamphlet as a whole was little more than an anthology of familiar ills and cures, long the staples of Cuban politics, especially as practiced by the late Eduardo Chibás, founder of the Ortodoxo party, to which Castro still nominally belonged.*

---

* Chibás had been one of the student leaders in the struggle against the Machado dictatorship from 1927 to 1933. In 1947, Chibás split the ruling Partido Revolucionario Cubano,

As Cubans understood it, *History Will Absolve Me* represented a program of radical social reform well within the framework of traditional Cuban left-wing politics. For at least twenty years, there had been a well-defined "left wing," even a "revolutionary left wing," outside of and opposed to the Communists. There was virtually nothing in the social and economic program of *History Will Absolve Me* that cannot be traced at least as far back as the 1932 program of the ABC—the largest of the anti-Machado organizations—or the 1935 program of Grau San Martín's Auténtico party, let alone the later propaganda of Chibás.

The 1932 program of the ABC had contained a seventeen-point economic plan that, among other things, had proposed the following: development and protection of small rural property holdings, gradual elimination of the latifundia, limitation on the acquisition of land by U.S. companies and measures leading to their nationalization, producers' cooperatives, nationalization of the public services, advanced social legislation, and preferential treatment for Cubans in commercial and industrial activities. The same program had put forward five fundamental principles: new men, new ideas and procedures, reconquest of the land, political liberty, and social justice.[4] The 1935 program of the Auténtico party had been based on the political trinity of "nationalism, socialism, anti-imperialism."[5]

After Castro had won power in 1959, it became customary to cite his *History Will Absolve Me* speech, or rather pamphlet, as if it were the only significant document in the whole period of his struggle for power. Some pro-Castro writers have even labored to show that it foreshadowed Castro's later Communism. Curiously, however, Castro himself has felt the need to explain why it had not been more radical. He had written the document "with care," he later said, in order to set forth a number of fundamental points without making the movement he wanted to build "very small and very limited." He intimated that his published words had not been as radical as his private thoughts: "If we had not written this document with care, if it had been a more radical program—though here it is certain that many people were a little skeptical of programs and often did not give them much attention—the revolutionary movement against Batista would not, of course, have gained the breadth that it obtained and made possible the victory."[6] On another occasion,

---

founded and headed by then President Ramón Grau San Martín, and organized an opposition, the Partido del Pueblo Cubano. The two parties were usually referred to as "Auténticos" and the "Ortodoxos," respectively. Chibás committed suicide in 1951. Fidel Castro became active in the party about 1950 and ran for one of the houses of the Cuban Congress on the Ortodoxo ticket in 1952, but the election was never held owing to Batista's coup on March 10 of that year.

Castro pointed out that *History Will Absolve Me* owed its permanent value to its "vivid denunciation of all the horrors and crimes of Batista's tyranny" rather than to its "theoretical value from an economic and political point of view."[7] He was undoubtedly right.

But he wrote something else in 1954, far less well known, that affords a much greater insight into his motivation. In that year, he sent a number of letters to Luis Conte Agüero, an Ortodoxo leader and popular radio commentator, appealing for aid in organizing his campaign for amnesty and confiding some of his innermost thoughts about his nascent movement. "I ought," he wrote on August 14, 1954, "to organize the men of the 26th of July and to unite into an unbreakable body all the fighters, those in exile, in prison, and in the street." They would constitute, he explained, "a perfectly disciplined human nucleus" and provide "the force necessary to conquer power whether it be by peaceful or by revolutionary means." Then he went on, with rare candor, "The conditions indispensable for the organization of a true civic movement are: ideology, discipline, and leadership. The three are essential, but leadership is basic. I don't know if it was Napoleon who said that one bad general in battle counts more than 30 good generals. It is not possible to organize a movement in which everyone believes that he has the right to issue public statements without consulting anyone else; nor can you expect anything from a movement made up of anarchic men, who, at the first disagreement, take the path they consider most convenient, breaking and destroying the machine. The apparatus of propaganda and of organization should be so powerful that it would implacably destroy anyone who tried to create tendencies, cliques, schisms, or rebellions against the movement."[8]

Of the three conditions, Castro obviously preoccupied himself with ideology the least. What really interested him were the other two conditions, "discipline" and "leadership," especially the latter. His axiom, "la jefatura es básica" (leadership is basic) was far more closely related to "leadership-principle" movements such as fascism and Peronism than to an ideology-and-party-conscious movement such as Communism. It is hard to imagine a Communist using the language of Castro in this extraordinarily revealing letter to Conte Agüero.

After Castro was released from the Isle of Pines in May 1955, he stayed in Cuba for only six weeks, when he went to Mexico to prepare for his invasion of the island. On July 19, less than two weeks after his arrival in Mexico, he called a meeting of his adherents and formally decided to launch the "26th of July Movement."[9] It is common practice in Latin America to name new movements after dates of symbolic events, but it is not without significance that Castro should have decided to follow this pattern. His date symbolized a heroic act or gesture, not a political philosophy or revolutionary tradition. The act or gesture was all his own, something that no one could ever take away from him, the bedrock of his "jefatura."

In August 1955, Castro sent a message to a congress of "militants" of the Ortodoxo party in Havana, in which, for the first time since its formal inception, he tried to explain publicly what the new movement stood for. He called it "Manifesto No. 1 of the 26th of July to the People of Cuba," and, in substance, it closely followed the line of *History Will Absolve Me*. It invited the support of all Cubans who wished "to reestablish political democracy and implant social justice." It undertook to realize all "reforms" within the spirit and letter of "our advanced" Constitution of 1940. It contained a fifteen-point program of these reforms, from "distribution of the land among peasant families" to "confiscation of all property of all grafters." Yet, in this manifesto, Castro made clear that he was still an Ortodoxo, "faithful to the purest principles" of Chibás, and hopeful of getting the support of the "best Ortodoxos." In order to stay within the party but organize his own movement outside it, he carefully explained that "we do not constitute a tendency within the party; we are the revolutionary apparatus of Chibasismo." In effect, he did not claim to represent a political tendency as much as a more effective *aparato* to overthrow the Batista dictatorship.[10] Inasmuch as Chibás himself had been a consistent, militant anti-Communist, anyone who claimed to be his loyal disciple, as Castro did, was bound to have some of Chibás's reputation rub off on him.

At the end of 1955, the Ortodoxo leadership decided to participate with other opposition groups in a final effort to reach agreement with Batista for a peaceful transition to constitutional government. As soon as the negotiations had broken down, Castro seized the occasion to make a final break with the Ortodoxo party. In his letter of resignation of March 19, 1956, however, he continued to take the position that he was breaking away organizationally, not politically. "For the Chibasist masses," he wrote, "the 26th of July Movement is not something distinct from the *Ortodoxia*." On the contrary, he insisted that the 26th of July Movement was the true repository of the Ortodoxo faith, the authentic embodiment of Chibasismo. Ostensibly, then, the 26th of July Movement came into the world to fulfill, not to betray, the true Ortodoxo political mission. (After the victory over Batista, Castro made a pilgrimage to the tomb of Chibás, where he declared that the 26th of July Movement "was the continuation of the work of Chibás, the harvest of the seed that he planted in our people.")[11]

Thus, Castroism as a movement may be said to have been created in

four stages. It was given its initial impulse and raison d'être by the
attack on the Moncada army post on July 26, 1953. Its conception matured during Castro's imprisonment in the Isle of Pines from October
1953 to May 1955. It was officially launched in Mexico on July 19, 1955.
And it severed its last ties with any other movement, to strike out entirely on its own, in March 1956.

## Programs in Limbo

It is impossible here to analyze, or even to touch on, all the programmatic statements made by Castro from March 1956 to the end of 1958.
Yet, it is noteworthy that in this period the 26th of July Movement continued to feel a need for a full "program" and various efforts were made
to fill the vacuum, though they have been relegated to a historical limbo
since the fall of Batista. At least two important documents were not
composed by Castro himself—the "Tesis Económica del Movimiento
Revolucionario 26 de Julio" written by Felipe Pazos and Regino Botí,
first published in Mexico City in the magazine *Humanismo,* in January
and February 1957, and the pamphlet "Nuestra Razón: Manifiesto-Pro-
grama del Movimiento 26 de Julio," published in Mexico City in the
summer of 1957 and written mainly by Mario Llerena. Probably the
most important single document, however, was the "Manifesto of the
Sierra Maestra," drafted by Castro and signed by him, Felipe Pazos,
and Raul Chibás on July 12, 1957.[12] This was actually the first and only
formal program to which Castro ever put his name, if we exclude *History Will Absolve Me* as such a program. Unlike the latter, the Castro-
Pazos-Chibás manifesto was published in Cuba's most popular magazine, *Bohemia,* in the issue of July 28, 1957, and thus reached many more
Cubans than any previous programmatic statement by Castro's movement.* In any event, the "Manifesto of the Sierra Maestra" was taken
to be an expression of Castro's more mature views in the heat of the
civil war, and Castro himself directed attention to it as the basic docu-

* The reader may wonder how it was possible for the most popular Cuban magazine to
publish this manifesto in the midst of the civil war. The answer is that the Batista regime
was much too repressive for any democratic spirit and not repressive enough to be an efficient dictatorship. Magazines such as *Bohemia* and newspapers such as *Prensa Libre* maintained a high standard of political independence throughout the Batista regime. *Bohemia* in
particular provided a forum for all political groups, published letters and statements by
Castro himself, and distinctly favored the anti-Batista side. After violent actions, such as the
Moncada attempt in 1953 and the Directorio Revolucionario's attack on the presidential
palace in 1957, the regime established press censorship for limited periods during which
*Bohemia* refused to publish any political articles whatever in order to avoid political control.
Batista subsidized and suborned many Cuban papers; his partial control of the press was then
"exposed" to provide a justification for Castro's total control.

ment of the period.[13] He issued several other political statements and gave interviews in the next year and a half, but they were not intended to serve the same purpose.

It is not hard to understand why the "Manifesto of the Sierra Maestra," despite its exalted title, has never been cited as evidence that Fidel Castro made the kind of revolution that he said he would make. This document was primarily a plea for the unity of all the anti-Batista forces. It sought to close the breach between those who had hoped to get rid of Batista by means of peaceful elections and those who believed that he could be overthrown only by violent methods. To allay suspicions that Castro himself was not exactly a passionate devotee of democratic elections, the Manifesto stated that they were precisely what the entire struggle was about. "Is it that the rebels of the Sierra Maestra do not want free elections, a democratic regime, a constitutional government?" it asked indignantly. And it answered: "We have been fighting since March 10 [1952] because they deprived us of those rights. We are here because we desire them more than anyone else." The Manifesto then proceeded to spell out in detail the steps to be taken to achieve the desired objective. It insisted on only one condition: "truly free, democratic, impartial elections." It urged that "a provisional neutral government" preside over the elections. To lay the basis for such a government, it proposed the formation of a Frente Cívico Revolucionario (Civilian Revolutionary Front), made up of representatives of all opposition parties and groups. It also told the future Frente what was expected of it: choice of an impartial, nonpolitical provisional president; rejection of any foreign mediation or intervention and request for U.S. suspension of all arms shipments to Cuba during the civil war; nonacceptance of any kind of military junta to replace Batista; commitment "to dissociate the army from politics"; and a "formal promise that the provisional government will hold general elections for all national, provincial, and municipal offices at the end of one year, according to the standards of the Constitution of 1940 and the Electoral Code of 1943."

In addition, the authors of the Manifesto demanded that the provisional government commit itself to a ten-point program, which included "absolute guarantees of freedom of information, of the spoken and written press, and of all the individual and political rights guaranteed by the Constitution"; an intensive campaign against illiteracy; an agrarian reform based on distributing barren lands and converting all renters and squatters into owners, with prior indemnification to the former owners; a "sound financial policy"; and "acceleration of the process of industrialization and the creation of new jobs."

It should be noted that the future provisional government chosen by the still unformed, all-embracing Frente Cívico Revolucionario was not asked to consider this program; it was told what its program would have to be—a peculiar beginning for a constitutional democracy, irrespective of the program's desirability.* It should also be more understandable why there was so much concern about the holding of elections in 1959 after the fall of Batista. Castro himself had encouraged the widespread belief that the central issue in the struggle was the inviolability of "truly free, democratic, impartial elections." If he could not be trusted to carry out this "formal promise," which he had demanded of the proposed Frente Cívico Revolucionario, it was hard to know what to trust in the first months of his regime.

As one reads Castro's succession of statements in 1956–58, the most striking thing about them is their increasing "moderation" and constitutionalism. For example, he had called for nationalization of the public utilities in *History Will Absolve Me* and again in "Manifesto No. 1" of 1955, but he withdrew this demand on at least two occasions in 1958.[14] In virtually every document of this period, he reiterated his determination to live up to the "full enforcement" of the 1940 Constitution, including, on one occasion, the rights of "free enterprise and invested capital" along with all the other constitutional rights. For the most part, he guaranteed elections in no more than a year after the fall of Batista, and, to show that he meant to restore a traditional constitutionalism, gave assurances that he intended to convert the 26th of July Movement into a regular political party, which would, after the revolution, "fight with the weapons of the Constitution and the Law."[15] His last important commitment came in the "unity pact" of July 20, 1958, which called for a common strategy of "armed insurrection," a brief provisional government, leading to "full constitutional and democratic procedure," and a minimum government program guaranteeing "the punishment of the guilty, the rights of the workers, order, peace, liberty, the fulfillment of international agreements, and the economic, social, and institutional progress of the Cuban people."[16] Significantly, Castro made very few programmatic statements in the second half of 1958, when Batista's regime was crumbling. The most important in this period was "Law No. 3 of the Sierra Maestra on Agrarian Reform," dated October 10, 1958, which he signed with Humberto Sorí Marín. It was a detailed working out of the principle that those who cultivate the land should own it, and made no mention of "cooperatives" or "state farms."[17]

---

* The expression used was "El gobierno provisional deberá ajustar su misión al siguiente programa" ("The mission of the provisional government will have to conform to the following program").

As far as most Cubans were concerned, Castroism was what these manifestoes, programs, pamphlets, and assorted declarations said it was. They had no way of looking into Castro's mind or analyzing his personality to know his real ambitions, motivations, and latent tendencies. Castroism was the creation of Fidel Castro, but he created and recreated it, partly in his own image and partly in the image of those whom he wished to win over.

## Private and Public

Castro and his closest associates have clearly admitted, and even boasted, that there was a marked difference between Castro and Castroism, between what the man privately thought and what he made the movement publicly stand for, especially in the struggle for power. We have already noted Castro's explanation of why *History Will Absolve Me* was carefully written in order that it should not appear to be too radical. In effect, he said that he had made it only as radical as could be politically effective or as a large number of Cubans would accept. The 1954 pamphlet was not the only case of political double bookkeeping. This practice started at the beginning of the movement, and became more marked as it developed.

For example, Castro came dangerously close to implying that he had been something of a "Marxist-Leninist" in the Sierra Maestra but had consciously concealed it. "Of course," he said, "if we stopped at the Pico Turquino [a height in the Sierra Maestra], when there were very few of us, and said, 'We are Marxist-Leninists,' possibly we would not have been able to get down to the plain. Thus we called it something else; we did not broach this subject; we raised other questions that the people understood perfectly."[18]

President Osvaldo Dorticós once played a variation on this theme. Soon after Castro had proclaimed the advent of the "Socialist Revolution" in Cuba on April 16, 1961, Dorticós interpreted this act to mean that Castro had merely given "a name to the facts that had already occurred." When this comment aroused some speculation, Dorticós explained: "In other words, to a large extent, an integral revolutionary theory was not formulated previously out of considerations of strategy, wise strategy, and because it would have required a great effort of ideological training, an effort that could be avoided because the best ideological teaching that the Cuban people have received has been the incontrovertible teaching by the events themselves."[19] These words suggest that the *timing* of the proclamation of "socialism" was purely "strategic" in the sense that Castro waited until he thought that he had enough popular support to put it over. Castro himself has often resorted to "objective conditions" to explain why he said or did something at one time and not at another, with the implication that he wanted to do it earlier but had waited until "objective conditions" made it feasible.

But the occasion for these "confessions" must be held in mind. They were made in the year that Castro professed himself to be a "Marxist-Leninist," and it was in his interest at this time to make his present seem to be a logical development of his past. None of Castro's statements on this delicate subject can be accepted or understood standing alone, and it is necessary to view all of them in their contexts and in relation to each other to get a reasonable facsimile of the truth. As I have tried to show elsewhere, Castro has given so many different versions of his evolution toward "full" Marxism-Leninism that it is foolhardy to jump to any conclusion on the basis of one or two quotations that, in any case, are open to more than one interpretation.[20] But the fact remains that Castro himself has encouraged the belief that he was guilty of dissimulation.

As we have seen, the Castro-Pazos-Chibás manifesto of July 1957 was a key document of the civil war, which particularly encouraged confidence in Castro's democratic convictions. Did Castro really believe in its pledges of free elections, freedom of the press, and all the rest, or did he merely subscribe to them for purely opportunistic reasons? If we may trust Che Guevara—who should know, since his close association with Castro dated from the Mexican period—the latter was the case. According to Guevara, precisely the "democratic" provisions of the document were virtually forced on a reluctant Castro by Pazos and Chibás (though he does not explain why Castro subsequently reiterated most of them independently, as in the *Coronet* article or in the reply to Jules Dubois' questionnaire). The only thing in the manifesto that Guevara has seen fit to praise unequivocally is a short passage that called the Sierra Maestra "an indestructible bastion of liberty." Otherwise, he complains that "we were not satisfied with the agreement," that it "limited our effort" and that it was "a small halt on the road." Castro signed the manifesto, Guevara explained, because it was "progressive at that moment" to get democratic support, though it "could not last beyond the moment." He justified Castro's failure to live up to the manifesto, or, as he put it, the need "to break the inconvenient fetters," on the ground that a "tacit pact" recognizing the "authority of the Sierra," apparently to determine the future revolutionary government, was later broken. Guevara had to make the pact a "tacit" one because he could not point to anything in the document itself to bear out such an understanding. In Guevara's authoritative version, then, Castro had really resented the "democratic" points in the manifesto because they might have tied his hands, and the only thing that had really interested him had been the alleged recognition of his future "authority."[21]

That power was the determining factor is even more strikingly demonstrated in Castro's explanation of his letter of December 14, 1957, to the Junta de Liberación Cubana denouncing the "unity pact" that his representatives had signed in Miami.* Ironically, Castro's main pretext for rejecting the December 1957 pact had been its failure to include some of the provisions of the July 1957 manifesto. After his victory, however, Castro told a different story. He revealed that he had not been interested in broad unity in December 1957 because he had had only 120 armed men, and therefore was not strong enough to dominate unified action. Later, when he was much stronger, he confided, he favored unity because he could dominate it. He even went on to say that he had actually decided to prevent any broad unity until the end of the war (though he signed just such an agreement in July 1958) because he could not get the official Cuban Communists accepted by the other groups.[22]

A peculiar light has also been cast on Castro's agrarian reform program of late 1958 by the Communist representative in the Sierra Maestra and later head of the Instituto Nacional de Reforma Agraria (INRA), Carlos Rafael Rodríguez. In the discussion on agrarian reform, according to Rodríguez, "some who were apparently extremist" had proposed eliminating the latifundia completely. But Fidel, "with an extraordinary tactical and strategic clarity," had rejected the proposal, on the ground that it would "range us against all the landowners of our country and the foreign imperialists" at a time when the fundamental task was Batista's overthrow. After he took power, however, Castro went ahead with his second step, "the liquidation of the internal enemy in agriculture"; he postponed the third step, the break-up of the "imperialist latifundia," until still later. For this reason, it appears, "Law No. 3 of the Sierra

---

* The Junta de Liberación Cubana had been formed on November 1, 1957, by representatives of seven anti-Batista groups, including Felipe Pazos, Lucas Moran, and Lester Rodríguez for the 26th of July Movement. It was, in part, a response to the demand for a Frente Cívico Revolucionario that Castro, Pazos, and Raúl Chibás had made in their "Manifesto of the Sierra Maestra" on July 12, 1957. The founders of the Junta signed a "Document of Unity," which embodied most, though not all, the points raised in the Manifesto. Castro's letter of December 14, 1957, repudiated the action of his three representatives in Miami and withdrew the 26th of July Movement from the Junta. At the time, it was generally believed that the main difference between Castro and the Junta had been the choice of the future provisional president. The Junta had selected Pazos, who, as a signer of the Manifesto and an outstanding, nonpolitical public figure, seemed a logical choice. But the choice had infuriated Castro, probably because he knew that he could not dictate to Pazos. In his letter of December 14 denouncing the Junta, Castro unilaterally proposed Manuel Urrutia as the head of the future provisional government. (The text of the letter may be found in Selser, pp. 125–40, and in English translation in Dubois, pp. 188–206.)

Maestra on Agrarian Reform," issued October 10, 1958, did not provide for wholesale expropriation. "It was necessary to conquer the enemy piecemeal," Rodríguez observed admiringly.[23] (Like Felipe Pazos and Raúl Chibás, Humberto Sorí Marín, who was Castro's first Minister of Agriculture and the co-signer of Law No. 3, realized that he had been used for purposes that he had never intended, suffered disillusionment and apparently joined the underground opposition. Less lucky than the other two, he was caught and executed.)

Thus Castro has suggested that he did not privately believe in principles and programs that he had publicly espoused, and he has suggested that he could not afford to espouse principles and programs that he privately believed in. He has intimated that he was much closer to "Marxism-Leninism" than he had ever let on, and he has confessed to his past political innocence—whichever seemed to suit his purpose best at the time. On the whole, he has been far more convincing in showing that he was not what he had pretended to be than in demonstrating what he had actually been.

## The Road to Power

Thus far, we have been considering Castroism before its assumption of power in terms of its "programs." There is reason to believe, however, that they were not the main sources of Castro's power or influence. They were not different enough from other programs to make Castro stand out; in fact, he deliberately cast his ideas in a fairly traditional mold in order to gain a mass following. If a graph were charted of the "radicalism" of his public statements from 1953 to 1959, it would go almost steadily downward.

What made Castroism distinctive was something else. For the most part, Castro's road to power was based on tactics, not on ideas. And his tactics were, by Cuban standards, at least partially different.

After Batista's coup in March 1952, the opposition had split into two main camps, the "insurrectionist" and the "electoralist." The former believed that armed struggle was the only way to get rid of the usurper; the latter wished to use peaceful methods that would somehow lead to new general elections. Castro was one of the "insurrectionists," but far from the only one. He was not even the first to plan an uprising. Castro was anticipated by Rafael García Bárcena, leader of the Movimiento Nacionalista Revolucionario (MNR), whose conspiracy was foiled by the police on April 5, 1953, on the eve of the planned uprising, more than three months before Castro's Moncada attempt. Aureliano Sánchez Arango's "Triple A" was based on armed struggle, as were many other groups in the next six years.

In general, however, the others aimed their blows at the center of Batista's power—at the main military base near Havana, Camp Columbia—or at Batista himself. García Bárcena in 1953 and Colonel Ramón Barquín in 1956 both tried to overthrow Batista by getting the backing of a part of the armed forces to take over Camp Columbia. The attack on the Presidential Palace in Havana by the predominantly student Directorio Revolucionario on March 13, 1957, was planned to get rid of Batista personally, in the expectation that his regime could not survive without him. The Directorio's slogan was "Golpear Arriba" ("Strike at the Top"), even after it had begun to wage small-scale guerrilla warfare in the Escambray mountains, early in 1958.[24]

Castro departed from these more traditional tactics. In 1953, he chose to attack the second-largest encampment, in Oriente, the province farthest from the capital, as well as a smaller post in the town of Bayamo, which was in the same province. Like the others, he did not contemplate and was not prepared for a long campaign; he, too, thought in terms of a spectacular pronunciamento and heroic act that would set off a popular uprising in Santiago de Cuba, at the eastern end of the island, rather than in Havana. His unorthodox move at first caught the army garrison by surprise, but he was unable to gain much advantage from it because the soldiers, once they were alerted, fought for Batista instead of going over to Castro's side. This was the risk that Castro took as a result of another unorthodox aspect of his Moncada tactics—to attack the regular army from the outside rather than conspire to win over a portion of the army from the inside.

Castro's second military plan—his "invasion" of Cuba from Mexico in December 1956—was basically a variation of the 1953 attack. He intended to have his boat, "Granma," disembark near the port of Niquero, again in Oriente province, where he expected reinforcements; after attacking Niquero, he was supposed to make an assault on the larger city of Manzanillo; at the same time, his supporters were to stage an uprising in Santiago de Cuba. A country-wide campaign of sabotage and agitation was to culminate in a general strike.[25] So little did Castro envisage a long-drawn-out guerrilla war in the Sierra Maestra that he had not made any effort to study the geography of the region or try to set up any kind of organization there.[26] The 1956 plan misfired because, as one of its participants, Faustino Pérez, put it, "everything went wrong." Of the 82 men in the "Granma," only a handful—the number varies from five to twelve—were able to strike out for the nearby mountains of the Sierra Maestra to escape capture.[27] In its conception this plan was far more complex than the Moncada attack, inasmuch as it attempted to coordinate a landing near Niquero with an uprising in Santiago de

Cuba. But in essence it was but another way of winning an urban base in Oriente province from which to attack the main stronghold of the Batista regime.

In effect, Castro backed into guerrilla warfare after all his other plans had failed. Yet this is what set him apart from the other anti-Batista conspirators. They would have withdrawn from Cuba to prepare another invasion or uprising. Castro and a few of his most trusted men went into the mountains to suffer privation and danger, slowly building up a small guerrilla force. In 1957 and the first months of 1958, however, no one, *not even Castro,* thought that Batista could be overthrown by guerrilla warfare. In February 1957, the pro-Castro, urban-based Resistencia Cívica was organized, and victory seemed so far away in the Sierra Maestra that Castro expected the main blow to come from the urban resistance, in the form of a general strike. In the manifesto of March 12, 1958, he still publicly affirmed that "the strategy of the decisive blow is based on the revolutionary general strike, assisted by armed action."[28] Thus, until the failure of the general strike the following month, Castro himself believed that guerrilla warfare was a subordinate, if indispensable, tactic.

Batista tried to follow up the failure of the general strike by launching an offensive in May 1958 to wipe out Castro's band in the Sierra Maestra. This offensive was the beginning of the end of Batista's regime. For this battle, Castro had only about 300 men, about 60 of them so poorly armed that they were almost useless.[29] At the end of July, after 71 days of fighting, Batista's offensive collapsed. The secret of Castro's victory must be sought in the next five months. Despite Batista's setback, his losses were relatively small and restricted to the eastern end of the island. Physically, the regular army was virtually intact. Morally, however, it had begun to crumble from top to bottom. The collapse of Batista's army was far more a political and psychological than a military phenomenon. Batista has charged that he was deserted by his military commanders, and they have accused him of quitting on them.[30] Batista's end came so suddenly that even Castro was surprised, for it was more a capitulation to a hostile people than a defeat by a superior enemy force. To a large extent, Castro cashed in on the cumulative effect of all the efforts to overthrow Batista. The failures of the many contributed to the success of the one. Without Castro's military pressure, Batista's regime would not have fallen; but Castro's military pressure was far from enough to bring about Batista's fall.

Paradoxically, Castro did not start fighting with any thought of guerrilla warfare; he did not believe that guerrilla warfare was the key to victory until almost the end of the struggle; and guerrilla warfare as a theory of Latin American revolution was born, or at least propagated, after Castro's victory, not before. Guevara has insisted at least three times that the Cubans were not inspired by the Chinese example and that they knew nothing of Mao Tse-tung's doctrine of guerrilla warfare while they were still fighting Batista.[31] The Cuban theory was an ex-post-facto rationalization of an improvised response to events beyond Castro's control. The response itself owed much less to the example of Chinese or other Communists than to Cuba's own revolutionary tradition: every Cuban schoolboy knew that the Cuban "war of independence" in the nineteenth century had been largely a guerrilla struggle in the very region of Oriente that became Castro's sanctuary.

Thus, armed struggle—away from the center of Cuban political and military power; against, rather than inside, the regular army; with the ultimate aim of stirring up a mass, general rebellion against the existing regime, rather than merely eliminating its head—was the distinctive mark of Castroism during the struggle for power.

## From Antagonism to Alliance

Ideologically, then, Castroism never had a life of its own. But tactically, as a form of armed struggle, it had something all its own. And as such, it could attach itself to different ideologies. Until 1956, Castro attached himself to the ideology, such as it was, of Chibasismo. In 1961, he publicly attached himself to the ideology of Marxismo-Leninismo. The transition from one to the other was a protracted, tortuous process, only the main lines of which can now be clearly drawn.

After the attack on the Moncada barracks in 1953, the Partido Socialista Popular (PSP), as the official Cuban Communist Party was called, issued a statement that said in part: "We repudiate the putschist methods, peculiar to bourgeois political factions, of the action in Santiago de Cuba and Bayamo, which was an adventuristic attempt to take both military headquarters. The heroism displayed by the participants in this action is false and sterile, as it is guided by mistaken bourgeois conceptions." The statement also condemned the repression that followed the attack because the PSP paid most heavily for Castro's failure.[32] PSP publications were immediately suppressed and the party itself was subsequently outlawed.

The Communists, in effect, did not regard Castro's tactics as basically different from those of the other middle-class groups that had attempted to overthrow Batista by force. "Putschism" was, by Communist standards, ipso facto "bourgeois," and a "putsch" in Santiago de Cuba was for them no better than a "putsch" in Havana. An official Communist organ referred to the Moncada operation as "dangerous and sterile" as late as October 1956.[33]

During his imprisonment in 1953–55, Castro was never taken to be a Communist; not only did he claim to be an Ortodoxo, but the Ortodoxos were glad to claim him as their own. He was embroiled for the first time in a bitter public controversy over the charge that he was a Communist in July 1956. It flared up as a result of an article in the Cuban magazine *Bohemia* by a Spanish Republican exile, Luis Dam, reporting the arrest of Castro and 21 others in Mexico. According to Dam, the Mexican police had obtained confirmation that "Fidel is a member of the Communist party and leader of the 'Soviet-Mexican Cultural Institution.' "[34]

Castro handled this accusation in a curious way. He cited a Mexico City newspaper denying the report attributed to the Mexican police, and he charged that the whole incident was a plot against him by the Batista regime and the U.S. Embassy. But he also, indirectly, hit out at the Cuban Communists: "What moral right, on the other hand, does Señor Batista have to speak of Communism when he was the presidential candidate of the Communist party in the elections of 1940, when his electoral squibs hid behind the hammer and sickle, when his photographs hung next to those of Blas Roca and Lázaro Peña, when half a dozen of his present ministers and confidential collaborators were outstanding members of the Communist party?"[35] It is, I think, hard to imagine a Communist, open or concealed, defending himself in this way. The most unfriendly thing one could do to the Cuban Communists at that time was to remind them of their old partnership with Batista, or, even worse, to spread the word that they were still in collusion with the dictator. Apparently, in striking back at Batista, Castro could not resist striking out at the Communists.

Years later, however, Castro was quoted by an American correspondent as saying that he had made contact with the "'old Communists" after he had left prison in 1955, and that "there was contact and collaboration" with them "especially when we were preparing in Mexico." Castro also stated that the Communists had agreed to "collaborate" with his group "when we started from Mexico."[36] This may very well be true, but it is far from being the whole truth or even the essential part of it. For one thing, if Castro first made contact with the Communists in Mexico and some form of collaboration began after that, the theory that he had always been a Communist or Soviet agent as far back as his university days must be given up. For another, Castro had never before believed in putting all his political eggs in one basket, and he did not do so in Mexico.* He made contact and sought to collaborate with every possible anti-Batista element in Mexico, but by 1964 he chose to emphasize only the Communists. In 1956, he had appealed to and obtained funds from such anti-Communist sources as Justo Carrillo Hernández, leader of the Montecristi Group, and former President Carlos Prío Socarrás. After all, he had bought the "Granma" with Prío's money, not the Communists'. Nevertheless, if we may trust this statement, Mexico may be considered the starting point of the Castro-Communist "collaboration." But it still had far to go to become a full-fledged alliance, judging from Castro's unflattering allusions to the Communist leaders in *Bohemia* in mid-summer of 1956 and their subsequent reaction to his invasion of Cuba.[37]

For the Communists did not approve of Castro's "Granma" expedition any more than they had approved of his Moncada adventure. They stated their position most clearly in a "Letter of the National Committee of the Popular Socialist Party to the 26th of July Movement," dated February 28, 1957, though not published until the following June.[38] In this key document, the Cuban Communists expressed their "radical disagreement with the tactics and plans" put forward by Fidel Castro. They paid tribute to his group's "valor and sincerity," but insisted that armed action was the wrong tactic. They argued in support of "resisting the government with every peaceful expression of the popular will." They deplored the terrorism, sabotage, and burning of sugar cane that Castro was then encouraging. Yet, the Communists noted, their disagreement with Castro was primarily over "methods and tactics." Among the existing political groups in Cuba, the "Letter" went on to say, the 26th of July Movement "came closest" to the Communists' "strategic conception," though it ironically complained that the 26th of July Movement had not yet taken a strong enough stand against "imperialist

---

* According to Juanita Castro, the sister of Fidel and Raúl Castro, "the scheme to communize Cuba was incubated in Mexico in 1955." She says that Fidel first "contacted" Soviet diplomats and the PSP leader Lázaro Peña in Mexico around the end of 1955 or the very beginning of 1956. She seems to attribute these alleged moves to the influence of Guevara, who, in that case, had worked very quickly, since he had known Fidel for only a very short time. But Juanita Castro did not have any direct knowledge of these events; she says that she later heard "many of the anecdotes and stories of this episode in conversations my brother had with his 'bosom' pals in Cuba." These statements were made by Juanita Castro in a speech in New Orleans on January 18, 1965 (I have quoted from the English transcript). Yet Lázaro Peña was one of the two Communist leaders mentioned so unflatteringly by Fidel as late as July 1956, in *Bohemia*. The problem seems to be not whether Castro and the Communists or Soviet representatives made some "first contacts" in Mexico, but how far they went in reaching a full understanding, and whether Mexico was the beginning or the culmination of Castro-Communist collaboration.

domination." Despite the tactical disagreement, then, the Communist leadership made a bid to the 26th of July Movement for a "closer understanding" based on a "coincidence" of strategy.

The tactical divergence was emphasized in another document of this period, a letter dated March 17, 1957, from the titular head of the PSP, Juan Marinello, to the American journalist Herbert L. Matthews. "At the present time, and with reference to the assaults on barracks and expeditions from abroad—carried out without depending on the people— our position is very clear: We are against those methods," Marinello wrote sternly. After mentioning the 26th of July Movement by name, he added: "We think that this group is inspired by noble intentions but that, in general, it is following erroneous tactics." The right tactics, the Communist spokesman said, would be "to mobilize the masses" through "strikes, demonstrations, civic protests of every kind." The culmination of such activities, he assured Matthews, would be "elections," for which he advocated a Frente Democrático de Liberación Nacional to form a government representing the workers, the peasants, the urban petty bourgeoisie, and the national bourgeoisie, all "under the leadership of the proletariat."*

If Castro and the Communists were still so far apart in the spring of 1957, after Castro was already fighting in the Sierra Maestra, it would appear that any "collaboration" which they may have arranged in Mexico a year or two earlier had not gone very far.

By early 1957, in effect, the Communists had begun to regard Castro's movement with mixed feelings. They were still convinced that armed struggle by a tiny band, far from the center of Cuban power and politics, was an exercise in futility. Yet they recognized a greater kinship with the 26th of July Movement than with any other existing group. They made a sharp distinction between "disagreement" over tactics and "coincidence" of strategical outlook, or more loosely, between immediate and long-range policy. While Castro seemed to be wasting his time in the Sierra Maestra, however, the immediate, "tactical" divergence effectively prevented Castro and the Communists from getting together.

But, by February 1958, the Communists decided to make a "half-turn" in their own tactical approach. In brief, they adopted a dual policy of simultaneously supporting both "the armed struggle in the countryside and the unarmed, civil struggle in the cities."[39] This decision apparently reflected a split in the Communist leadership and a compromise between

* This letter is quoted, in a somewhat different translation, by Herbert L. Matthews, *The Cuban Story* (New York, 1961), pp. 51–52. The original letter is now in the Columbia University Library. I have cited some passages not used by Mr. Matthews.

the opposing factions.* In any case, the PSP ordered a number of young Communists to join Castro's forces in the Sierra Maestra.⁴⁰ An old-time Communist, Osvaldo Sánchez Cabrera, was sent to Castro's headquarters as the first go-between.⁴¹ Nevertheless, these overtures did not mean that the Fidelistas were ready for a full alliance with the Communists. The abortive general strike of April 9, 1958, was carried out by the 26th of July Movement without Communist backing. The Communists blamed the failure of the strike in Havana on the "unilateral strike call," which was issued by the 26th of July leadership "without counting on the rest of the opposition or on the workers themselves."⁴²

It is quite clear that an internal struggle took place inside both the 26th of July Movement and the Communist PSP before they were able to get together. In the 26th of July Movement, the struggle was waged between the civilian leadership of the *llano* (plain), which was anti-Communist, and the military leadership of the *sierra* (mountain), which was pro-Communist. The failure of the April 1958 strike served to discredit the former and give the latter a free hand. In the PSP the struggle raged between the old-line partisans of peaceful, "electoral" opposition and the new-style believers in armed, "insurrectionary" struggle. As late as June 28, 1958, the National Committee of the PSP put out a statement advocating an end to violence and settlement of the strife "by means of democratic and clean elections, respected by all, by which the people can effectively decide by means of the vote and the results of which would be honorably respected."⁴³

But by this time, Batista's offensive in the Sierra Maestra was petering out, and the odds were changing in favor of Castro. A turning point in Castro-Communist relations apparently took place in June–July 1958 or thereabouts. While Castro was negotiating with the other opposition groups for the "unity pact" that was signed in Caracas on July 20, he was simultaneously negotiating with the Communists and surreptitiously moving toward a second "unity pact" with them—surreptitiously because the democratic opposition groups would have nothing to do with the Communists. The former did not know, and even when they were told, would not believe, that Castro had accepted the Communists as allies.⁴⁴

On June 5, 1958, the Communist leader Carlos Rafael Rodríguez sent an article from Havana to the French Communist organ *La France*

---

* At the trial of Marcos Rodríguez in March 1964, Carlos Rafael Rodríguez remarked that he had opposed the line of Aníbal Escalante (*El Mundo,* March 25, 1964). The indications are that Carlós Rafael won out when the Party Secretary, Blas Roca, went over to his side.

*nouvelle,* in which he made known that negotiations were going on for a trade union agreement. He named several groups, including the 26th of July Movement and the Communists.[45] Castro then invited the opposition groups to send representatives to the Sierra Maestra, but only the Communists and the Directorio Revolucionario responded.[46] Rodríguez himself went to the Sierra Maestra in July, and a younger Communist leader, Luis Más Martín, went the following month.[47] The trade union negotiations, which must have been initiated at the end of May or beginning of June, evidently did not go too smoothly because an agreement was not reached until October, over four months later.[48] This agreement took the form of enlarging the Frente Obrero Nacional (FON), which had been a united front of the non-Communist opposition groups, into the Frente Obrero Nacional Unido (FONU). The FONU symbolically accepted the Communists into the trade union united front, but apparently accomplished little more than this.[49]

The Castro-Communist alliance, then, was first realized some time in 1958. This does not mean that some Castroites and some Communists did not work for such an alliance before 1958. But as movements they were inhibited from working together as long as an important section of the 26th of July Movement was anti-Communist in principle and the Communist leadership was anti-insurrectionist in practice. By the summer of 1958, however, the former had suffered an irreparable blow by virtue of its own failure to win power through a general strike, and the latter had immeasurably increased its maneuvering power by backing, at least partially, an "insurrectionary" policy. The dividing line between Castro and the Communists had increasingly narrowed down to a single issue: "armed struggle." The Communists had to cross this line and go over to Castro's side to make a full alliance possible. But whereas "armed struggle" was the raison d'être of Castroism, it was a purely tactical question, not a matter of principle, for the Communists. They could concede the point to Castro without, in their own minds, having made a more serious mistake than having misjudged the "objective circumstances" and the "relation of forces." The Castro-Communist alliance left the Communists' ideology intact. It did not leave intact Castro's ideology, or whatever he had professed to be his ideology.

## From Alliance to Fusion

First there was the Castro-Communist alliance, then there was the Castro-Communist fusion. About two years passed between the first stage and the second, and again only the main lines of the process can be clearly drawn.

We now know that Castro had decided on "fusing" with the Communists by the end of 1960, though the decision was not made public for another half year. On December 2, 1960, Castro presided at a meeting setting up the Escuelas de Instrucción Popular to train cadres for the future "united party." According to Lionel Soto, the Communist director of these schools, this meeting was the first formal manifestation of the "integration of the revolutionary forces."[50] This decision to fuse with the Communists was of such import and magnitude that it could not have been taken without long forethought and preparation. We will be able to interpret the events of 1960 far more realistically when we know more about the actual genesis of this decision and not merely its first "formal manifestation." One of the most striking aspects of this entire process was, and still is, the reluctance of the Cubans to tell much about it. Few Cuban secrets have been so well guarded as this one, as if the truth were still too upsetting to be revealed. The Cuban leaders have preferred to pursue a policy of facts first and names afterward, as Dorticós put it, or to rationalize their actions by depicting them as reactions, as if they had never done anything to encourage precisely those actions to which they wished to react.

In many ways, the process of Castro-Communist fusion was similar to the process of Castro-Communist alliance. In both cases, struggles took place within both the 26th of July Movement and the Communist Party. In the former, the struggle between the pro-Communist and anti-Communist factions occupied most of 1959. Almost all the internal crises in the Castro regime that year—the defection of Major Pedro Díaz Lanz, the first head of the Air Force, in June; the dismissal of Manuel Urrutia, the first President, in July; the arrest of Major Hubert Matos, the commander of the Rebel Army in Camagüey province, in October; Castro's personal intervention to save the Communists from total rout at the trade union congress in November; the removal of two ministers, Faustino Pérez and Manuel Ray, who refused to go along with Matos's arrest, in November; the replacement of the President of the National Bank, Felipe Pazos, by Che Guevara, the same month; and the sentencing of Matos to an oppressive twenty-year prison term in December—all turned on the issue of Communism. It is significant that the Communist organ *Hoy* had launched a campaign against Urrutia as early as March and against Matos in June of that year.[51] Invariably, the days of those attacked by the Communists were numbered, and events bore out the direst foreboding of the anti-Communists.[52]

In the Communist leadership, the main struggle was over the balance of power in the new "united party." In order to achieve fusion, the Fidelistas had to pay homage to the old-time Communists' ideological pre-eminence, and the old-time Communists had to pay tribute to the Fidelistas' tactical superiority. Yet, in practice, the question remained whether the new party should be based on those who had been the long-time guardians of the orthodox ideology or on those who had been the long-derided executors of the successful tactics. In 1961, the pendulum swung in favor of the orthodox, as indicated by Castro's humble admissions of ideological backwardness, his pledge of allegiance to the "collective leadership" of the party, and the staffing of the new party's training schools almost exclusively with old-time Communists.[53] In March 1962, with the purge of the old-time Communist leader Aníbal Escalante, the pendulum swung the other way. Thus there have been different phases in the relationship between Fidelistas and Communists, before and after fusion, in their former names and in their latest incarnations as "new" and "old" Communists.

Again the question arises how Castro's private beliefs accorded with his public utterances. On the surface it would seem that in the first few months of his regime he was torn between conflicting tendencies within himself and his movement. At different times he encouraged both the pro-Communist and anti-Communist wings of the movement and managed to give each of them reason to believe that he was merely waiting for an opportune moment to take a strong stand against the other. He characterized Communism in a way that would soon be a crime in anyone else's mouth. On April 23, 1959, for example, he classified fascism, Peronism, and Communism as different kinds of "totalitarianism."[54] On May 21, 1959, he talked of Communism as a system "that solves the economic problem, but that suppresses liberties, the liberties that are so dear to man and that I know the Cuban people feel." He said that the Communist states "sacrificed" man as "pitilessly" as the capitalist states. He accused the Cuban Communists of complicity with "counterrevolutionaries" in stirring up unrest.[55] Yet a few months later it was political suicide in Cuba to say anything against the Communists, and Castro himself led the campaign in their behalf.

Had it been a hoax or the real thing? In practical effect, it hardly matters. Either way, Castro succeeded in allaying the apprehensions of the anti-Communist wing of his movement. Just as he had said that he could have come down from the Sierra Maestra to the plain if he had called himself a "Marxist-Leninist," he could not have gained the time he needed to consolidate his personal power if he had prematurely called himself a "Marxist-Leninist" in 1959. Still, it is hard to imagine a covert Communist choosing to characterize the Communist movement in general and the Cuban Communists in particular in the terms used by Castro in the first months of 1959. And, in his "I am a Marxist-Leninist" speech of December 2, 1961, Castro found it necessary to allude to these past transgressions and to beg indulgence for them on the ground that he had been a victim of "imperialist propaganda."

In the struggle for power, as we have seen, Castro never tried to give his movement a distinctive doctrine or ideology. After he took power, however, Castro did make one attempt to put forward an embryonic ideology or doctrine that he could call his own, a doctrine summed up in the term "humanism," which for a time served as the trademark of his revolution. The term's background and fate are most revealing.

There had been, in Cuba, a "humanist movement," founded in 1950 by a well-known intellectual, Rubén Darío Rumbaut. This movement was an offshoot of what was known as the Catholic Left, and its promoters hoped that it would prepare the way for a Cuban Christian Democratic Party. They were inspired by, among others, the French Catholic social philosopher Jacques Maritain. But the movement never took fire, and "humanism" did not amount to much politically until Castro suddenly appropriated the term, apparently during his visit to New York in April 1959.

For Castro, "humanism" seemed to be an alternative to both "capitalism" and "Communism," a third way. "Neither dictatorships of men, nor dictatorships of classes, nor dictatorships of groups, nor dictatorships of caste, nor oligarchies of class: government of the people without dictatorship and without oligarchy, liberty with bread and without terror—that is humanism," he said in New York on April 24, 1959.[56] "We believe that there should not be bread without liberty, but neither should there be liberty without bread," he said in Montreal a few days later. "We call that humanism. We want Cuba to be an example of representative democracy with true social justice."[57] In this period he also said that "capitalism may kill man with hunger" and "Communism kills man by wiping out his freedom."[58]

At first the Cuban Communists tried to avoid a clash with the new "humanist" vogue.[59] But when a section of the 26th of July Movement took up the new slogan—for it was little more than that—as the long-awaited, independent and indigenous Fidelista doctrine, and especially when the 26th of July trade union section swamped the Communists in union elections on a humanist program, the Communists decided to fight back. Aníbal Escalante criticized it as "ideological confusion,"[60] a dereliction for which Castro may never have forgiven him. At the time, however, Escalante prevailed. Castro dropped the term and never used it again. Its life span was only about two or three months.

Thus the one and only attempt by Castro to enunciate an ideology—

214                                                      THEODORE DRAPER

or even the slogan of an ideology—of his own was characteristically un-original and pathetically short-lived.

## Armed Struggle or Peaceful Transition

After the purge of Aníbal Escalante in March 1962, however, Castro made one notable attempt to assert his individuality within the world Communist movement. The occasion was provided by the missile crisis of October 1962, which was resolved by Soviet Premier Nikita Khrushchev and President John F. Kennedy at some cost to Castro's pride and influence. Unable to relieve his feelings at the expense of the Soviets, Castro took out most of his rage on the Latin American Communist leaderships, which with few exceptions had been resisting following the Cuban "example" while profiting from it. In a speech on January 16, 1963, Castro paid them back and made his most outspoken bid for the leadership of Latin American Communism. He accused some of his Communist brethren of spreading "false interpretations" and distorting the "historic truths" of the Cuban revolution in order to justify their policy of "peaceful transition." He maintained that the "objective conditions" for revolution already existed in most of Latin America, and that only the absence of the "subjective conditions," or revolutionary will, held it back. He accused other, unnamed, Latin American Communists of such egregious vices as "conformism" with imperialism and "fear of revolutions."

In the same speech, Castro instructed the Latin American Communists on how to make the revolution. His ideas may be summed up in four points:

(1) "The masses make history," but they must be "launched into the battle" by "revolutionary leaders and organizations."

(2) The Cuban masses had been launched into the struggle by "four, five, six, or seven" guerrillas.

(3) The "objective conditions" for such a struggle exist in "the immense majority of Latin American countries," and only the "subjective conditions"—that is, the "four, five, six, or seven" willing to launch the armed struggle—are lacking.

(4) "Peaceful transition" may be "possible," but there has not yet been a single case of it on record, and, in any event, armed struggle must take place in most Latin American countries.

Thus, the true face of Castroism showed itself within the Communist movement at a moment of crisis. In effect, on the single issue of "armed struggle," Castroism reasserted itself—this time inside the Communist movement. It had distinguished Castro from the official Cuban Communists before 1958, when they did not think that armed struggle could overthrow Batista, and now it distinguished him from most Latin American Communist leaderships, which did not think that they could overthrow the existing regimes in their countries through armed struggle. The basic issue was the same; only the context—all of Latin America instead of Cuba—had changed.

Castro did not have an easier time convincing most of the old Latin American leaderships than he had had convincing the Cuban Communists. The only countries in which he could induce the local Communist party to adopt his tactics were Venezuela and Guatemala. Elsewhere, Castroism merely threatened the established parties with splinter groups and factional struggles. In Argentina, for example, at the Twelfth Congress of the Communist Party, February 22–March 3, 1963, the main resolution of the Congress did not fail to pay tribute to the Cuban revolution for having "qualitatively changed the character of the freedom revolution in Latin America." As for immediate tactics in Argentina itself, however, it chose "to conquer power by the peaceful road" through a "National Democratic Front" of workers, peasants, students, progressive professionals and intellectuals, the petty bourgeoisie, and even sectors of the "national bourgeoisie."[61] In February 1963, the outstanding Brazilian Communist leader Luis Carlos Prestes journeyed to Moscow and then flew directly to Havana. It was Prestes's first visit to the Cuban capital—the major old-time Latin American Communist leaders did not hurry to make the pilgrimage—and what had brought him there was clearly intimated in an interview published in the old-time Cuban Communist organ *Hoy*.

"There are persons," said Prestes, without naming names, "who mistakenly believe that the initiation of an armed struggle in Brazil to depose the government would constitute the best support for Cuba. In the present conditions of Brazil, this would be completely wrong. It would isolate the Communists from the masses and facilitate the work of those who are pressing the government in the direction of breaking relations with the Cuban Government." Prestes added, in case some "persons" might imagine that he was speaking only about Brazil: "For Marxism-Leninism, revolution is not synonymous with violence; it is fundamentally a change of classes in power; and that is possible, in certain countries of Latin America, in present conditions, without civil war and without armed insurrection."[62]

One of the problems that Castro took with him to Soviet Russia, where he arrived on April 27, was undoubtedly the growing tension between the Cuban and the other Latin American Communist parties.

The outcome was a statement, signed by Castro and Khrushchev on May 23, in which one passage related directly to the intra-Communist dispute in Latin America and obviously represented a compromise formula. The key sentence in this respect reads: "The PURS [Cuba's Partido Unido de la Revolución Socialista, or United Party of the Socialist Revolution] and the CPSU [Communist Party of the Soviet Union] consider that the question of the peaceful or non-peaceful road toward socialism in one country or another will be definitely decided by the struggling peoples themselves, according to the practical correlation of class forces and the degree of resistance of the exploiting classes to the socialist transformation of society." Another relevant sentence reads: "The working out of the concrete forms and methods of the struggle for socialism in each country is the internal affair of the people of each country."[63] In short, the Cubans were to stop telling the other Latin American Communists how to make a revolution as part of the price of the general agreement reached by Khrushchev and Castro at this time.

This modus vivendi, Communist-style, lasted about six months. In August 1963, even Major Ernesto Che Guevara assured a group of Latin American sympathizers that "armed struggle" was to be undertaken only when and where the necessary "objective conditions" existed, and the decision was up to the revolutionaries of each country.[64] In the September 1963 issue of the Cuban theoretical magazine *Cuba Socialista,* Guevara raised the question: "Is the method of guerrilla warfare the only formula for taking power in all America? Or will it be, in any case, the predominant form? Or will it simply be one more formula among all those used for the struggle?" He still insisted that "there are fundamental arguments that, in our view, determine the necessity of guerrilla action in America as the central axis of the struggle." But he conceded that "the peaceful struggle" could succeed in "special situations of crisis." In his book *La Guerra de Guerrillas,* one of the basic premises had been that all the conditions for making a revolution were not always necessary because the insurrectional center ("el foco insurreccional") could create them.[65] Now he advised that "violence should be unleashed exactly at the precise moment when the leaders of the people have encountered the most favorable circumstances." At one point he tried to generalize as follows: "An analysis of the foregoing, taking a panoramic view of America, would have to come to the following conclusions: In this continent, there exist in general objective conditions that impel the masses to violent actions against the bourgeois and landlord governments; there exist crises of power in many other countries and some subjective conditions also. It is clear that in the countries in which all the conditions are found it would even be criminal not to seize the opportunity to take power. In other countries, in which this is not happening, it is permissible that different alternatives should present themselves and that the decision applicable to each country should emerge from theoretical discussion."[66]

It seems clear, from this rather tortuous and highly qualified line of reasoning, that Guevara was attempting to hold onto his original extreme line in principle while modifying it considerably in practice. As long as each Party could decide for itself which conditions required which tactics, the Cuban "road to power" could be honored more in the breach than in the observance.

Two months later, in December 1963, the *World Marxist Review,* the international organ of the pro-Soviet Communist parties, published an article by the Chilean Communist leader Luis Corvalán entitled, "The Peaceful Way—A Form of Revolution." Whereas Guevara had made grudging admissions that the "peaceful road" might be applicable in some circumstances, Corvalán made grudging admissions that the "violent road" might be equally applicable. For Corvalán, the important thing was the coming Chilean elections, in which the Communists had succeeded in putting together a "Popular Front" based on a "peaceful," "democratic" approach to the Chilean electorate. Thus Corvalán was concerned with preaching against "adventurism," denigrating the importance of violence or armed struggle, extolling maximum flexibility in tactics, and emphasizing that both objective and subjective conditions had to be "ripe" for a successful revolution.

The Chilean leader was especially wrathful because the Chinese Communist Party had sent the Chilean Party a letter that had sharply contrasted Corvalán's "peaceful way" to Castro's "revolutionary way." In reply, Corvalán cited the Khrushchev-Castro declaration of May 23 to the effect that "forms and methods" are the business of each individual Party. Thus Castro had temporarily put himself in a position of being used by both sides. "No Communist party that accepts the thesis concerning the peaceful way repudiates the way of armed uprising a priori," Corvalán protested. He also made it clear that if the Chilean Communists ever won power, one way or the other, Chile would end up as another Cuba. Still, on the burning question of tactics, there was no doubt where Corvalán stood: "In upholding the peaceful way our Party aims at solving the tasks of the revolution without civil war or armed uprising. On the other hand, whether a struggle is revolutionary or not is not determined exclusively (and often not even mainly) by the number of violent actions, by the predominance or absence of armed struggle."[67]

By the end of 1963, then, it was quite clear that the Moscow formula of May had worn somewhat thin. Both sides were using some of the same language to say quite different things. Still, as long as each Party was permitted to make up its own mind without interference or reproach by other Parties, the formula avoided open clashes and served a useful purpose. But the Cubans could not hold their fire for long. In January 1964, Guevara was his old self again. To an Italian correspondent in Havana, he said: "I maintain that the war of liberation will necessarily assume a violent form in almost every one of these [Latin American] countries—in almost all, I say. There is no other way. Violence is the only form in which their political will can manifest itself."[68]

Castro himself was somewhat more cautious. In an important interview with foreign correspondents during the celebration of the ninth anniversary of the Moncada affair, he was asked to comment on Chile just before the election. "In general, the political and revolutionary leaders of each country do not ask anyone what to do, and we ourselves do not ask anyone about anything," he replied in the spirit of the Moscow agreement. "But on the theoretical level, I will say that there is no one road to make the revolution; I believe that there is more than one road, and that these roads are determined by circumstances."

He went on: "In some countries, as, for example, Chile, where legal methods of struggle are open, I believe that the road they are following in Chile, the constitutional and legal road, is a correct road. In those countries where all legal methods are closed and objective conditions exist for making the revolution, then it is necessary to have recourse to the methods of armed struggle in order to conquer revolutionary power. And if I were a Venezuelan, and if I were a Colombian, that is what I would do."[69]

All of which seemed quite fair and reasonable. But no sooner had the Communist-backed Popular Front in Chile suffered a setback in the September 1964 elections than Castro changed his tune. He quickly held forth again on "the inevitable road of revolutions, in many circumstances the inevitable road of armed revolutionary struggle.[70]

Thus, until the Moscow agreement of May 1963 the Castroite position on the question of "armed struggle" versus "peaceful transition" had clearly favored the former. Then began a period of over a year in which Castro apparently modified his position to bring it closer to that of the major Latin American Communist parties, those in Argentina, Brazil, and Chile. Even if Guevara seemed to undercut the new line by making essentially superficial concessions, he did make some effort to broaden his approach, and in any event it could be said that only Castro spoke officially and conclusively for Cuba. But the circumstances of the shift, and the hasty Cuban reaction to the disappointing Chilean elections, showed that the motivation had been practical rather than doctrinal. The Venezuelan Communist movement had already paid a heavy price for its terrorist tactics; the Castroite tendency in Brazil had virtually fizzled out; the Chilean elections made it imperative for the largest Communist party in Latin America to muffle the Castroite chorus in its rear. The lack of suitable theaters of action for armed struggle in Latin America and Cuba's own overriding economic needs in 1963 made it necessary for Castro to tone down his previously contemptuous references to "peaceful transition." Ironically, the Castroite obsession with violence and terrorism—and, as Venezuela showed, all the revolutionary rhetoric of "armed struggle" really boiled down to in practice was sheer terrorism—had threatened the unity and force of the larger Latin American Communist parties more than it had the existing regimes.

But after the Chilean elections, circumstances again changed, and with this came another change of line. Despite the opportunistic moderation of 1963–64, it was never a secret that "armed struggle" had remained the distinguishing characteristic and most strident war cry of Castroism within the Communist movement of Latin America, wherever, as in Venezuela, the Castroite tendency controlled Communist policy. If it did not have that, Castroism would lose its identity in the Communist mass. That is why, as long as Castro wishes to assert himself as an independent force within Latin American Communism, he can temporarily modulate, but he cannot abandon, his basic position.

## Power and Ideology

Historically, then, Castroism is a leader in search of a movement, a movement in search of power, and power in search of an ideology. From its origins to today, it has had the same leader and the same "road to power," but it has changed its ideology.

If Castroism were merely an extension of its leader, it would be classified among the traditional caudillo-based movements of Latin America, in which power is its own justification. But Castro is not a traditional caudillo; he is a new type of caudillo with a need to justify his power ideologically. Yet Castro's ideology has never come out of himself. He has only produced a "road to power," which has attached itself to different ideologies. He won power with one ideology and has held it with another. This is perhaps the most peculiar aspect of the Castroite phenomenon.

The three schools of thought mentioned at the outset explain this phenomenon in different ways. The first contends that there was no change in ideology, at least in Castro, that he was always a Communist, but a secret one. The second maintains that there was a natural, consistent development from his pre-Communist to his post-Communist ideology. The third—at least as I understand it—believes that Castro did not have an ideological core of his own and filled the vacuum in himself with different ideologies to serve his power in different ways at different stages of his political career.

Castro himself seems increasingly to have adopted the third view. For example, on January 2, 1964, he stressed the unpreparedness of both the Cuban leadership and the Cuban people for building socialism, and their lack of "organization, tradition, habits, customs, ideas, and mental attitude" for the new task. In a similar vein, Guevara had previously remarked that the revolutionary leaders had been "only a group of fighters with high ideals and little preparation."[71]

The old-time Communist leaders have agreed on a revealing formula to define Fidel Castro's "great historical merit." As one of the oldest and most authoritative of them has written, it has consisted essentially in his ability "to find the right road for achieving victory, that of the armed struggle of the people, the only possible road in the conditions of Cuba in 1952–58."[72] As late as January 1964, the former Communist General Secretary Blas Roca paid tribute to Castro's "great historical merit" in virtually the same terms, always emphasizing that he had found the right road to power, rather than what he had done with power.[73] In effect, Castroism gave Communism total power in Cuba, and Communism gave Castroism an ideology of total power. In a previous period, Castroism might well have adopted a different ideology of total power. In this sense, Castroism has never been self-sufficient or homogeneous; it has been made up of elements from different traditions and movements; it has mainly contributed means and sought elsewhere for ends.

Thus, the reason for Castroism's coalescence with Communism can be explained less by what Castroism was than by what it was not. It was not a movement with a serious political thought or a serious political thinker. It has had a leader with great gifts of popularization, demagogy, and dissimulation, with a contagious sense of mission and "jefatura," with the physical attributes of a warrior-hero. But he has also had a deep, persistent feeling of intellectual inadequacy and inferiority, a tendency to depend on others for fundamental values or systematic theorizing, an inherent political superficiality and instability. Before taking power he could put his name to fine democratic aims and principles without believing in them—not because he was profoundly committed to other beliefs, but because he did not believe in anything very profoundly.

But it is only in Cuba that Castroism has gone through enough stages to make its relationship with Communism clearly visible and openly avowed. In other countries, one may detect Castroite tendencies that reflect earlier stages of Cuban Castroism and that still maintain a seemingly tenuous or ambiguous relationship with existing Communist movements. Thus, non-Cuban Castroite groups may resemble the Cuban Castroism of 1955 or 1957 much more than the Cuban Castroism of 1961 or 1965. The former may seem to be a revolutionary mood rather than a movement; it may be distinguished by its "pure" adherence to armed struggle or direct action without the (temporary) encumbrance of an ideology; it may even, like its progenitor, claim to be an alternative rather than a road to Communism. But it is much more difficult for any non-Cuban Castroism to pretend to be democratic and non-Communist, as Cuban Castroism once pretended to be, precisely because the latter has demonstrated what such professions were worth. The success of Cuban Castroism in turning itself into a Cuban form of Communism has, ironically, hindered Castroite groups elsewhere from achieving success in quite the same way. The hopes and illusions on which Cuban Castroism once fed can hardly be made to order for any other Castroite group, and we may even get a Castroite tendency somewhere that promises to avoid the mistakes and excesses of Fidel Castro.

There are, it seems to me, two main dangers to be avoided in any analysis of Castroism today. One is to separate it from the world Communist movement, and the other is to equate it with everything else in the world Communist movement. It is just as logical to say that Fidel Castro cannot be a Communist because he is a Castroite as to say that Mao Tse-tung cannot be a Communist because he is a Maoist or that Tito cannot be a Communist because he is a Titoist. On the other hand, it is just as illogical to deny the peculiar characteristics of Castro's Communism as it is to deny the peculiar characteristics of Mao's or Tito's, Khrushchev's or Khrushchev's successors'.

In short, Castroism today represents a tendency within the world Communist movement. There is no such thing as Castroism per se. Indeed, the term Castroism is not used in Cuba today, and Castro himself seems very coy about acknowledging the existence of Castroism. It is necessary to distinguish between the "ism" of the genus "Communism" and the "ism" of a species such as Castroism. But, for better or worse, the different Communist tendencies are also called "isms," and this practice is not likely to be given up.

In this sense, Castroism may be distinguished from other Communist tendencies by its leadership, its history, its geographic sphere of influence, its language, and its "road to power."

(1) The inspiration and source of authority of the Castroite tendency is Fidel Castro, not the Soviet leadership, Mao, or anyone else. Castro has his own personal cadre and independent following in Cuba, and, to a lesser extent, elsewhere, which have given him a margin of maneuverability vis-à-vis the old-time Communists in Cuba and the other Communist states and parties.

(2) Castroism is the only tendency within world Communism that came into the movement from the outside and did not develop organically from within, as Maoism or Titoism did. In Cuba it has needed world Communism to give it a doctrine, a social and economic pattern, and material assistance, but it feels that world Communism needs it externally for expansion in Latin America.

Castro and his closest associates have repeatedly spoken of Cuba as the "example" that most of Latin America must follow in order to make the revolution. Many of the Communist parties of Latin America date from the early 1920's (one, the Mexican, from 1919), and the old leaderships were brought up on the proposition that the "example" to follow, with some modifications and adaptations, were the Russian Revolution and the Russian Party leadership. The "example" of the Chinese Revolution was the first great challenge to the Russian prototype, but Castro hopes that the Cuban "example" will supersede both of them. The ultimate authority, of course, on who is and who is not correctly following the "Cuban example" will be found in Havana, not in Moscow or in Peking.

(3) In effect, Castro has staked out for himself a Communist sphere of influence. He has, on occasion, made nothing less than a bid to be recognized as the Communist leader of Latin America, to be treated eventually on a par with the Soviet leadership and Mao Tse-tung. This may smack of delusions of grandeur for the leader of a country as small and weak as Cuba, but it is precisely Castro's point that numbers are not important. If a dozen men could start a revolution in Cuba, why should not little Cuba be able to set off the revolution in Latin America, or at least claim credit for it?

(4) Guevara has pointed out that Cuba has "something" for Latin Americans that no other Communist power can match. "That some-

thing," he said, "which speaks to them in Spanish, in its own language, and which explains in a clear form what they have to do to achieve happiness, is called the Cuban Revolution."[74] The same idea, less obtrusively, but no less unmistakably, has been publicly voiced by Blas Roca: "The Cuban Revolution established the first socialist country in America and has made the first Marxist-Leninist revolution in the Spanish language. And that is for all time."[75] Language, in fact, reinforces and perhaps even outweighs geography as a factor in the Castroite sphere of influence. The language factor indefinably exacerbates and nationalizes whatever other differences may exist among the various Communist tendencies.

(5) Finally, the Castroite "road to power" is not the traditional Communist one. In the orthodox Communist view of the past, revolutionary force or violence has been considered the last, not the first, stage of the revolutionary struggle. Objective conditions created the basis for armed struggle; armed struggle did not create objective conditions. As the veteran Argentine Communist Victorio Codovilla has said of the Chinese Communists, but which applies just as well to the Cubans, "they stake everything on armed struggle alone," and especially on "partisan warfare." Codovilla, who served for many years as a Comintern functionary, agreed that "in certain conditions partisan action as a component of the mass movement is a form of the popular struggle" and a "justified and necessary form"; but, he insisted, armed force is only one of many admissible forms of struggle, and "if the objective conditions are not favorable for waging an armed struggle, partisan action will end in failure and in the long run will damage the revolutionary movement."[76] This is not the language of Castroism, which had previously advocated the use of force always and almost everywhere by a handful of guerrillas even in countries with a weak Communist party or outside the party altogether.

In view of the existing confusion in some quarters, it may be well to emphasize that the difference between Codovilla, an outstanding representative of the Communist "old guard," and Castro, the exemplar of the Communist "new wave," is not one of "armed struggle" versus "peaceful transition" in principle. The difference is over when, where, and in what circumstances, it is necessary or advisable to use force. The "old guard," men like Luis Carlos Prestes of Brazil, has painful memories of the heavy price paid years ago for the misuse of force, and considers the stakes too high to be risked lightly. Soviet Russia and not Communist China has, after all, given Castro the material assistance and military equipment that have made his belligerence possible. The difference, then, is not one of abstract doctrine; thus far the "old guard" and the "new wave" have found it possible to live with such differences of doctrine as do separate them. Nevertheless, factional struggles in the Communist movement have flared up and have raged out of control for less cause. The antagonism between "old" and "new" Communists in Castro's Cuba should not be pooh-poohed. For historical, personal, and tactical reasons, it is one of the most divisive elements in Castro's regime, and potentially one of the most explosive.

In historical perspective, then, I would suggest that Castroism represents a particular case of cross-fertilization, as yet difficult to assess with finality, of a Latin American revolutionary tradition and the European Communist tradition, just as Leninism represented a cross-fertilization of the Russian revolutionary tradition and the European Marxist tradition. I say "a particular case" because it is not yet certain that the Cuban phenomenon is typical or representative of Latin American Communism as a whole. I say that it is as yet difficult to assess with finality because it is still of relatively recent vintage and in constant flux. If the Cubans should ever achieve their ambition and truly carve out for themselves a Latin American sphere of influence—which still seems to be a long way off—it will mark a further division of the Communist world into regional oligarchies. Castroism has given world Communism cause for both exhilaration and apprehension. It has created new opportunities and new tensions. It represents growing pains and growing contradictions. All that it is safe to say at present is that the end is not yet in sight.

# The Prospects for
# Pluralistic Communism

The history of world Communism, conceived as a united movement with a common doctrine and strategy formulated from a single center, is at an end. One hundred years after the foundation of the First International, and fifty years after Lenin proclaimed the need to form the Third in order to replace the Second, the doctrinal and organizational unity of the "world party" created by him has been irretrievably broken by the rival claims to leadership of the two Communist great powers, and the resulting schism has opened up new possibilities of independent development to many nonruling Communist parties, and even to some now in power. International Communism no longer has a single worldwide organization, a single center of authority, or a single orthodox doctrine.

But if the history of "world Communism" is at an end, the history of Communism in the world is not. Now, as before the schism, a nuclear world power, the Soviet Union, is ruled by a Communist party; it exerts its regional hegemony over a number of East European countries (as well as over Outer Mongolia), partly through its ties to the Communist parties ruling them; and it seeks to retain, and in part revive, its guiding influence over the majority of other Communist parties in the world, including the ruling party of Cuba. The greatest regional power in Asia, the Chinese People's Republic, is governed by its own form of Communism, controls the Communist regime of North Korea and—perhaps less completely—that of North Vietnam, and is actively engaged in laying the doctrinal and organizational foundations of a new revolutionary International with its center of gravity in the underdeveloped continents; in this effort, it already enjoys the support of some of the leading Communist parties of Asia as well as of considerable sections in Latin America. Further, a number of the nonruling Communist parties, regardless of their allegiance to either side and often in proportion to their growing independence, continue to play a major political role in their own countries, and at least a few of them must be considered serious potential contenders for national power; and even where no effective Communist organization exists at all, elements of the Communist ideology exert a substantial influence on the political and intellectual elites of underdeveloped countries.

This contrast between the dramatic breakup of the Communist "monolith," and the continued importance and even vitality of its pieces, raises a fundamental question about the significance of the whole event. Are we simply confronted with a new plurality of Communist states and parties of a familiar type, each pursuing its own separate interests in power politics but each retaining the same structural characteristics and ideological goals? Is it conceivable that Communism should have ceased to be truly international—that is, worldwide and single-centered—without otherwise changing its nature? Or should the schism be viewed as both an effect and an additional cause of divergent trends of development in different parts of the Communist world, so that we are dealing with increasingly different types of Communist regimes and increasingly different versions of the Communist doctrine, each of which exerts its attraction in different social and cultural conditions? In other words, will the terms "Communist party" and "Communist regime" continue to have clearly definable basic meanings despite the inevitable national variations of detail, or will they eventually become as ambiguous as the term "socialism" has become since the break between Communists and Social Democrats after the First World War?

Clearly, we cannot evaluate the prospects for the various Moscow-oriented, Peking-oriented, or independent forms of Communism without considering the prospects for the further internal transformation of each of them. A first approach to an answer may emerge if we ask what factors have been decisive for preventing continued all-inclusive cooperation among independent Communist states, and for causing their differences to assume the form of a doctrinal schism.

### The Inevitability of Divergence

Any inquiry into the nature of the schism must begin by recalling the "Caesaro-papist" character of modern totalitarianism, its inseparable unity of state power and ideology. In any totalitarian Communist regime, the rulers must justify their rule in doctrinal terms, while for the subjects, loyalty to the faith and obedience to the state coincide. Accordingly, the unity of the Communist world party, such as we knew it for more than three decades, was built around the existence of a unique center of both political power and doctrinal authority—the Soviet Union.

This uniqueness was ended, and the foundations of worldwide Communist unity undermined, by two events: the rise of a second Communist great power in China, and the blow inflicted on Soviet authority by Khrushchev's "secret speech" of 1956. The emergence of a plurality of sovereign Communist states, each with different national interests and internal problems resulting in differences of ideological outlook, was bound to put an end to the centralism of the Communist secular church, as was first proved when Communist Yugoslavia established its sovereignty in conflict with Stalin. With the rise of Communist China, the unique position of the Soviet Union as a command center for all Communist parties became a thing of the past; this was recognized implicitly in Stalin's dealings with China, and it has been made explicit by his heirs.

At first, both Soviet and non-Soviet Communists hoped to be able to preserve unity of policy without a unique center of power, and respect for Soviet doctrinal authority without subordination to Soviet organizational discipline. They might have succeeded for some more years because of the historical role of the Soviet Union and the Bolshevik party as the original model for Communists everywhere; but the chances of such success were critically impaired when Khrushchev, setting out to destroy the myth of Stalin's infallibility, destroyed forever the belief in the infallibility of the Soviet Communist Party and thus precluded himself from inheriting Stalin's worldwide prestige. The shock of de-Stalinization was the direct cause of the East European crisis of October 1956; and although the Chinese Communists then worked actively to help restore Soviet leadership, in the hope of decisively influencing its future use, they never forgot that it rested henceforth on borrowed authority. The "secret speech" was certainly not the original cause of the Sino-Soviet conflict, as the Chinese have since claimed; but by damaging beyond repair the traditional prestige of the Soviet Communist Party, it provided the basis for Peking's challenge to Moscow's worldwide leadership, which was to turn that conflict into a schism.

The emergence of a plurality of sovereign Communist powers, and the vacuum of international authority created by de-Stalinization, were thus basic factors in making the disintegration of the organization and doctrine of world Communism possible: given these two conditions, any major differences of national interest and internal ideological needs between the two principal Communist powers might lead to open political and doctrinal conflict between them, for each would now decide its policies independently and seek to justify them in ideological terms. The only way to maintain a modicum of unity within this new pluralistic constellation would have been a common effort to tolerate the inevitable political and doctrinal differences, to develop a looser form of international cooperation based on pragmatic compromise and ideological nonaggression. This would have required that neither Moscow nor Peking claim a position of world leadership founded on a monopoly of orthodoxy for its own interpretation of the doctrine; for such claims, being no longer based on unique power or unquestioned tradition, could now be made with equal justification by either side, and could only lead to mutual accusations of heresy. But once such accusations were publicly raised in the forum of the international Communist movement, not only the international influence of the Soviet and Chinese leaders but even the legitimacy of their rule in their own empires would be at stake in the factional struggle thus opened—and this would make retreat and compromise impossible and organizational and doctrinal schism inevitable.

An awareness of these dangers seems, in fact, to have been the basis for the compromise reached by the Soviet and Chinese leaders in early 1959, at the time of the Twenty-first Congress of the CPSU, when both sides temporarily agreed to hold to their different views about the People's Communes without engaging in further polemics; and when the Soviets responded to the Chinese ideological attacks throughout 1960 not only by rebutting them but by declaring their willingness to renounce their worldwide "leading role," they were probably groping for a return to such a solution.[1] It may indeed be said that although the Soviets have never abandoned their claim to be in the orthodox Leninist tradition, they have in recent years been more interested in avoiding outside ideological criticism than in enforcing worldwide ideological conformity; provided they were left a free hand to develop their own domestic, imperial, and worldwide policies, they have been increasingly willing to tolerate a measure of political and even doctrinal variety among their allies and comrades.

Conversely, it has been the Chinese who have consistently proclaimed the need for complete ideological unity based on a single doctrinal authority, first seeking to maintain the Soviets in that role, and later challenging them to ideological debate; and when the Soviets formally abandoned the "leading role" during the Moscow conference of 81 Communist parties in order to end the debate, the Chinese chose to see this new compromise as only another stage in a continuing ideological struggle to impose their own views on the world Communist movement, including the Soviet Union. It was this Chinese determination to replace the discredited authority of the "revisionists" in Moscow—not by toleration of differences but by claiming for themselves the role of sole fountainhead of Leninist orthodoxy—that led to the collapse of the compromise during the Twenty-second Congress of the CPSU in 1961, and, foiling all later attempts at an ideological truce, made it impossible to preserve a looser form of worldwide Communist unity on a pluralistic basis.

This contrast between the willingness of the Soviet leaders to adjust their policy, even though inconsistently and with many hesitations, to the new pluralism of Communist power, and the Chinese insistence on restoring complete doctrinal unity under one central leadership, has been crucial for the growth of the schism and may be expected largely to determine its future course. In part, it is obviously to be explained by the disproportion of material power between China and the Soviet Union—the dependence of the former on the economic, military, and diplomatic aid of the latter, and her inevitable dissatisfaction with the extent of that aid. The Soviets, confident that their superior power would normally prevail in any compromise reached by quiet diplomacy among allies, were clearly interested in keeping relations on this pragmatic level and avoiding the embarrassment of ideological disputes. The Chinese, frustrated in their more discreet efforts to influence Soviet policies, were increasingly tempted to try and put pressure on their powerful ally by ideological attacks—by questioning the orthodoxy of Soviet behavior in the forum of the international Communist movement. There is no need here to recount in detail the frustrations suffered by Peking in 1958-59—the disappointment of Chinese hopes for massive Soviet capital aid, the lack of Soviet regard for Chinese prestige in the Lebanon crisis, the limitation of Soviet military support for the Chinese attack on Quemoy, the Soviet refusal to help China become an atomic power, the critical Soviet neutrality toward China's border conflict with India, and the Soviet efforts to establish a basis for a dialogue with the United States—nor to retrace their translation into ideological terms. Yet in the course of 1960 the Chinese Communists found that their ideological attacks were not leading to an increase in Soviet aid, but to its total cessation. Hence their decision to continue the struggle even after the compromise of the Moscow declaration cannot be explained simply by considerations of power politics: by 1961 Mao must have been convinced that Khrushchev's outlook had become incurably "revisionist"—that they differed not only about particular policies but about the basic tasks of a Communist party regime in building "socialism" at home and in promoting the advance of the world revolution.

In fact, these different concepts concerning the central issues of Communist doctrine and strategy have been made increasingly explicit in the programmatic documents published by both sides since the Twenty-second Congress of the CPSU.[2] Of course, this recent elaboration of increasingly complete rival interpretations of Marxist-Leninist doctrine has been largely a result of the factional struggle for control of the world Communist movement. But it would be superficial to see these competing systems as mere ideological superstructures erected to justify a personal or national rivalry for world leadership; for while the rival systems are new in their present form, they grew out of differences of outlook that existed long before the schism, and indeed were largely responsible for causing it by leading Moscow and Peking to develop different ideas about the possible forms of international unity. Nor can these differences of outlook be understood as merely reflecting differences of national interest in the field of foreign policy; they are as much an expression of different domestic needs resulting from the different roads traveled and the different stages reached by the two leading Communist regimes in their "construction of socialism."

The full importance of these different internal needs of the Communist regimes becomes clearer when we recall that it was primarily for internal reasons that Khrushchev embarked on the difficult and dangerous path of de-Stalinization. The central domestic task facing Stalin's heirs—and especially Khrushchev, as the chief exponent of the efforts to restore the primacy of the Party over all other power machines—was to adapt the rule of the CPSU to the needs of a growing industrial society. Khrushchev had understood at an early stage that Soviet society could not develop further without drastic changes in the methods of governing it, notably a renunciation of mass terrorism that would involve a major reduction in the role of police coercion in daily life, and a major increase in the role of material incentives for the ordinary workers and peasants; and he quickly found that the bureaucrats trained by Stalin could not be induced to change their methods unless the legend of Stalin's infallibility was destroyed first. The very fact that Khrushchev wanted to accomplish the change in the name of an ideological party forced him to justify it by an ideological break.

But the unforeseen consequences of de-Stalinization did not remain confined to the damage to Russia's international authority; internally, too, the renunciation of mass terrorism and the new emphasis on encouraging a steady growth of productivity led to further changes in the dynamics of Soviet development. Under Stalin, the creation of the material skeleton of an industrial society had been accompanied by periodic violent transformations of the social structure; these "revolutions from above," intended in theory as thrusts toward the goal of a classless society, served in practice to prevent any consolidation of the body social that might weaken the power of the totalitarian state. Toward the end of his life, Stalin had proclaimed that the achievement of true communism would require, apart from quantitative advances in productivity and corresponding increases of real income and reductions of working time, one more major structural change: the transformation of collective farm property into all-national property, which would end the distinction between collective farms and state farms, between collective peasants and state workers.[3]

As late as the Twenty-first Party Congress in 1959, Khrushchev, in outlining his own program for the building of communism, accepted the disappearance of the distinction between collective farms and state farms as a precondition for reaching the goal, and he announced a catalogue of measures aimed at bringing about this structural change.[4] Yet while Stalin had envisaged an abolition of all monetary exchanges between the collective farms and the state and their replacement by barter contracts as the crucial step in this transformation, Khrushchev's reforms had tended for years to raise agricultural productivity by making all costs and prices comparable in monetary terms; and he showed himself anxious to accomplish the new structural change without a setback to productivity, hence without violent upheaval. In short, Khrushchev was seeking to combine the dynamics of ever-new structural change, required by Communist doctrine, with the dynamics of economic rationality, imposed by the need for competition with the non-Communist world at the stage of development reached by Soviet society; and experience soon showed that the two were in conflict, for every local advance in structural change promptly resulted in losses in agricultural output.

By the time of the Twenty-second Congress in 1961, economic rationality had won. In the new party program, structural change was no longer demanded as a precondition for the transition to Communism, but only anticipated as a byproduct of the long-term rise in productivity.[5] Now, for the first time, the effort to build Communism was defined purely in terms of quantitative economic improvement, no longer in terms of the deliberate use of state power as an instrument of social transformation. Correspondingly, the Soviet state was no longer described as a "dictatorship of the proletariat" exercised by its vanguard, the Communist Party, but as a "state of all the people" led by that party. The significant revision here was not the admission that state and party had ceased to be "proletarian," which had been clearly implied in the Stalin Constitution of 1936 and in the party statute of 1939, but the claim that the party regime had ceased to be a "dictatorship": it was intended to emphasize the change of political climate brought about by the end of mass terrorism, and to assure the Soviet people that while one-party rule would continue indefinitely, the era of violent social upheavals staged in the name of the Party's goals—of the "class struggle" inside the Soviet Union—was over for good. The new formula thus expressed the conviction of the Soviet leaders (both before and after the fall of Khrushchev, whose successors have promptly reaffirmed their loyalty to the party program and to the decisions of the Twentieth and Twenty-second Congresses) that at the present stage of development, their rule could better be justified by disguising rather than by emphasizing its dictatorial character—that henceforth the stability of their regime and the growth of its material power would be better served by a more relaxed form of autocratic rule than by the extreme of totalitarian tension.

Finally, the Soviet thesis that world war is not "fatalistically inevitable" and may even be "eliminated from the life of mankind" before the end of imperialism, and the increased verbal stress on "peaceful coexistence" even during acutely critical periods in East-West relations, have (apart from their truth content and their role in foreign policy) a function in this domestic context. A regime that seeks to impose bitter sacrifices in a climate of internal tension will tend to project the cause of this tension into the outside world, and to justify its domestic harshness by pointing to an imminent external danger. But a regime that seeks to appeal to the self-interest of its subjects in order to achieve a steady growth of productivity will want to encourage a sense of security among them—and this must mean security not only from police persecution but also from imminent war. Of course, this requirement may at times conflict with the need to justify special efforts and sacrifices imposed by the armaments race: but on the whole it is remarkable how hard the Soviet leaders have tried in recent years to reassure their people that peace can and will be preserved.

In Communist China, on the other hand, the entire recent development of the country has been dominated by Mao's conviction that his rule can only be maintained if ideological militancy is kept up in an atmosphere of the besieged fortress. It would be an oversimplification to attribute this conviction directly to the comparative youth of the Chinese revolution, or to the lower level of China's economic development; for it should not be forgotten that China became an active and successful pioneer of the coexistence campaign in Asia in 1954, and that in 1956 and early 1957 Mao had experimented with permitting intellectual criticism of his regime in the "Hundred Flowers" campaign, and even with tolerating the expression of popular grievances, as a safety valve for "nonantagonistic contradictions" in Chinese society. Students of Communist China seem to agree that it was his shock at the flood of domestic opposition that those experiments brought to light, even more than the shock of the Hungarian revolution, that caused Mao to turn, in June 1957, to a policy of deliberately maintaining a climate of internal tension and irreconcilable ideological struggle.[6]

From that moment, he seems never to have looked back. The second session of the Eighth Party Congress of the CCP in the spring of 1958 brought the Great Leap Forward—a program to achieve fantastic simultaneous increases in agricultural and industrial production, mainly by mobilizing "mass initiative"—and the preparations for the People's Communes. By the end of the summer, the total transformation of rural life by driving the entire peasantry into communes within a few months, in conditions where long hours and poor rewards were enforced by militarization of labor and egalitarian propaganda, was proclaimed as the next step in an "uninterrupted revolution" that was to lead to full communism within a short time.[7] Mao's insistence on branding "revisionism" as the main danger in the international Communist movement during the Moscow conference of November 1957 must be seen largely within this domestic Chinese context. The fact that the Chinese delegation at this conference, when it sought not yet a quarrel but the closest possible cooperation with the Soviet leaders, behind the scenes expressed serious doctrinaire qualms about Khrushchev's 1956 formula of the "peaceful" or "parliamentary" road to socialism, indicates the Chinese fear of any theory that might appear, even remotely, to blur the picture of an irreconcilable worldwide struggle.[8] Clearly, the Chinese felt that any such appearance might interfere with their determination to maintain the atmosphere of the besieged fortress at home; and that same determination must have been an important contributing factor in causing them to engage in various national conflicts with their Asian neighbors in the following years.

It is particularly significant that even after the catastrophic economic results of the Great Leap Forward and the People's Communes forced the Chinese Communist leaders to revise their expectations and correct their immediate policies, they refused to change the general climate of their internal development. Under the whip of hunger, they abandoned the attempt to achieve a massive increase in heavy industrial production without corresponding capital investment, by means of country-built furnaces, and they once again gave priority to agriculture. The internal organization of the People's Communes was greatly loosened, and they were turned into units of administration rather than of actual production. The belief that by means of those communes full communism could be reached in less than a generation was dropped, and it was stressed that the way ahead would be long and arduous.[9]

Yet at the same time, and despite the demands for a more far-reaching reversal of the line voiced by a "right-wing" minority in the leadership at the Lushan session of the Central Committee in 1959,[10] Mao and his supporters have continued to insist on such basic features of their "general line" as the need to develop China by its own strength, the rejection of any attempt to reward scarce technical cadres by increased income differentiation during the main period of industrial construction, the preservation of the communes as a "germ" for higher communist forms, and the preference for militarization of labor over any consistent policy of material incentives.[11] To the outsider, such policies seem unlikely to solve China's tremendous economic problems; but to Mao and his team, they have the merit of preserving the atmosphere of intransigent ideological struggle against all dangers of *embourgeoisement*. It is indeed remarkable that the same insistence on extreme egalitarianism and uninterrupted revolution, which was justified in 1958 by the promise of a rapid transition to full communism, has now come to be based on the opposite argument—that the danger of a new privileged class attempting a "capitalist restoration" will persist during the entire long transition period of "five to ten generations" or "one or several centuries," and that it can only be held at bay if the regime continues the most vigilant class struggle throughout that time.

In the ninth and last official Chinese "Commentary" on the "Open Letter" of the Central Committee of the CPSU of July 14, 1963 (issued on its first anniversary), which reads like a political testament of Mao Tse-tung, this argument is used to attack the "revisionist" outlook of the 1961 CPSU program, and above all to condemn the thesis that after the destruction of the former exploiting classes the "dictatorship of the proletariat" can be replaced by a "state of all the people." Indeed, while in a Soviet context that thesis serves the rulers' need to give their subjects an increased sense of security from further violent upheavals, the implied promise of such security must appear to the Chinese rulers in *their* context as dangerous encouragement for opposition to their own harsh regime. In the framework of Marxist-Leninist doctrine, renunciation of dictatorship can be justified only by the ending of the class struggle following the final disappearance of "antagonistic classes." Conversely, the open defense of permanent dictatorship requires proof that the class struggle must still continue, and the Chinese provide it by claiming that new capitalist elements will arise again and again until the final achievement of communism, and that the struggle against them may enter particularly acute phases at any time during that long period.

This gets Mao Tse-tung close to Stalin's notorious thesis—developed in his 1937 speech to the Central Committee as a justification for his blood purge, and specifically denounced in Khrushchev's secret speech 19 years later—that the class struggle must become more acute with the progress of socialist construction.[12] The internal Chinese meaning of the argument becomes transparent in the concluding section of Mao's "testament": there the Chinese Party is urged to train loyal successors to the first generation of revolutionaries lest revisionist careerists should gain power and, by relaxing the struggle against the neo-capitalist elements, turn the country away from the true socialist path.

Once again, it is this internal need for unrelenting struggle that accounts for the  peculiar dogmatic character of Chinese opposition to Soviet propaganda of "peaceful coexistence" and the "peaceful road" to Communist power. Stalin, after all, was also concerned to limit his foreign policy risks and to avoid world war, and there is no evidence whatever that the Chinese are seriously bent on provoking a nuclear holocaust. But Stalin did not *talk* so much about "reasonable" imperialists understanding the need for peace, nor did he exchange friendly visits with American presidents; and it was just this talk and these visits of Khrushchev's that appeared particularly objectionable to Mao because of their effect on the ideological climate within the Soviet Union and the bloc. Similarly, Stalin did in fact experiment with the "peaceful road" to power in the first postwar years, both in authorizing the use of "parliamentary" forms for the consolidation of Communist rule in the East European "People's Democracies," and in encouraging the West European Communist leaders to see how successfully they could imitate the example without the presence of the Russian army.[13] But Stalin did not make the successful example of the Prague coup d'état of February 1948 the basis of a general *formula* about the possibility of a peaceful conquest of power, as Khrushchev did in his report to the Twentieth Congress of the CPSU—and Mao fears that such a formula might make the task ahead appear easier and the struggle less bitter both to Communists in underdeveloped countries with revolutionary possibilities and to those in the Communist countries themselves. In the international as in the domestic field, Mao's central charge against the "revisionists" is that their slogans lead to the ideological disarmanent of the Communist ranks.

What all this amounts to is that a different concept of the domestic tasks and nature of a Communist regime entails a different concept of the "world revolution" and of its own role in it. The classical justification of totalitarian Communist rule is the need for permanent social revolution at home and permanent irreconcilable conflict with the non-Communist world, both of which are interpreted as aspects of the class struggle; because the stakes in this struggle are survival or death, it is bound to assume violent forms at crucial moments and can only be conducted effectively by a ruthless dictatorship acting as its international High Command. But if the class struggle is ended at home and domestic social revolution is beginning to give way to peaceful economic evolution, the domestic effort can no longer be presented as merely a sector of a single worldwide struggle, and the link to the international Communist movement is loosened, even ideologically. This change has made it easier for the Soviets to accept the facts of Communist pluralism and to renounce their traditional "leading role." But by the same token, the Chinese Communists' continuing commitment to unceasing revolutionary struggle at home maintains their need for seeing themselves as part of a worldwide revolutionary front; and when this front appeared to be threatened with disintegration because its former commanders had left their posts, the Chinese were willing to assume the command.

### The Prospects for a Maoist International

It has taken years of successive disillusionments for the Chinese leaders to become aware of the full implications of their sense of mission. In 1956–57, they had begun to feel ideologically superior to Stalin's heirs, but had still wanted to keep them in the "leading role" and to guide them quietly behind the scenes. In 1959, following a series of disappointments over Soviet policies, they had begun to criticize their allies in the forum of the international Communist movement, hoping to bring effective pressure to bear on them. By late 1960, having met unexpectedly stubborn resistance, they had come to think in terms of a protracted factional struggle, which, after repeated compromises, would eventually enable them to become the recognized leaders of the world Communist movement; but they probably still thought that a split could be avoided. It seems likely that it was only the Twenty-second Congress of the CPSU —which produced the clash with the Soviet leaders over the Albanian issue and the memory of Stalin and brought the adoption of the Soviet Party's new program—that finally convinced Mao and his team that the Soviet leaders were incurable "revisionists," and that it was the Leninist duty of the Chinese Party to prepare for a split and the creation of a new truly revolutionary International. At any rate, both the ideological output and the organizational tactics of the Chinese changed after this event: ideologically, they broadened the area of the dispute to defend Stalin's memory and to attack Khrushchev's domestic policies; organizationally, they began to prepare positions for an impending break rather than for a long-term internal debate, and worked openly to discredit the Soviets among the nationalists of the underdeveloped countries.

While thus looking toward a split, the Chinese leaders were still trying to avoid the onus of the initiative and also to delay the date: the longer they could work with a separate factional platform and organization inside a formally united movement, as the Bolsheviks had worked inside Russian Social Democracy until 1913, the better, they felt, would be their chances to extend their influence—provided they did not make any more ideological concessions for unity's sake. But when the double crisis of the autumn of 1962—over the Soviet missiles in Cuba and the Sino-Indian border war—showed that the alliance between the two main Communist powers had been eroded to the vanishing point, the course of five European Communist party congresses in the following months made it clear that the Soviets, too, now regarded a split as inevitable and would hasten it if they could. In the circumstances, the bilateral talks held in Moscow in June and July of 1963 were viewed by both sides not as a last chance for reconciliation, but as a final confrontation before the break. On the eve of the talks, the Chinese published their "Proposal for the General Line of the Communist Movement," with its all-out attack on the "revisionist" CPSU program, and the Soviets replied one month later with the "Open Letter" that contained among other charges the specific accusation that the Chinese were supporting splitting activities in various Communist parties. Expulsions and counterexpulsions had in fact begun in a number of countries, and the time had come to justify the organizational schism on grounds of principle. After the Sino-Soviet talks had failed and the Soviets had signed the nuclear test ban agreement with the United States and Britain in late July, the Chinese were ready for that: they called the agreement a betrayal, they began to disclose parts of the secret prehistory of the conflict, and they built up the case for splitting Communist parties that had fallen into the hands of "revisionist traitors."

By the beginning of September 1963, the Chinese Communist press began to publish approving reports about the formation of anti-revisionist splinter groups in various countries.[14] At the same time, the first clearly Peking-financed organs of Communist dissidence made their appearance outside China, after French and Spanish editions of the

"Peking Review" had prepared the way several months before. Later that month, the Indonesian Party leader, D. N. Aidit, reporting on a two-months journey through the leading Communist capitals on his return, proclaimed the principle that true Marxist-Leninists, if expelled by a revisionist party leadership, were entitled to form a new Communist party, and that such "circles, magazines, and new parties," if found to be truly Marxist-Leninist, deserved the support and solidarity of established parties under Marxist-Leninist leadership.[15] On October 26, the deputy head of the Chinese Party's propaganda department, Chou Yang, declared in a speech in Peking that the splitting of revisionist-led parties by Marxist-Leninists sprang from an "inexorable law"—for the surprising dialectical reason that the Communist movement, like everything else, "tends to divide in two." The speech was published two months later,[16] and, more important, its principal arguments recurred in early February 1964 in the seventh of the Chinese Party's official commentaries on the Soviet "Open Letter," entitled "The Leaders of the CPSU are the Greatest Splitters of All Time"; with the full authority of the Chinese Party, this document took the line that in any split between "revisionists" and "Marxist-Leninists," regardless of the factual circumstances, the political guilt rests with the revisionists—in other words, that a pro-Chinese minority cannot do wrong when it splits a pro-Soviet Communist party. During the same period, finally, the Soviet and Chinese Parties had also changed roles with regard to the project of another Communist world conference:[17] in 1962 the Chinese had urged and the Soviets evaded it, but from October 1963 it was the Soviets who sought a showdown conference to achieve a clear majority vote against the Chinese views, and the Chinese who worked to prevent it while they were building up their own new International.*

The Chinese were not, in fact, explicitly speaking of the need for a new international organization; on the contrary, in their polemics against the Soviet leaders they kept stressing the independence and equality of all Communist parties, denying the right of even the most powerful

---

* Both Soviet efforts to call the conference on the broadest possible basis, if at the price of some postponement, and Chinese efforts to prevent other Parties from attending it have continued after Khrushchev's fall; so has the support of each side for breakaway groups from Communist Parties whose leaders have opted for the other. On December 12, 1964, the CPSU announced that the preparatory meeting of the "editorial commission" for the world conference, to which 25 other Parties had been invited, would start on March 1, 1965. Rival congresses of the pro-Moscow majority and the pro-Peking minority of the Indian Communist Party were held by the latter in Calcutta at the beginning of November and by the former in Bombay in mid-December. The Ninth Congress of the Japanese Communist Party, held at the end of November, criticized Khrushchev's successors for not abandoning his policies and confirmed the expulsion of a pro-Soviet minority, which sub-

outside party to interfere in any party's internal affairs and asserting that there could be no return to the times of the Comintern with its single command center. In practice, however, they behaved exactly as the Soviet leaders had behaved in the formative years of the Comintern. They used their authority to redefine the principles of revolutionary doctrine and strategy, and to decide which party or splinter group was "truly" revolutionary in accordance with those principles. They used their diplomatic missions and publishing offices in various countries to make contact with dissident revolutionary groups, to subsidize their activists by employing them, and to finance their publications.

They also indicated their willingness to combine fission with fusion: just as Lenin, in his effort to rally all militant revolutionaries, had appealed to revolutionary syndicalists even if they had no Marxist traditions and had rebuked the "intellectual arrogance" of those old-line Marxists who wished to reject them on those grounds, so the Chinese were now saying that the Algerian FLN had proved itself a more revolutionary force than the Algerian Communist Party, and Castro a better revolutionary leader than the old Cuban Communists.[18] For the new International in its initial stage, what mattered most was clearly to attract the most militant revolutionary elements of any country, regardless whether they came from inside or outside its established Communist party. This was most clearly shown in the one directly international organ that was created, also in September 1963, on the Chinese line and with Chinese money: the monthly "Revolution," published in several languages from Paris as a magazine for Africa, Latin America, and Asia, based its appeal on no narrower doctrine than that of violent anticolonialism. In fact, the Chinese leaders are convinced that this must also be the main basis of the appeal of the new International as a whole.

---

sequently announced the intention of holding a rival congress in the spring. *The Times* (London), December 3, 1964.

When the preparatory international meeting was finally held in March 1965 on a "consultative" basis, the Communist parties of China, Korea, Vietnam, Japan, Indonesia, Albania, and Rumania refused to attend. Though the colorless communiqué took no stand on the disputed issues of substance, appealed once more for an end to public polemics, and virtually conceded that no world conference would be called without the prior agreement of the Chinese and their supporters, the Chinese subsequently denounced the meeting as a "splitters' conference" because it had admitted delegates of the official, pro-Moscow Communist parties of India, Brazil, and Australia despite the existence of rival, pro-Chinese parties; they also announced their intention to intensify support for such parties of the "revolutionary left" and to continue polemics until the complete capitulation of the "revisionist" Soviet leaders. (Communiqué in *Pravda*, March 10, 1965; joint editorial of *Red Flag* and *People's Daily*, March 23; Chou En-lai interview with K. S. Karol, *New Statesman*, March 26, 1965.)

Long before the factional struggle began, the Chinese had decided that their main chances of expanding their international influence lay in the underdeveloped countries of Asia, Africa, and Latin America. As early as the end of 1939, Mao had first expressed the view that the revolution in all colonial and semicolonial countries would follow the same "laws" as in China; and on the morrow of final victory in the civil war, Liu Shao-chi had proclaimed the Chinese revolution as a model for all those countries at the Peking conference of Asian and Australasian trade-unionists.[19] During the years that followed, China's authority among the Asian Communists had grown, apparently with toleration from Stalin; and after Stalin's death the Bandung conference had greatly increased China's prestige among Afro-Asian governments, and the formation of the "Afro-Asian Solidarity Committee" had given her access to useful machinery for influencing the most militant revolutionary elements of both continents.[20]

By the time the factional struggle with the Soviets opened in 1959–60, colonial "wars of national liberation" had become, in Peking's concept, a vital means for diverting the strength of the imperialists—above all the main enemy, the United States—and wearing them down; now they also became a useful lever for disrupting the Soviet diplomacy of "peaceful coexistence," that is, for interfering with any plans for a Soviet-American dialogue. In the April documents of 1960, which constituted Peking's first coherent factional platform, the need to support anti-imperialist uprisings without regard to the risk of escalation or to the consequences for overall diplomatic relations with the enemy became one of the central theses. When the Soviets advised the Algerian FLN to negotiate with de Gaulle, they could be accused of opportunism; when they supported Cuba with economic aid and demagogic threats against the United States, they could be embroiled with the Americans; when they got involved in the Congo troubles, both lines could be pursued by Peking in turn. In any violent colonial conflict, Chinese interest was clearly on the side of militancy, while Soviet interest was divided between the wish to inflict defeat on the imperialists and the need to control the risk; and the Chinese missed no chance for pointing out the difference to the Communists and sympathizers from the countries concerned. It is hardly surprising that both at the 1960 Moscow conference of 81 Communist parties and at the meetings of the World Federation of Trade Unions and the World Peace Movement, the Chinese line found a sympathetic echo chiefly among some of the delegates from the underdeveloped continents, and that support for it proved much stronger in the Afro-Asian Solidarity Organization than in any other international "front."

It is true that some of the revolutionary movements which thus received Chinese support were by no means Communist-controlled and could be described as corresponding to the "Chinese model" only in that they were anti-imperialist, peasant-based, and above all violent. But as the bulk of the Communist parties of the advanced industrial countries took sides against China in the factional struggle, it became increasingly obvious to Peking that all the chances for revolutions, whether under Communist or non-Communist leadership, were concentrated in the colonial, ex-colonial, or semi-colonial countries, while in the advanced countries, however large their Communist parties, there seemed to exist no immediate potential for revolutionary struggle at all. In Western Europe and North America the Communist parties, except for insignificant minorities, had welcomed Khrushchev's "revisionist" thesis of the "peaceful road" to power. But the Communists of Vietnam and Laos were fighting a civil war under Chinese guidance. The Cuban Communists had, however reluctantly, joined Fidel Castro's revolution, and the Venezuelan and various other Latin American Communists were trying to imitate its partisan strategy. Strong factional opposition to the "peaceful road" strategy had developed—originally, it seems, independent of any Chinese stimulation—among the Brazilian Communists since 1957 and among the Indian Communists since 1958, while the Japanese Communists were expelling a "revisionist" group at the very moment of the Twenty-second Congress of the CPSU.[21] Both the early struggle for national liberation in countries where the Communist parties were weak or nonexistent (as in Africa) and the later Communist-led struggle against the continuing influence of the "imperialists" in formally independent countries thus seemed to offer the scene of irreconcilable, violent conflict that was required by the Chinese vision—and with it corresponding chances for Chinese leadership.

Once the Chinese had determined on preparing for a new, truly revolutionary International, it was natural that they should recognize this geographical shift in the main theater of the world revolution. They did so by adopting, in early 1963, the formula that the countries of Asia, Africa, and Latin America now constitute "the main focus of global contradictions" and "the storm center of the world revolution," and that the struggle of their peoples would be "decisive" also for the ultimate victory of the proletariat of the advanced industrial countries.[22] They have since stuck to this formula in the face of all Soviet charges of "racialism" and all warnings against weakening the colonial liberation struggle by "isolating" it from the cause of the advanced "socialist" countries and from the movement of the Western industrial proletariat.[23] This thesis is basic for the possibility of a new, Sino-centric International in that it denies to the conflict between the Soviet-centered "socialist world system" and the imperialist powers its role as the main axis of the international class struggle. But it also constitutes the germ of a new doctrine that is incompatible with the teachings of either Marx or Lenin.

For Karl Marx, it was axiomatic that the victory of socialism would be brought about by the industrial proletariat of the most advanced countries on the basis of the highest level of economic development that capitalism could achieve. Lenin broke with this concept by seizing power in backward Russia on the ground that Russia constituted "the weakest link" in the imperialist chain, and by proclaiming the alliance between the revolutionary proletariat of the industrial West and the nationalist revolution of the colonial East; but he never left any doubt that he regarded the class struggle of the proletariat as the decisive force, compared with which the nationalist movements of the colonial and semi-colonial countries would be mere auxiliaries. The new Chinese doctrine reverses this relationship, treating in fact the working class of the advanced countries as mere auxiliaries of the peoples of the underdeveloped countries, and unreliable auxiliaries at that; it thus adopts a position that was explicitly criticized by Lenin and Stalin in the early years of the Comintern, when similar views had been expressed by Sultan Galiev and for a time also by the Indian Communist M. N. Roy.[24] Nor can the Leninist orthodoxy of the new Chinese position be rescued by the fiction that the leading role of the proletariat in the new International will be assured by the leadership of the Chinese Communists: for though Lenin himself evolved a similar fiction to justify the possibility of Soviet regimes in Asian territories without an industrial working class, he never regarded such territories as the central part of the international revolutionary front. Moreover, the Bolshevik Party in Lenin's time, though in fact independent of working-class interests thanks to its centralist organization, was at least based on a predominantly proletarian membership and allied with important sections of the West European proletariat. In the case of Mao's party today, however, the claim to represent the industrial proletariat has become wholly fictitious: it rests not on its history, its composition, or its international influence, but only on the vestigial notion that whoever conducts a militant revolutionary struggle against imperialist monopoly capitalism expresses *ipso facto* the true class consciousness of the proletariat.

Yet just in its conflict with both Marxism and Leninism, Mao's new doctrine is based on a recognition of some of the decisive historical facts of our time. In the 40 years since Lenin died, the workers of the advanced industrial countries have become less and less revolutionary, with the result that in no such country have the Communists been able to lead a victorious revolutionary movement. By contrast, it is in the underdeveloped countries that huge masses of people, living in extreme insecurity on the edge of starvation, can be said to have "nothing to lose but their chains," and their despair has offered opportunities for a number of victorious revolutions, including Communist revolutions. The course of contemporary history has thus made it impossible for the Communist leaders to be faithful to Lenin's Marxist belief in the industrial working class and to Lenin's passion for revolutionary struggle at the same time, though they have tried hard not to admit the fact to themselves. Under the pressure of their conflict with the Soviets, the Chinese leaders, whose links to European Marxism and to the industrial proletariat have always been tenuous, have at last made a choice: their new International will be wholly revolutionary, but only marginally proletarian.

What, then, are the chances that further revolutions of the underprivileged peoples will in fact lead to the victory of totalitarian parties committed to permanent, irreconcilable struggle against the "imperialists," and that the Chinese Communists will be able to guide the development of these new totalitarian regimes for any length of time?

In trying to answer the first part of the question, it may be useful to group the bewildering variety of prerevolutionary crisis situations in these countries into a few main types. First, there are the few African populations still struggling against direct colonial rule or formal white supremacy. Second, there is the much larger number of politically sovereign, "semi-colonial" countries whose problems of economic and social development, difficult enough in themselves, are complicated by the existence of foreign capitalist combines holding key positions in the national economy—combines that often have no positive interest in the overall development of the country concerned and sometimes are directly opposed to it. Third, there are the newly independent countries whose regimes, quite apart from any influence of foreign capital, are proving for various reasons unable to create a functioning administration and a sense of national loyalty, yet are continuing to enjoy Western "imperialist" support simply because they are in power and often appear as the only available alternatives to Communist victory.

In the first type of situation, Communist leadership has hitherto been exceptional: only in the Vietnamese uprising against French rule did the Communists lead from the start. The Chinese Communists themselves emphatically recognize that such a contingency, however desirable, should not be a condition for their support of an anti-imperialist revolt: for years they have gone out of their way to extol the Algerian FLN, despite its non-Communist ideology and leadership, as a model for other oppressed nations;[25] and while hoping for stronger Communist influence among the underground movements in South Africa and the Portuguese colonies, they will similarly support them in any case. Yet the FLN in power has shown no desire to continue militant conflict with the West for conflict's sake; whether it will eventually return to such conflict will depend neither on the memories of its heroic period nor on Chinese advice, but on the obstacles it encounters in trying to develop its country and on the ability of its leaders to cope with them. Generally speaking, the "first phase" of the anti-colonial revolution—the struggle for political independence—is unlikely to result in Communist regimes of any kind.

The second type of prerevolutionary situation is widespread both in Latin America and in the Middle East, and examples occur in all underdeveloped regions. The histories of Mossadegh's rule in Persia and of Kassem's Iraqi revolution as well as of Nasser's Egypt, and of Perón's Argentina as well as of the Bolivian and Venezuelan revolutions, offer examples of the political explosions that may result if independent national development has to be achieved against the joint resistance of native oligarchies and foreign capitalist interests. So far, Fidel Castro's Cuban revolution has been the only one of this type that has actually issued in Communist rule, yet it seems to have greater potentialities as a model than that of Ho Chi Minh among the first type; for while non-Communist movements for political independence have almost universally succeeded, many of the non-Communist revolts against "semi-colonial" dependence have failed. Regardless of Castro's cautious maneuvering in the Sino-Soviet conflict, the close affinities betwen the "Fidelist" guerrilla strategy as taught by Guevara and Mao's type of partisan warfare are notorious, and throughout Latin America today the influence of the Fidelist and the Chinese model tend to merge.[26] On the whole, the prospects that further revolutions against "semi-colonial" dependence may turn Communist are serious, because here the link between nationalism and anticapitalism is inherent in the situation; they can be reduced only if the Western powers, and particularly the United States, go out of their way to dissociate themselves from the vested interests of Western private corporations in those countries.

Yet there are indications that the "classical" chances for Chinese-inspired Communist revolutions arise in the third type of crisis: the one that occurs where the leaders of a newly independent country fail, for whatever reason, to create a viable state and, *a fortiori,* to solve the problems of economic development—particularly if those leaders, after successfully conducting the original struggle for independence, have meanwhile been accepted by the West. After all, Mao's original conquest of China was the victory of such a "second wave" revolution—one that exploited the failure of the once revolutionary Kuomintang to cope with the immense difficulties of Chinese unification and modernization after decades of war and civil war. Today, comparable failures are offering opportunities for a variety of promising strategies to Chinese-oriented Communist parties in several Southeast Asian countries. The Indonesian Communists were seeking, for a long time successfully, to profit from the administrative and economic ineffectiveness of Sukarno's "guided democracy" by first collaborating with him, involving him in conflict with the West, infiltrating his machinery of government, and finally inheriting his power; the Vietnamese Communists have profited from the different but equally marked ineffectiveness of the bureaucratic-military regime in South Vietnam to expand their guerrilla warfare in the teeth of all American support for their opponents. These "second wave" opportunities are not identical with the "second phase" of the anti-colonial revolution foreseen by Leninist theory: just as in China in the forties, they arise not from the class struggle of the proletariat against the rule of the "national bourgeoisie," but from mass despair in a climate of general political decay. (The Chinese do not even hesitate to exploit the weakness of some of the new states by promoting purely tribal revolts, as now in the Congo!) But as China's own case has shown, the chances of the "second wave" revolution are nonetheless real for not fitting into the traditional Leninist schema.

We must thus reckon with the prospect that further totalitarian revolutions of a more or less "Chinese" type may be victorious in various parts of the underdeveloped world, and we can be sure that Mao's China will give them any aid and encouragement of which it is capable. But it does not follow that the regimes emerging from such totalitarian movements, or even the movements themselves before the seizure of power, will be willing to submit to Chinese leadership in the way in which all Communists submitted to Soviet leadership for several decades. There are, in fact, at least three major obstacles to this.

First, the revolutionary movements on which the Chinese tend to lean are much more strongly nationalist than those with which Lenin built the Third International: after all, the Comintern arose from a reaction to the "betrayal of internationalism" by the official socialist parties in the First World War, whereas the new "Sinintern" is to be largely based on the "betrayal of the national liberation struggle" by the Soviets.

Second, for many of the movements in question, China is not the only available, nor even a sufficient, source of support: Castro may well regard China as more reliable than Russia, but he has to rely on Russia nevertheless, because the Soviets can offer him so much more of what he needs.

Third, Russia was the unique model for all Communists until at least 1949. Now Russia has lost her uniqueness, but that does not mean that China has automatically gained it, even in the eyes of those Communist parties and governments that incline to her side of the schism.

The Chinese Communists themselves are sufficiently aware of these limitations to disclaim any thought of returning to a "world party" with the rigid, single-centered discipline of the Comintern. They may in fact exert close organizational control over the pro-Chinese splinter groups in the West that depend on them for funds and publicity, and over such traditionally dependent Communist underground parties as those of Malaya and Thailand, most of whose members are Chinese. Their influence may be dominant in helping the left wings of the Indian, and of course of the Nepalese, Communists to organize their separate parties, and it has been traditionally strong with the Communist Party in Japan; but they could not afford to interfere in the least with the autonomy of the powerful Communist Party of Indonesia, which made a point of taking its time and listening to both sides before it officially joined the "Chinese camp." Again, North Korea behaved for a number of years like a Chinese satellite, but the Communist rulers of Albania have joined the Chinese cause by their free decision and have made an independent contribution to the dispute, and North Vietnam, for all her dependence on Chinese backing in her military struggle in the South, could not simply be ordered to take the Chinese position but had to be slowly—and perhaps incompletely—won over.

But while the Chinese Communists can and do renounce any claim to disciplinary subordination in their new International, they cannot renounce the claim to ideological leadership: they have always believed that no united international movement is possible without a recognized ideological authority, and as we have seen, the schism means to them that they now have to play this role. The logic of this claim to ideological leadership has not only driven them to elaborate their version of the Communist doctrine more and more thoroughly, just as the Leninist version of Marxism was thoroughly elaborated only in the context of the worldwide break with the democratic socialists; it has also compelled them to find a doctrinal justification for their own claim to uniqueness—that they are the only great power actually engaged in building socialism and eventually communism.

It is in that context that Mao's charges of July 1964 about the "restoration of capitalism" not only in Yugoslavia but also in Russia itself acquire their true international significance. They serve not only to denounce the "Khrushchev clique" and to explain to the Chinese Communists that they must in future stand alone without counting on the Soviet alliance, but also to "prove" to the Communists and revolutionary nationalists of the underdeveloped regions whom China wants to lead that there is no alternative. If Russia is going capitalist again thanks to the alliance between the re-emerging private businessmen and kulaks, the corrupt bureaucrats and grafters, and the "revisionist traitors" at the top who tolerate and protect them; if Russia's new spirit of less visible controls and increased emphasis on material incentives and comforts is a capitalist spirit, as Mao's "testament" of July 1964 claims, then the schism is not merely about questions of strategy and tactics, not even merely about orthodoxy versus heresy: it is a conflict between a socialist and a capitalist power.[27] The Soviet Union is not merely an unreliable ally—it is ruled by traitors who have joined the enemy camp. To China, as the only great power still following the true path of socialism, has fallen the task of carrying the banner; henceforth, to struggle for socialism means to accept China's leadership.

Yet this argument for the uniqueness of China contains both dangers to her own development and weaknesses from the viewpoint of her international attraction; for it depends on a rigidly egalitarian and military concept of the road to socialism that rejects all privileges for scarce technical, economic, and administrative cadres and deprecates any belief in material incentives in favor of a cult of collective enthusiasm and heroic poverty. Unless this dogma is radically revised (which might conceivably occur after Mao's death), it will add to the many objective difficulties of China's economic development a self-made obstacle that could well prove unsurmountable; indeed, one is tempted to wonder whether it does not really express a half-conscious tendency of the Chinese leaders to give up the near-hopeless struggle for industrializing China without major foreign aid and to seek instead to conserve their political order on the present low economic level by glorifying its social justice and collective discipline.

But such a "socialism" of "high-minded but hungry people sitting around an empty table in complete equality," as Khrushchev once expressed it, would lack one of the main attractions hitherto exerted by the Communist bloc on the intelligentsia of the underdeveloped countries—the attraction of a model for quick modernization. Indeed, the passion to catch up with Western productivity and power implies at least a partial acceptance of Western values; conversely, Mao's increasingly complete rejection of those values is incompatible with that obsession with material productivity which the Bolsheviks took over from their Western teacher, Karl Marx, and the new nations from their former imperialist rulers. It is, of course, conceivable that the Chinese reversal of the order of priorities will appeal to some of the political elites in Asia and Africa, particularly in countries where the problems of economic development appear increasingly insoluble; Communism of the Chinese type would then become not a model for development, but a model for accepting its failure and reacting by a final extrusion of the influence of Western civilization. But short of either such a generalized withdrawal from the present fascination with economic development, or a radical change in Chinese economic and social doctrine, it would appear that Communist China's chances of being accepted as a guide for "building socialism" in developing countries are much poorer than its chances of serving as a guide for the revolutionary seizure of power.

If this is true, it limits severely the prospects of maintaining Chinese authority in a new International. For it means that while revolutionary movements in the underdeveloped world will gladly accept Chinese ideological guidance along with other forms of support, successful revolutionary governments will, unless physically dependent on China, tend to keep their own counsel and refuse to recognize Peking's "leading role." Whenever possible, they will continue to accept support from both Russia and China, as Cuba was doing and Vietnam still is doing; and if they are forced to make a choice, those who are not in China's physical power sphere may well prefer the protector that demands the least ideological conformity and offers the most material help. This means that Castro's Cuba, despite its interest in guerrilla revolutions, is unlikely to join a Chinese-led International. It also means that though the Indonesian Communists may be expected to become one of the most important founder members of such an International, a Communist-governed Indonesia would hardly submit to China's ideological authority for long. The Chinese effort to build up a new International may have an important stimulating effect on Communist and semi-Communist revolutionary movements in the underdeveloped world. But the new body itself will be unstable, and may decay much more rapidly than its parent.

## The Transformation of the Soviet Camp

We may assume that the Soviet decision to take measures against the Chinese faction even at the risk of an open break dates from the clash at the Twenty-second Congress, just as did the Chinese decision to prepare actively for the split. The diplomatic rupture with Albania and the quiet expulsion of Molotov, Malenkov, and Kaganovich, the leaders of the "anti-party group,"[28] showed a new realization of the urgent need to deprive Mao's factional allies of any influence in the European Soviet bloc, though in both cases there were also hesitations and inconsistencies indicating a sense of the political risks involved and perhaps a disagreement about tactics within the Soviet leadership. With the issuing of a number of documents and reports on the dispute by the French, Italian, and Belgian Communists in early 1962,[29] a more active campaign was also set in motion among pro-Soviet Communist parties outside the bloc. Finally, the determination of the Soviet leaders to make no further concessions for the sake of compromise became visible in December 1961, in the open voting down of a Chinese-sponsored resolution at the Stockholm session of the World Peace Council, and again the following spring, in the refusal to entertain the Chinese-supported "neutral" proposals for an early Communist world conference unless all participants would pledge themselves to abide by majority decisions.[30]

Nevertheless, throughout most of 1962 the Soviets were not attacking their principal opponents by name in their own press; like the Chinese, they were maneuvering to avoid responsibility for the break even while accepting its inevitability. Only after the public Chinese attacks on their own conduct of the Cuban missile crisis in the autumn of that year did the Soviets encourage explicit criticism of the Chinese at the congresses of European Communist parties and join in it; and only after the Chinese had, in the summer of 1963, come out with their root and branch condemnation of Soviet domestic policy and of the CPSU program, and had at the same time weakened their own propagandist appeal by opposing the ban on nuclear tests, did the Soviets conclude that it was now in their interest to complete the formal and final split, and therefore to call a world conference.

The Soviet decisions first to risk, then to promote, and finally to hasten the split thus took place in interaction with two other major developments in Soviet policy: the climax and final failure of Khrushchev's attempt at a world political breakthrough, followed by the turn to a new effort at Russo-American détente; and the growing preoccupation of the Soviet leaders with the need to improve the performance of the Soviet and East European economies—including their performance in the satisfaction of consumers' wants. The Soviet leaders' concept of the form that relations among the "loyal" Communist parties should take after the break with the Chinese has been shaped by this new situation, and by the somewhat contradictory needs arising from it, as well as by the growing awareness of their irrecoverable loss of authority and by the difficulty of rallying parties for an International that was no longer all-inclusive.

On the whole, both the collapse of Khrushchev's worldwide offensive and the bitterness of the conflict with Peking seem to have inclined the Soviet leaders to make their links with other Communist parties less rigid than at any time since 1920—to seek a loose and broad fraternal alliance rather than unity on a strict and narrow doctrinal basis. After the Cuban crisis, a decisive advance of the "world revolution" appears far more distant than Khrushchev believed in the preceding years; after the schism, the relevance to Soviet greatness of further Communist revolutions, even where they are possible, appears far more doubtful than before. Now that experience has shown that the Soviet Union may not be able to control the policy of other revolutionary powers, the Soviet leaders must be increasingly concerned that other powers should not attempt to control their own by forcing on them ideological arguments in an international framework; and that means that they must now favor a form of international association founded on broadly defined common objectives and mutual ideological nonaggression rather than on the search for precise doctrinal unity. Finally, the greater the toleration for differences of opinion in such an alliance, the broader support the Soviets may hope to rally for it in the face of Chinese obstruction.

This is, of course, a "revisionist" concept of what the links between a Communist power and the international movement ought to be like; it corresponds closely to what the Yugoslavs, with growing support from the Italian Communists, have advocated in recent years. In fact, the first indications that the Soviets were moving toward that sort of concept were furnished by their demonstrative rapprochement with Tito's regime since 1962 and by their defense of it against Chinese attacks—on the grounds that fraternal solidarity was possible without complete ideological agreement.[31] Since then, the Soviets have further developed this argument by insisting that Yugoslavia, despite some "errors," was still a "socialist" country and that the same applied to Albania on the opposite pole[32]—thus making clear their own willingness to remain in a common international association with both "revisionist" and "dogmatist" parties and governments, provided only that all would refrain from hostile polemics against the Soviet Union. Yet the fact that this decision was not easily reached is attested by the notorious affair of the 1963 May Day slogans, which in their original version failed to describe Yugoslavia as "building socialism" and had to be corrected in this sense three days later[33]—in the middle of polemics conducted against the Chinese on this very point.

By 1964, the Soviet concept of the future form of fraternal relations among Communist parties had further to be clarified in the context of the effort to call another Communist world conference. Here the question of Yugoslav participation did not arise immediately, because the first step proposed was a preparatory meeting of the same 26 parties that had prepared the Moscow conference of 1960; and among these, Yugoslavia had not been included following her failure to subscribe to the declaration of the 1957 conference. But now the Italian Communists voiced openly, and some of the ruling East European parties internally, doubts about the usefulness of such a conference that amounted to the setting of conditions for their participation. The Italians joined with the Yugoslavs in demanding that the condemnation of "revisionism" as the main danger in the declarations of 1957 and 1960 must be cancelled; they called for assurances that the conference would be used for a constructive examination of new international developments and not for an "excommunication" of the Chinese deviators; and they flatly opposed the principle of an international discipline that would oblige the minority of such a conference to carry out decisions taken by a majority of the Parties present.[34]

The Soviets, in their turn, were clearly inclined to drop the anathema against revisionism once the new conference met, even while they were still basing their preparations on the continued formal validity of the 1960 decisions; and they denied any intention to hold a conference of excommunication when they sent out their invitations.[35] But they tried to avoid an explicit climbdown on the principle of majority decisions, which they had so far defended against the Chinese. On August 10, 1964, a *Pravda* editorial pointed out that the conference must at least result in a binding pledge of mutual ideological nonaggression: "Even if we do not succeed in working out full agreement on all questions and in finding a common language, there is every reason to agree at the conference that the Communist parties will undertake to heed each other's opinions, to collaborate conscientiously in those areas where their positions and interests coincide, and to refrain in the future from any action harmful to the Communist parties that aggravates their difficulties and brings happiness only to our class enemies." And when Togliatti, in his last memorandum to Khrushchev, restated the case for preferring full autonomy

over international discipline, and the Italian Central Committee published the text after Togliatti's death despite Soviet objections, the Soviet
leaders manifested their continued indecision by publishing the text of
the Italian leader's "testament" in *Pravda* on September 10, but the next
day publishing the theses of their own Institute of Marxism-Leninism
on the centenary of the First International—theses that defended the
"obligatory observance of the decisions adopted within the International,
with subordination of the minority to the will of the majority," as one
of the "principles of proletarian internationalism" that retain their importance today. Subsequently, however, Khrushchev's successors had to
postpone the preparatory meeting, originally scheduled for December 15,
1964, until March 1, 1965,[36] and to declare it "purely consultative" in order
to assure the participation of at least 18 of the 25 foreign Parties invited.
The communiqué published by *Pravda* on March 10 indicated that any
hope for future majority decisions had been definitely abandoned, and
that the intention to call a world conference without the pro-Chinese
Parties if necessary had at least temporarily been dropped—in response
to the insistence both of the more independent-minded pro-Soviet Parties, led by the Italians, and of the "neutral" Cubans on the "principle
of unanimity."

Such a decision implies a major sacrifice of principle on the part of the
Soviets. For it recognizes the "equality and independence" of all national
Parties to an extent that will by its very nature exclude not only any return to organizational discipline, but any return to Soviet leadership
based on doctrinal authority. In some ways, the new fraternal alliance
of the pro-Soviet Parties will thus be little more than what Lenin contemptuously called the Second International—a "letter-box." Yet as it
would in fact be grouped around the Soviet Union, it would still be a
channel through which the latter, by virtue of the prestige of its military
and economic power, could exert considerable influence on important
movements in many countries; and it would enable the Soviet leaders to
tell their own people that though Moscow has ceased to be the headquarters of an embattled army of the world revolution, their country is
still the beloved and admired stronghold of the great majority of the
world's progressive forces. Such an arrangement would therefore be in
harmony with an internal situation in which the Soviet leaders, while
trying to legitimate their rule increasingly by their domestic economic
achievement, still feel the need for an international legitimation as well.

Moreover, the Soviets may well calculate that what will be lost in ideological conformity may be more than regained in breadth of influence
in areas where Marxist-Leninist orthodoxy has hitherto acted as a self-
imposed limitation on the Communist appeal to nationalist revolution-

ary movements. In fact, since the late months of 1963, Soviet writers have begun to underpin the tactical efforts for closer relations with some of the ruling parties of ex-colonial countries by admitting the possibility— also first put forward by the Yugoslav and Italian revisionists—that some of these countries, having embarked on the "non-capitalist road of development" thanks to the sincere anti-imperialist and pro-socialist orientation of their ruling parties, might actually advance toward "socialism" without the leadership, or even the separate existence, of a Communist party.[37] Their views were given solemn official sanction when "Comrade Ben Bella" was hailed, during his visit to the Soviet Union in the spring of 1964, as the head of a party and government engaged in "building socialism"; and they were embodied in a resolution of "representatives of the Communists"—not the Communist parties—"of the Arab countries" later that year.[38] This suggests that the Soviets may seriously hope to get some of these ruling left-wing nationalist parties—parties that have never accepted a commitment to "Marxism-Leninism" but feel that they share their anti-imperialist and "socialist" outlook with the Communists—to join a reconstructed, loose International, or at least to take part in regular international conferences, particularly if the participation of Yugoslavia proved that this could be done without joining a Soviet-commanded military alliance at the same time.

For at least two years, however, the described tendency of the Soviet leaders to put their international party relations on a looser but broader basis had to contend with the simultaneous Soviet desire to tighten the ties of control in the region where inter-party relations matter most—the Soviet bloc proper in Eastern Europe.

Both the Sino-Soviet conflict and the growing Soviet emphasis on economic performance have contributed to this countertrend. The need to eliminate pro-Chinese factions in the Soviets' own power sphere led to demands that all the East European states should follow the Soviet rupture with Albania, to fairly open pressure for the removal of Chervenkov and his followers at the time of the Bulgarian party congress in late 1962, and to more discreet urgings to make de-Stalinization belatedly effective in Czechoslovakia. At the same time, the Soviet leaders reacted to the—for them—surprising success of the West European Common Market by pressing for speedier progress toward a rational "socialist division of labor" within the Comecon. By 1962 Khrushchev had come to realize that the complete independence of the national planning machineries of the member states was in fact favoring autarchic nationalist tendencies to the detriment of the bloc. Thus when, at a meeting held in Moscow in June 1962, he called for the creation of a new Executive Committee of the Council for Mutual Economic Aid consisting of party leaders as well as for the forming of a number of supranational economic organs, he was not simply looking for the best institutional forms for bloc-wide rationalization; he was seeking to enlist the loyalty of the party leaders in the struggle to overcome the vested interests of the national planning bureaucracies.[39] As soon as one of these leaders, the Rumanian Gheorghiu-Dej, refused to cooperate in sacrificing his country's heavy industrial projects to a Soviet-sponsored supranational plan, the Soviets found that in this region at least, they were still in need of their traditional "leading role." But they also found, much to their surprise, that the decay of their authority had gone so far that they could no longer enforce it even on a recalcitrant "satellite" by any means short of physical power—and this they were now unwilling to use.

The surprise of the Soviets was not unnatural. They had accepted the fact that they could not control sovereign Communist states that had arisen from independent revolutions; that had been proved not only by the conflict with China, but by Yugoslavia's defiance of Stalin and Albania's challenge to Khrushchev. But they had never regarded the East European Communist regimes that owed their existence to Soviet military domination of that region as sovereign states; it was, after all, the obvious fact that these regimes depended on Soviet external protection for maintaining their domestic rule that had earned them the Western label of "satellites." When after Stalin's death Khrushchev had introduced a number of reforms in this empire—ending its brutal exploitation, reducing detailed Soviet supervision, and even granting the local Communist leaders some representation in collective organs of military and economic coordination—he had meant to modernize the form but not to abandon the substance of Soviet control; and he had still stuck to this concept when he restored the unity of the bloc after the October events of 1956.

In fact, of course, those events had shown the first serious weakening of Soviet control in this area, owing to the crisis of Soviet authority that followed de-Stalinization. The Polish Communists' change of leadership amounted to a first step toward emancipation from satellite status. Yet the Hungarian uprising proved once again to all the East European Communist regimes that their very survival would be in danger without Soviet protection. On the basis of these experiences, the 1957 reconstruction of the bloc granted the satellites greater domestic autonomy than Khrushchev had originally intended, but at the price of strict subordination to Soviet foreign policy and ideological authority. At the same time, the Soviets had begun to work for a more differentiated division of labor, not only for economic reasons but also as a means to strengthen the ties of self-interest that would bind each member state to the bloc.

This settlement worked well enough at first: during the next five years, nothing dramatic happened in Eastern Europe, if we leave the Albanian issue aside. Yet it would appear in retrospect that it was just this period of quiet consolidation that prepared the ground for the "de-satellitization" of Eastern Europe. As most of the Communist rulers used their autonomy to make life more tolerable for their subjects, while the Hungarian experience caused a general loss of hope for an over-throw of Communist rule, the growing resignation of the peoples led to a loss of fear and a growing self-assurance among the Communist leaders that reduced their sense of dependence on Soviet protection. Con-versely, as some of those leaders became bolder in standing up to the Soviets on behalf of national interests, they came to be accepted by growing sections of their own people, with however many reservations, as national spokesmen, and their need to hold down their subjects by force was correspondingly lessened.

The pace of the process and the mixture of its ingredients have, of course, differed from country to country, according to the history of each regime, its assets for trade relations outside the bloc, and the degree of its continuing sense of danger from the West. In Hungary, the shock of 1956 has made the leaders probably more inclined to make conces-sions to their people but less inclined to quarrel with the Soviets than any of their neighbors. In Poland, fear of German "revanchism" has contributed both to close cooperation with the Soviets and to a renewed "hardening" of the regime. Economic dependence on the bloc is a for-midable tie for Bulgaria, while Rumania's resources give her possibil-ities for extra-bloc trade that combine with the total absence of threats from the West to encourage her independence. But nowhere has the simple satellite relationship to the Soviets survived, with the one excep-tion of Eastern Germany. There, the magnetism of a free and prosper-ous state comprising three-quarters of the German people makes impos-sible any national identification of the forcibly separated fourth quarter with its Soviet-imposed rulers.

The Soviet bloc in Eastern Europe thus had already moved a con-siderable distance away from the old type of subordination to Soviet leadership in the direction of a classical alliance, centered around the military and economic preponderance of a leading power but limited by various national interests, when the open Chinese challenge to Soviet authority and the threat of a split accelerated the change and forced it into the consciousness of the participants. Outside Albania, none of the

East European regimes showed any inclination to side with China on the issues in dispute, the wistful hankerings of some bureaucratic cliques for the Stalinist past notwithstanding.[40] But nearly all of them felt that if they decided to reject the Chinese views, this would be their own free decision made in the light of their own experience and interests, not the result of an automatic loyalty to Soviet authority, and that it would also be their own affair when and how they wished to give expression to this decision. Hence there has been considerable differentiation both in the handling of state relations with Albania and in the form and timing of public polemics with China by the East European Communists, and considerable reluctance to endorse the Soviet call for another world conference without an assurance of Chinese participation. The East European Communist leaders realized that Sino-Soviet rivalry *within* a factionally divided movement gave them increased freedom of maneuver in relation to the Soviets, and they were unwilling to sanction a formal and final split so long as there was danger that this might lead to a revival of Soviet claims for doctrinal authority—at least for their own area.

The issue was brought to a test by the Rumanian resistance to Soviet plans for bloc-wide economic integration. The Rumanian objections to these plans, which were due to Rumania's special economic interests as an industrially underdeveloped country whose chances for independent industrialization were favored by highly saleable raw material resources, were not shared by the other East European states; in fact, the plans in question were largely based on Polish proposals. But the Rumanians raised the question of principle whether a sovereign Communist government could be forced to submit to supranational planning against its will; and the Chinese, by publicly supporting their stand for the economic sovereignty of any "socialist" state,[41] made it impossible for the Soviets to use physical pressure against them, as this might have driven many wavering parties to the Chinese side. The Soviets' loss of uncontested authority, skillfully exploited by the Rumanians in their "objective" presentation of both the Soviet and Chinese points of view and their attempts at "mediation," thus hampered Khrushchev even in using the weight of Russian economic and military power against a rebellious ex-satellite,* and when Khrushchev tried to achieve a change of

---

* In June 1963, the Rumanians were the only East European Communists to publish large extracts from the Chinese "Proposal for a General Line" before the Soviets did. In March 1964, a Rumanian high-level delegation traveled to Peking and Moscow to attempt mediation, and the Soviet leaders postponed the publication of Suslov's CC report of February 14 in the meantime.

leadership in the Rumanian party during a "private" visit, he failed utterly.

In the spring of 1964, after the failure of Rumanian "mediation" and simultaneously with the belated publication of Suslov's indictment of the Chinese, Khrushchev for the last time publicly suggested the discussion of "organizational forms to improve the continuing exchange of opinions and the coordination of foreign policy between the member countries of the Council for Mutual Economic Aid."[42] It was after this that the Rumanian Central Committee, in its resolution of April 1964, while siding with the Soviets on the main issues of the conflict with China, haughtily criticized the conduct of both sides and also took the occasion to erect the rejection of any form of supranational planning into an "ideological principle."[43] It followed up the resolution with a campaign of information meetings for party cadres with strong anti-Soviet and anti-Khrushchev undertones,[44] and with the demonstrative sending of high-level delegations to Washington and Paris. When the Soviets decided after a brief hesitation to swallow their pride, stop all polemics with the Rumanians, and in fact drop the idea of majority decisions on supranational planning,* it meant that they had abandoned their hope for restoring a more tightly knit control in Eastern Europe; the Rumanians, by using Khrushchev's need to compete with Mao, had not only won their own battle for economic independence, but had ensured that in any Soviet plans for future international cooperation the "broad and loose" concept would prevail—without exceptions for Eastern Europe.

Communism in Eastern Europe is thus likely to survive the schism with a structure that is no longer based on either totalitarian doctrinal unity or one-way imperial control, but on an alliance of differentiated and independent but broadly "like-minded" states accepting a limited measure of leadership from the hegemonial power. Within this region, the growth of pluralism and its reluctant acceptance by the Soviet Union will prove compatible with the preservation of unity to the extent that the ruling parties share common interests. But whenever the constellation of interests should change—for instance by the growth of new opportunities for extra-bloc trade following internal economic reforms in some of those states, or by the disappearance of some of the fears under-

---

* The Soviet retreat began with the Moscow session of the Council for Mutual Economic Aid in July 1963, which endorsed the Rumanian projects for heavy industrial development. Following a flare-up of polemics in the spring of 1964, the Soviet press and radio stopped all criticism of Rumania in July 1964, just before the visit of a high-level Rumanian delegation to Moscow. For the Rumanian statement on this visit, which produced no joint communiqué, see *Agerpress*, July 14, 1964.

lying the alliance—such a structure would have little strength to resist further centrifugal tendencies. Moreover, the lack of a universally recognized model will leave the impulse for further internal revolutionary transformation—the characteristic dynamism of totalitarian regimes—seriously weakened in all of them, and will strengthen the receptivity to "revisionist" economic reforms aimed at improved performance in most of them—particularly if such reforms should first be adopted by the Soviet Union.

It has been suggested above that the increasing preoccupation of the Soviet leaders with economic improvement rather than permanent revolution at home has made it easier for them to accept the facts of Communist pluralism abroad and to seek a looser form of association with the international revolutionary struggle. It is equally true that the irretrievable loss of the Soviet Communists' "leading role" in a single worldwide movement, and the fading of the grandiose visions of a speedy, worldwide revolutionary advance under Soviet leadership, have favored the tendency to shift the ruling party's primary source of legitimation to its role as the architect of domestic economic progress.

The first major step in that direction was taken within a few weeks after the Cuban missile crisis that ended Khrushchev's hopes of a speedy overturn of the world balance of power, at a time when Chinese taunts about a "Munich" were still reverberating in his ears. At a plenary session of the Central Committee in November 1962, Khrushchev took as his text (or rather as his pretext) a recently rediscovered draft of Lenin's dealing with the primacy of economic tasks after the seizure of power, and used it to justify a sudden and radical reorganization of the entire party machine into parallel industrial and agricultural sectors: henceforth, the primary duty of the heads of party organizations on all levels was to consist in raising output in their area of responsibility.[45] Technically, the plan was an improvisation of doubtful value; politically, it hurt many vested interests; and ideologically, it had a distinctly revisionist flavor, tending as it did to turn the party's main attention away from the needs of ideological struggle at home and abroad. It is thus hardly surprising that the winter of 1962–63 seems to have brought more resistance to Khrushchev's new "line" in high places than had been noticeable at any time since his 1957 victory over the "anti-party group"—resistance carried on in the name of the primacy of politics over economics and of the importance of tightening the party's control on the ideological front.[46] Yet Khrushchev rode out the storm, and after the Chinese attack on the party program was able to go ahead with his policy; and by the time of the Central Committee meeting of February 1964, it was Suslov, the party's leading doctrinaire, who declared that the *international* duty of the Communists of the "socialist countries" consisted in building up the new society at home so that it should become an attractive example for the masses elsewhere.[47]

Suslov put forward that discovery in his report on the conflict with the Chinese Communist leaders; it was part of his rebuttal of their attempts to proclaim that the underdeveloped continents had become the new "storm center of the world revolution" and to deny that the conflict between the imperialists and the advanced countries of the "socialist camp," above all the Soviet Union, was the main contradiction of the present epoch. But in order to defend his thesis of the central role of this conflict despite the inglorious end of Khrushchev's offensive, and despite the evident absence of revolutionary chances in the advanced Western countries, Suslov had to reinterpret the conflict as being fought out mainly in terms of economic competition. This interpretation, of course, had been used often before in propagandist speeches and interviews addressed to Western audiences; but never had it been given the dignity of a serious doctrinal statement before the leading organ of the party. With that, it became indeed a commitment to a new international "economism" that is as far removed from Lenin's concept of the "world revolution" as is the Chinese vision of a revolutionary front centered on the underdeveloped nations. Thus under the pressure of the need to systematize the doctrinal justifications for the divergent development of the two powers, the disintegration of Leninism proceeds in both directions. To China's final rejection of its Marxist elements—the link between the revolution and the industrial working class of the advanced countries— corresponds a Soviet emphasis on the importance of economic superiority for the victory of socialism that often sounds like an echo of the Marxist arguments once used against Lenin by his Menshevik critics.

At the same time, the Soviets' growing concentration on economic results, and especially results of a kind that are to benefit the consumer, creates a materialist spirit that is bound to weaken the pressure for tight ideological control of all spheres of life, and to strengthen the argument for reforms that are in conflict with received dogma but in accord with practical experience. Before the November Plenum of 1962, the Libermann proposals for reducing detailed bureaucratic planning and giving industrial managers freedom and incentive to reduce costs and improve quality in response to market indicators had been eagerly discussed, and an experiment was authorized even then; during the months of the counterattack of the doctrinaires, nothing more was heard of the matter. Yet by 1964 the counterattack had petered out, and the Libermann discussion was resumed with increased boldness and evident official support; practical measures in this direction have even been speeded up since Khrushchev's fall.[48] The trend is clearly in the direction of a "Titoist" type of market economy in a planned framework—though the changeover must be infinitely more difficult in Russia after decades of detailed bureaucratic planning on a gigantic scale.

With all due allowances for the differences in scale and power, it may thus be predicted that a Soviet Union whose international ties have been loosened by the schism and the growth of pluralistic Communism, and whose ruling party is increasingly thrown back on the need for justifying its rule by achievements of value to its own people, will evolve in the same revisionist direction in which the Yugoslav Communists evolved when Stalin had cut them off from the world Communist movement and when their survival depended on success in broadening their own domestic support. This evolution still takes place under the imperative of the self-preservation of the party regime; indeed, the overthrow of Khrushchev and the subsequent cancellation of the 1962 reorganization can best be understood as an attempt to ensure its survival. But self-preservation now requires that this regime should change both in its justification and in its methods. The totalitarian regime, once characterized by permanent revolution carried out by mass terrorism and guided by ideological goals, is being eroded into an evolutionary authoritarianism in which the party still wields a monopoly of political power but is reluctantly yielding sectors of economic and intellectual life to autonomous social activity. As the hegemonial power of the Soviet Union in the East European bloc has survived the doctrinaire authority of the Soviet Communists over the former satellite parties, so the institutional power of the Soviet party at home survives the erosion of its ideology. Yet in the long run, it is not very plausible that the monopolistic power of an ideological party should be required for so unideological a purpose as the promotion of peaceful economic progress; hence its preservation may become more difficult in each new crisis of succession. The Chinese may well be right in wondering how long a theocracy can hold on to power after the disintegration of its faith.

The changes in the international outlook of the Soviet leaders could be summed up in the thesis that Khrushchev's attempt at a revival of the Leninist faith in "world revolution" has collapsed under the impact of his dual failure to achieve a breakthrough in world politics or to maintain the unity of world Communism, and that the Soviet Union is now returning to a concentration on "Communism in one bloc" that recalls Stalin's "socialism in one country." But just as Stalin's skepticism about the progress of world revolution did not prevent him from using the foreign Communist parties as instruments of his policy, so the present and future Soviet leaders will wish to use the largest possible number of international party links as channels for Soviet influence—at least so long as the Soviet Union itself is governed by a party regime. In the circumstances, the Soviet leaders themselves cannot expect to compete successfully with the Chinese for the allegiance of totalitarian revolutionary parties involved in making serious bids for power in the underdeveloped areas of the world. But they start with the support of the overwhelming majority of the Communists in the advanced countries of the West; and they clearly wish to maintain or develop alliances with the largest possible number of already *ruling* revolutionary parties in the underdeveloped countries—whether these be nominally Communist, as in Cuba, or nominally non-Communist, as in Algeria.

Yet it is precisely the Communist parties in the advanced Western countries that find themselves cast farthest adrift by the decay of Soviet authority and the disintegration of the Leninist faith. For decades, these parties have stubbornly clung to a totalitarian revolutionary doctrine and corresponding forms of organization in a situation offering no revolutionary prospects, keeping their faith alive by hitching it to a foreign model; how are they to survive the admission that neither the doctrine nor the model has universal validity?

Faced with this threat to their ideological foundations, many of the smaller Communist parties in the West have at first reacted by trying to ignore the schism, pretending as long as possible that there was still a single Communist world movement under Soviet leadership—and then by pleading with the protagonists to restore unity at any price and not to force them to make a choice. But these are short-term evasions, likely to be followed by a further sectarian splintering of the Communist splinter parties and by their progressive disappearance from the arena of effective political activity.

It is different, of course, with the Communist mass parties of France and Italy. They have not been working in conditions of a prerevolutionary crisis either, at any rate not since the end of the postwar upheavals; and even during that critical period the task assigned them by Stalin was not to attempt the revolutionary seizure of power but rather to influence national policy and entrench themselves in the state machine by joining in "coalitions of liberation." But they benefit from the fact that important strata in their nations, including the majority of their industrial working classes, are traditionally disaffected—in the sense not of being ready for revolutionary action but of refusing to feel themselves as part of the democratic state.[49] This mass attitude, which has its roots in past history rather than in present economic and social conditions, was revived when the Communists, and in Italy also the Nenni Socialists, were pushed back into opposition in 1947; and the Communist parties have been skillful in exploiting it, satisfying at the same time the ideological needs of those disaffected masses by their revolutionary phraseology, and their practical needs, particularly in Italy, by a militant reformist policy in the trade unions, cooperatives, and municipalities (in a manner recalling the similar dual role of the "revolutionary" Social Democrats of Germany until 1914, of Italy until the victory of Fascism, and of Austria until the Dollfuss coup of 1934). But just because this kind of pseudo-revolutionary mass disaffection is a historical hangover rather than a reflection of present conditions in the Western world, both parties have largely depended on the Soviet myth for maintaining it.

Yet the inner atmosphere of the French and Italian Parties, and the view taken by their leaders of their own role, have been as different as their history. The French Party emerged from Stalin's continuous purges with thoroughly Stalinist and thoroughly mediocre leaders, apt only to maintain the members' hatred of the "bourgeois state" and their loyalty to the Soviet Union with unswerving conviction, and to combine the comfortable role of an entrenched permanent opposition with the smug certainty that they were thereby rendering an important service to the "socialist fatherland." The Italian Party, whose old cadres were shielded from some of Stalin's excesses by their underground existence and by Togliatti's tactical skill, and whose younger elements were recruited after the war, never became equally fossilized; and its able leaders were both too ambitious and too conscious of the contribution made to the rise of Fascism by the purely negative opposition of the "maximalist" Socialists to feel happy with a similar policy. Much more than their French colleagues, they had seen their early participation in the government as a possible road to the "legal" conquest of power; much more, too, they chafed under the domestic isolation to which the Cold War and Italy's NATO membership condemned an avowedly pro-Soviet party.

This difference of background made it inevitable that the two parties should react very differently to the series of shocks beginning with de-Stalinization and leading up to the present disintegration of world Communism. To the French leaders, any weakening of Soviet authority was a net loss, because their vested interest in the Soviet myth was overwhelming. They reluctantly accepted de-Stalinization because they would not oppose the present Soviet leaders, but they dwelt as little as possible on the critique of the past. Similarly, they accepted Khrushchev's 1956 doctrine of the "peaceful" or "parliamentary" road to power; but though the Soviet leader had obviously proclaimed it at least partly in order to make his French and Italian comrades once again eligible for government participation, the PCF made no serious efforts to overcome the barriers maintaining its domestic isolation. They rejected Togliatti's suggestion of a "polycentric" future for Communism and insisted on Soviet leadership; they praised Soviet intervention against the Hungarian "counterrevolution"; they willingly endorsed the second excommunication of the Yugoslavs. Finally, when the conflict with the Chinese developed, they again "followed the baton" and took the Soviet side all the way; and while they no doubt deplore the split, they became the first major party to give unconditional support to the Soviet proposal for a new world conference.[50]

The Italian Communists, on the other hand, while sensitive to the blow inflicted on the Soviet myth by de-Stalinization, have from the start also grasped the chance of greater "polycentric" autonomy implied in the weakening of Soviet authority.[51] They welcomed it all the more eagerly because they hoped that visible proof of their independence would remove the principal obstacle to winning a share of power along the "peaceful road." If they did not succeed, it was not because they lacked domestic flexibility but only because they proved not to be independent enough to disavow the Soviet intervention in Hungary. They did indeed adopt the Yugoslav version, defending the final intervention without claiming that the uprising had been "counterrevolutionary" from the start; but this nuance did not even convince Nenni and his Socialist party. In fact, the shock of Hungary, following so closely on the shock of de-Stalinization, was probably decisive for Nenni's evolution toward an autonomous, democratic policy, culminating in his joining a government coalition without the Communists.

Yet it seems in retrospect that ever since then the leaders of the Italian Party have been waiting for their chance to become *really* independent. They did not break relations with the Yugoslav "revisionists" after their second excommunication in 1958. They objected behind the scenes to the concessions made to the Chinese at the Moscow world conference of 1960.[52] They were ahead of the Soviets in recognizing the success of the West European Common Market, which their trade union leaders experienced in its favorable effect on Italian wages, and in calling for a realistic (i.e., reformist) adjustment to it.[53] They developed the doctrine of the "parliamentary road" to the point of specifically promising that not only "other parties" but even "opposition parties" could continue to function after a hypothetical Communist victory.[54] Without actually quarreling with the Soviets, they thus went consistently ahead of them in promoting "revisionist" ideas inside the fold.[55] They were rewarded by being made the main target of open Chinese attacks after the Yugoslav "outsiders" and before the Soviets were attacked by name.

Since the end of serious attempts at a Sino-Soviet compromise, the Italian Communists clearly believe that the hour of real independence has come—and this, to them, means the hour when the Soviets can frankly be treated as a respected but no longer infallible ally. During the municipal elections of the spring of 1963, the Italian Communists openly criticized the then current Soviet campaign to restore ideological discipline among writers and artists. More important, when the Soviets began to call for a new world conference, the Italians, in open agreement with the Yugoslavs and in confidential consultation with the Poles, expressed misgivings about its usefulness and finally agreed to participate only on conditions: there should be no formal excommunication of the Chinese; there should be a frank discussion and toleration of differences but no attempt to impose a general line on the parties attending by majority vote; and the conference should be devoted to a constructive examination of recent international developments rather than to a factional settling of accounts.[56] The Italians have thus been an important factor in pushing the Soviets toward the "letter-box" type of International; and, by their posthumous publication of Togliatti's last memorandum to Khrushchev, they have served notice that they intend to remain an important force for filling this revisionist form with an equally revisionist content.

The Italian example seems to illustrate two of the conditions that any Communist party will have to fulfill if it is to survive as an important force in the West. It will have to accept the disappearance of Soviet doctrinaire authority and to convince both its followers and its opponents that its support of Soviet policies is not unconditional—that its traditional Soviet sympathies no longer imply subordination. And it will have to adapt its program and policy to the political, economic, and social situation in the advanced Western democracies, and to convince its potential partners that its program is meant to be carried out in the institutional framework of Western democracy under the rule of law. In short, it will have to be independent, and it will have to be thoroughly revisionist: in the second half of the sixties, to be unconditionally pro-Soviet and to wait for Moscow's doctrinal pronouncements will no longer be enough for a great party—not even in France.

It remains doubtful, however, whether even the fulfillment of these two conditions will suffice to assure an effective role for Communist parties in the West—at least so long as by "Communist parties" we mean parties with the centralistic, undemocratic internal structure originally imposed by the Comintern on all its sections. Next to their dependence on a foreign center and to their refusal to be bound by constitutional rules, this totalitarian form of organization has always been a basic objection to the acceptance of the Communists as possible partners by other political forces, and hence an obstacle to their full participation in the democratic political game;[57] yet it is such participation that they must crave if they can no longer look for salvation from beyond the frontiers. On the other hand, the centralistic form of organization was originally justified by the need to forge an instrument for the revolutionary conquest of power, and to ensure disciplined obedience to the world headquarters in Moscow: if the political reasons are really gone, why not the organizational corollary? Already the question is beginning to be asked not only from outside, but from inside the parties concerned. Among the Italian Communists, the avowedly revisionist group around Amendola and Alicata has advocated the principle of "majority and minority platforms" ever since the Twenty-second Congress of the CPSU, and to advocate such a principle for more than two years without being silenced by organizational measures goes quite a distance toward achieving it in practice.[58] Even the French Communists lately experienced, for the first time in many years, a kind of opposition from their students' organization, whose leaders were frankly looking to the "revisionists" in Rome.[59]

Of course, we must expect resistance to organizational change to be stronger than on any other issue. Here, not only the vested interests of the party machines are at stake, but ultimately their distinctive Communist character—their "being" as distinct from their "consciousness." A party which renounced that would really become just a militant sort of democratic socialist party, and it might eventually find that its only remaining reasons for separate existence were of a historical, not to say sentimental, kind. In a discussion on roads to left-wing unity organized by the Italian Communists, Amendola has gone so far as to state that unity could not be achieved "either on social democratic or on Communist positions," adding: "A political organization that has not reached its objectives in half a century must seek the reasons for this failure and know how to transform itself."[60] Other Communists have of course attacked this as an abandonment of basic principles; but the open question is precisely whether parties with the distinctive characteristics once transferred to Western Europe by the Bolsheviks will be able, in a non-revolutionary situation and in the long run, to survive the fading of the belief in the unique salvational mission of the Soviet Union.

What of the prospects for Soviet influence on the Communist or left-wing nationalist one-party regimes of ex-colonial countries, and for their further political evolution under that influence? At the moment, it remains improbable that the ruling parties of Cuba, Algeria, Mali, Guinea, and other countries will wish to join even a loose Soviet-sponsored International: they all wish to be formally neutral as between the Soviets and the Chinese, and some of them also between the Soviets and the West. Whether these objections will retain their force depends on many unforeseeable factors— on China's economic successes or failures and the degree of her involvement in warlike conflicts in the first case, on Western development aid and the degree of its detachment from private vested interests in the second.

But formal participation in international conferences, or even in a new kind of international association, is not the only form in which influence may be exercised by means of "interparty relations"; in some cases, such relations may be very effective without being exclusive or even formalized. Kemal Ataturk's Republican People's Party never dreamt of affiliating with the Comintern, and the episode of the Kuomintang's admission to it as a "sympathizing party" came near the end of its real cooperation with the Communists; yet for a time, an important formative influence was exercised by the Bolshevik model in both cases. For years, the Yugoslavs have maintained informal party relations both with the Russians and with some of the new ruling parties in Africa, above all the Algerian FLN. The Soviets receive from time to time fraternal delegations from Ghana, Guinea, and Mali,[61] but the Chinese may do the same. Castro will certainly maintain party relations with both Moscow and Peking as long as possible. In short, pluralistic Communism means not only the decay of the old International and the extremely difficult efforts to form two rival new Internationals of very different types; it will also mean a profusion of bilateral and multilateral criss-cross contacts, not all of them visible to the naked eye.

In fact, just in the case of the new ruling parties of ex-colonial countries, we have to bear one more type of relationship in mind—what may be called "licensed infiltration" or "the party within the party." The Communists in Cuba who merged their organization with that of the victorious Castro were regarded as poor revolutionaries, but they quickly gained influence by having a rather more precise program than their new companions; and some of their leaders probably still feel a basic loyalty to Moscow. The Algerian Communist Party was banned in 1962; but from April 1964 to June 1965 its newspaper appeared, under the same editors, as an organ of the FLN, and Communists boasted of having substantially influenced the FLN's new program when they attended the drafting convention as representatives of affiliated "mass organizations."[62] Soviet specialists on these countries now state in their theoretical articles that a non-Communist one-party regime need not be reactionary, provided that its internal structure permits "conscious proletarian elements" to exert a growing influence on its policy.[63]

Once more, we are reminded of the Kuomintang in the early twenties, when Soviet aid and advice were combined with the "bloc within" tactics of the Chinese Communists; but the present experiment takes place *after* the victory of the national revolution, and its purpose may well be different. It seems at least doubtful whether Moscow looks on the Communists in some of these countries as future leaders of an independent mass movement and aspirants to power in their own name; conceivably it has come to regard the exertion of influence on the ruling groups by this channel as a preferable alternative to the development of rival parties in conflict with them. Nor should it be taken for granted that the ambitions of the Communist cadres in all these countries are more far-reaching: their training has given them a sense of superior "scientific" insight that is valuable in their present role, but they might find it very difficult to fight the nationalist-socialist myth of the established leaders with a myth of their own. Indeed, the weakening of Soviet authority will be a far less serious handicap for such backroom advisers than for would-be political leaders: the latter can no longer point to Russia as the unique model of true socialism, but the former may still point to it as an impressive model of economic development.

In the era of pluralistic Communism, the prospects for Soviet influence on the postrevolutionary regimes of underdeveloped countries may thus be improved precisely to the extent that the Soviets may be less committed to replace them ultimately by Communist party regimes—in other words, that they come to adopt the attitude of the Yugoslav revisionists toward these countries. In what direction, then, may we expect that influence to be exercised? Internally, it will favor the "noncapitalist road"—the expropriation of foreign firms, the building up of the nationalized sector, radical land reforms; but the Soviets may be cautious about recommending either agricultural collectivization or their own type of detailed administrative planning. Internationally, they will use the slogans of anti-imperialist solidarity but also those of peace and disarmament; they will aim at winning the diplomatic support of these countries, in the United Nations and elsewhere, but will be cautious about pushing them into armed conflicts with the West which they could not sustain alone and in which the Soviets would not wish to become involved. Generally, they will try step by step to replace Western political, economic, and cultural influence in these countries, while respecting their military neutrality and some degree of ideological independence. To most of the countries concerned, this policy of a "Cold War with muffled drums" may prove more attractive than the more militant policy of the Chinese.

## Some Conclusions

In trying to sum up the results of our analysis, the first and most definite conclusion that seems to emerge is the answer to our initial question. The Sino-Soviet schism is *not* a mere phenomenon of power conflicts within a basically unchanged Communist world; it both reflects and promotes divergent trends of development in the Soviet Union and China, and these have already led to essential changes of policy and doctrine on both sides. Hence there will also be less and less of an unambiguous meaning to the concept of a "Communist" party or regime. Even today, one can no longer define this concept by Leninist doctrine, for Leninist orthodoxy, polemically claimed by each side, has in fact been abandoned by both of them: neither the Chinese attempt to transfer the revolutionary mission of the industrial proletariat to what Toynbee has called the "external proletariat" of Western civilization, nor the Soviet thesis that socialism will ultimately defeat imperialism by economic competition, can in truth be described as Leninist.

Our second conclusion concerns the new international alignment resulting from the schism. The trend is not toward a simple split into two clear-cut and stable new Internationals. The Chinese will indeed try to form a new International of actively revolutionary parties based on their own model and doctrinal authority, and may have substantial initial success in countries whose internal situation offers chances for new totalitarian revolutions; but such an International is likely to be unstable owing to the strength of nationalist motives in each participating movement and to the limited attraction of the Chinese model of economic development. The Soviets are aware that their only chance to rally broad international support is to form a loose alliance without a very precise doctrinal platform and possibly even without a clearly defined membership. One result of this is to make it doubtful how long an "orthodox"

Soviet interpretation of the Communist doctrine will survive at all as an effective influence on Communist thought outside the Soviet Union. Another result is that a number of Communist parties, like the Cuban and perhaps even the Rumanian Party, may stay outside both "camps" at least for a time, or may choose a form of association with the Soviets that carries no obligations whatever, and that a number of bilateral criss-cross contacts between parties inside either camp, or outside both, may continue for a considerable time. In the communiqué of the consultative conference of 19 Communist parties held in Moscow in March 1965, the Soviets conceded explicitly that all such contacts with their Chinese rivals are legitimate, thus abandoning any claim to exclusive ties.

A third conclusion is that in this world of uncertainty and flux, the comparatively most stable inter-Communist relations will be those within the immediate power sphere of each of the protagonists—in other words, hegemonial relations of military and economic cooperation in Eastern Europe, and of military, economic, and subversive cooperation in East and Southeast Asia. Even though the East European Communist regimes, except for East Germany, can no longer be described as Soviet satellites and have acquired a measure of real independence, the ties of interest underlying the regional alliance continue to be more real than any other ties among Communist parties are likely to remain.

A fourth tentative conclusion is that, contrary to a widespread impression, the schism is not tending to produce a clear-cut division of spheres of influence, with the Soviets guiding the Communists of the West and the Chinese those of the underdeveloped world. While the prospects of any form of Communism in the West appear increasingly doubtful, both Moscow and Peking regard the underdeveloped world as the chief arena of their competition, and both compete for influence on revolutionary nationalist as well as Communist movements there. In that competition, the Chinese are likely to have more attraction for totalitarian revolutionary movements still fighting for power, but the Soviets may have an advantage with ruling revolutionary parties because they can offer them more and demand fewer risks.

One final question, which is perhaps not strictly within the scope of this essay, has been touched upon all the time by implication: I mean the future of the conflict between the Soviets and the Western powers. If the "world revolution" no longer has a clearly defined meaning from the viewpoint of Soviet interest; if its promotion ceases to be an objective that is directly and actively pursued; if even its importance as a legitimation of the party dictatorship becomes secondary; if Soviet internal development seems to require a climate of security rather than of permanent tension—what becomes of the need for maintaining a state of permanent conflict with the non-Communist world as such, over and above the pursuit of Russian national interests? A totalitarian ideological dictatorship needs that conflict; a thoroughly de-ideologized, authoritarian regime would no longer need it. The long-term trend of Russian internal development seems clearly to run from the former to the latter, and the breakup of world Communism has certainly strengthened that trend. It would be foolish for the West not to notice, and welcome, the tendency toward such a change. But it would be equally foolish, and far more dangerous, to regard the change as accomplished before we have direct and unmistakable proof of it.

* * *

This essay has dealt with the pluralistic decay of the former organizational and doctrinaire unity of international Communism under the impact of the Sino-Soviet schism. It has not been concerned with the development of state relations between the Soviet and Chinese governments, except inasmuch as conflicts of national interest have been one major factor in bringing about the schism; in particular, it has not dealt with the future of the Sino-Soviet alliance or the possibility of direct territorial conflict between the two major Communist powers. The schism and interstate relations are evidently connected, as I have pointed out, in the sense that there would have been no schism without the existence of two or more sovereign Communist powers with conflicting interests; in that sense it would be absurd to view the schism as due to "purely ideological" causes. But the effects of the conflicts of national interest and of the divergence of internal development between Moscow and Peking on the organizational and ideological structure of international Communism can be studied separately from the course of state relations between China and the Soviet Union.

When this essay was first presented in the fall of 1964, those state relations were developing in a climate of undisguised hostility. Following the Chinese denunciation of the 1963 nuclear test ban agreement between the Soviet Union, Britain, and the United States as an act of "betrayal," and after the series of subsequent disclosures concerning past conflicts between the Chinese and Soviet governments, Mao Tse-tung had in July 1964 publicly raised a number of territorial issues and had simultaneously accused the Soviet Union of "concentrating troops on her frontier" with Sinkiang; and Pravda, in reprinting Mao's statements and rejecting his demands on September 2, had not denied the accusation.[64] In retrospect, the explosion of a Chinese nuclear device in Sinkiang during the following month suggests the possibility that Mao—rightly or wrongly—may have feared that the Soviets intended to forestall this event by military action against the site of the preparations, which was, of course, known to them.

Since the actual explosion of the Chinese bomb and the simultaneous fall of Khrushchev, there has been no sign of an ideological reconciliation between Moscow and Peking; but an immediate lowering of the temperature of interstate hostility has been followed by Soviet attempts at a revival of diplomatic cooperation. Soviet propaganda for a Communist world conference and Chinese opposition to it continued, and so did Chinese-supported actions to split pro-Soviet Communist parties and Soviet-supported actions to split the pro-Chinese Communist Party in Japan. But indications of acute tension on the Soviet-Chinese frontier declined considerably; and by the beginning of February 1965, Premier Kosygin's visit to Hanoi brought evidence not only of continued Sino-Soviet rivalry for influence on the Vietnamese Communists, but also of the Soviet effort to revive cooperation in this area against the United States.

There is nothing in this course of events that affects the basic analysis offered in this essay. The conflict of interests between the Soviet Union and Communist China has not destroyed their common interests in opposing the non-Communist world, and their alliance has therefore continued formally, even during the most acute phases of the conflict, as an "alliance in reserve."[65] It makes divergence and schism inevitable, but it is compatible with a fairly wide range of diplomatic situations— from the massing of troops on the frontier to anti-Western cooperation. The breakup of international Communist unity does not mean the inevitability of acute interstate conflict; it merely means that cooperation is no longer a matter of course, but will depend on the balance of conflicting and common interests at any given moment—just as among any other two great powers in the world. How that balance develops will depend, among other factors, on the character of Western policy, particularly in the areas of common concern to Russia and China.

### Note to the Second Printing, August 1966

The tendencies toward a growing divergence in the development of Soviet and Chinese Communist policies and doctrines, and toward an increasing pluralistic differentiation of other Communist parties and governments under the impact of this conflict, have continued during the period since the present volume first went to press. On the Soviet side, the Twenty- third Party Congress has shown that Khrushchev's successors, while more careful to hold on to the levers of political control and social discipline, remain determined to continue on the road of nonrevolutionary economic progress and to uphold the "revisionist" doctrines expressing its requirements. On the Chinese side, the purges of 1966 seem to mark a new stage of the commitment not only to the principle of "permanent revolution" at home, but to the rejection of such requirements of economic rationality as strict professional division of labor or advancement and income differentiation according to performance as "capitalist," in the name of the attempt to rely on military command and ideological enthusiasm rather than on material incentives; while internationally, the Chinese Communists have expressed more clearly than ever their belief that the revolutionary conquest of the "countryside of the world"—the underdeveloped continents—must precede any decisive change in the industrially advanced "cities of the world." The persistent rejection by the Chinese of all Soviet offers of a "united front" against the "imperialists," both on a party and on a state level, and the contrast between these tactical offers and the internal Soviet anti-Chinese statements anticipating their rejection, are an expression of this continued divergence.

At the same time, the Soviets, with their greater tactical flexibility, have regained some international influence at Chinese expense, so that the low point of that influence, marked by the Moscow "consultative meeting" of March 1965, appears in retrospect as the starting point of a limited recovery. By abandoning pressure for binding majority decisions on issues of doctrine, strategy, and organization or for an early world conference, and by concentrating on practical cooperation on the broadest possible basis while the Chinese insisted on purely doctrinal unity, the Soviet leaders have succeeded in drawing the Cuban Communists to their side, and improving relations with the Vietnamese Communists to a point where these have returned to strict neutrality between the two Communist "camps." Moreover, since the Korean, the Japanese, and the "left" Indian Communists have markedly reduced their dependence on Chinese authority, and the once powerful Indonesian Communist Party was virtually destroyed after the failure of its 1965 bid for power, Chinese efforts for creating a new, Peking-centered International appear to have suffered a major blow and to have been thrown back, for the time being, to the cadre-building stage.

However, the partial recovery of Soviet influence remains conditional on Soviet recognition of the new pluralistic independence of a growing number of Communist parties, and it is this independence which is the basic new phenomenon—in Europe as well as in Asia and Latin America. Even the French Communists, who had been unconditionally and uncritically pro-Soviet for so long, have since the death of Maurice Thorez made undeniable steps along the "Italian road" to critical independence. The Rumanian Communists now combine membership in the Warsaw Pact not only with neutrality in the Sino-Soviet conflict, with an independent economic policy and considerable freedom of diplomatic movement, but with outspoken public criticism of the disastrous role of Comintern interference in their earlier history. Finally, the failure of the key experiment in "licensed infiltration" in Algeria, where the Communists were deprived of their influence and once again driven underground after the overthrow of Ben Bella, has not caused the Soviet leaders to abandon their policy of "fraternal cooperation" with non-Communist, ruling national-revolutionary parties in underdeveloped countries: clearly, exerting influence on many, broadly like-minded forces is now regarded in Moscow as more important than maintaining strict disciplinary control over a narrow sector.

# Notes

*Leninism*

1. The three letters quoted are dated December 25, 1916, January 19, 1917, and January 30, 1917. Unfortunately, the Marx-Engels Institute, which has the letters of Inessa Armand, has withheld them from publication and refuses to let any scholar who has not been housebroken consult them. But Lenin's replies (of which more below) give us some notion of her argument. For more on this, see my book *Marxism: One Hundred Years in the Life of a Doctrine* (New York, 1965), Chapter V, "What Lenin Made of the Testament of Engels," and my article "Lenin and Inessa Armand," *Slavic Review,* March 1963, pp. 96–114, or *Encounter,* February 1964, pp. 83–91.

2. Bertrand de Jouvenel, *On Power* (New York, 1964), p. 121.

3. Letter of January 10, 1913.

4. Italics here and throughout this chapter are as they are found in the original. Lenin, *Sochineniya,* XII, 378–89. All references are to the Fourth Russian Edition of Lenin's *Collected Works,* published in thirty-five volumes during Stalin's regime, between 1941 and 1952. After Stalin's death, four additional volumes of things omitted or suppressed were published. Where they are referred to, the volume number and date will be given.

5. An interesting discussion of some of the character traits of Lenin and the psychological and political problems they raise may be found in Lewis Feuer's review of four books on Lenin in the *New Leader,* August 3, 1964, pp. 18–21. For some of the judgments cited in this paragraph I am indebted to his article. Rosa Luxemburg's unfavorable view of Lenin is in Rosa Luxemburg, *The Russian Revolution and Leninism or Marxism?* (Ann Arbor, 1961). The remarks on Lenin's "chess moves" are in Angelica Balabanoff, *Impressions of Lenin* (Ann Arbor, 1964). Trotsky's early views on Lenin are in his *Report of the Siberian Delegation to the Second Congress* and *Our Political Tasks,* both published in 1904. Bebel's and Adler's reactions are cited from Feuer's review article.

6. Peter Struve, "My Contacts and Conflicts with Lenin," *Slavonic and East European Review,* April and July 1934.

7. Maxim Gorky, *Memories of Lenin* (Moscow, 1931), p. 41.

8. Lenin, *Sochineniya,* XXIV, 137–39.

9. *Ibid.*

10. Lenin, *Sochineniya,* XIV (*Materialism and Empiriocriticism*), p. 312.

11. Three versions of Marx's speech, as reported in newspapers of the period, are given in the *Bulletin* of the International Institute of Social History, No. 1 (Leiden, 1951). In 1891, when Britain was at the height of her imperial power, Engels reiterated this, and added France to the roster of such countries "where popular representation concentrates all power in itself, where one can do constitutionally what one will as soon as one has the majority of the people behind one; in democratic republics like France and America, and in monarchies like England ... where the dynasty is powerless against the will of the people" (1901–2), *Neue Zeit*, XX, 5–6, 9–13.

Lenin was eager to explain this away concerning America and more particularly England since, after he took power, the British Empire was his main target and the "main enemy." In debates with Kautsky and arguments with Bertrand Russell and Macdonald of the I.L.P. of Great Britain, he contended that Britain had become more imperialist, more bureaucratic, and more militarist since Engels' death, so that labor could no longer hope to come to power peacefully. On this, history has given the verdict to Marx, Engels, Kautsky, Macdonald, and Russell, and not to Lenin.

12. Marx, *Werke*, VII (Berlin, 1960), 244–54. It has been translated as both *Address* and *Circular*. Actually it was a conspiratorial circular letter of instructions not intended for publication. Evidence that conspiratorial agents of the Blanquists were being used by Marx as emissaries of the Central Committee to the various branches is to be found in a second circular dated June 1850, *Werke*, VII, 305–12. On the relations of Marxists to Blanquists at this moment, and on the Blanquist character of the March *Circular*, see Nikolaevsky and Maenchen-Helfen, *Karl Marx, Man and Fighter* (Philadelphia, 1936), pp. 208ff.

13. One other document of the 1848 period from Marx's hand is worth noting for its "Leninist" spirit of statism and centralism, *The Demands of the Communist Party of Germany*, a leaflet composed by Marx in consultation with Engels in Paris in March 1848. It contained 17 demands as a supplement to and enlargement of the immediate program of the *Communist Manifesto*. Point 1 read: "All Germany is declared a single, indivisible republic." The demands are notable for their statism and their element of compulsion. The "armed people" is to serve not only in defense but also in "labor armies" and as "a means for the organization of work." Feudal estates, mines, etc., are to become state property; mortgages are to be taken over by the state, which is to receive the interest payments thereon; leased lands are to be taken by the state and the rents paid to the state; agriculture is to be conducted by the state on a large scale with modern "scientific methods" and with the use of armies of agricultural laborers directly responsible to the state and under its command, the state to receive the product of their labor and devote it to the public welfare. Stalin could have made these proposals his gospel, as Lenin and Trotsky thought of doing under war communism and in the pre-NEP period of demobilization of the armies of the Civil War. For the text of the *Demands of the Communist Party*, see *Werke*, V (Berlin, 1959), 3–5.

14. Republished by Engels in 1895 under the title *Class Struggles in France, 1848–1850*.

15. The best account of this society is in Nikolaevsky and Maenchen-Helfen, pp. 208–11. This account is the more remarkable for its objectivity in that this whole period of Marx's development, which Nikolaevsky seems to narrow down pretty much to the period from March to June 1850, is profoundly distasteful to the

authors of the biography, inclined as they are to see Marx as the "democratic" and "scientific" socialist of the mature period, and a natural opponent of Blanquism.

16. Engels, "Program of the Blanquist Commune Refugees," in *Volkstaat*, June 26, 1874; *Werke*, XVIII (Berlin, 1962), 529.

17. Marx, *Werke*, VII (Berlin, 1960), 614.

18. Marx and, for most of his life, Engels were more attracted to the Russian Populists and Terrorists of the Narodnaya Volya than to the Russian Marxists as represented by Plekhanov. When Vera Zasulich put questions to him for Solomonic judgment, Marx was equivocal in the letter he sent, and vacillating in the many preliminary drafts he did not send. For these drafts see *Marx-Engels Arkhiv*, I (Frankfurt, 1926), 309–42.

19. Tsarist Russia between 1885 and 1914 developed industrially at a faster rate of growth than England, France, and Germany, and, during part of the period, faster even than the United States. On this, see Alexander Gerschenkron, "The Rate of Industrial Growth in Russia," *Journal of Economic History*, VII, Supplement 7, 144–74, and his essays on economic growth republished in book form in 1963. Russia's average percentage increase in her industry was 5.72 per annum, America's 5.26, Germany's 4.49, the United Kingdom's 2.11. From the Emancipation to 1900, Russian industrial productivity increased more than seven times, German almost five times, French two and one-half times, English a little over twice. In his "Development of Capitalism in Russia" (*Sochineniya*, III, 428), Lenin exults at some of these facts, concluding: "From these figures it is clear what a technical revolution is going on at the present time in Russia, and what an enormous capacity for the development of the productive forces heavy capitalist industry possesses. . . . We see that the development of the metallurgical industry in Russia goes even more rapidly than in Western Europe, and to some extent even faster than in the United States. . . . The development of capitalism in young nations is significantly *faster* as a result of the example and aid of older countries." In the last two "five-year periods," as Gerschenkron demonstrates, industrialization developed still faster, even though, with the downfall of Count Witte, state aid diminished. Thus, gradually and for the first time in Russian history, society began to develop independently of the state and to reverse the "oriental-despotic" relations in which the state was stronger than society. During the same last period, further industrialization was accompanied by a rising standard of living for labor and peasantry, and the beginnings of political freedom. What happens then to the unconscious apologetics of those of our Western Sovietologists and *political* economists who are advancing the theory that a totalitarian dictatorship is "necessary" to rapid industrialization?

20. *Sochineniya*, I, 272.

21. *Ibid.*, XV, 41.

22. This is one of the advantages to Lenin accruing from his conception of the party as a classless intellectual elite or "vanguard of the proletariat," rather than a party of the proletariat itself. An intellectual elite can "stand on the shoulders of a number of revolutionary generations of Western Europe," but a backward Russian working class cannot.

23. *Sochineniya*, XV, 31.

24. *Ibid.*, VIII, 262.

25. *Ibid.*, IX, 14.

26. *Ibid.*, 32.

27. *Ibid.*, VIII, 505; IX, 9, 15–17, 81.

28. *Ibid.*, XXVII, 46–53. This statement was made in 1916, before Lenin called his

party *Communist*. The same passage contains Lenin's famous pronouncement on the possibility of a "peaceful road to socialism." It reads: "However, we cannot reject the *possibility* that in special cases, by way of exception, for example in some little state after its great neighbor has already carried through a social revolution, there *may be* a peaceful yielding of power, if they have convinced themselves of the hopelessness of resistance, and prefer to keep their heads fastened to their necks. It is much more probable of course that, even in little states, socialism will not be realized without a civil war. Therefore, the only program . . . must be recognition of such a war, even if in our ideal there is no place for the use of force on people."

29. *Ibid.*, XXXI, 326.

30. All the above are from *Iskra* and *Zarya*, written when these were journals for which there was as yet no party. *Sochineniya*, IV, 345–46, 369; V, 7–9, 481.

31. The instructions of Lenin on the Third Congress and on the Armed Detachments are in *Sochineniya*, VIII, 157–70, 327–415; IX, 257–59, 315–17, 389–93.

32. *Ibid.*, VIII, 87–91.

33. *Ibid.*, IX, 389–93.

34. *Ibid.*, XXV, 264.

35. *Ibid.*, 313–16.

36. *Ibid.*, XXVI, 266.

37. *Ibid.*, 375.

38. *Ibid.*, 457–59.

39. *Ibid.*, XXIV, 265.

40. *Ibid.*, XXIII, 279–80.

41. *Ibid.*

42. *Ibid.*, 448.

43. *Ibid.*, VII, 365–66.

44. *Vospominaniya o Lenine*, I (Moscow, 1956), 313.

45. Lenin to the Ninth Congress of his own party in April 1920, and to the Second Congress of the Communist International, *Der zweite Kongress . . . Protokoll* (Hamburg, 1921), p. 576.

46. *Sochineniya*, VI, 221–23. See also VII, 365–66.

47. *Leninskii Sbornik*, VI, 134, 137; *Vtoroi Ocherednoi Sezd* (Geneva, 1903), p. 241. The *Sbornik* wrongly attributes the speech to Rozanov. When another delegate spoke of the "rights of Party members," Lenin wrote in his notes for reply (the notes are reproduced in the *Sbornik*): "*There are no rights in Party membership*. RESPONSIBILITY."

48. *Sochineniya*, VI, 211–15.

49. *Ibid.*, 223.

50. *Ibid.*, XXVII, 477.

51. *Ibid.*, 303–4; XXX, 155, 339.

52. On this see Leopold Haimson, *The Russian Marxists and the Origins of Bolshevism* (Cambridge, Mass., 1955).

53. "The task of the bourgeois politician," wrote Lenin icily, "is to assist the economic struggle of the proletariat. The task of the Socialist is to make the economic struggle assist the Socialist movement and the victory of the revolutionary labor party." *Sochineniya*, IV, 273. This was the abyss that separated Lenin from Axelrod and from Rosa Luxemburg.

54. *Ibid.*, 347–48.

55. *Ibid.*, 431.

56. *Ibid.*, 354–56.

57. *Ibid.*, 392.

58. *Ibid.*, 398.

59. *Ibid.*, 441.

60. *Ibid.*, XXVII, 427–28.

61. *Ibid.*, 421.

62. *Ibid.*, 442–43.

63. *Ibid.*, XXVII, 54; XXXII, 222; XXVII, 69.

64. As Lenin told the Eleventh Congress of his party: "When we say 'state,' that state is us, it is the proletariat, it is the vanguard of the working class." *Sochineniya*, XXXIII, 249. What could be clearer—or more confusing?

*Stalinism*

---

1. S. V. Utechin, *Everyman's Concise Encyclopedia of Russia* (London, 1961), p. 514.

2. His exact words, when I said good-bye to him in January 1925, were: "They will kill me." See "Ultima verba de Léon Trotski," *Preuves,* March 1959.

3. See "Staline et Trotski" (Letter from B. Souvarine to *Courrier socialiste*), *Contrat social* (Paris), May 1960, and *Sotsialisticheskii Vestnik* (New York), April 1960.

4. The 1905 dispute amounts to a quibble over words. At that time Lenin wrote, among other things, "When the democratic revolution breaks out, we will immediately bring to bear all our strength—the strength of an awakened and organized proletariat—to get the socialist revolution under way. We are for *uninterrupted* revolution. We will not stop halfway." Lenin, *Polnoe sobranie sochinenii,* 5th ed., XI (Moscow, 1960), 222. On the other hand, the first edition of the *Malaya Sovetskaya Entsiklopediya,* VI (Moscow, 1930) defines permanent revolution as a "theory advanced by Marx and Engels, and later Lenin, to describe the course of the revolution's development." (Column 438).

5. See B. Souvarine, *Stalin: A Critical Survey of Bolshevism* (New York, 1939), p. 390.

6. See "Sur l'origine de la légende du 'trotskisme': Attestations documentaires," *Biulleten Oppozitsii* (*bolshevikov-lenintsev*), Paris, February–March 1930. Letters from Trotsky, Preobrazhensky, Pyatakov, Rakovsky, and Elzin.

7. At Stalin's death in 1953, the population of the U.S.S.R. had reached only 188 million. It should have been in the neighborhood of 344 million in 1948, according to the estimates made in 1912 by Edmond Théry on the basis of official data (cf. *La Transformation économique de la Russie,* Paris, 1914). These data rectified those of Vacher de Lapouge made in 1890 on the basis of calculations by Emile Levasseur, projecting 320 million for 1950. Allowing for territorial adjustments and wartime losses, the population deficit caused by a rise in the death rate and a drop in the birth rate consequently exceeded 100 million lives. See B. Souvarine, "Abomination de la désolation," *Figaro,* November 23, 1956; and Paul Barton, "Le Déficit démographique en U.R.S.S.," *Contrat social,* November–December 1959. The Polish Communist André Stawar concluded that the concentration camps alone were responsible for the loss of 100 million people. *Preuves-Information,* October 10, 1961.

8. Engels had used the expression in speaking of the capitalist past; Lenin gave it a new twist in applying it to the future. Stalin latched onto it to justify the unjustifiable violence that promoted barbarity instead of combating it.

9. "On the Industrialization of the Country and on the Rightist Deviation," Stalin's speech of November 19, 1928, to the Central Committee of the Communist Party, in *Sochineniya,* XI, 245–90 (Moscow, 1949). There Stalin reiterates Lenin's idea, which dated from October 1917, in "Grozyashchaya katastrofa" (The threatening catastrophe). *Polnoe sobranie sochinenii,* 5th ed., XXXIV, 151–99 (Moscow, 1962).

10. Stalin, J., "O proiekte Konstitutsii Soiuza SSR" (On the Project of the Constitution of the USSR), report to the Eighth Congress of Soviets, November 25, 1936 (Moscow, 1945).

11. For these decrees, see the following issues of *Izvestiya*: February 27, 1927;

January 25, 1931; August 8, 1932; June 9, 1934; and April 8, 1935. See also *La Peine de mort en U.R.S.S.: Textes et documents* (Paris, 1936). This brochure was reproduced in large part in *Contrat social,* January 1963.

12. In a speech before the Central Committee on January 19, 1925, he described his policy in a way that would apply equally well in 1939: "Our banner is, as before, the banner of *peace.* But if war comes, we shall not sit on our hands; we shall have to intervene, but we shall be the last to do so. And we shall intervene in order to throw a decisive *weight* in the balance." "Rech' na plenume TsK RKP(b)" (Speech before the Central Committee) in Stalin, *Sochineniya,* VII (Moscow, 1947), 14. Italics in the original.

13. In his annotations to Hegel's *Science of Logic,* Lenin admits that "the theoretical, abstract exposition of the transition from quantity to quality is so obscure that it is beyond comprehension." *Polnoe sobranie sochinenii,* 5th ed., XXIX (Moscow, 1963), 107. Nevertheless, he used the expression whenever he found it convenient.

14. Lenin, *State and Revolution,* Chapter 2.

15. For this passage, from a speech Bukharin made in Petrograd in the spring of 1923, see Lucien Revo, "La Révolution de la culture," *Bulletin communiste* (Paris), January 11, 1924.

16. General A. V. Gorbatov, "Gody i voiny," *Novyi Mir* (Moscow), No. 4 (1964).

17. In editing Lenin's collection *O mezhdunarodnom rabochem i kommunisticheskom dvizhenii* (Moscow, 1958), Stalin's heirs took the liberty of suppressing Lenin's reports and speeches to the Second, Third, and Fourth Congresses of the Communist International, as well as various writings that the title indicates should have been included. Thus, on this essential point, Khrushchev and his cohorts proved to be convinced adepts of Stalinism.

18. De Gaulle made this statement on July 24, 1964.

19. Among Lenin's last writings, considered part of his Testament by those who were closest to him, see "K voprosu o natsional'nostyakh ili ob 'avtonomizatsii,' " *Sochineniya,* 4th ed., XXXVI (Moscow, 1957).

20. Stalin had used these expressions in 1925 at the Fourteenth Congress of the CPSU and at the next Congress, in 1927. He repeated them in "Conversation with the First Delegation of American Workers," September 9, 1927, and several times later. See Stalin, *Sochineniya,* X (Moscow, 1949), 92–148; "Interview with Mr. Roy Howard," March 1, 1936 (Moscow, 1936); "Replies to American Journalists," March 31, 1952; and finally, "Replies to Mr. James Reston," December 21, 1952, *New York Times,* December 25 and 26, 1952. See also François Houtisse, *La Coexistence pacifique* (Paris, 1953).

21. The letter to Péguy dated Nov. 17, 1901, was printed as "Question de méthode," in *Cahiers de la quinzaine,* and in the introduction to Jaurès's *Etudes socialistes* (Paris, 1901), pp. xxxix–xc.

## Khrushchevism

1. *Let Us Live in Peace and Friendship—The Visit of N. S. Khrushchev to the U.S.A.* (Moscow, 1959), pp. 191–92.

2. *Ibid.,* p. 338.

3. Nikita Khrushchev, *Communism—Peace and Happiness for the Peoples* (Moscow, 1963), II, 365.

4. Quoted in Thomas P. Whitney, *Khrushchev Speaks* (Ann Arbor, Mich., 1963), p. 5.

5. *Ibid.*, p. 4.
6. *Pravda*, February 3, 1955.
7. *Ibid.*, February 15, 1956.
8. *Ibid.*, November 29, 1957.
9. *Ibid.*, February 15, 1956.
10. *Ibid.*, January 25, 1961.
11. *Ibid.*, February 15, 1956.
12. Nikita Khrushchev, *For Victory in Peaceful Competition with Capitalism* (London, 1960), p. 327.
13. *Pravda*, March 10, 1963.
14. *Ibid.*, December 18, 1962.
15. *Ibid.*, March 10, 1963.

## Maoism

1. Comments in this and the following paragraph are Mao's as made to Edgar Snow in 1936 and published in *Red Star Over China*, rev. ed. (New York, 1944), pp. 126–60. Keeping in mind the danger of distortion after the fact, this young Mao is plausible.

2. Mao, a lesser figure among the Party's fathers, would now have men believe he had been the primary force in establishing the CCP. He stated in July 1964 that he (Mao) had "organized" the Party.

3. Chu Teh later (in January 1935) described their condition in his notebook: "Corn, with bits of cabbage, chief food of people here. Peasants too poor to eat rice. Sell it to pay rent and interest. Rice seized by militarists as 'war rice tax.' ... Peasants call landlords 'rent gentry' and themselves 'dry men'—men sucked dry of everything." Cited in Agnes Smedley, *The Great Road: The Life and Times of Chu Teh* (New York, 1956), p. 315.

4. Interview with Edgar Snow, July 23, 1936.

5. Regarding the real importance of the ideas derived from Chu Teh and other military men, CCP materials conceal the collaborative origin of Mao's military code, so that he alone is credited with its formulation.

6. Conrad Brandt, Benjamin Schwartz, and John K. Fairbank, *A Documentary History of Chinese Communism* (Cambridge, Mass., 1959), p. 22.

7. "For pure military strategy and tactical handling of a great army in retreat, nothing has been seen in China to compare with Chu Teh's splendid generalship of the Long March" (*Red Star Over China*, p. 389). However, CCP materials in 1965 depict Marshal Lin Piao as second in importance only to Mao during the Long March. This further revision of history is intended as a reward for Lin because of his defense of Mao at the Lushan Plenum in 1959. Lin had earlier been eulogized for "applying creatively the thought of Mao Tse-tung." *Red Flag*, August 1, 1963. (Unless otherwise noted, all Chinese periodicals cited are published in Peking.)

8. Mao recently (January 1965) denied to Edgar Snow that he had written *Dialectical Materialism*, which bears his name. For two English translations of Mao's fragment—originally printed in *Min Chu* (Shanghai), March 1940—see Karl A. Wittfogel and C. S. Chao, *Studies in Soviet Thought* (Dordrecht, Holland, 1963), pp. 251–77; and Dennis J. Doolin and Peter J. Golas, "'On Contradiction' in the Light of Mao Tse-tung's Essay on 'Dialectical Materialism,'" *The China Quarterly*, July–September 1964, pp. 38–46.

9. In his January 1965 interview with Snow, Mao insisted that he gave "lectures"

on practice and contradiction in 1937 but avoided the matter of whether he presented his essays then *in essentially the form* they have now taken. He also avoided the key point regarding the failure of the CCP to publish any of his philosophical essays in his selected works prior to 1951.

10. *Where Do Man's Correct Ideas Come From?* (May 1963).

11. The Poles' version of Mao's speech, as reported by Sidney Gruson, appears to be authentic. *New York Times,* June 13, 1957.

12. At several key points, the Maoist defense of Stalin in fact makes him look small. The Chinese say that Stalin had confessed to his errors on China policy but that Mao had made "no" mistakes since he became the dominant CCP leader in 1935.

13. Joint article, *People's Daily* and *Red Flag,* September 13, 1963.

14. Mao's timetable was indicated by Lu Ting-yi in his speech of November 26, 1964.

15. *On the Intraparty Struggle* (July 1941). Liu's work in building the covert apparatus within KMT-controlled cities in the late 1920's and 1930's is one of several major contributions he has made in helping Mao to shape the CCP into a narrow and disciplined combat party.

16. *Oppose the Party "Eight-Legged Essay"* (February 1942). Party theorists have claimed that this scare device combined with confession is "an important creative result of Comrade Mao Tse-tung's thought on the matter of solving the contradiction between right and wrong in the party and an important contribution to the Marxist-Leninist theory of party building." *Red Flag,* January 23, 1963. On the premise that theory means a view that informs practice directly, this claim is valid.

Philip Bridgham points to the Liaoning Province Party purge as one means of realistically gauging the intensity of intraparty struggles. The provincial party "rectification conference" lasted 103 days in 1958, as members vigorously "exposed, criticized, and thoroughly smashed" the activities of an "anti-party faction" under the personal guidance of Party General Secretary Teng Hsiao-p'ing and Politburo member Li Fu-ch'un. *Liaoning Daily,* October 31, 1958 (in *Survey of China Mainland Press,* U.S. Consulate General, Hong Kong, #1925, January 2, 1959).

17. Mao acted on his earlier view that gentry murder created a revolutionary psychological impact on peasants. He had said that: "When a big local bully or big member of the bad gentry is shot, the entire rural county is stirred. It is a very effective way of purging rural feudal remnants." *Report of an Investigation into the Peasant Movement in Hunan,* March 1927.

18. Po I-po used these phrases, which indicate the nature of the psychological atmosphere the CCP leaders had created for the drive, in his report on the results. *Bright Daily,* January 10, 1952.

19. "Regarding the appraisal of the great movement for the suppression of counterrevolutionaries—made by the Central Committee, which also affirmed certain policies of the suppression of counterrevolutionaries—Wang Cheng and Sung Li expressed doubts and rejected them. Wang Cheng doubted the claim that in the first movement . . . the achievements were the main feature and the defects and mistakes were only of local significance. Sung Li also rejected the claim . . . regarding the 1955 drive in the Lushun-Dairen municipality." *Liaoning Daily,* October 31, 1958.

20. Mainland students visiting Hong Kong for the lunar New Year in 1961 reported that they had witnessed the executions. *South China Morning Post* (Hong Kong), February 19, 1961.

21. "Some comrades raise the issue that 'in the war era ... sacrifices were natural, but today we are engaged in construction and still are getting the worst of it.'" (*Peking Daily*, January 8, 1962.) The Peking municipal party organ also reflected the cadres' desire "to enjoy the fruits of their labors now and suffer later." (*Ibid.*, December 11, 1961.)

22. *People's Daily*, January 11, 1960.

23. John Wilson Lewis, *Leadership in Communist China* (Ithaca, N.Y., 1963), p. 87. Only the second half of this sentence applies in practice.

24. Thus CCP theorists insisted in November 1959, during the retreat, that the communes had been a "creation of the masses," and Chou En-lai insisted in late December 1964 that the old fallback policies of 1959–62 were really advocated by others.

25. For a discussion of "Law as a Weapon in Class Struggle," see *People's Daily*, October 28, 1964.

26. Six regional bureaus of the Central Committee were established by the Ninth Plenum in order to ensure more effective central CCP control over policy implementation (especially economic) at the provincial level and below. The regional bureaus, headed by senior party officials, were charged (according to Charles F. Steffens) with seeing that central directives were effectively executed by the provincial party committees, which had been the focal point of "flexible" interpretation of Politburo policy.

27. The communiqué of the Tenth Plenum was carried after the meeting in *People's Daily*, September 29, 1962.

28. Mao is quoted thus in *Red Flag*, March 31, 1964.

29. *People's Daily*, February 1, 1964.

30. *Ibid.*

31. *Ibid.*, April 4, 1964.

32. Mao Tse-tung, "Note on 'The Seven Well-Written Documents of Chekiang Province Concerning Cadre Participation in Physical Labor,'" May 9, 1963. Cited in joint article, *People's Daily* and *Red Flag*, July 14, 1964.

33. *Ibid.*

34. Speech titled "The Fighting Tasks Confronting Workers in Philosophy and Social Science," given October 26, 1963. This important speech was published in both the *People's Daily* and *Red Flag* on December 27, 1963; it was broadcast the previous day—Mao's seventieth birthday—by Radio Peking.

35. "The kind of life advocated by Comrade Feng Ting, which would provide good things to eat and wear, good places to live in, and cordial relations between husband and wife and between parents and children, does not conform with the Communist ideal." *China Youth*, October 31, 1964.

36. "It is clear that class struggle will go on for a long time in a socialist society until communism is attained.... We must be prepared to carry on an uninterrupted revolution for from five to ten generations before we can bring about communism." (Lu Ting-yi, Politburo alternate and now Minister of Culture, made these remarks on November 26, 1964.)

37. Mao's attack on Chinese traditional values has been extended to the idea of *respect* for the dead, and his propagandists now praise the extension of class analysis to the dead. "We should make a class analysis of those who have died.... Thoughts about exploiters and oppressors should end with their death. What is there about them worthy of mourning?" *China Youth*, January 1, 1965.

For a novel view of Maoist class analysis, see the conclusion drawn by Joseph R.

Levenson, *Confucian China and Its Modern Fate: The Problem of Intellectual Continuity* (Berkeley, Calif., 1958), p. 145: "They introduce class-analysis, not joyously to kill the traditional Chinese culture, but in the latest of a series of efforts, all of which have previously failed, to exorcize the spectre of decay."

38. This directive was attributed to Mao's statement at the Tenth Plenum. See Hu Yao-pang's report to the YCL congress given on June 11, 1964.

39. Dennis Bloodworth dispatch from Singapore, *Washington Post*, December 13, 1964. Ch'en Yi repeated Mao's reply to a French pianist's praise for China's young musicians: "The Long March veteran reflected a moment and then said: 'But they have no combat experience.'" *New York Times*, January 3, 1965.

40. See Li Ssu-kuang's article on "revolutionizing" scientific and technical work in *Red Flag*, October 1, 1964.

41. *Ch'ien Hsien*, September 1964.

42. "If China bows to United States imperialism, permitting the imperialist army to take her territory [Taiwan], our international prestige would drop 10,000 feet in one fall." *Work Bulletin*, April 25, 1961. Any discussion of Sino-American relations that avoids Mao's refusal to renounce the use of force against Taiwan is not a real discussion of these relations.

43. Mao's public statement of May 14, 1960, contains this phrase.

44. *People's Daily*, June 24, 1964.

45. *Red Flag*, June 30, 1964.

46. The CCP "Open Letter" to the CPSU of June 14, 1963, includes kings, princes, and aristocrats in the anti-American united front.

47. *Work Bulletin*, April 25, 1961.

48. "Open Letter" to the CPSU, June 14, 1963.

49. That Khrushchev had made such a suggestion at the time is implied in the *Work Bulletin* of April 25, 1961, and is made explicit in Peking's formal statement of September 1, 1963: Khrushchev said that "depending on what basis you took, there is more than one way to solve every complicated question. For example, after the October Revolution, there was established in the Soviet Far East the Far Eastern Republic, and Lenin recognized it at the time; this was a temporary concession and sacrifice, but later on it was united with Russia." The formal statement warned that the CCP "has not forgotten and will not forget" this plan for "two Chinas."

50. CCP declarations that they, unlike the "revisionists" (i.e., the Soviet leaders), always act with an eye to the needs of "international" revolutionary forces rather than on the basis of Chinese national interests were dramatically refuted by many Soviet writers in fall 1963. They exposed the contempt Mao had shown for the domestic position of the Indian Communists in striking at Indian forward posts and then demanding that the local Communists support the PLA attack politically in the face of angered critics.

51. "Unity, struggle, and even a split, and new cohesion on a new basis—such is the dialectics of the development of the international working class movement." Joint article, *People's Daily* and *Red Flag*, February 4, 1964.

52. *People's Daily*, March 4, 1965.

53. See Note 34.

54. "It is quite possible that, with a change in conditions, other parties will go into the front ranks of the movement." Joint article, *People's Daily* and *Red Flag*, February 4, 1964. Here, "other parties" is the Maoist locution for the CCP.

55. This is similar to the tactical formula Mao had employed during the Chinese

Communist revolution, which depicted the "national capitalists" as allies of the CCP because of their "dual character"—that is, as exploiters but at the same time opponents of foreign imperialism.

56. This declaration was made by the Vietnamese Communist Liberation Front in a radio broadcast of March 8, 1965.

57. "Basing themselves on the changes in the Soviet Union, the imperialist prophets are pinning their hopes of 'peaceful evolution' on the third and fourth generations of the Chinese Party. We must shatter these imperialist prophecies. From our highest organizations down to the grass roots, we must everywhere give constant attention to the training and upbringing of successors to the revolutionary cause." Joint article, *People's Daily* and *Red Flag*, July 14, 1964.

## Castroism

1. Francisco de Armas, "Como Se Editó en la Clandestinidad la Primera Edición de La Historia Me Absolvera," *Hoy*, July 21, 1963, section 2, pp. 2–3. The author attributes the information in his article to Melba Hernández.

2. Luis Conte Agüero, *Cartas del Presidio* (Havana, 1959), p. 37. The author of these letters was actually Fidel Castro.

3. At least two different and seemingly contradictory stories have been told about the genesis of *History Will Absolve Me* in its published form. The first one claimed that it had been based on "shorthand notes" or the "record of the shorthand reporters" at the trial. A later version, given in the Appendix to the 1964 edition, says that it was a "reconstruction" made "little by little," with no mention of help from shorthand notes, which presumably would have made such a piecemeal reconstruction unnecessary (Havana, 1964, pp. 205–6). Unless the original transcript is produced, it will be impossible to tell how closely it resembled the "reconstruction."

4. Carlos G. Peraza, *Machado, Crimenes y Horrores de un Régimen* (Havana, 1933), pp. 215–50, for the text of the ABC program.

5. Ramón Grau San Martín, *La Revolución Cubana ante América* (Mexico, 1936), p. 104.

6. *Revolución*, December 2, 1961.

7. *Ibid.*, March 28, 1962.

8. Conte Agüero, *Cartas del Presidio*, pp. 60–61.

9. René Ray, *Libertad y Revolución* (Havana, 1959), p. 11.

10. From a copy of this Manifesto in my possession. It apparently has never been reprinted in full, but excerpts may be found in Luis Conte Agüero, *Los Dos Rostros de Fidel Castro* (Mexico, 1960), pp. 104–7, and in *"...y la luz se hizo"* (Havana, 1959), pp. 86–90.

11. *Bohemia*, January 18–25, 1959, p. 103.

12. The "Tesis Económica" and the "Manifesto of the Sierra Maestra" may be found in Fidel Castro, *La Revolución Cubana: Escritos y Discursos*, edited by Gregorio Selser (Buenos Aires, 1960), pp. 119–24 and 393–422. I have been told by Raúl Chibás, brother and political heir of Eduardo Chibás, that the Manifesto was written mainly by Castro. Felipe Pazos, who had been President of the National Bank of Cuba, had resigned immediately after Batista's coup, in 1952. He again served in the same post in 1959. Regino Botí was Minister of Economy in Castro's government from 1959 to 1964.

*Nuestra Razón* may be found in Enrique González Pedrero, *La Revolución Cubana* (Mexico, 1959), pp. 89–130. This pamphlet is dated November 1956, but I have been assured by Llerena that this date was put on it for reasons of expediency and that it was not actually published until after he had arrived in Mexico City, in June 1957.

13. In his "Carta a la Junta de Liberación Cubana," dated December 14, 1957 (Selser, pp. 130 and 138), and in the Manifesto of March 12, 1958 (Selser, p. 144). It is significant that *History Will Absolve Me* was never mentioned in this period.

14. In the article signed by Fidel Castro in *Coronet,* February 1958, and in his May 1958 reply to the questionnaire of Jules Dubois, *Fidel Castro* (Indianapolis, Ind., 1959), p. 263. Significantly, the text of Castro's reply to Dubois was included in Selser's semi-official pro-Castro anthology, pp. 147–51.

15. Dubois, pp. 264–65.

16. Selser, pp. 152–55 (English translation in Dubois, pp. 280–83).

17. González Pedrero, pp. 139–56.

18. *Revolución,* December 22, 1961.

19. *Verde Olivo,* June 25, 1961, p. 29.

20. Theodore Draper, *Castro's Revolution: Myths and Realities* (New York, 1962), pp. 144–54.

21. *Pasajes de la Guerra Revolucionaria* (Havana, 1963), pp. 100–105.

22. *Revolución,* December 2, 1961.

23. *Obra Revolucionaria,* August 31, 1962, p. 6.

24. From "Proclama del Directorio Revolucionario desde la Sierra de Escambray: Al Pueblo de Cuba," dated February 25, 1958 (copy in my possession).

25. Faustino Pérez, *Bohemia,* January 11, 1959, p. 38.

26. Fidel Castro, *Revolución,* December 2, 1961.

27. Twelve became the legend. But Castro has also said that the first survivors of the "Granma" numbered as many as "the fingers of one hand" (*Revolución,* July 27, 1963).

28. Selser, p. 144.

29. Fidel Castro, *Revolución,* December 2, 1961.

30. Fulgencio Batista, *Respuesta* (Mexico, 1960), especially pp. 91–145; José Suárez Nuñez, *El Gran Culpable* (Caracas, 1963), pp. 155–74; Esteban Ventura Novo, *Memorias* (Miami, Fla., 1960), p. 25; Florentino E. Rosell, *La Verdad* (Miami, Fla., 1960).

31. *Obra Revolucionaria,* August 25, 1960, p. 16; *Revolución,* August 21, 1963; *ibid.,* November 23, 1964.

32. *Daily Worker* (New York), August 5, 1953.

33. *Carta Semanal,* October 10, 1956 (quoted by Andrés Valdespino, *Bohemia,* June 26, 1960, p. 43, in a controversy with the Communist leader Carlos Rafael Rodríguez, who did not challenge it).

34. *Bohemia,* July 8, 1956, p. 87.

35. Fidel Castro, "¡Basta Ya De Mentiras!," *Bohemia,* July 15, 1956, p. 84. Blas Roca was the Communist General Secretary and Lázaro Peña the Communist trade union leader.

36. Barnard L. Collier, *New York Herald Tribune,* August 23, 1964.

37. Daniel James seems to share the view of his informants that "in Mexico Castro received his final indoctrination in Communism and that the July 26th Movement, which had ostensibly been created as an instrument of Cuban nation-

alism, was largely in Communist hands." (*Cuba: The First Soviet Satellite in the Americas,* New York, 1961, pp. 55–56.) To bolster this point, he quotes from a Mexican writer, Mario Gill: "The first stage of the revolution of the Sierra Maestra was completed in Mexico: the theoretical and technical preparation of the invading group." (*¡Cuba Si! ¡Yanquis No!,* Mexico, 1960, p. 104.) Even as it stands, this sentence proves nothing about Castro's Communist indoctrination inasmuch as Gill does not characterize the "theoretical and technical preparation." But, inexplicably, James mistranslates the key word, *"inició"*; "was completed" should read "began."

38. *Carte del Comité Nacional del Partido Socialista Popular al Movimiento 26 de Julio* (copy in my possession).

39. Aníbal Escalante, *Fundamentos,* August 1959, p. 12. The February 1958 "turn" was also mentioned by Carlos Rafael Rodríguez, in *Hoy,* April 15, 1959, p. 3.

40. Two of the young Communists sent to the Sierra Maestra, Pablo Ribalta and Hiram Prats, were named at the Marcos Rodríguez trial (*El Mundo,* March 25, 1964).

41. His role was revealed only after he was killed in an airplane accident in January (*Verde Olivo,* January 22, 1961, p. 79, and July 2, 1961, p. 12).

42. "Declaraciones del PSP: Las Mentiras del Gobierno Sobre la Huelga y la Situación," leaflet signed by the Comité Nacional del Partido Socialista Popular, dated April 12, 1958.

43. "Srs. Miembros de los organismos dirigentes del 'Movimiento 26 de Julio,' del PRC (a), de la Organización Auténtica, del Directorio Revolucionario, del grupo 'Montecristi,' del PPC (O) y del PNR," signed by the National Committee, Juan Marinello, President, Blas Roca, General Secretary.

44. Letter from Angel del Cerro to Theodore Draper, September 2, 1962. According to del Cerro, who then represented the Montecristi Group in Havana, Carlos Rafael Rodríguez returned from his first trip to the Sierra Maestra and told the "Caracas Pact" representatives in Havana that Castro wanted the Communists included, but no one believed him and he was not accepted.

45. Carlos Rafael Rodríguez, "Entre la colère et la peur," *La France nouvelle,* July 17–23, 1958.

46. Testimony of Carlos Rafael Rodríguez at the Marcos Rodríguez trial, *El Mundo,* March 25, 1964.

47. *Hoy,* January 11 and 15, 1959.

48. Joaquin Ordoqui, *Elementos para la Historia del Movimiento Obrero en Cuba* (Havana, 1961), p. 35, gives the date as October 1958. The Communist trade union leader Ursinio Rojas stated that the negotiations were initiated in "June and July 1958" and concluded in "October and November" of that year (*Fundamentos,* March 1959, p. 22).

49. *Bohemia,* February 15, 1959, p. 88.

50. *Cuba Socialista,* February 1963, p. 30.

51. *Hoy,* March 5 and June 12, 1959.

52. The fates of Treasury Minister Rufo López-Fresquet and Luis Conte Agüero were similarly foreshadowed (*Hoy,* May 5 and June 30, 1959).

53. Interview with Castro, *L'Unità* (Rome), February 1, 1961; *Revolución,* March 26, 1961; *Revolución,* December 2, 1961; Lionel Soto, *Cuba Socialista,* February 1963, pp. 62–63.

54. *Guía del pensamiento político económico de Fidel* (Havana, 1959), p. 30.
55. *Revolución*, May 22, 1959.
56. *Guía del pensamiento político económico de Fidel*, p. 48.
57. *Hoy*, April 28, 1959.
58. *Revolución*, May 22, 1959.
59. Blas Roca, *Hoy*, May 10, 1959.
60. *Hoy*, June 30, 1959.
61. *XII Congreso del Partido Comunista de la Argentina: Resolución* (Buenos Aires, 1963), pp. 4 and 9.
62. *Hoy*, March 9, 1963.
63. "Declaración Conjunta Soviético-Cubana," *Cuba Socialista*, June 1963, pp. 17–18.
64. *Revolución*, August 21, 1963.
65. Che Guevara, *La Guerra de Guerrillas* (Havana, 1960), p. 11.
66. "Guerra de Guerrillas: Un Método," *Cuba Socialista*, September 1963, pp. 1–17. The entire article, as may be seen, lends itself to different interpretations depending on which sentence is emphasized, which may have been Guevara's intention. The passage quoted above, however, has had an even more complicated career in translation. Unfortunately, the only publicly available English translation appeared in the *Peking Review*, January 10, 1964, pp. 14–21. At key points, this version significantly changed Guevara's meaning. For example, Guevara had used the expression "las siguientes conclusiones," which became, in the Chinese Communist organ, "the inevitable conclusion" instead of, simply, "the following conclusions." More seriously, Guevara wrote: "En este Continente existen en general condiciones objetivas," etc. The Chinese translated this as follows: "There exist everywhere in this continent the objective conditions," etc. By using the term "everywhere" for Guevara's "en general" (in general), the Chinese translation significantly distorted the meaning of the original, even though the sentences immediately following belie the intention of Guevara to assume objective conditions for violent action in every Latin American country.
67. *World Marxist Review*, December 1963, pp. 3–10.
68. Gianni Corbi, "I Niños Malos," *L'Espresso* (Rome), January 26, 1964.
69. *La Tarde* (Havana), July 29, 1964.
70. *Obra Revolucionaria*, 1964, No. 20, p. 24.
71. *Hoy*, July 16, 1963.
72. Fabio Grobart, *Cuba Socialista*, July 1963, p. 55.
73. Blas Roca, *ibid.*, January 1964, pp. 11–12. Blas Roca used this formula for the first time in 1960 (Partido Socialista Popular, *VIII Asamblea Nacional*, Havana, 1960, p. 44).
74. *Revolución*, March 25, 1963.
75. *El Mundo*, October 14, 1964.
76. Victorio Codovilla, *Information Bulletin*, Supplement No. 3 to *World Marxist Review* (Ontario, 1963), pp. 33–34.

*Prospects for Pluralistic Communism*

1. In his report on the 1960 Moscow conference of Communist parties (*World Marxist Review*, January 1961), Khrushchev stated that the "leading role" formula had been omitted from the conference's statement at the Soviet delegation's request.

The Chinese Communists have since disclosed that Khrushchev had already rejected the formula in a banquet speech during the meeting of the bloc's party leaders on February 4, 1960, and again at the Bucharest meeting of delegates from ruling Communist parties on June 24, 1960. See Notes 11 and 12 to the Chinese seventh "Commentary" on the CPSU "Open Letter," entitled "The Leaders of the CPSU Are the Greatest Splitters of All Time," *New China News Agency* (hereafter cited as *NCNA*), February 4, 1964.

2. The most important systematic statements are, on the Soviet side, the "Open Letter from the CC of the CPSU," *Pravda*, July 14, 1963, and the report made to the CC by M. A. Suslov on February 14, 1964, *Pravda*, April 3, 1964; on the ideologically more prolific Chinese side, "More on the Differences between Comrade Togliatti and Us," March 4, 1963, "A Proposal for the General Line of the International Communist Movement," June 14, 1963, and the nine "Commentaries" on the CPSU "Open Letter," issued jointly by the editorial staffs of *Red Flag* and *People's Daily* on September 6, 13, and 26, October 21, November 18, and December 12, 1963, February 4, March 30, and July 14, 1964. All these were issued by *NCNA* on the dates cited and also as pamphlets by the Foreign Languages Press, Peking; all documents published between June and November 1963 are reproduced in whole or in part by William E. Griffith, *The Sino-Soviet Rift* (Cambridge, Mass., 1964).

3. Stalin, *Economic Problems of Socialism in the USSR* (Moscow, 1952).

4. See Khrushchev's report to the Twenty-first Congress on the Seven-Year Plan, in *Pravda*, January 28, 1959.

5. See the English text of the program adopted by the Twenty-second Congress and Khrushchev's report of October 18, 1961, in *Current Soviet Policies IV: The Documentary Record of the Twenty-second Congress of the CPSU* (New York, 1962).

6. See, e.g., Roderick McFarquhar, "Communist China's Intra-Party Dispute," *Pacific Affairs*, December 1958, and his *The Hundred Flowers Campaign and the Chinese Intellectuals* (New York, 1960); Donald Zagoria, *The Sino-Soviet Conflict* (Princeton, N.J., 1962); and Harvard University, *Communist China 1955–59: Policy Documents with Analysis* (Cambridge, Mass., 1962).

7. See the resolution of the CC of the CCP of August 29, 1958, on the "People's Communes," *Peking Review*, September 16, 1958.

8. The confidential memorandum on the issue of Khrushchev's "peaceful road" to socialism, submitted to the Soviet delegation by the Chinese delegation at the 1957 Moscow conference, has been published as an annex to both the first and the eighth CCP "Commentaries" on the Soviet "Open Letter" (*NCNA*, September 6, 1963, and March 30, 1964).

9. For the main stages of these practical retreats without ideological revision, see the CC resolution on the communes of December 10, 1958, *Peking Review*, December 23, 1958; Liao Lu-yen, "Taking Agriculture as the Foundation," *ibid.*, September 14, 1960; the communiqué of the Ninth CC Plenum virtually ending the Great Leap Forward, *ibid.*, January 27, 1961; the *People's Daily* editorials of October 1, 1961, and January 1 and March 29, 1962; and the communiqué of the Tenth CC Plenum, *Peking Review*, September 28, 1962.

10. See David Charles, "The Dismissal of Marshal P'eng Teh-huai," *China Quarterly*, October-December 1961.

11. See in particular the ninth "Commentary" on the CPSU "Open Letter," entitled "Khrushchev's Phony Communism and Its Historical Lessons for the

World," *NCNA,* July 14, 1964. The last part summarizes the "main content" of Mao Tse-tung's theories and policies in 15 points.

12. English text of Stalin's 1937 speech is in his *Mastering Bolshevism* (New York, 1937). For Khrushchev's "secret speech," see *The Anti-Stalin Campaign and International Communism,* a selection of documents edited by the Russian Institute, Columbia University (New York, 1956).

13. See, for example, Maurice Thorez's interview on the "legal road" to "people's democracy" in France with *The Times* (London), November 18, 1946, and Stalin's 1945 musings about "socialism under the English monarchy" as reported by Djilas, *Conversations with Stalin* (New York, 1962). Addressing the East Berlin congress of the SED in January 1963, Khrushchev called on the British Communist leaders to give witness that Stalin himself had inspired their 1946 platform advocating the "peaceful road." *Neues Deutschland,* January 17, 1963.

14. For a reliable timetable of Chinese splitting activities, see Kevin Devlin, "Rival Communist Parties," in *World Today* (London), June 1964.

15. Aidit's speech of September 29 formed the basis of his report to the Central Committee of his party in December. The official summary of this report was quoted in English by the Indian CP weekly, *New Age,* January 19, 1964.

16. *The Fighting Task Confronting Workers in Philosophy and the Social Sciences* (Peking, 1963).

17. For the attitude of both sides toward a world conference during the earlier phase, see the letters of the CC of the CPSU of February 21 and March 30, 1963, and that of the CC of the CCP of March 9, 1963, including their references to earlier correspondence, in *Peking Review,* March 22, 1963, and William E. Griffith, *The Sino-Soviet Rift* (Cambridge, Mass., 1964). For the later phase see the exchange of letters for the period from November 29, 1963, to May 7, 1964, as published by *NCNA* on the latter date, the Soviet CC's letter of June 15, 1964, in *Tass,* July 15, 1964, and the Chinese CC's reply of July 28, *NCNA,* July 30, 1964.

18. See the Chinese eighth "Commentary" on the Soviet "Open Letter," entitled "The Proletarian Revolution and Khrushchev's Revisionism," *NCNA,* March 30, 1964.

19. Mao Tse-tung, "The Chinese Revolution and the Chinese Communist Party," in *Selected Works of Mao Tse-tung,* III (London 1954), 96; Liu Shao-chi's speech is in *World Trade Union Movement,* December 1949.

20. See the present writer's chapter on China in Zbigniew Brzezinski, ed., *Africa and the Communist World* (Stanford, 1963).

21. On the Brazilian split, see the Devlin paper cited in Note 14 above, and the same author's "Boring from Within," *Problems of Communism,* No. 2, 1964; on the Indian opposition, see Harry Gelman, "The Indian CP between Moscow and Peking," *ibid.,* No. 6, 1962, and "Indian Communism in Turmoil," *ibid.,* No. 3, 1963; on the Japanese party, see Branko Lazitch, "Un 'Conciliateur' dans le mouvement communiste international: Le Parti communiste japonais," *Est et Ouest,* May 16–31, 1963.

22. "More on the Differences between Comrade Togliatti and Us," *Red Flag,* March 4, 1963.

23. In the "Open Letter" of the Soviet CC, *Pravda,* July 14, 1963, and again in Suslov's report to the Soviet CC of February 14, 1964, *Pravda,* April 3, 1964.

24. For Lenin vs. Roy, see the different versions of Roy's theses on the colonial

question in the Protocol of the Second Congress of the Comintern, and the account in E. H. Carr, *The Russian Revolution 1917–23*, Vol. III (London, 1953); for Sultan Galiev, see his articles in *Zhizn Natsionalnostei*, October 5 and 12 and November 2, 1919, and Stalin's attack on him in *Sochineniya*, V (Moscow, 1947), 301 *et seq.*

25. This was still repeated during Chou En-lai's African tour; cf. the reports of his speeches on Algiers Radio, December 26, and *NCNA*, December 27, 1963.

26. See Ernst Halperin, "Castroism—Challenge to Latin-American Communists," *Problems of Communism*, No. 5, 1963.

27. The ninth "Commentary" on the Soviet CC's "Open Letter" ("Khrushchev's Phony Communism"), *NCNA*, July 14, 1964.

28. The fact of this expulsion was officially mentioned for the first time in Suslov's report to the CC of the CPSU of February 14, 1964, published in *Pravda*, April 3, 1964.

29. *Interventi della delegazione del PCI alla conferenza degli 81 partiti comunisti e operai*, published in Rome in January 1962; *Contribution de la délégation française à la conférence des partis communistes et ouvriers, Moscou, novembre 1960*, circulated to party members in France in November 1961; and the two series of articles by Jean Terfve and Ernest Brunelle published in January 1962 in *Le Drapeau rouge* (Brussels).

30. On the Stockholm vote, see the account of the Italian participant Velio Spano, in *Unità*, December 23, 1961; on the refusal of the later Chinese proposals, see the correspondence on the conference project cited in Note 17 above.

31. See the defense of the rapprochement with Tito in *Pravda*, February 10, 1963, against the attack in *People's Daily*, January 27, 1963.

32. In the "Open Letter" to all party organizations and Communists of the Soviet Union, *Pravda*, July 14, 1963 (English version in the *New York Times*, July 16).

33. *Pravda*, April 8 and 11, 1963.

34. See in particular the communiqué on Togliatti's visit to Tito and Togliatti's press conference in *Unità*, January 22, 1964; the Italian Party's statement following the publication of Suslov's report, *ibid.*, April 5, 1964; Togliatti's report to the CC of April 22, and his posthumously published memorandum to Khrushchev, *Rinascita*, September 4, and *Pravda*, September 10, 1964.

35. See the letter from the CC of the CPSU to the Chinese Party of June 15, 1964, *Tass*, July 15, 1964, and the invitation to the preparatory conference sent out on July 30, 1964, and published by the Chinese with their reply of August 30, *NCNA*, August 30, 1964.

36. *Pravda*, December 12, 1964.

37. See the Khrushchev interview with journalists from Algeria, Burma, and Ghana in *Pravda*, December 22, 1963, and the editorial comment in *Aziya i Afrika segodnya*, No. 2, 1964; the articles on Algeria by V. Kaboshkin and Yu. Shchirovsky, *Kommunist*, No. 16, 1963, and by G. Mirsky, *New Times*, No. 17, 1964; on Egypt by G. Mirsky, *New Times*, No. 2, 1964, and the editorials on Khrushchev's visit there in *New Times*, No. 23, 1964, and in *Kommunist*, No. 8, 1964; the programmatic May Day article by G. Mirsky, *New Times*, No. 18, 1964; and the report of a systematic discussion on the subject in *Mirovaya ekonomika i mezhdunarodnie otnosheniya*, Nos. 4 and 6, 1964.

38. See the communiqué on the visit in *Pravda*, May 7, 1964, and the communi-

qué of the meeting of Arab Communist representatives in *ibid.*, December 11, 1964.

39. See his argument in Nikita Khrushchev, "Vital Questions of the Development of the Socialist World System," *World Marxist Review*, No. 9, 1962.

40. For an informative survey of these elements, see R. V. Burks, "The Thaw," *Encounter*, August 1964.

41. See the Chinese "Proposal for the General Line of the International Communist Movement," *NCNA*, June 14, 1963.

42. In his speech in Hungary on April 3, 1964.

43. Text published by the Rumanian News Agency *Agerpress*, April 27, 1964.

44. See R. V. Burks in the paper cited in Note 40 above; also J. F. Brown, "Miss Rumania," *Der Monat* (Berlin), July 1964.

45. Khrushchev's report to the CC of November 19, 1962.

46. For the links between the "ideological campaign" of that winter and resistance to Khrushchev in the party leadership, see, for example, Priscilla Johnson, "The Regime and the Intellectuals," *Problems of Communism*, No. 4, 1963; Carl Linden, "Khrushchev and the Party Battle," *ibid.*, No. 5, 1963; Richard Lowenthal, "Reaktion und Fortschritt in der Innenpolitik," *Osteuropa*, No. 11, 1964.

47. Text of Suslov's report is in *Pravda*, April 3, 1964.

48. See M. Gatovsky's report on such a discussion in *Voprosy ekonomiki*, No. 2, 1964; V. Nemchinov in *Kommunist*, No. 5, 1964; V. Trapeznikov in *Pravda*, August 17, 1964; and O. Volkov, *Pravda*, August 23, 1964. Cf. also Libermann's interview with Borba, Belgrade, July 9, 1964. For the post-Khrushchev practice, see the report of Kosygin's speech to the Supreme Soviet on the 1965 Plan, Moscow Radio, December 9, 1964.

49. Cf. Richard Lowenthal, "Secessio Plebis," *The Twentieth Century* (London), May 1951.

50. See the French CC resolution of October 6, 1963, reported in *L'Humanité*.

51. See Togliatti's interview with *Nuovi Argumenti*, June 16, 1956, which coined the phrase, and his report to the Italian CC reported in *Unità*, June 24, 1956; English texts are in *The Anti-Stalin Campaign and International Communism*.

52. See *Interventi della delegazione del PCI alla conferenza degli 81 partiti comunisti e operai.*

53. See the Italian Communists' theses for the Moscow conference on contemporary capitalism, *Unità*, August 29, 1962; their comment on the discussions, *ibid.*, September 3–4, 1962; their theses for the Tenth Congress of their own party, *ibid.*, September 13, 1962; and their subsequent polemics with the WFTU leadership before and during its Leipzig conference in December of that year. See also the relevant section in Giorgio Galli's chapter on Italian Communism in William E. Griffith, ed., *Communism in Europe*, Vol. I (Cambridge, Mass., 1964).

54. See the theses for the Tenth Congress of the PCI and the chapter by Galli cited in the previous note.

55. For a detailed discussion of the evolution of relations between Italian and Soviet Communists that takes a somewhat more cautious view of Italian Communist independence, see Galli, "Italian Communism," in Griffith, *Communism in Europe*.

56. See Note 34 above.

57. See, for instance, the series of articles on the issue published by the French Socialist *Le Populaire* in December 1963.

58. See the report of the debates in the Italian CC session following the congress,

*Unità*, November 12, 1961 (full English extracts in A. Dallin, ed., *Diversity in International Communism*, New York, 1963), and the chapter by Galli cited in Note 53 above.

59. See for details "La Crise de l'union des étudiants communistes," *Est et Ouest*, No. 297, April 1–15, 1963; Jean-Pierre Morillon, "Le Conflit des étudiants communistes français avec la direction du P.C.F.," *ibid.*, No. 308, November 11–15, 1963; "Le Parti communiste italien et la politique anticolonialiste," *ibid.*, No. 325, July 16–31, 1964.

60. *Rinascita*, November 28, 1964.

61. For the first time on the occasion of the Twenty-second Congress of the CPSU.

62. On the newspaper, see the announcement in *Alger Républicain*, April 19–20, 1964, and the approving report in *Pravda*, April 22, 1964; on Communist claims of having influenced the FLN program, see Luigi Longo's report in *Rinascita*, January 25, 1964.

63. See, e.g., M. Kremnyov in *World Marxist Review*, No. 8, 1963; W. Sheppard, *ibid.*, No. 3, 1964; G. Mirsky in *New Times*, No. 17, 1964; and V. Kaboshkin and Yu. Shchirovsky in *Kommunist*, No. 16, 1963, and the debate in *Mirovaya ekonomika i mezhdunarodnie otnosheniya* cited in Note 37 above.

64. See Mao's interview with a delegation of Japanese Socialists on July 10, 1964, reported on Kyoto Radio on July 13, and in *Pravda* on September 2, 1964.

65. Cf. Richard Lowenthal, "Factors of Unity and Factors of Conflict," *Annals of the American Academy of Political and Social Science*, Vol. 349 (September 1963).